SECTION V: CONTRACTORS
    Chapter 1: Official Service Contractors   357
    Chapter 2: Registration & Data Management   373
    Chapter 3: Housing Management   405
    Chapter 4: Air & Ground Transportation   421
    Chapter 5: Audio-Visual Services   433
    Chapter 6: Exhibition Shipping   445

SECTION VI: ON-SITE OPERATIONS
    Chapter 1: Staffing & Communications   457
    Chapter 2: Crisis Management & Security   471
    Chapter 3: Green Meetings   491
    Chapter 4: Evaluation   507

SECTION VII: APPENDICES
    Chapter 1: Exhibition Industry Certifications   521
    Chapter 2: Exhibition & Event Industry Organizations   539
    Chapter 3: Index   545

Forward

Since 1928, IAEM has provided quality and value to its members and the industry through leadership, service and education. As a part of that tradition, the First Edition of the *Art of the Show* textbook was published through the IAEM Foundation in 1997. Since the Second Edition was published in 2001, world events and a subsequent world recession have rocked the industry worldwide. In order for events to survive and grow, exhibition organizers all over the world must continue to explore new ways to attract attendees, and how to provide exhibitors with a positive return on investment. IAEM will continue to serve the exhibition industry by providing relevant and valuable information that will further the industry and the growth of all parties involved.

From the beginning, the *Art of the Show* textbook has explored how exhibitions and events are evolving as a global marketing medium, but the Third Edition now brings this focus to every chapter. Written by industry professionals, it is a standard tool in university and college classrooms around the world where exhibition and event management is studied. The textbook has been translated into Korean and Mandarin Chinese languages. We expect that international usage and distribution will continue to increase because of the need for highly qualified, educated exhibition industry professionals. The goal of this textbook is to provide the basic information necessary to manage a successful exhibition anywhere on the globe.

IAEM is once again proud to be the publisher of a new edition of the *Art of the Show* because it gives you, the reader, a leading edge on the future of exhibitions and events.

I.R. (Sandy) Angus
Chairman of the Board of Directors, 2006
International Association for Exhibition Management
Chairman, Montgomery Exhibitions, London, England

Preface

The First Edition of this textbook was written in 1997, nearly a decade ago. Students who are just embarking on their careers will find it hard to believe that (way) back then, only a few of us "early adapters" were as dependent on e-mail as we all are now. No one had a cell phone that could send and receive e-mail. Not many of us – or our attendees and exhibitors – used the Internet to book our hotel and airline reservations. Most shows did not have Web sites. Air travel, although already a frequent occurrence for those in the exhibition industry, was still occasionally a pleasant escape from the ordinary work day.

Indeed, we are well aware that the exhibition industry has changed over the past decade-technically, economically, and in response to many global factors. And so, when we set out to create the Third Edition of the *Art of the Show*, we knew that the textbook needed some significant updating. However, we thought we would simply sprinkle in references to new technologies in a few of the chapters. Instead, we quickly found ourselves creating almost a totally new book because there was so much new information to present. Fortunately, our collection of industry experts made this thoroughly revised and updated edition possible. On behalf of IAEM, I thank each one of them for taking time out of their very busy professional lives to provide an update on the state of the exhibition industry within each of their specialties. Likewise, without the work of the editor of the first and second editions, Sandra L. Morrow, CEM, CAE, PhD, there would not have been an *Art of the Show* to update, and we continue to be in her debt for her vision and the standards she set in creating the definitive textbook on the exhibition industry.

Speaking of change, one important editorial decision we made was not to include lists of vocabulary terms in this edition due to the advent of the excellent on-line resources available, especially at the Convention Industry Council site (www.conventionindustry.org). And in another move to make use of Internet technology, we have only included two teaching aids in the newest edition of *Art of the Show*, the learning objectives at the beginning of each chapter, and the (hopefully provocative) questions for discussion at the end of each chapter. IAEM's goal is to develop a Web site for curriculum materials in use by teaching faculty around the world. IAEM also plans to post an assortment of historical and standard documents on its Web site.

In addition to being current, our other mission has been to think globally and there is more information in this book on exhibitions outside the United States, than in the previous editions. We recognize that readership is now global. We have tried to include as much information as possible about exhibitions worldwide (including totally new information about the history of exhibitions in China, created just for this edition). We have also tried to expand our vocabulary to include terms not commonly used in the U.S. exhibition industry.

But while thinking globally, we have used what we consider to be the most widely accepted industry terms, recognizing there are nuances attached to many. For instance, although show organizer is our preferred term for the person with overall responsibility for an exhibition, we have also used show manager, exhibition manager, and on occasion event planner, with roughly equivalent meaning. Similarly, we prefer exhibition since the term encompasses both trade and consumer shows, although convention, show and event are widely accepted alternatives and those terms are also found in this text. Perhaps over time, usage will be consolidated into a core group of universally accepted terms.

We look forward to getting feedback from students and faculty who use this new edition. Please send your comments and suggestions for future updates to iaem@iaem.org. Without doubt, I am privileged to work on this project and I am sincerely grateful to IAEM for the opportunity.

Penny Kent

Penny Kent, CEM
September, 2006

Ms. Kent has nearly 30 years of experience in the exhibition industry. She started her career at a major city-owned convention center, later was responsible for producing a 2,000 booth medical convention for 30,000 attendees, and has been in sales for a third party housing provider for the last 12 years. She also taught a course called "Introduction to Conventions and Expositions" at the junior college level for 10 years, utilizing previous editions of the *Art of the Show*. She is also past chairperson of the IAEM Services Inc. Board of Directors

Acknowledgements

The LVCVA and the Las Vegas Convention Center have played an integral role in the advancement of both Las Vegas as a business destination and the convention and exhibition industry as a whole during their nearly 50 years in existence.

In the early 1950s, community leaders in Southern Nevada realized that the cyclical nature of tourism caused a significant decline in the number of visitors to the destination during midweek, during the summer months and over the holidays. Those leaders established the Clark County Fair and Recreation Board, which later became the LVCVA, and focused on attracting convention and trade show business to the destination to bolster visitation during those critical periods.

In April 1959, the vision of those early leaders was well on its way to becoming a reality when the Las Vegas Convention Center opened with a 20,340-square-foot rotunda, 18 meeting rooms and 90,000 square feet of exhibit space. The center was completely funded through a room tax, ensuring that locals did not foot the bill. The center hosted eight conventions and 22,519 delegates in its first year of operation.

That early foresight put Las Vegas on the map as a convention destination, and the LVCVA continually built its reputation as a major player in the convention and trade show industry from that first year.

Since that opening, the Las Vegas Convention Center has undergone approximately a dozen expansions and renovations and has grown with the destination. Today, the 3.2-million-square-foot center contains more than 2 million square feet of exhibit space and 144 meeting rooms.

Over the past half-decade, the LVCVA and Las Vegas Convention Center have continued to grow both in size and reputation through the industry. The number of conventions and delegates has consistently grown over that time, with two more major convention facilities opening in the destination – the Sands Expo Center and Mandalay Bay Convention Center.

Today, Las Vegas is recognized as a leader in the convention industry in several categories, including the most Tradeshow Week 200 shows at 44 in 2005, the most available guest rooms at 133,000 and growing, three of the 10 largest convention facilities and more than 9.5 million square feet of exhibit space.

The LVCVA is consistently recognized as a leader and innovator in the industry, operating the Las Vegas Convention Center and Cashman Center, as well as providing sales and marketing support for all of the facilities in the destination. More than 22,000 conventions, trade shows and meetings were held in Las Vegas in 2005, with more than 6 million delegates attending.

Being a leader is not good enough, however, for Las Vegas. Destination representatives are constantly seeking out ways to improve the destination and the experience for its convention industry clientele. The LVCVA leads trade show missions to destinations around the globe, seeking to assist its convention clients in exposure to and attendance from international destinations. These trips help expose shows to key industry participants in new and emerging markets, as well as marketing the destination both for convention and leisure travel.

The destination continues to reinvent itself to further benefit visitors, with new resorts and amenities being added to the inventory regularly. There is currently more than $30 billion in planned and under construction development projects in Las Vegas, and two of the major convention facilities are planning major renovations or expansions in the coming years. The Las Vegas Convention Center is under going a major renovation project that will make the center a world-class facility for the next 50 years. The Sands Expo Center is planning a renovation and expansion that will add more meeting and exhibit space to the continually in-demand destination.

Las Vegas has played an integral role in the growth and maturity of the trade show and convention industry. Starting with the foresight of community leaders in the 1950s, who determined that the Las Vegas Convention Center was the key to growth in Las Vegas, and continuing through the billions of dollars in investment in the industry today, Las Vegas continues to be a leader in the industry and will be for many years to come. The Las Vegas Convention and Visitors Authority (LVCVA) is pleased to be the signature sponsor of this textbook, given its influence in the exhibition industry over the past 50 years.

Contributors

The following exhibition industry professionals contributed their time and expertise to this textbook. Our special thanks to the Chapter Contributors:

Stuart Aizenberg, CEM	Director of Trade Shows & Associate Director of Membership, *National Automatic Merchandising Association*
I.R. 'Sandy' Angus	Chairman, *Montgomery Exhibitions Ltd*
Susan Bennett	Manager, *Strategic Account Sales & Industry Relations ExpoExchange*
Carina Bloom	Marketing and Operations Director, *Regent Exhibitions Ltd*
MaryAnne Bobrow, CAE, CMP	Managing Partner, *Bobrow & Associates*
Cathy Breden, CAE, CMP	Chief Operating Officer, *International Association for Exhibition Management*
Patrick Buchen, CEM	President & CEO, *Adjuvant Expos Inc*
Jack Buttine	President, *John Buttine Exhibition Insurance*
Amanda Cecil, Ph.D., CMP	Assistant Professor, *Indiana University, Department of Tourism*
Gary Clark	Vice President, Communications, *AVW-TELAV Audio Visual Solutions*
Jonathan 'Skip' Cox	President, *Exhibit Surveys Inc*
Paul Cunniffe	Director of National Accounts, *GES Exposition Services Inc*
Robert Dallmeyer	President, *RD International*
Jeff Ducate	VP of Sales, *CMAC*
Doug Ducate, CEM, CMP	President & CEO, *Center for Exhibition Industry Research*
Cindy Ferguson, CEM	Director of Marketing, *Association of Progressive Rental Organizations*
Christine Fletcher, CEM	Executive Producer, *Encore Event Management*
Francis Friedman	President, *Time & Place Strategies Inc*
Steven Hacker, CAE	President, *International Association for Exhibition Management*
Jennifer Hoff, CEM	Vice President of Operations, *National Trade Productions Inc*
Susan Hueg, CEM, CMP	NBM Business Development, *National Business Media Inc*
Gerald Kallman Sr.	Managing Director, *Kallman Global Consulting*
Penny Kent, CEM	Director of Sales, *Travel Planners Inc*
Michael Kovac	Director of Sales & Marketing, *Rock-It Cargo USA LLC*
E. Jane Lorimer, CME	Managing Director, *Lorimer Consulting Group*
Curtis Love, Ph.D.	Assistant Professor, *UNLV - College of Hotel Administration*
Brian Monroe	Director of Sales & Marketing, *Myrtle Beach Convention Center*
John Plescia, CMP, CEM	Event Operations Manager, *Orange County Convention Center*
Vincent Polito	Senior Vice President, *Reed Exhibitions*
Garet Robinson	Airline Manager, *Travel Planners Inc*
Mark Roysner	Attorney at Law, *Roysner & Associates / Legal Consultants to the Exhibition & Meetings Industry*
Chen Ruowei	Chairman, *China International Exhibition Center*
Stephen Schuldenfrei	President, *Trade Show Exhibitors Association*
Chuck Schwartz, CEM	Chairman, *ConvExx*
Patti Shock, Ph.D.	Professor, *UNLV - College of Hotel Administration*
Stephen Sind	President & CEO, *Global Event Strategies LLC*
Julia Smith, CEM	Vice President of Sales, *GES Exposition Services Inc*
John Smith, CFE	Adjunct Faculty, *Georgia State University*
Amy Spatrisano, CMP	*Meetings Strategies Worldwide & Green Meetings Industry Council*
Zhao Weiping	General Manager, *Messe Frankfurt (Shanghai) Co., Ltd.*
Liu Zhiyong	Deputy Secretary General, *China International Exhibition Center*

Many thanks also to the *Art of the Show* Advisory Task Force

Robert Dallmeyer	President, *RD International*
Karen Howe, CEM	Executive Director of Meetings & Convention Department, *National Safety Council*
Penny Kent, CEM	Director of Sales, *Travel Planners Inc*
Curtis Love, Ph.D.	Assistant Professor, *UNLV - College of Hotel Administration*
Peter Nathan, CEM	President, *PWN Exhibicon International LLC*
Susa Schwartz, CEM	Executive Director, *ConvExx*
Richard Stone	Chief Executive Officer, *ACT/EXPOCAD*
Jack Withiam, Jr., CEM	Executive Vice President & General Counsel, *George Little Management LLC*
M.T. Hickman	Program Coordinator, *Richard College, Dallas Community College District*
Jennifer Hoff, CEM	Vice President of Operations & Conferences, *National Trade Productions*
Amanda Cecil, Ph.D., CMP	Assistant Professor, *Indiana University, Department of Tourism*
Robbi Lycett, CEM	Vice President, Conventions & Conferences, *Biotechnology Industry Organization*

In Memory Of:
Sandra Lynn Morrow, CEM, CAE, Ph.D.
Educator, exhibition organizer, and author of The Art of the Show, First and Second Editions. Her tireless work on behalf of IAEM and the exhibition industry will never be forgotten and without whom this Third Edition would not be possible.

As Always, our appreciation for the help and support received from the IAEM staff. And special gratitude for copy editing service provided by: Joanne McCoy, President, The McCoy Group.

Section I: Overview

Introduction

F R E E M A N

September, 2006

To those who seek to learn about our industry:

Since the earliest days of fairs & bazaars, to today's sophisticated exhibitions, face-to-face marketing remains the single most effective vehicle a company can utilize to further their selling efforts. Therefore, I believe that the exhibition industry is a healthy, integral part of our economy, and will only continue to grow in the future.

Nowhere else can a company bring a new product or service to the marketplace as quickly, reach an audience pre-determined to have interest, or have the ability to demonstrate its benefits as in a face-to-face environment. Whether a small "mom and pop" organization, a start-up entrepreneurial entity, or a large, global corporation, participation in an exhibition brings real and unique results to both sellers and buyers.

Face-to-face marketing also works across all industries. From medical specialists and television programming executives, to stationery suppliers and high-tech manufacturers, there is truly an event designed to serve everyone's needs in a unique way.

The future of the exhibitions industry is bright, in part because the industry responds quickly to changing conditions in our national – and global economy. Part of the excitement of participating in this industry is this change, and adapting to new marketplace conditions. One such development is the recent emphasis on supplemental methods of face-to-face marketing through private shows, mobile marketing, and dedicated corporate events, often in partnership with an exhibition.

Career opportunities within the industry continue to develop and grow as well, and offer exciting choices for those with a variety of skills and backgrounds. I think one of the biggest challenges our industry faces is, it is still often "invisible" to the general business and public eye, despite its multi-billion dollar impact on our economy. This textbook, and other educational efforts put forth by IAEM and related professional industry organizations, is a big step towards a better understanding.

Congratulations on your enthusiasm in learning more about this industry. I hope you will find it as exciting, challenging and rewarding as all of us do at Freeman.

Sincerely,

Donald S. Freeman, Jr.
Chairman and CEO
Freeman

Chapter 1
Exhibition Industry Outlook

"Trade fairs are privileged forums which offer us the opportunity to meet not only our customers and potential clients, but also the leading decision makers and journalists in our business sector. And in comparison with advertisements, when participating in an exhibition, we can more convincingly demonstrate the technical quality of our products."
– Françoise Sortais Manager,
Show & Event Coordination Michelin Company, France

Section I: Overview

IN THIS CHAPTER YOU WILL LEARN

- The historical role of exhibitions in the US economy
- The three primary catalysts to the growth of the exhibition industry in the 20th century
- Key economic factors affecting tradeshows
- Challenges and trends in the exhibition industry in the 21st century

INTRODUCTION

For a business sometimes called an "invisible industry," exhibitions play an extraordinarily large role in the US economy. For an introductory overview of where this industry has been and where it is going, there could be no better contributor to this text than Steven Hacker, who brings many years of leadership and exposure to the industry's best thinkers and most successful exhibition organizers. Although there are many potential threats ahead, his analysis points to the continuation of exhibitions as a critical force in the world economy.

CONTRIBUTOR

Steven Hacker, CAE, President, International Association for Exhibition Management

Since the launch of the world's first niche commercial trade fair, which many believe was the Leipzig (Germany) Book Fair in the middle 15th Century, exhibitions and trade fairs have served as remarkably reliable mirrors of the industries and market sectors that they serve. These events, intended to bring buyers and sellers together, almost always reflect the underlying conditions of their industry sectors.

For example, if a particular segment of commerce is doing exceedingly well, expect to see many exhibitions competing aggressively against each other for the attention of key buyers and sellers. Typically, one will also see both the launch of new exhibitions, and the expansion of existing events, including the cloning of successful events, the creation of regional events, and the introduction of related events that broaden the scope of an existing event's market coverage.

Likewise, when economic circumstances are particularly harsh in an industry, one expects to see retrenchment, contraction, plummeting attendance, and in the case of weaker exhibitions, the collapse of the event entirely. In summary, this ebb and flow of exhibition industry activity over time is nothing more than the predictable and entirely normal evidence of supply and demand economics at work.

Exhibitions and the US Economy

Despite a series of economic recessions – including a relatively severe downturn in the late 1980s – the US exhibition industry averaged about six percent annually from the mid-1970s through the early 1990s. At the close of the 20th century, the American exhibition industry seemed virtually immune to market fluctuations and changing economic cycles.

Many industry observers attribute the remarkable growth and expansion of the US exhibition industry during the latter half of the 20th century to the introduction of purpose-built exhibition halls like McCormick Place in Chicago, and dozens of others like it. These buildings constructed especially with large exhibitions in mind provided new platforms upon which to launch events.

Concurrent with this development was the extraordinary expansion of the US economy, and the launch of entirely new industries such as telecommunications, information technology and consumer electronics.

Adding additional power to the surging growth of the domestic exhibition industry was the introduction in 1960 of jet-powered passenger aircraft, which compressed transcontinental travel from nine hours to less than five.

Commercial jet passenger travel brought buyers and sellers together in ways that no one could have imagined before.

These three catalysts allowed corporations to fully engage exhibitions as a unique and powerful way to introduce new products and services, measure competition, meet existing customers under favorable circumstances, launch new advertising and public relations campaigns and build corporate image.

Despite this incredible period of growth and expansion, however, the laws governing economics inevitably came into play in the latter portion of 2000. The convergence of a seriously slumping world economy, and the dramatic and nearly catastrophic collapse of the dot.com economy in the US, began a downturn in the exhibition industry.

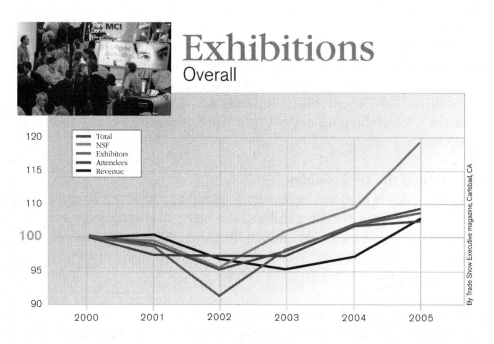

The tragic events of September 11, 2001, brought nearly 40 years of growth to an immediate halt, bringing with it the exhibition industry's first serious contraction. Measured by the Center for Exhibition Industry Research's (CEIR) Index, it took four years for the industry to fully recover. The CEIR Index reports from 2000 through 2005 reflect the industry's post 2000 recovery:

The exhibition industry's recovery from the effects of the serious global economic recession of 1999-2001, the collapse of the IT industry beginning in 2000, and the impact of the terrorist attacks of 2001 would have been more robust had it not been for the presence of additional factors that delayed its full recovery.

For example, the revenues generated from the more than 10,000-13,000 exhibitions conducted each year in the US were further reduced as a result of the scores of corporate mergers and acquisitions that occurred in the early years of the 21st century. Among the casualties of this trend were millions of buyers whose jobs were eliminated, and who would otherwise have attended exhibitions as buyers.

This same trend among Fortune 1000 companies also helped to decrease the number of exhibitors during the same period. Not only were there fewer corporations selling, there were fewer buyers as well. The newly-created companies frequently had many fewer employees than their pre-merged counterparts, which reduced the number of potential exhibition attendees significantly.

At the same time, international travel to the United States plunged dramatically due to changes at US Customs check points in the wake of September 11th. According to data reported by the Travel Industry Association, the share of US International tourism declined 36 percent between 1992 and 2004, at the same time that world tourism increased by 52 percent. In 1992, the US received 9.4 percent of worldwide travelers. By 2004, that number had dropped to only 6 percent.

Rather than be subjected to some of the newly-initiated practices of the US Immigration Service (photography, fingerprinting and iris identification), many international buyers and sellers who heretofore attended US exhibitions chose to participate in comparable events in other nations. Only the weakness of the US dollar compared to other currencies during this time, and the inherent power of the country's economy helped to stem losses that might have been even higher had the US dollar gained in strength.

Globalization of the Exhibition Industry

As the economics of the nations of the world have become linked in a global trading network, the exhibition industry has become a global industry. Driving change in many industries – especially in the manufacturing sectors – is China, whose economy has been expanded by seven to ten percent annually. Not far behind is India, with dozens of emerging economies across Asia and the Pacific trailing. It is becoming apparent that future economic growth is slowly but dramatically shifting to the east.

Many exhibition organizers in the United States are now recognizing the opportunities that exist in Asia and the Pacific, and are beginning to expand in that direction. Even so, they trail far behind their colleagues from several important German show organizers (called "messes") who established operations in the region beginning in the 1980s and 1990s. Nevertheless, the sheer size and power of the US economy suggests that the US interest in China especially can quickly make up any ground lost to the Germans.

Although the list of possible threats to the future of the exhibition industry is long and growing, perhaps the most serious threat involves issues related to domestic and international travel. First and foremost, the stability of the airline industry is of paramount concern. With legacy airlines struggling to stay in the air, it becomes questionable if some cities can maintain an adequate air list to service events, especially the larger ones. Many second and third tier cities have had the number of air carriers and flights that service them reduced, some quite drastically.

The cost of travel is an equally troubling concern. In addition to rising costs associated with petroleum fuels, the tax burden upon travelers has been increasing at an alarming rate. It is common for the cost of a hotel room to be inflated by 20 percent or more as the result of a variety of taxes imposed by city, county and state tax authorities. The prevailing view is all too often that "visitors don't vote," so levying a tax burden on them makes for a convenient way to raise revenues for cities, counties, and states.

Finally, and perhaps most concerning of all, is that along with the ease of travel comes the opportunity to spread communicable diseases, rapidly and perhaps even catastrophically. As evidenced by the highly-publicized outbreaks of SARS in China and Toronto in 2002-2003, the mere threat of a contagious epidemic is sufficient to wreak havoc in an industry that is so dependent upon the freedom and will to travel.

Exhibition Industry Challenges

As corporate marketers have had to demonstrate a more robust return on investment to senior management, more demands have been put upon show organizers to develop metrics to illustrate the value of exhibitions. This relatively new trend presents some interesting challenges to the industry. Using tools like circulation numbers and Nielsen ratings, other business-to-business media like print advertising, broadcast television or radio can be easily measured to reflect the frequency of impact. It can be very difficult, however, to measure the results achieved by a company's participation in exhibitions in many instances.

If selling product is the principal objective, and if the event is a product-selling event, assessing effectiveness of the company's participation is a relatively simple matter of recording the number of orders taken, and tallying the total. On the other hand, many exhibitors who participate in tradeshows for a variety of reasons come to events without a clearly defined set of objectives in mind. For example, how is it possible to accurately measure the impact an exhibition has an the exhibitor's image or goodwill among customers? How can the value of sales resulting from exhibiting be determined if the selling cycle is elongated, and the path to purchase convoluted through many different districts and regions of one exhibiting company's own structure?

Another complication is the evolution of the marketing and advertising industries themselves as the result of technology and changing demographics. Traditional forms of advertising and marketing are being displaced by new and often experimental techniques. One of the newest and potentially most effective forms of marketing ad advertising is engagement. Loosely defined, it is an interactive form of communication in which the buyer engages with the seller using some form of electronic communication such as Web sites, PDAs or smart phones. It remains to be seen if engagement will truly alter the terrain, but the American Advertising Foundation-- along with several other powerful organizations in the advertising industry-- are trying to develop new ways to measure the metrics of engagement.

This is important to the exhibition industry because the tradeshow experience is one of the principal and most effective ways to engage buyers and sellers.

A growing exhibition industry requires sufficient purpose-built venues in which to house its events. In the decade between 1995 and 2005, the inventory of US exhibition space has increased materially. In 1995, an estimated 60 million square feet of exhibition space was available in the United States. By the end of 2005, more than 85 million square feet was available, with more expansions and new construction still ahead.

The presence of more exhibition venues, accompanied by more aggressive competition for events, has contributed to driving costs of rental and usage down for exhibition organizers. While the organizers of large events have more choices than ever, they still have far fewer venues to consider. For larger events, the need for housing and the requirements of exhibit space become exponentially more difficult. Unless a city can offer both the requisite amount of exhibition space and the number of hotel rooms available at the same time, a larger event may have to seek space elsewhere. These needs are driving a growing interest in many communities to build more exhibition space, and convenient housing to accompany it.

The Future for Exhibitions

Despite a recent pause in industry growth, the forecast for the future of the exhibition industry remains quite promising for several reasons.

Buyers who come to today's exhibitions typically have very specific objectives in mind before they come to an event. While the number of corporate buyers attending events from any one company are typically fewer in number than before 2000, more decision-makers are attending.

A survey of corporate exhibitors in 2004 by Exhibit Surveys, Inc. revealed that 84 percent expected their exhibiting budgets to remain the same or increase in the future. Only 16 percent believed their budgets for exhibiting would decrease. The same survey reports that 32 percent of buyers believe that exhibitions are either "Very or Extremely Important" to the purchase decision. Moreover, 67 percent think that exhibitions are a "Very or Extremely Important" platform to increase awareness.

While there is concern about the rising number of proprietary corporate marketing events, such as technical conferences of exhibitions, road shows held by a single corporation, mobile truck exhibits, and permanent briefing and demo centers, this same survey indicates that 76 percent of buyers still think exhibitions are the most valuable of these kinds of events. This is probably because – of all the venues being evaluated – an exhibition presents the buyer with the broadest range of seller selections. Exhibitions remain the most effective way to evaluate, compare and shop for products.

At the same time, many exhibition organizers have increased the size of their events by enhancing the conference and education components that are offered. This has been a particularly effective strategy for industries such as pharmaceuticals and medical practice in which there is a requirement for certification or continuing education credit.

As buyers' time has been reduced, and travel costs have increased, the opportunity to co-locate events becomes a more attractive and viable option for exhibition organizers. This trend is likely to accelerate as time and expense continue to become critical issues.

New business expansions are taking place at an unprecedented pace. Each year, millions of Americans are opting out of corporate employment to create their own small businesses. For the nation's more than 11,000 exhibitions, this means millions of potential new exhibitors eager to use tradeshows as a way to launch their businesses and introduce new products. Throughout the history of the exhibition industry in the US, it has been the small business owner, especially those in launch mode, who have powered the growth of the exhibition floor.

SUMMARY

Despite the issues that potentially threaten the exhibition industry's future, and the many challenges and uncertainties named, the long-term forecast remains bright with promise and opportunity.

QUESTIONS FOR DISCUSSION

① What is it about tradeshows that have made them continue to exist over so many centuries?

② Given future developments in communications technology, do you think exhibitions will become extinct?

③ What type of potential disaster (such as a pandemic or terrorism) do you think would have the worst impact on the future of the exhibition industry?

Section I: Overview

Chapter 2
Careers in the Exhibition Industry

"Leadership and learning are indispensable to each other."
– John F. Kennedy

Section 1: Overview

IN THIS CHAPTER YOU WILL LEARN
- What kinds of jobs are available in the exhibition industry
- Skills and characteristics required to be successful
- Jobs that get "a foot in the door"
- Average Compensation

INTRODUCTION

A career in the exhibition and event industry can be rewarding, challenging and ever-changing. There are opportunities for world travel, and working with different people and cultures, which can be very exciting. But it is certainly not a normal nine-to-five position since show organizers often work long hours in advance of an event and at the show site. And it does not stop there. Each year, organizers must reinvent their exhibitions to stay ahead of the competition and strategically position their shows to grow. In his book, *The World is Flat*, Thomas L. Friedman points to technological advances and the increased competitiveness of emerging markets. For the exhibition industry, this means that there will be ongoing challenges and opportunities for the industry and the people employed in it. As the saying goes, "You are only as good as your last show."

CONTRIBUTOR

Cathy Breden, CAE, CMP, Chief Operating Officer, International Association for Exhibition Management

What Jobs Are Out There?

There are many ways in which a person can enter the exhibition industry. In North America alone, there are over 13,000 exhibitions every year, from small table top exhibitors to huge exhibitions with 3,000 or more exhibitors. With an estimated 1.5 million exhibiting companies, and over 100 million attendees, there are many pathways to a career in the exhibition and event industry.

The United States is not the only market where opportunities exist for career development. Europe has an established exhibition industry, and in the emerging market of China, there is an estimated 567 exhibitions. In fact, Asia produces almost 1,800 exhibitions, with an annual growth rate estimated at between 12 and 14 percent. Future job opportunities in Asia will be plentiful, especially for people who can speak a local language.

Exhibition Organizer Side

The industry is comprised of the show organizers who create and manage the exhibitions, and suppliers who provide products and services to support the exhibitions. Suppliers that serve exhibitions include convention centers and other exhibition facilities, hotels, housing and registration service providers, transportation companies, official services contractors, audio-visual companies, technology companies and specialized advertising and insurance agencies. Some industry professionals began their careers in the industry as suppliers, gaining valuable experience, and then moved into a position as an exhibition organizer. But the reverse is also true; it is possible to enter the industry as a show organizer, and then move to the supplier side.

Exhibitor Side

There are also jobs within the companies who exhibit at shows. Common job titles often include the words marketing/ communications/advertising manager, specialist, or administrator. These people, depending on their positions within the company, may manage tradeshow logistics and operations, handle the advertising or administer the public relations programs for a few or a large number of events. They may be involved in setting strategy, determining which events they are going to exhibit in, and monitoring budgets and developing methods for determining the return on investment resulting from their participation in all marketing channels.

Other possible positions in an exhibiting company may include people who have operational and logistical responsibilities. Individuals in these positions may provide input into developing strategy, organizing pre-show sessions or post-show meetings, planning special events, supervising the booth set-up on site, attending and working the event.

The detail work of managing and implementing an organization's exhibiting program requires someone who is very detail-oriented, and also has the ability to work with outside vendors. Individuals in these positions are responsible for working with freight companies and service contractors, keeping track of where their exhibit booth(s) may be at any given time, making sure the booth will arrive on time, ensuring that all the collateral and promotional giveaways arrive on time, ordering furniture and carpet, telephone lines or Internet access, ordering refreshments, scheduling staff and training them to work the booth. Some organizations may participate in 50 events in one year, resulting in a lot of travel!

Supplier Side

There are many other paths to take when beginning a career in the exhibition industry, including gaining valuable experience with event registration companies, convention centers, local convention and visitor bureaus, and hotels. Hotels often have entry level positions that require no previous experience in the business and often promote from within. For example, one prominent hotel executive started her career as a secretary in the catering department of a large hotel and rose through the ranks.

Official services contractors provide exhibition management and exhibitors with a wide range of services. In addition to designing and setting up the show floor, the official services contractor coordinates all the services provided to exhibitors, including pipe and drape and carpeting, and coordinates move-in and move-out procedures. They may also provide the signage, installation and dismantling of booths, and work with labor unions in the US to provide the labor for setting it all up.

Because every event usually has an official services contractor, there are many entry level opportunities for people in sales, account management and operations. Some common titles include operations director/manager, account executive, exhibit service manager, sales director/manager. Positions with a service contractor, as with most suppliers, generally require a moderate amount of travel.

What Skills Does It Take?

Opportunities abound for persons seeking a dynamic and challenging career in the exhibition and event industry. Employers are looking for individuals who are enthusiastic, creative, have a good attitude, and are team players. Having an entrepreneurial mindset – the ability and interest to constantly look for opportunities in the marketplace for the organization – is also helpful.

By their very nature, all jobs in the exhibition industry require that the people employed in the industry:

• be detail-oriented

- have the ability to develop and follow timelines
- be able to effectively manage multiple tasks
- be customer-focused
- be enthusiastic
- have a good attitude and "can-do" spirit
- be team-oriented.

It would be unrealistic, however, to expect that everyone on staff will have all the key characteristics; that is why team orientation is so important throughout the exhibition industry. Each person on the team will have his or her own unique set of skills and characteristics and complement someone else's. Understanding that someone is really good at analyzing the details, but may not be very good at interacting with customers, is what makes a team effective.

Sales positions often provide a way for college graduates with degrees in business-related disciplines to gain entrance into an organization that produces exhibitions. People with good selling skills are always in high demand. A person who sells the exhibit booths for events must have a good telephone voice, be enthusiastic, able to understand and articulate the value proposition to exhibitors, build relationships with exhibitors, have a good customer service focus and be able to close a sale.

Marketing majors are also in demand, with the most important skill set being the ability to create and implement a marketing strategy. Marketing staffs also need to be able to understand targeted and one-on-one marketing, as well as be able to keep abreast of new advancements and how people want to receive information. As technology advances, blogs, podcasts, and other methods of digital marketing will become outdated, and new ones will take their place. After entering the job market in a marketing assistant position, and learning as much as possible about a specific exhibition, the industry it is in, and the marketplace it represents, new opportunities will become available.

Advancing to an exhibition director or group exhibition director position requires an advanced set of knowledge and skills. These positions usually direct and manage the support staff, and the event itself. In addition to having the ability to see the "big picture" as well as the minutiae, the director must have a positive attitude, outstanding communication skills, and the flexibility to effectively supervise and motivate his or her team to produce an outstanding event. Although the director needs to be strong and assertive, it is still important to be open to discussing issues, thoughts and new ideas. The director also needs to be able to think and act quickly, if necessary, and communicate effectively in difficult situations, such as when an exhibitor is not pleased with the customer service, has a problem on site, or expresses displeasure with the outcome of their participation in the show itself. The key to a good show director is having business skills such as communication and creativity, along with the ability to analyze long term opportunities and threats to the event.

How Much Does It Pay?

The value of a college degree is documented in *Expo Magazine's* 2005 biennial salary survey for the US. The sixth such survey sponsored by *Expo Magazine*, the study revealed that individuals with a college degree earn 12 percent more than those with no degree, and persons holding an advanced degree earn 20 percent more than those with only a four-year degree.

Salaries for jobs on the exhibition organizer side of the industry vary depending on a variety of factors, including geographic location, organization type (corporate show producer, independent show producer, and not-for-profit association show producer), industry served, size of show and revenue generated, years of experience, gender, and job title.

As might be expected, independent show producers tend to earn a higher salary and make larger bonuses than the not-for-profit association show organizers, given the fact that salaries for those working for associations tend to lag behind market. The gender gap still exists with men earning 41.5 percent more than females. Experience plays a big part of earnings, with the median salary for persons with less than three years of experience earning a median salary of $40,000. However, salaries increased 44 percent during the first ten years in the industry, and 51.9 percent over the next ten years.

For people entering the job market through an exhibiting company, the same salary variables hold true as for the exhibition organizer. Bonuses tied to performance are used by most exhibiting companies, regardless of whether the person is in a sales, marketing, or operations position. Bonuses are a good way for companies to reward employees beyond merit increases, and can be motivate staff to perform at even high levels.

Where to Look

Many of the major associations have job boards on their Web sites, with positions listed ranging from entry level to experienced mid-management level positions. Many also list opportunities for internships to obtain hands-on experience, and to help determine if the exhibition and event industry is a good fit for the job-seeker.

Finding a job in the exhibition industry is just like any other industry. A good place to start is to review the professional certification programs offered by each organization.

Most have student membership rates and student chapters. Get involved. Join one or more, and become engaged in the work of the association. Sixty to 70 percent of all jobs are found by networking. Once employed by an organization, keep the following thoughts in mind:

- Salary surveys indicate that people working toward or completing an advanced degree earn more money.
- Organizations will reward employees with a higher salary or a bonus for attaining professional certifications.

In fact, many employers will view advanced degrees and professional certifications as professional development, and may cover all or part of the expense.

Why Join Professional Organizations?

Although knowledge and credentials will go a long way toward getting into the exhibition industry, joining an association will provide access to a lifetime of learning and leadership skills. It can also aid in the hiring process by providing networking connections with influencers and decision-makers. Finding a job is made a lot easier if connections and relationships are made. IAEM (International Association for Exhibition Management), PCMA (Professional Convention Management Association), ESCA (Exhibitor Services and Contractor Association), DMAI (Destination Marketing Association International), and ASAE (American Society of Association Executives) are some of the key organizations touching on the exhibition industry.

Section 1: Overview

SUMMARY

For thousands of people worldwide, a career in the exhibition industry provides opportunities that other more traditional business careers do not provide. Planning, producing and selling products and services relating to exhibitions provides endless opportunities to learn about new industries and products, to meet new people, to travel to new places and to confront new challenges and gain new skills. There are many routes to the top for the enthusiastic and ambitious person in the exhibition industry.

QUESTIONS FOR DISCUSSION

① Do you think employers should value degrees and professional certifications more than life experience?

② What would be the absolute best job you could imagine in the exhibition industry?

③ What might be the very first step in getting to your dream job?

Chapter 3
Defining Exhibitions

"Expositions are the timekeepers of progress. They record the world's advancement. They stimulate the energy, enterprise and intellect of the people, and quicken human genius. They go into the home. They broaden and brighten the daily life of the people. They open mighty storehouses of information to the student. Every exposition, great or small, has helped this onward step"

– President William McKinley, 1901

Section I: Overview

IN THIS CHAPTER YOU WILL LEARN
- About the CEIR Census of the exhibition industry
- Various types of exhibitions
- Three interdependent components of an exhibition
- Why attendees and exhibitors go to exhibitions

INTRODUCTION

As the exhibition industry has grown, the demand for specialists certified in all aspects of the creation, organization and production of exhibitions has also increased. Today, this area of specialization is a full-fledged profession, whose credentialed practitioners are called show organizers, show managers, and exhibition managers. These managers possess a flair for creativity, a passion for excellence, and a showman's heart, but most of these professionals will tell you that their greatest strength lies in being knowledgeable, flexible generalists with gamblers' instincts.

CONTRIBUTOR

Doug Ducate, President & CEO, Center for Exhibition Industry Research; Sandy Morrow, PhD, Editor, 2nd Edition, Art of the Show

The social, cultural and economic impact of exhibitions is far greater than was ever imagined by McKinley in 1901 as mentioned in the quote that begins this chapter. The Center for Exhibition Industry Research (CEIR) is continually updating their estimate of the scope of the industry. CEIR estimates that the total number of exhibitions held each year around the world is between 25,000 and 30,000, with the combined US and Canadian total representing 50 percent of the global total.

Exhibitions have come to mean many things to many people. They are often called tradeshows, exhibitions, trade fairs, expos, public shows, and of course, exhibitions. The term "exhibition" generally covers all types of events that bring buyers and sellers together, and is the term that is recognized globally. These events are created specifically for the purpose of displaying and selling goods to end users in a particular market segment, and they all share a common purpose: to provide a time-sensitive, temporary marketing environment where the buyer comes to the seller.

In 1994, the Trade Show Bureau (TSB) changed its name to the Center for Exhibition Industry Research (CEIR). CEIR continued to conduct and publish research to support its parallel mission of promoting the use of exhibitions to bring products to market. By the end of the 20th century, exhibitions were second only to print advertising in domestic marketing expenditures. It was that growth that prompted CEIR to undertake two related projects to quantify the US exhibition industry.

In 1999, CEIR commissioned the first census of the industry. The Census set out to identify the number of exhibitions held that year in the United States and Canada. It was published by CEIR in July 2001.

The process of garnering support for the project included the necessary step of defining what was to be counted. Twelve industry associations participated in that process. In the end, they all agreed that for purposes of the survey, an exhibition would be defined as an event with ten or more participating companies comprised of more than 3,000 net square feet of exhibit space. Business-to-business exhibitions are those produced primarily for a business audience, or for buyers of the goods and services being displayed. They usually are not open to the public. Business-to-consumer events (also known as consumer or public shows, or "gated" events) are open to the public. An admission fee may or may not be charged.

The tables that follow present some of the information revealed by the first Census.

The original plan called for updating the CEIR Census in ten years. The tragic events of September 11, 2001, and some of the unrelated challenges that followed – such as the continuing recession and the SARS epidemic – had a significant negative impact on business throughout the world. Industry consolidations and other major factors cast doubt on the continued reliability of the 2000 Census. As a result, CEIR updated the Census in 2005. The following data relates to Census II.

U.S. & Canada Totals

Number of Events: 14,124

By Type of Venue	Number	Percent
Exhibition/Convention Center	6,769	48%
Hotel	4,483	32%
Conference Ctr/Other/Not Classified	2,871	20%

Event Venues

- ■ Exhibition/Convention Center
- ■ Hotel
- ▨ Conf Ctr/Other/Not Classified

Net Square Feet of Exhibit Space*:	3,000-9,999	10,000-24,999	25,000-49,999	50,000-99,999	100,000+	All Sizes
Number of Events	5,524	4,122	2,054	1,230	1,194	14,124
Percentage of Events	39%	29%	15%	9%	8%	NA
Average Net Square Feet	5,433	14,669	33,358	65,677	250,168	37,900

* Includes estimates.

Total for U.S. & Canada		
Measurement	N	Total
Net Square Feet	14,124	535,294,876
Number of Exhibiting Companies	14,124	1,616,791

Note: N for the Total for U.S. & Canada is the number of events in U.S. & Canada, from which totals were projected.

Event Orientation

- ▨ Business-to-Business
- ■ Business-to-Consumer

Events by Month*

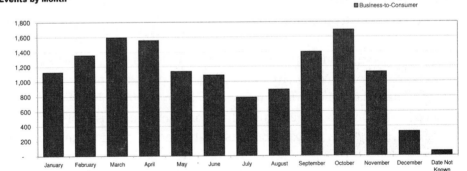

* Events classified by start date.

The companion product to the CEIR Census is the CEIR Index. Unlike the Census, which is admittedly a snapshot in time, the Index was designed to be a tool to measure continuing changes in four industry metrics for the business-to-business events, creating an exhibition industry-specific version of the Dow Jones®. Those four metrics are:

- Net square feet of space sold
- The number of exhibiting companies

- Professional or qualified attendance
- Revenue

In order to have enough history to clearly identify trends, data collection that began in 2000 was not published until 2004. The Index is published quarterly to compare quarter over quarter results, and to track actual growth. Data is published for the Industry as a whole, then divided into eleven (11) Industry Segments. The following tables illustrate the Index data.

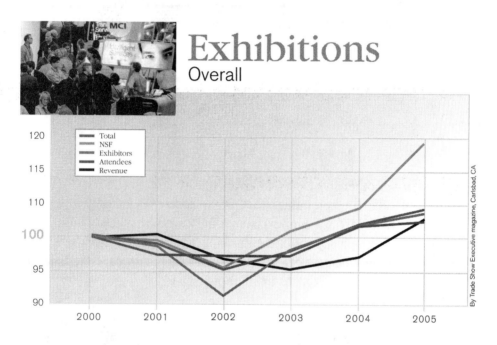

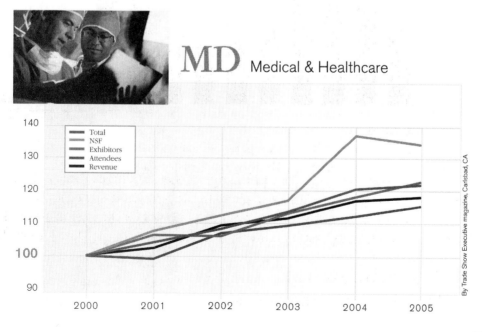

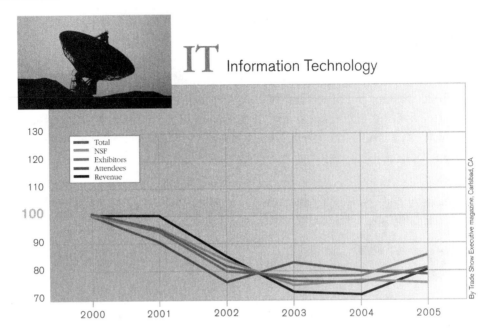

IT Information Technology

By Trade Show Executive magazine, Carlsbad, CA

There is not another industry that rivals the exhibition industry in terms of the number of different companies that organize events. Some two-thirds of the exhibitions held in the US and Canada are owned by associations, with most associations producing only one exhibition a year. The largest single organizer controls less than 4 percent of the market. This makes the task of doing something as simple as conducting a census much more difficult.

On a global basis, the task is even more daunting. Definitions vary among organizers and countries. And while it is relatively easy to convert square feet to square meters, it is much more difficult to agree upon what qualifies an attendee as a legitimate buying influence, and who can validate the published numbers. The *Union Des Fiores Internationales* (UFI), a Paris-based organization that serves fairground owners and trade fair operators around the world, is undertaking such an effort using the CEIR template.

The Exhibition by Many Names

In North America, exhibitions are generally categorized according to the markets they are created to serve. Exhibitions have historically been placed in six major categories: industrial, business-to-business, health care, scientific and engineering, consumer and international. *The Tradeshow Week Data Book* uses an industry classification system as follows: medical and health care; computer and computer applications; home furnishings and interior design; sporting goods and recreation; education, building and construction; engineering; landscaping and garden supplies; telecommunications; and industrial. For purposes of our discussions, exhibitions will be generally classified as trade (business-to-business), consumer, combined and international.

EXHIBITION

1. An event at which products and services are displayed. The primary activity of attendees is visiting exhibits on the show floor. These events focus primarily on business-to-business (B2B) relationships.

2. Display of products or promotional material for the purposes of public relations, sales and/or marketing. See TRADE SHOW. See Also CONSUMER SHOW, GATE SHOW, PUBLIC SHOW.

TRADE SHOW

An exhibition of products and/or services held for members of a common or related industry. Not open to the general public. See EXHIBITION. Compare With GATE SHOW, PUBLIC SHOW, CONSUMER SHOW.

EXHIBITION

See Exhibition.

GATE SHOW

Exhibition open to the public usually requiring an entrance fee. See CONSUMER SHOW. See Also PUBLIC SHOW. Compare With TRADE SHOW.

CONSUMER SHOW

Exhibition that is open to the public, usually requiring an entrance fee. See EXHIBITION. See Also GATE SHOW, PUBLIC SHOW. Compare With TRADE SHOW.

Tradeshows

Tradeshows or business-to-business exhibitions may encompass all ten classifications of exhibitions. Trade exhibitions do have certain distinguishing characteristics that set them apart from consumer or combined exhibitions. The exhibitor is typically a manufacturer or distributor of products or services specific or complementary to those industries. The typical buyer is an end user within the industry segment hosting the exhibition. Attendance is restricted to these buyers, and is often by invitation only. Business credentials or pre-registration are usually required to qualify the buyer as a legitimate member of the trade or industry. An access or registration fee may also have to be paid prior to admission to the event.

In other words, not just anyone can attend a trade exhibition. Trade exhibitions may be as short as a single day or as long as seven to ten days, depending on the markets being served. Some are held semi-annually. Most are held annually, a few biennially. Some large-scale industrial exhibitions are held once every three to seven years. Many trade-only exhibitions have also become a source of professional education for business attendees. Trade-only exhibitions make up approximately 51 percent of the exhibitions produced in the US.

Consumer Exhibitions

Consumer exhibitions are exhibitions that are open to the general public. They represent an expanding marketing opportunity for consumer-based companies. Exhibitors are typically retail outlets or manufacturers looking to bring their goods and services directly to the end user. Consumer exhibitions play a prominent role in consumer product marketing. In fact, many companies use consumer exhibitions as a testing ground for new products and a forum for expanding positive public relations efforts. Based on industry classifications, consumer exhibitions include home furnishing and interior design; sporting goods and recreation; landscape and garden supplies; education, computer and computer applications; automobile exhibitions, and wellness and health care events, among many others.

Attendance at consumer exhibitions is not usually restricted, nor is a registration fee required. However, an entrance or gate fee is often charged. Consumer exhibitions are sometimes also referred to as gate shows or public shows. Like their trade counterparts, consumer exhibitions are now offering educational programming as a part of their overall package. Home and Garden and Consumer Electronic shows have played a leading role in offering educational seminars to the paying public. Consumer exhibitions comprise approximately 14 percent of the exhibitions produced in the US.

Reprinted with special permission of King Features Syndicate.

Combined or Mixed Exhibitions

A combined or mixed exhibition is a combination of trade and public shows. This is an exhibition that is open both to the trade and to the public. Exhibitors are typically manufacturers or distributors. The typical trade buyer is an end user within the targeted industry segment. The public attendee may be a small business owner buying at wholesale, or a member of the general public. Sometimes, the hours available to each attendee type differ, allowing trade buyers the opportunity to investigate products and make buying decisions without the pressure of potential customers knowing the wholesale cost of goods. In the consumer electronics field, the buying hours are the same for both.

To accommodate the diverse needs of a mixed audience, many exhibitors, especially manufacturers, will have resellers or retail vendors within their exhibits to service the ultimate end user – the consumer. Combined shows make up 35 percent of exhibitions produced, and this number is expected to increase in the next decade.

International Exhibitions

International exhibitions are more commonly known as trade fairs, and usually take place outside the US. Historically, trade fairs have been the primary marketing medium of exporting countries. Initially, trade fairs were horizontal in their organization, with various products and services in specified industry groupings. A vertical organization is more commonplace today, with the exhibits being confined to one industry or a specialized segment of a specific industry. Attendance at trade fairs tends to parallel that of trade exhibitions. Buyers are usually business members of an industry, and often must be pre-qualified to attend the fair.

International trade fairs represent a cost-effective and efficient way of getting US-made goods into the global marketplace. US companies are increasingly recognizing the marketing opportunities international trade fairs represent.

Photo courtesy of Regent Exhibitions Ltd 2006

Interdependence of the Buyer, Seller and Organizer

We have identified three major groups in our discussion of trade exhibitions so far: the buyer (exhibition attendees), the seller (product suppliers and exhibitors) and the organizer (the individual or corporation who puts the exhibition together). Each of these groups brings a unique perspective to the world of exhibitions. More importantly, the relationship among the three groups is one of interdependence. Without any one piece of this triangle, the exhibition cannot happen. An exhibition cannot function with only two of the three. All are needed to provide the balance and harmony necessary to create an exhibition.

The Buyer

William McKinley called exhibitions the timekeepers of progress. The modern day exhibition is not only a timekeeper of progress, it is the harbinger of change. Nowhere is change more constant than in the product and service mix presented at exhibitions. As technology moves at an ever-quickening pace, the exhibition continues to be a primary marketing medium used to bring new and innovative ideas to end users. In spite of the Internet, Web brochures and email alerts, attendees still view exhibitions as one of the environments where they can view change in action and in person.

Attendees (also called buyers) come to exhibitions expecting to see new solutions. They expect to learn how new ideas will make their lives easier, improve on-the-job efficiency and solve problems. They and the organizations that send them to the event expect innovations that will lead to cost-effective production methods back home. Moreover, attendees have come to view exhibitions as a way to view the changing world within a safe, microcosmic environment, and decide whether or not they are ready to include these changes in their business and personal lives.

Reprinted with special permission of King Features Syndicate.

The Seller

Without attendees, there would be no exhibition. Conversely, without sellers (also called exhibitors) there would be nothing for attendees to see.

From the exhibitor's perspective, an exhibition provides the ideal environment to present new products. It represents a three-dimensional environment where a product's features can be demonstrated in real time to as wide or as narrow an audience as is desired. The concept of being able to bring the product to the end user, and to show how it works via people-to-people interaction, is a critical thread that runs through the heart of the exhibition industry.

The exhibition provides the opportunity for increased commerce and the inherent promise of sales. Exhibitors set up displays for the express purpose of advancing their businesses, and they usually won't return unless they get results. Exhibitions offer an effective and efficient way to promote buying by the targeted end user.

Exhibitions afford the opportunity to explore and attain competitive information and advantage, giving exhibitors a way to benchmark themselves against others in their field. The exhibition environment is the ideal medium in which to learn about a competitor's products, how they market and gain market share, and to compare efforts at a grassroots level.

Another way exhibitors use exhibitions is as a way to stay in touch with existing clients, as well as to develop new relationships. An exhibition is the most cost-effective medium available for bringing buyer and seller together. The manner in which business is done on the exhibition floor provides the opportunity to talk one-on-one with clients, to aid in client problem solving and to gain immediate and personal feedback for players in the organization who do not normally have direct contact with their clients and customers.

The Organizer

Seen from the organizer's perspective, an exhibition usually represents two things. The first, and perhaps most obvious, is a source of revenue. Depending on the type of ownership, the revenue generated serves either as additional funding to finance various other activities, as is the case with most association-owned exhibitions ("nonprofit" organizers); or as a means of adding profit to the bottom line, as is the case with private-owned exhibitions ("for-profit" organizers). Regardless of the status of the organizer, the bottom line is crucial.

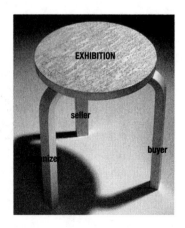

The second and perhaps less obvious rationale for hosting exhibitions from the organizer's point of view, lies in the challenge of creating a thriving temporary marketplace that has significant impact on a particular segment of an industry. Many exhibition managers thrive on the challenge of identifying a void in the marketplace and creating an exhibition to fill that void. The successful exhibition organizer recognizes the void before the competition does, and is first out of the gate with a totally new venue or a "spin-off" of an existing exhibition.

If two competing exhibitions are launched at the same time, it is not necessarily the larger exhibition or the bigger company that wins market share. Successful exhibitions are run by exhibition managers who skillfully combine technology, market savvy and the needs of all the players – attendees, exhibitors, and organizers alike – into a single successful and memorable event.

SUMMARY

Although there are many names for the variety of events that bring buyers and sellers together, and many reasons for their success, together they comprise a significant sector of the economy. As the industry has grown, an entire profession has come into being based on the expertise and knowledge it takes to put these exhibitions together, and this textbook is your key to acquiring that knowledge.

QUESTIONS FOR DISCUSSION

① What was the most recent exhibition event you attended and what was your primary reason for attending?

② Why do buyers prefer exhibitions to online purchasing?

③ Why do you think the exhibition industry is sometimes referred to as "the invisible industry"?

Chapter 4
A History of Exhibitions

"Gentlemen, the Exposition of 1851 is to give us a true test and a living picture of the point of development at which the whole of mankind has arrived..."

– Albert, Prince Consort, 1851

Section I: Overview

IN THIS CHAPTER YOU WILL LEARN
- How exhibitions started and what they have in common
- Why the Crystal Palace and the Eiffel Tower were constructed
- What still-existing US association mounted the first US convention
- Why the industry grew so dramatically in the 20th century
- Some of the history of exhibitions in China.

INTRODUCTION

Fairs and Expositions are but one of the many types of events that have evolved from one of the basic functions of humanity: the buying and selling of goods and services. In fact, the modern exhibition isn't all that different from local trade fairs which have been occurring in all cultures since ancient times. The modern exhibition shares roots with the many Fairs and Expositions of all types that have developed over the centuries. Although there were dire warnings in the late 20th century that exhibitions would become obsolete with the advent of technology, exhibitions continue to thrive because they meet an essential human need to interact, often called "face to face" marketing.

CONTRIBUTORS ON EURO-AMERICAN HISTORY

Robert Dallmeyer, President, RD International and Doug Ducate, President and CEO of Center for Exhibition Research (CEIR)

CONTRIBUTORS ON CHINESE EXHIBITION HISTORY

Mr. Zhao Weiping, General Manager, Messe Frankfurt (Shanghai) Co., Ltd.; Translated by Liu Zhiyong, Deputy Secretary General, CAEC; Edited and revised by Chen Ruowei, Chairman, CAEC

Throughout recorded history, whenever and wherever goods and products were conceived and produced, some variety of what we today call an exhibition was initiated to bring buyers and sellers together for mutual benefit. The Egyptian, Greek, and Roman marketplaces were the first examples. In fact, trade fairs were mentioned twice in the Bible's Old Testament.

These fairs became commonplace in the European Middle Ages. They featured agricultural products, arts and crafts, and hand-made specialties. Churches used them to celebrate religious holidays and liturgical seasons. Several European countries, including Germany and France, claim to have hosted the first western trade fairs. Records show that Leipzig had a fair in 1165. In 1259, Cologne began holding trade fairs twice each year, and the Champagne region of France hosted a major fair during the same period. Frankfurt's Book Fair, which is still held today, became famous following Gutenberg's invention of the movable type letterpress in 1445. An historical anecdote from 1530 finds the intellectual Erasmus of Rotterdam complaining about his need to meet publishing deadlines for an upcoming Frankfurt Book Fair, proving some things never change.

During the European Renaissance when goods were still made by hand, examples of handicrafts were presented in "Sample Fairs," where orders were taken for later delivery. Daniel Defoe, author of Robinson Crusoe, wrote an essay about attending a fabric fair in the early 1700s.

Exhibitions in Europe gained prominence during the Industrial Revolution. Mass production of goods in the 1750s gave birth to capitalism, as well as intense competition to find buyers for these new goods. Improved transportation enabled more buyers and sellers to attend exhibitions in diverse geographic areas, which were generally held in or around transportation hubs.

In 1798, the newly-formed French Republic mounted an exhibition of clocks, ceramics, chemical products, and other manufactured goods. These were displayed in temporary buildings constructed along the Seine. As in certain tradeshows today, nothing was for sale at the event, and the main purpose was to boast of French product superiority, which the makers no doubt hoped would lead to future sales.

The 19th Century

Meanwhile in the US, the first recorded fair was in Pittsfield, Massachusetts in 1814. The Berkshire Agricultural Society hosted a showcase of agricultural and regional products, particularly the handicrafts and furniture of the local Shaker religious group.

London's Great Exhibition of 1851 was created to showcase Great Britain's industrial, military, and economic superiority. Queen Victoria's German husband and Consort Prince Albert – a quote from whom appears at the beginning of this chapter – was the genius behind the event, held in London's Hyde Park in a specially designed "Crystal Palace." Made of over one million feet of glass and containing over 13,000 exhibits from around the world, this huge, iron-framed structure was considered the first modern exhibition facility. More than six million people attended, making it so profitable that it provided the initial funding for several current London landmarks including Albert Hall, the Science Museum, the Natural History Museum, and the Victoria and Albert Museum.

The Exhibition of the Industry of All Nations opened in New York City two years after the event in London with its own Crystal Palace – a somewhat smaller version – housing several thousand exhibits. It was also a highly successful event.

Interestingly, in the 1980's a real estate developer named Trammel Crow built a replica of the Crystal Palace in Dallas, Texas, to house wholesale showrooms and exhibitions, primarily in the hi-tech industry.

In 1876, The International Exhibition of Arts, Manufactures and Products of the Soil and Mine opened in Philadelphia. This celebration of the United States' 100th anniversary showcased American intellectual and material progress through successes in science, industry, and culture. It introduced Alexander Graham Bell's latest invention, the telephone.

Exposition Universelle de 1889 in Paris

The Typewriter Show was launched in Madison Square Garden in 1903. One of the hidden purposes of the exhibition was to prove that women could operate this new invention, a fact that business and industry leaders (all male) found hard to believe. One of the first exhibitors to sign up for the exhibition was a desk manufacturer, who cannily realized that these new typewriters had to be placed on something to be operated. Renamed The Business Show in 1908, the exhibition was later managed by the Business Equipment Manufacturers Association as the BEMA Show.

Four years after the Soil and Mine Show, the Professional Photographers of America held its first convention with exhibits in Chicago, the first exhibition by a founding member of the International Association of Exhibition Managers (IAEM). Two hundred attended and five exhibited, including George Eastman of Kodak.

To celebrate their Revolution's centennial, the French produced the *Exposition Universelle de 1889* in Paris. It showcased their industrial and cultural achievements, with one central attraction: the Eiffel Tower. Intended as a temporary structure with no other purpose than to present the engineering genius of Alexander Eiffel, this marvel of iron was hailed as the world's tallest structure. More than 80 other structures surrounded the Tower on the *Champ de Mars*. The most impressive was the *Galerie des Machines*, a 1,452-foot-long structure with the largest open floor area of any building ever constructed, designed to showcase the latest heavy power machines and technology. Lit by new electric lights, it had overhead traveling walkways, which allowed visitors to look down on the exhibits. All the nations of Europe, South America, the United States, and the French Colonies were represented, showcasing their cultural specialties and industrial achievements. The French government commissioned August Rodin to create his famous sculpture, The Kiss, for the event.

The decorative style Art Deco was derived from the title of the *Exposition Art Decoratifs et Industriels Modernes* held in Paris, France in 1928. It was not so much a design movement, but rather a shared approach to styling. The interplay of geometric forms, abstract patterns of zigzags, chevrons and sunbursts, rendered in brilliant colors, as well as the use of bronze, ivory and ebony, were some of its characteristics. It was inspired by non-Western art, particularly that of Africa and Egypt, which was enjoying a swell of popularity after the discovery in 1922 of Tutankhamun's tomb. The cubist paintings of Picasso and Braque captured the imagination of the designers, and the *l'Esprit Nouveau* pavilion, designed by Swiss architect le Corbusier; was touted as the model of Modernism.

As the Gay Nineties brought the century to a close, 54 cities on every continent had hosted major exhibitions. The importance of exhibitions in the economic growth of nations and industries was firmly established. This would serve as a launch pad for the startling advances about to take place in the 20th century.

The 20th Century

In 1895, some 15 years after the Photographers Association's exhibition, a Detroit journalist proposed that various businesses join together to attract exhibition business to Detroit in much the same manner as the Chamber of Commerce. After the very successful World's Fair in St. Louis in 1904, the St. Louis Convention Bureau was formed. Likewise, following the Democratic National Convention in Denver in 1909, the Denver Convention Bureau was launched.

By 1914, approximately 15 cities had created agencies to attract convention business to their cities. They formed the National Association of Convention Bureaus in 1914. It is interesting to note that the word "visitor" was not added to the names until the 1970s. It is not a coincidence that NACB was created the same year Henry Ford opened the first assembly line manufacturing plant in the world that led to making the automobile affordable for the middle class. A more mobile America portended great things for a national convention market.

The Exposition: "A Timekeeper of Progress"

1925 Society of Automotive Engineers Trade Show, New York. Photo courtesy of Art Weldy, Exposition Planning + Production, Inc., Pittsburgh, PA.

1950's Christmas Gift & Hobby Show, Indianapolis. Photo courtesy Patrick Buchen, CEM.

After a pause during World War I, the US convention business took off in the "Roaring 20s." For the most part, these events were large meetings which, like political conventions, were primarily held in hotels. In 1927, however, Minneapolis built an "Auditorium" to host these large events. Kansas City followed soon after, opening the Kansas City Municipal Auditorium in 1935.

The Exposition: Technology's Showplace

BREDE INC. — 1927
MINNESOTA DENTAL

Photo courtesy Brede Exposition Services, Minneapolis, MN.

Emerging technologies have always found a ready home at expositions. Advances in technology are evidenced in these photographs. Photo courtesy of Einzig Photography, New York, NY.

Another significant event occurred in 1927 that was an important part of the development of the US exhibition business. The Palmer House Hotel in Chicago was opened, offering, in addition to the traditional guest rooms and meeting space, two floors of dedicated show rooms. These rooms were leased to traveling salesmen, enabling them to invite their customers to come to them to view products instead of them going to each customer. The hotel provided services such as electrical power, draped tables, food and beverage, nightly cleaning, security services and bell staff to carry the merchandise to be displayed to and from the room. That model was replicated by facilities and contractors some 40 years later when the first convention centers were built.

The Exhibition: A History Lesson in Marketing

1993 Frankfort Auto Show. Photo courtesy Kelsey-Hayes, Livonia, MI.

The Great Depression took its toll on the US convention business during the 1930s, and World War II further depressed the meetings market. In fact, the industry did not begin to recover until well after World War II ended in 1946. When it finally did begin to recover, meeting organizers suddenly had to compete with returning soldiers for hotel rooms in virtually every major city.

The displacement of conventions led to a summit meeting of four industry associations: the IACVB (International Association of Convention & Visitor Bureaus; now called The Destination Marketing Association), ASAE (American Society of Association Executives), AH&MA (American Hotel & Motel Association, now called American Hotel & Lodging Association), and HSMA (Hotel Sales & Marketing Association). The Convention Liaison Council was formed soon thereafter, and producing the Group Room Booking Model and the Housing Reservation Service – both under the aegis of IACB. That was the early beginning of a national meetings market and targeted sales campaigns by hotels and local convention & visitor bureaus.

Another significant event followed World War II when, in 1947, then Secretary of State George C. Marshall introduced the Marshall Plan to rebuild Europe. This commitment of some $20 billion had a caveat that American-made goods would be bought and shipped on American flag vessels to Europe. This had two impacts that affected the exhibition business. Some of the money was used by France, Italy, and West Germany to build Fair Grounds with exhibition centers to establish a base for future commerce. Second, Europeans got exposed to American-made products. The giant Trade Fairs held in Europe (many of which are still in existence today) became the model for the business-to-business exhibition industry in the United States.

War-torn Germany's 1947 economy was characterized by industrial ruin and chronic food shortages. However, the Marshall Plan called for Germany to become economically self-reliant as soon as possible. The British occupation authorities, working with the commander-in-chief of the American zone, organized the first *Export Messe Hannover.*

It was set up in the outskirts of the Hanover fairground in five enormous halls where aircraft wings were manufactured during the war. The fair opened on August 18th and closed on September 7th, 1947. Thirteen hundred exhibitors, with exportable post-war products bearing an official "Made in Germany" sticker, were visited by 736,000 attendees from 53 nations during those 21 days. Many buyers were flown into Hanover on military planes (both British & American), and were quartered in a nearby British transit camp at the government's expense. Almost 2,000 export agreements were signed, having a value of $31.6 million US dollars. In the ensuing years, the Hanover Fair was the symbol of Germany's economic miracle, becoming the largest trade fair in the world. Its logo, the profile of Hermes, the God of Trade, is recognized around the globe.

During the 1950's, two significant events completed the platform necessary to create a national convention market. First, the National Interstate Highway System was completed in 1956, offering a network of roadways connecting the entire country. Second, the commercial introduction of the jet airplane made short-term cross-country travel feasible.

Expositions: An Ever-evolving Industry

Photo courtesy Brede Exposition Services, Minneapolis, MN.

Signs of the Times — The evolution of the sign from an information source to an integral part of the exhibit design. Photo courtesy of Freeman, Dallas, TX.

The first convention and exhibition center designed to attract national events, McCormick Place, was opened in Chicago in 1964. First-generation "boxes with docks" like this huge building was called, began springing up in various cities that already had airlift and a reasonable inventory of hotel rooms. A Hotel Occupancy Tax (HOT) was created by various taxing entities across the country, effectively taxing visitors and dedicating the revenue to servicing the bond debt incurred to build these facilities. The facilities themselves were seen as "loss leaders," because of the economic benefit to the region that came from the money visitors spent while they were in the local area. Because these facilities allowed destinations to compete for this lucrative regional and national exhibition business, new facilities began to spring up across the United States.

Professional societies saw the enhanced value an exhibition could add to their annual meeting programs, and trade associations saw the value exhibitions offered by producing flagship events for their industries. The competition to attract attendees and sell booth space to exhibitors was keen because of the many new opportunities arising, and the market exploded overnight.

Pipe and drape has literally become the backbone of the US exhibition industry. Reportedly the brainchild of Bill Brede, founder of Brede Exposition Services, pipe and drape was created in the early 1930s for a client with a traveling pet show who needed a way to delineate exhibit booths that did not involve building expensive, labor-intensive hard wall structures. Brede's initial invention used interlocking brass railings and machine-sewn draperies. Following World War II, less expensive aluminum was substituted for the piping.

Although Brede patented his innovative method, he allowed the industry to use it for exhibitions throughout North America. This drastically reduced the time required for exhibit installation and dismantling, allowing facilities to schedule many more exhibitions during a calendar year. In effect, Bill Brede's pipe & drape invention permitted the exhibition industry to enjoy its phenomenal growth during the 20th century.

In spite of burgeoning growth and although considered by those participating to be a viable marketing alternative, conventions did not have the greatest of reputations. Convention organizers chose exotic locations to hold their events, hoping the location would attract exhibitors and attendees. Trips to exotic destinations, however, were thought to be frivolous in those days when most still took vacations by automobile, and many business people viewed them as more entertainment than business. By the mid-1970s, the previously fast-growing exhibition industry had slowed and was struggling with challenges ranging from not being considered a serious marketing endeavor, to not even showing up on marketing managers' radar screens.

Expositions: Change Agents Through Innovation

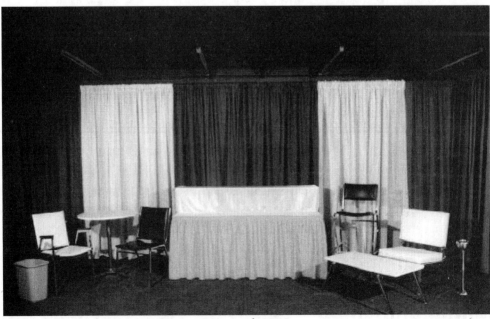

Photo courtesy Brede Exposition Services, Minneapolis, MN.

The ever-changing demands of creating a marketplace that reflects the latest in trends and technology is best exemplified on the exhibit floor where custom-designed modular displays now dominate, having replaced the standard pipe and drape display system. Photo courtesy Freeman, Dallas, TX.

In 1978, a small group of industry leaders got together and developed a strategy to combat the "entertainment versus business" image problem, and raise awareness about the exhibition industry. They asked the National Association of Exposition Managers (which is now IAEM) to create an event at which to expose their plan. The result turned out to be the largest gathering of hospitality industry associations held to date: the 1977 NAEM Annual Meeting in Las Vegas.

The idea was simple and not particularly original. The group knew that there were agencies created to promote marketing dollars being spent with their industry. Two of the largest and most well known were the Radio and Television Bureau, and the American Newspaper Bureau. The proposal was simply to create a Trade Show Bureau (TSB) to promote the use of trade exhibitions to bring products to market. The idea received enthusiastic approval, and TSB was launched.

From the outset, TSB faced a major problem. Before the organization's founding, there had been no definitive work done to document the industry, or prove the industry claims. Print media had well-established circulation audit practices, and the radio and television market had Nielson and other rating systems to document their claims of listening and viewership. TSB was faced with the daunting task of promoting the use of exhibitions, a marketing medium with no track record and no data to support marketing success. As a result, before TSB could begin to promote the industry, its first mission had to be conducting research.

Commercial publishers were also alert to the fast-growing meetings and exhibitions business, and several vertical publications were introduced to serve the market. Some of them took on the task of publishing schedules of events, and even quantifying the industry as to the number of exhibitions held each year.

In 1986, Bob Black, the publisher and founder of *Tradeshow Week* presented a paper at Cornell University that was the first scientific work designed to quantify the industry. The paper reported that there were 2,733 events with 10,000 or more net square feet of exhibit space sold. The author also suggested that there were probably another 2000 events with fewer than 10,000 net square feet. Black's work allowed the industry to move forward with a general estimate that there were some 4,000 to 5,000 events with exhibitions held each year in the United States.

Between 1986 and the end of the 20th Century, the exhibition industry in the United States flourished. By 2000, the modern industry had survived two general economic recessions in the US, and proven it was both resistant and resilient when it came to recovery.

Expositions: Then and Now

1927 Industry-only exposition.
Photo courtesy of Brede Exposition Services, Minneapolis, MN. The 1990s exposition.

Photo courtesy of Einzig Photographers, Inc., New York, NY.

Modern Times

During the late 20th century, significant changes were also taking place in the international community. The Cold War had ended, and trade was beginning to open up among countries that had previously refused to trade for political reasons. Many of the "controlled economy countries" such as China and Russia were accustomed to doing business with other countries, not companies. Most of the trade exhibitions produced in those countries were hosted events sponsored by another government. For example, China would host an exhibition of Yugoslavian or French goods. That country in return would host an exhibition of products made in China. Since these events were government sponsored and organized, the products exhibited covered a very broad range.

When China opened its doors to the United States in 1977, entrepreneurs saw many opportunities to produce events in China. However, it was not until the first US event was produced in Beijing in 1979 by the US Department of Commerce that private requests were considered. The approval process was frequently based upon the Chinese need for the products proposed to be shown. In 1981, the US-based Society of Petroleum Engineers produced an exhibition in Beijing displaying equipment used in exploring for and producing oil and gas. That event was significant in that it broke through three separate barriers simultaneously. First, it was produced by an organization instead of a government. Second, the exhibits applied to a single industry. Third, it was truly an international event with companies from ten different countries.

Section 1: Overview

During the last 25 years of the 20th century, further expansion of the international exhibition industry occurred with the advent of developing countries. As the world entered an extended period of relative peace, aid poured into countries who suffered from famine, disease, and a poor standard of living. The countries began to build their own economies, and seek improvements in the quality of life. The two early signs of a developing nation became the launch of a national airline, often with only a few aircraft, and the building of an exhibition center to welcome international events.

That model still exists today, as exhibitions continue to demonstrate that they are the fastest, most efficient way to bring products to markets. Even in countries that do not trade with one another, exhibitions are sometimes permitted to bring goods related to basic human needs such as heath care and food to market. The US exhibitions being held in Cuba are examples of this practice.

HISTORY OF EXHIBITIONS IN CHINA

The history of China's exhibitions can be traced back to the ancient bazaars held more than 2000 years ago. Originating from a religious gathering first held during the Western Zhou Dynasty (1100-771 B.C), an annual, three-day bazaar was held in the Fengchushan Village Temple Fair in the Qishan area of the present Shanxi Province.

In addition, Dadu had more than 30 bazaars during the Yuan Dynasty (1271-1368 A.D.) Now located in present-day Beijing, Zhonggulou, which means "drum-bell's tower" is the place where the prosperous bazaar in Yuan Dynasty was located.

Bazaars remained prosperous during the Ming Dynasty (1368-1644 A.D.). Regular fairs were held at local temples, including Chenghuangmiao, Longfusi, Huguosi and Baiyunguan. State-controlled bazaars were also held with the participation of nomadic tribes in the North.

When China entered into the Qing Dynasty (1644-1911 A.D.), the temples of Baitasi, Longfusi and Huguosi) had become the three most famous fair sites in Beijing. Some specialized bazaars based on the traditional model, such as the rice bazaars in Wuxi (Jiangsu Province) and Wuhu (Anhui Province), emerged. Another typical specialized bazaar was the medicine fair in Anguo (Hebei Province), which was held twice a year – once in the spring, and again in the autumn. These specialized medicine fairs represent the trade exhibition of today in its embryonic form.

In 1905, the Ministry of Industry and Commerce of the Qing Dynasty set up The National Exhibition Hall of Industrial Development at Qianmen in Beijing to showcase the industrial products from different provinces. Meanwhile, the business promotion marketplace was established for the sale of commodities.

Many regard this as the earliest exhibition in China. It was divided into various specific-use areas, including a provincial hall, textile hall, tea hall, arts & crafts hall and national defense hall. The exhibition lasted three months, and hosted over 200,000 visitors.

In 1912, in the early days of the Republic of China (1912-1949 A.D.), the Beijing government changed The National Hall of Industrial Development of Qing Dynasty at Qianmen into the "Commodities Hall." Later changed into a trade fair venue, China's earliest exhibition hall became a marketplace.

In August, 1921, the Shanghai General Chamber of Commerce set up the Commodities Display Hall. Held in the autumn once a year, the Shanghai General Chamber of Commerce held the China Pod Silk Fair in Shanghai for the first time in October of 1922. .

In 1925, Wuhan Expo was held, followed by the Sichuan Homemade Products Expo in 1928. In 1929, the Xihu (Westlake) Expo was held for the first time in Hangzhou, which was the largest scaled exhibition in China's history. In 2000, the Xihu Expo was resumed and is now held once every year. Before the Sino-Japanese war (1937-1945), some other trade fairs were also held in other parts of China.

From the 1950s to the early 1980s, except for some domestic trade fairs, the exhibitions in China were mainly solo foreign national exhibitions served for diplomatic purpose. In the mid-1980s, China's exhibition industry started to develop international tradeshows with market orientation. Especially due to the rapid development of China's economy in the past twenty years, China has become a leading market for the exhibition industry in Asia.

QUESTIONS FOR DISCUSSION

① What do you think a village fair in Medieval Europe was like? Describe who the buyers and sellers were, the types of products they offered for sale and the location of the fair.

② What do you think George Eastman (founder of Kodak) was doing when he visited the Professional Photographers Association show in 1880? What was he looking to gain from attending the exhibition?

③ Explain the benefits for a city to host a world fair? What negative impacts could it have on the city?

④ Are you surprised to hear that there is a history of exhibitions in China? Discuss.

Section I: Overview

Chapter 5
Varieties of Exhibitions

"In the business world, the rearview mirror is always clearer than the windshield."

– Warren Buffett

Section I: Overview

IN THIS CHAPTER YOU WILL LEARN

- Multiple ways exhibitions are structured and managed
- Why exhibitions are critical to many associations
- How the type of event influences the content
- Various business models for expansion of exhibitions

INTRODUCTION

It is no longer easy to classify types of exhibitions and exhibition organizers. New rules of competition, changing economic environments and other competitive forces have contributed to a blending of many of the traditional types. Some experts say show organizers will be challenged in the future to be less in competition with each other, but better positioned to fend off increasing competition among other marketing methods. This may result in even more combinations and blurring of the distinctions between types of events and ownership.

CONTRIBUTOR

Vincent Polito, Senior Vice President, Reed Exhibitions

Chapter 5 — Varieties of Exhibitions

Associations and Exhibitions

The majority of exhibitions are hosted by non-profit associations. Very often, the single biggest financial resource for any association is its own exhibition. These events (often called conventions, as they include both meetings and an exhibition) are important because they raise the capital the organization or association needs to pursue its core mission throughout the year. In some cases, associations outsource some or all of the production of the event to third-party producers. And in a few cases, an association has sold its exhibition to an independent show producer. But the majority of exhibitions produced by non-profit associations are also owned by the association. This practice allows the association to maintain its focus on the goals and initiatives that will most benefit its members.

There are associations for nearly every product group, every industry and profession and many, many other interest groups. For example, a trade association comprised of product manufacturers will host an exhibition at which its members are the exhibitors, and attempt to attract the buyers of its member's products for education as well as commerce. Depending on the industry's own cycles and other factors such as the complexity and type of products, actual sales may take place at the show in the booth itself, or much later. Some sales may not be finally confirmed until two years or more after the exhibition. Actually, when the attendees are the association members, commerce may occupy a secondary or tertiary priority to educational programming or networking. Sometimes an exhibition also gives the exhibitors opportunities to provide training to the attendees or delegates on their own products and may also take the opportunity to request certain modifications or product enhancements to the manufacturers.

In addition to bringing buyers and sellers together to do business, an association convention allows the entire membership an opportunity to get together to discuss other common issues and association tasks such as advocacy and lobbying. An association's annual meeting also allows a retrospective look at the prior year, and a "look ahead" at the issues most relevant for the coming year, giving the association an important, high-profile opportunity to set its agenda and goals for the future.

Independent or For-Profit Producers

Independent producers are for-profit companies that often design and produce exhibitions around particular market trends they have identified. In certain industries, they produce the largest and most prominent event in that industry, even when there is an association producing a competitive event. In other cases, one or more associations may sponsor an event they do not own, but for which they provide a large percentage of the content, community and commerce, and production of the exhibition is outsourced to an independent third party not affiliated with any of the sponsoring associations.

All industry events are designed to highlight important developments in the industry in question. These developments often focus around changing or evolving technologies, and a focus on new products and education can be seen as key drivers for participation. Therefore, industries with constant product innovation and evolving ways of doing business, coupled with either buying or selling groups that have a predisposition to gather as a group, tend to be fertile ground for successful events. Events where there are multiple strong competitors also provide a strong element for success.

Integrated Media Companies

A subset of for-profit producers who also produce exhibitions are integrated media companies. Through sponsorships and combined marketing efforts, industry-specific media publications can help tradeshows target a specific audience. The publication lends credibility to the event by substantiating its content, and is able to reach a larger percentage of its target market, because the addition of an exhibition offers advertisers and readers a face-to-face extension of the magazine. Brand recognition and the extension of the face-to-face aspect add to the exhibition's positive reputation by increasing its capacity to attract and maintain market share for both the publication and the exhibition.

Corporate Exhibitions and Events

Frequently, a corporate exhibition is produced as a way to gather a company's major customers. A corporate exhibition is typically an event that brings together customers and prospects around a single company's products and services. In the technology arena, this can be a "User-Group Meeting," although this concept has evolved to include the offering of additional products and services from both the corporation as well as its partners. This is favored by the corporation as a way to provide an additional intimacy and depth of engagement between a company and its partners that may not be possible at an association or independent exhibition.

Occasionally, these corporate events are held for a smaller subset of the company's customers in a "road show" format, which is really a series of small or micro-sized exhibitions spread out over a larger geographic area.

Hybrids

Each of the above three examples can be combined with one another to form its own class. For example, multiple associations may join together to produce an event. This is most effective when buying associations combine with selling associations to create a marketplace approximately once a year – more or less depending on product and association needs. Independent producers may also come together through various partnership arrangements to create marketplace environments with one another.

Companies who serve the same client base – each with a different product or service – may come together to create a corporate event. For example, if one company serves a common customer set with products, and the other with separate but related services, they may decide that a cooperatively-produced event would maximize everyone's use of time, and enhance attendee value. Similarly, corporate events often find greater success when they align themselves strategically with events produced either by independents or associations.

Franchising, Cloning and Geographic Expansion

Like any brand that is seeking to expand – McDonalds or Sheraton Hotels are two noteworthy examples – there are multiple approaches to expansion for exhibitions.

Franchising

The first is through a franchise agreement. Through a franchise agreement, a show organizer would contract to have its show's brand licensed to a franchise owner to produce the event. This could be done by way of an upfront license fee, or by negotiating the return of a percentage of revenue and/or profit made by the franchise owner's event. In either case, brand standards are developed; however, the actual production and ownership of the event lies with the franchise owner (licensee) and not the original company (licensor). In return for the fee, the licensor gives up a significant measure of control. Done well, this allows expansion without significant increase in expense. Done poorly, it can have a negative backlash to the original event.

Cloning

A frequent occurrence in the technology arena, cloning occurs when larger multinational companies or associations choose to extend their exhibitions nationally or internationally, using a "sister office" to produce the same event in another location in another country. In this case, there are usually plenty of checks and balances, but the sister companies and association affiliations needed to accomplish the cloning of an event must be of comparable scope and resources to the originators. While control over the event is maintained without adding significant additional expense when cloning, like a long-distance personal relationship, there may be challenges.

Geographic Expansion

Simple geographic expansion is a high-risk/high reward proposition. For example, imagine a company that chooses to produce an additional event in a new city, which of course means taking on all the additional expense. This could be in the form of opening a new office, or simply adding resources at the home office to produce the additional event out of town. Such a method ensures maintenance of brand standards and reliable execution, but has higher expense metrics and the disadvantage of not knowing the local "lay of the land." The advantage is that all rewards belong to the home office.

Co-locations, Partnerships and Joint Ventures

Event organizers and other industry leaders and influencers will at times produce an event together. This, too, can take on a variety of formats.

Co-location

The easiest and simplest format to explain, co-location, happens in three ways. The first occurs when two unrelated events share services at the same venue at the same time. There is no overlap and money is saved by sharing expenses. Another method of co-locating occurs when two related events that share a common or directly-related customer set join together to present one mutual exhibition. In this case, two distinct events exist, but the belief is that satisfaction of both attendees and exhibitors will increase as a result of the synergy created by the interaction of the two, distinct events. In this scenario, revenues for each event are handled separately, but the expenses are likely shared for the economies of scale reasons as in the first.

The third form of co-location looks like a single event to everyone but the show organizers. Conference programs can be jointly or separately developed, but in this case, the exhibit floor is most often a single floor with only the most subtle distinctions among the different areas – such as the use of different carpet colors in the aisles – and the attendee moves freely through the entire show. In this form of co-location, there needs to be a level of revenue and expense sharing based on either the relative size of the events or investment level.

Partnership

A partnership can be two events coming together to form a single event. While clear elements of each may be visible, there is still a seamless event floor and a single education program. For the organizers, there is likely a single Profit & Loss sheet for the event, although an actual record of expenses or revenue may be difficult to determine. In the best scenario, an exhibitor used to exhibiting at only one of the events may purchase more space as a result of the two events coming together.

Joint Venture

Joint Venture occurs when two groups come together to create a totally new exhibition. It may involve two existing exhibitions combining under a new name, or two new concepts coming together to produce a new exhibition. In either case, show organizers usually agree to split revenues based on a division of certain income elements such as conferences and exhibits, or they agree to share profits based on percentages.

Types of Content

It is also helpful to recognize that all events can be broadly classified in one of the following categories: trading, sourcing or learning.

Trading

Exhibitions that result in immediate sales activity are categorized as trading events, commonly called tradeshows. At these events, the transaction takes place at the event where an order is placed immediately, or soon thereafter. These events are often retail in nature, and are scheduled based on the buying cycle in a specific industry. For example, gift shows may be produced to showcase merchandise for retailers in preparation for the holiday season, or golf exhibitions in anticipation of the golf season. Industries that are constantly introducing new product innovations are most typically trading events.

Sourcing

Sourcing events often have longer selling cycles, and transactions may not take place as quickly. Although these events are used to accelerate the selling cycle, the actual transaction may be harder to directly link to the exhibition participation either due to the complexity of the transaction, or because of product life cycles. This exhibition experience is likely centered around comparative shopping, or the reviewing of vendors and their products without an immediate sales transaction. This presents a challenge for exhibitors looking to quantify the return on investment (ROI) metrics, because the sourcing event is harder to measure than the trading event. Many medical shows are sourcing events, and no sales are allowed in the exhibition area.

Learning

Learning events emphasize or require significant product or service education. Often existing in cooperation in markets where trading events also flourish, training and education are key components to learning events. Service and technology industries have several learning events. In some cases, a trading event will exist for the purchasers of a certain product type, and a learning event will also exist for the users of that particular product type. For example, there are several shows where owners of pizza establishments come to buy and sell, and also to learn the latest trends in making and selling pizza.

Virtual Exhibitions

Toward the end of the last century, there was some legitimate fear that the concept of virtual exhibitions would cause considerable damage to the exhibition industry. What transpired was a lot of unnecessary anxiety. The Virtual Exhibition – taking (or attempting to take) all the attributes of an actual exhibition and moving them to the desktop via online participation – has taken place with some pockets of success, but without any significant impact to date. Actually, the more successful virtual events are usually extensions of existing exhibitions, and are not stand-alones or replacements of them.

The Gourmet HOUSEWARES SHOW®

May 8-10, 2007
Orange County Convention Center
Orlando, Florida
(Part A)

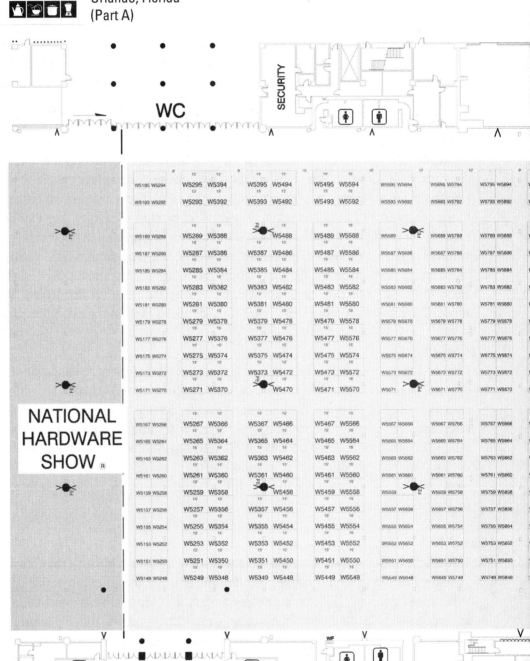

WC

SECURITY

NATIONAL HARDWARE SHOW ®

ENTRANCE

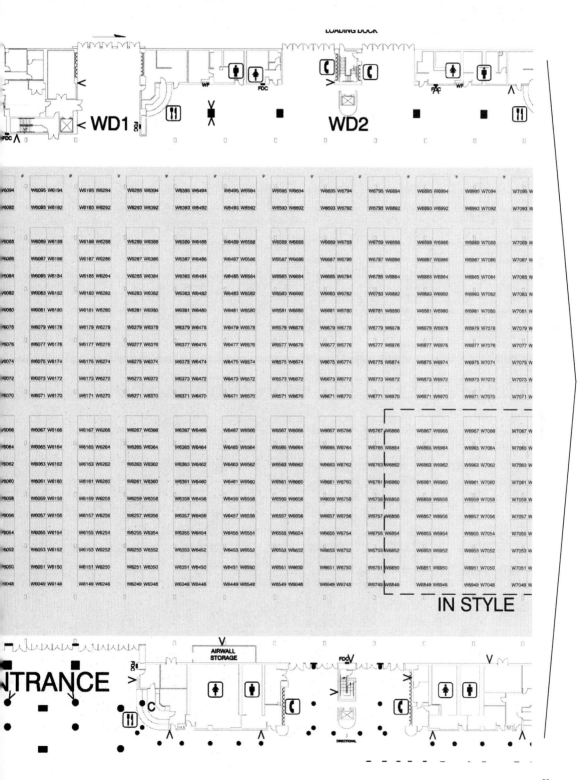

The Gourmet HOUSEWARES SHOW®

May 8-10, 2007
Orange County Convention Center
Orlando, Florida
(Part B)

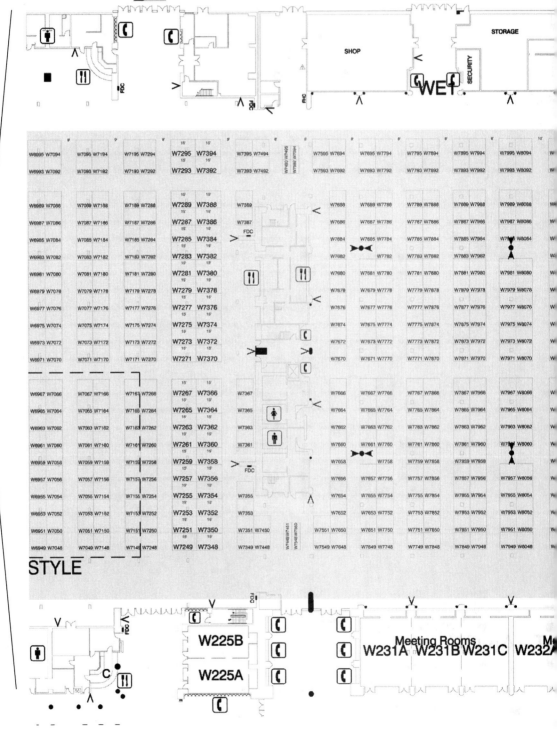

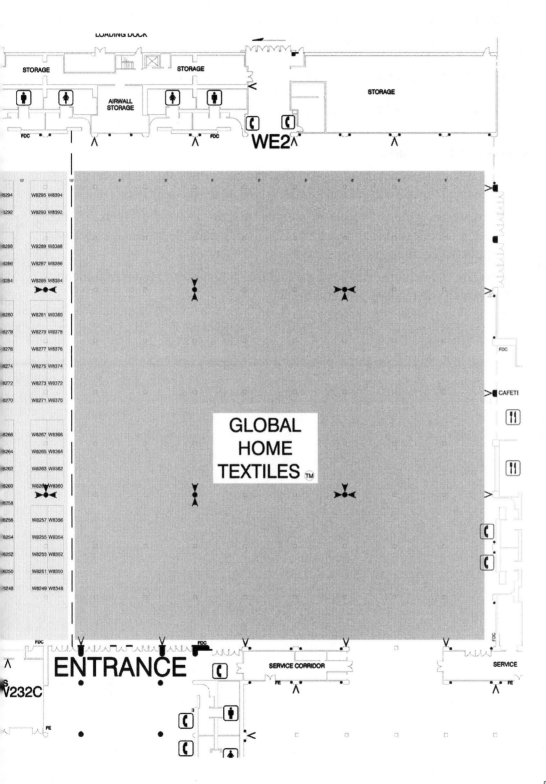

Section I: Overview

SUMMARY

While other communication vehicles of more recent vintage – the Internet, for instance – have claimed *content, community and commerce* as a rallying cry, the exhibition has long been designed around those very same principles. All event types have some blend of content, community and commerce. Exhibitions where commerce is the leading attribute are focused on transactions between buyer and seller. Events where content is the main event place a priority on education and training over any interaction between exhibitors and attendees. Events with a community focus are often built around networking activities.

QUESTIONS FOR DISCUSSION

① Why would an independent producer of tradeshows find it easier than an association to create a new exhibition focusing on an emerging trend?

② When do most consumer shows about boating occur and when do most consumer shows about skiing occur? How is this example of sales cycles similar to the example about gift shows above?

③ What are the benefits of buying a franchise? Name several types of franchises with which you regularly do business.

Chapter 6
Exhibitions Worldwide

*"The International Monetary Fund defines globalization as
"the growing economic interdependence of countries worldwide
through increasing volume and variety of cross-border transactions
in goods and services, free international capital flows,
and more rapid and widespread diffusion of technology."*
– Wikipedia

Section 1: Overview

IN THIS CHAPTER YOU WILL LEARN
- Differences in how exhibitions operate around the world
- Business models for expanding an exhibition globally
- Geographic trends in the exhibition industry

INTRODUCTION

We live in a global economy. Many of our customers – both sellers and buyers – do business globally, in one way or the other. Some manufacture in their home market and export, or manufacture in other countries to serve markets outside of their home markets. Others sell in other markets, or import from other countries to sell in their home market. Thousands of products and services crisscross the globe continuously. As our customers' industries become more global, the exhibition industry should look across borders as well in order to provide these global customers with new opportunities.

CONTRIBUTOR

Steve Sind, President and CEO, Global Event Strategies with additional input from Gerald Kallman, Sr., Managing Director, Kallman Global Consulting, and I.R. (Sandy) Angus, Chairman, Montgomery Exhibitions, Ltd.

Differences Around the World

For all outward appearances, an exhibition in Tokyo looks very similar to one in Munich or Orlando or Sao Paulo. The inscription on the header or fascia may look strange or different, but globalization has rendered all tradeshows inherently similar and familiar. However, there are still many differences in structure, philosophy and culture.

Organization

In Germany, nearly all exhibition venues are owned by quasi-government agencies. The mammoth Munich Fair Grounds is owned by the city of Munich and the State of Bavaria, with a minority interest held by the local Chamber of Commerce. Therefore, the hall owner also serves as the show organizer. In the past, these situations blocked outside organizers from renting or using the facilities, but guest events are now welcomed at all the German venues.

Culture

Cultural differences come into play particularly in Asia, where colors take on more significance, and traditions can have an impact on the success of an event. For example, at an environmental exhibition in Taiwan – in keeping with the environmental theme and to liven up the hall – the show organizer flew in a planeload of bright yellow forsythia blossoms. They were carefully arrayed throughout the hall until, on the night before opening, a local partner noted that yellow is the color of mourning in Taiwan, and the entire plan was (literally) trashed. This might also illustrate the value of having a local partner or advisor when venturing abroad! In his book *Dos and Taboos,* Roger Axtell has a wealth of good advice on these pitfalls, including how to handle visiting dignitaries who may be on hand for the ribbon-cutting, or to create some celebrity buzz for the event.

Hospitality

Hospitality of another sort is common at European shows, or where European companies are exhibiting. Although hospitality suites at nearby hotels are unknown in these cases, on-site entertaining takes on new proportions. Important guests might be offered a wide array of food and beverages, including wine, beer or other libations, all prepared on site. Hospitality "chalets" are common at European air shows and other events with large outdoor participation, such as construction equipment exhibitions. These facilities allow entertaining on a grand scale at a venue (usually an airport or air field), which is devoid of normal amenities.

Rules and Regulations

With the exception of universal fire codes and some height restrictions – and these are often flexible at best – show organizers outside the United States do not pay much attention to the sight lines and other regulations typically observed in the US.

Walls that are eight feet or two-and-a-half meters high can extend to the aisle, and island stands might be completely enclosed by solid walls with just one entrance where buyers are checked before being admitted to the exhibit itself. This format works well at sporting goods or fashion events, when new lines are introduced only for the benefit of bona fide distributors, agents or major retailers.

Unusual venues such as an open aeroplane hanger offer special challenges when exhibiting internationally. At FIDAE 96, an aerospace show in Santiago, Chile, a full-scale replica of the Wright Flyer, visible at right, was the centerpiece of the USA pavilion. Photo courtesy of Kallman, Associates, Inc., Waldrick, NJ.

Logistics

On the simplest level, most countries outside the US operate on the metric scale. Thus, a booth – more commonly known as a "stand" in Europe, Asia or South America – will be demarcated in meters rather than feet. Multiplying the length by the depth will give you the area of the stand in *square meters* (one square meter is approximately 10.8 square feet.)

On a more complex level, electrical service in practically every country outside of North America is delivered at 220 volts as opposed to 110 volts. The frequency of the alternating current is 50 Hertz (Hz) rather than our standard 60 Hz.) As a result, an appliance wired for use in the US will not operate in a German tradeshow, for example, without appropriate adaptor plugs or transformers.

Another thing not found outside the US is pipe-and-drape furnishings. Rather, custom-built displays or stand systems relying on aluminum supports and in-fill panels (or hard walls) are the norm. In Southeast Asia, many are fabricated right on the show floor. Stand builders have become proficient and very creative with using in-fill panels, combining them frequently with curved elements. Plexiglas panels and startling lighting effects are used to present products and concepts in a one-time display.

Labor Unions

Another difference between American exhibitions and those held outside the US is the absence of a strong labor union presence. In Amsterdam, for example, an organizer can take care of minor adjustments and alterations on the show floor, or carry a carton to a stand in Singapore without breaking any labor agreements. While US labor unions and show organizers have generally come to terms, there is currently little or no organized labor interference anywhere else in the world, with the possible exception of England.

How to Go Global

There are two directions to take when going global. Neither is mutually exclusive; going one way does not preclude going the other:

Inbound

Inbound refers to bringing exhibitors and visitors from outside the host organization's own country into an exhibition. This requires structured sales, marketing and promotional programs similar to those in place for domestic sales and marketing. Establishing a strong global sales network of agents is critical in securing the number of companies necessary to globalize the exhibition, and result in an event with a relatively high margin. To accomplish this, a sound strategy is required.

- Identify the key markets where the export of goods and services to the home market is large enough that the companies from other countries need to be there, since their buyers are there
- Select the right sales agents in these markets, either specialist agents selling exhibit space across many sectors, or specialists in one industry sector
- Develop a sales promotion program and package with a global look and feel that uses market data to address the needs and interests of exhibitors from outside the US
- Perhaps most importantly make the global sales team an integral part of the total sales effort. Map out a sales plan with the global sales agents, include them in all team messages, give them adequate sales tools, and communicate frequently. Promote them on your Web site as your global sales offices. Make every effort to keep the event on the top of their minds all the time.

As another part of the sales strategy, contact the embassies and commercial offices of the exhibition's targeted markets to make them aware of the event. Find out who can get the information back to their head offices, and who is able to provide information to their companies visiting their offices. At the same time, have an agent make direct contact with the counterparts. This cross-communication can lead to having pavilions from many different countries in the exhibition, sponsored by the various governments and associations.

On the attendee or visitor side, it is best to focus on a few key markets. In these markets, develop contacts with the embassy and commercial office to assist in identifying key associations and government organizations that could potentially sponsor a buyer group, as well as provide lists of potential visitors. For US organizers, consider applying for the US Department of Commerce's International Buyer Program. As with exhibitor promotion efforts, develop materials that will entice buyers from abroad and provide special incentives.

Outbound

Outbound refers to developing a global business by taking an event and its exhibitors to other geographic markets, and/or developing a new portfolio of exhibitions outside the host organization's own country. This requires a much greater commitment than bringing exhibitors and visitors into a domestic exhibition, but the rewards are also greater. This activity requires a strategic focus on the long term growth of a business, and becomes an integral part of its overall strategic plan. Taking an event into global markets adds value to its customers by providing new sales and marketing platforms, and offering them a well-known and established brand.

Business Models

There are seven basic business models to consider in globalizing an exhibition. The right choice depends on the market situation, the opportunities, and the amount of risk an organizer is willing to take. These models do not differ substantially from models which an organizer may already have used, but they are complicated by different cultures in each new market, language, distances, and time zones – making the process a bit more difficult and time consuming:

Licensing the brand

Licensing a brand is much like a franchise. The show organizer owns the brand and all the intellectual property, and agrees to provide certain support and data to a licensee/partner while the licensee/partner organizes the event for a certain term. This not only creates a local presence in a new market, but contributes to the development of a global brand. This is a relatively quick and easy way to enter a market, and offers the lowest risk with some significant returns over time.

The key is selecting the right partner, one with whom the show organizer is comfortable and vice versa. While licensees have all the liability, and can organize the event according to local market situations, they must maintain strict quality standards set by the owner to ensure that the brand maintains the look, feel and quality that have been established.

This model is based on a limited but renewable term, usually five years. The licensee keeps all the profits after their costs and fees, while the owner of the show gets his or her revenue off the top in the form of fees and royalties. Depending on the size of the event, this revenue can be fairly substantial over time, with minimum effort and few up-front costs. Owners can add to this revenue stream by having a sales agreement with the licensee that gives them exclusive rights to sell space to companies in their home market. This may make sense for some, but it should be studied carefully in light of the additional attention, staff time, and resources it will require.

Postcard advertising the American Pavilion at the 1997 Paris Air Show at which 120 American companies were represented. Photo courtesy of Kallman Associates, Waldwick, NJ.

Arab Dental Show 1996 in Dubai gave 25 American companies entry into the growing Middle East market supported by the U.S. pavilion walk-on stand package. Photo courtesy Kallman Associates, Waldwick, NJ.

Organizing a US Pavilion

This model is utilized mostly by associations who understand that there are opportunities that exist for their members overseas that do not require assuming all of the financial liability and risk of running a stand-alone event in another country. The opportunity to organize a pavilion in an event overseas can come from several initiatives, but generally results from conversations with exhibitors or members, a direct approach from the overseas event organizer looking to form a US pavilion or from another strategic partner.

The decision-making starts with determining the right markets for the industry sector, and thoroughly researching the existing events in these markets and selecting the right one(s). In some cases, a show organizer might know of the leading event; surveying an event's prospective exhibitor base – informally, at first – will help to gauge the level of interest. If this preliminary query results in 15-25 positive replies, then it is time to approach the organizer. It is a bit easier when an organizer outside an event's home marketplace approaches show management, as the indications are immediate that there is interest in expanding globally.

When organizing a US pavilion, the selling/pricing model is typically a discount from the organizer, and then a mark-up or a commission-based structure for sales to pavilion participants. As for responsibilities, the overall organizer provides the space and all the marketing material which may need to be supplemented. The owner's own staff works with contractors for freight and booth design.

SEE FIGURE 1

Because owners can negotiate to pay only for the space used, this approach is a relatively low risk way to create a global opportunity for customers and members, gain exposure in other markets for domestic events, and build awareness for the event's or organization's brand. Due to this model's dependence on significant staff time however, the potential for considerable financial gain is limited. Therefore, the strategic benefit must outweigh the financial one.

Joint Ventures

A preferred business model of many organizers and their potential global partners, the joint venture commits both parties financially as they work to achieve the same overall goals and objectives. This model gives organizers a local, committed partner with a strong vested interest in the event's success. With a joint venture, organizers move up the risk ladder, although the financial rewards over time could be much greater than the previous three models

Typically, a joint venture is established through an agreement in which the organizer/owner of the original event owns its brand and license, but the organizer/

FIGURE 1

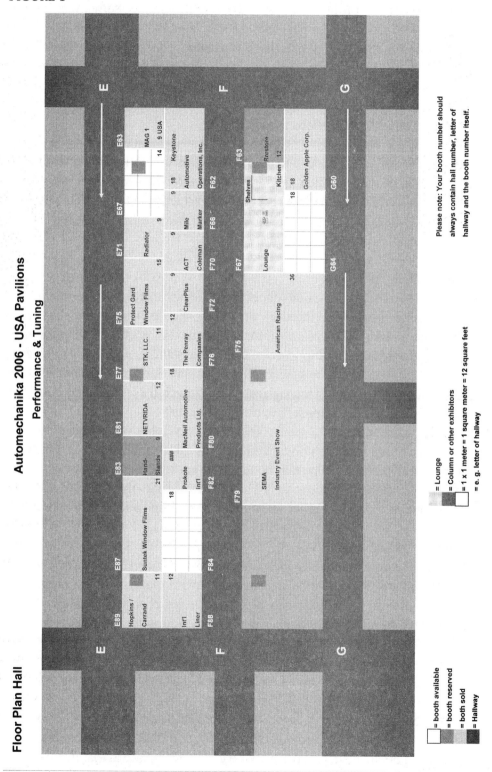

Courtesy of Messe Frankfurt

owner and his/her partner in the joint venture both own the new event. There is a division of equity, profits and costs, however the partner sometimes receives an additional management fee plus sales commission, and perhaps a small incentive if the show comes in under budget or on target. The partner generally does the organizing, including all the marketing and promotional materials, in-territory sales and operations, while the owner provides the educational programming and sales within the show's home marketplace. In the end, the organizer has more control over the event than in previous models.

This partnership can also lead to additional launches of the same brand into other countries in the geographic region, thus increasing the show organizer's return on investment. While the financial risk is quite a bit larger, and more staff time will be required – including re-assigning some existing and hiring additional staff – the financial rewards are definitely higher.

Management contracts

With this model and those that follow, the stakes are increased because the financial liability is now entirely on the show organizer's shoulders, and the risk is increased. There are a variety of pitfalls with management contracts, including the need for greater resource time and long distance direction and management. However, the rewards at the end could be significantly higher, since organizers receive 100 percent of the profit after costs and management fees. However, it is absolutely critical to find the right partner, as each must have trust in the other.

The partner usually works on a fixed fee plus sales commission, to which a small percentage of the bottom line may be added in order to provide additional incentive to save money on the cost side as well. The partner provides the local, "on-the- ground" staff resources, local and regional sales and marketing, and any operational support.

Launching Independently

A variation on the previous model, launching independently carries even more risk, since everything will need to be done remotely. In this model, the show organizer drives the entire process, from planning to sales to operations, often spending several weeks on location to line up contractors, the venue, media sponsors, and strategic partners. In addition, there is no substitute for being a resident in the market when it comes to developing strong industry relationships; sometimes, remote organizers find this impossible when operating from outside the area, especially at a very long distance.

For these reasons, this model is not recommended unless there is at least one person in the market who can provide assistance, such as a staff person from a sister association or other strategic partner who is already in place in that market.

The Trends Geographically
North America and Europe

New venues are being created throughout the world, and many cities in North America are constantly updating, improving or even completely rebuilding their venues to remain competitive. In the early years of the 21st century, there were approximately 40 new venues either in the planning or construction stage in North America, reflecting the continued support of cities for the tradeshow and convention business.

While all the major US destination continue to host significant events, the truly international exhibitions take place in cities where organizers know they will draw a global audience. The North American tradeshow industry has continued to grow, but there can be no doubt that the perception of what visitors require when attending a tradeshow has changed. The idea of an exhibition alone is no longer enough to draw large numbers of people and to attract a global audience; the venue must offer peripheral forms of entertainment.

Europe has continued to expand its tradeshow market by building new venues, but not on the scale of the US and Asia. Growth for the major global exhibitions in Europe has been flat in recent years, and, in many cases, those brands have been taken to Asia where they are gradually beginning to rival the mother brands. This has resulted in the German tradeshow industry moving large numbers of people and resources primarily into the Chinese market.

South America

South America has seen spectacular changes of fortune during the past five years, and will likely maintain its current growth pattern as more of its large populations are lifted above the poverty level. Sao Paulo remains the center of the Brazilian market, where a major portfolio of established events continues to grow. There are other major cities in South America that have also established tradeshow markets, but it is likely that the most significant future growth area will be Brazil.

Asia and China

In Southeast Asia, venues continue to expand and replace older facilities, creating some of the best exhibition space in the world. This growth was initially centered on Singapore and Southeast Asia, but has also moved north to China, Hong Kong and Macau – three emerging locations which have ambitiously begun to create ideal conditions for a tradeshow market.

The continued building of exhibition space in some parts of China has created a massive surplus and lower occupancy rates, therefore increasing competition between cities. The massive building programs in the Pearl River Delta and other parts of China have put millions of square meters of available space into quite small geographical areas. Despite a 20 percent growth in the tradeshow market, and challenges connected to a lack of regulation and dual pricing policies, exhibiting companies see Asia as a vital platform which they cannot afford to ignore.

While there are many similarities between India and China, the development of India's exhibition industry is not parallel. Without the same level of government support and infrastructure as in China, it has been difficult for the Indian exhibition industry to reflect the same growth as its general economy has enjoyed.

The Russian market has seen substantial growth in recent years but has been held back by a lack of venues. The discovery of spectacular resources and oil and gas is now transforming Russia into a capitalist economy where tradeshows are seeing significant growth, and demand is outstripping supply.

Middle East

Despite a tenuous political climate in some parts of the region, the Middle East continues to expand on the colossal cash surpluses generated by oil prices with ambitious plans to make it a world center for the tradeshow industry. Dubai and Abu Dhabi are both seeking to create a market which they believe is ideally placed between America, Europe and Asia, where safety, weather, hotels and all the other ingredients for a successful industry will be present

Unpredictable Factors

Tradeshows in particular are very vulnerable to a number of outside influences which are associated with discouraging buyers from traveling. Most prominent among these would be pandemic disease. Equally threatening are terrorism and natural disasters, both of which have had dramatic effects on areas such as New York and New Orleans in particular. However, the resilience of the marketplace continues to defy those elements which have affected it. The growth of the industry globally will depend on organizers' ability to promote the medium, control costs and deliver a return on investment formula with which both exhibitors and visitors are familiar.

SUMMARY

Regardless of the language spoken, the originality or banality of the booth or stand, or the product or service being promoted, the objective of the exhibition is the same. Wherever an exhibition takes place, sellers greet buyers, and business is done. A host organization's strategy and business philosophy determines how best to participate in the various global markets, each offering different levels of risk and reward.

QUESTIONS FOR DISCUSSION

① If you have visited exhibitions both inside and outside the US, what were the major differences you personally observed?

② Why do you think it came to be called a "booth" in the US and a "stand" in Europe?

③ Why might it be more advantageous for exhibitors to provide hospitality at the stand instead of in a hotel suite?

Chapter 1
Exhibitions and the Marketing Mix

"It happens about 70 million times a year. All over North America,
somebody is walking into a tradeshow to buy or to sell."

– Tradeshow Bureau

Section II: Business Issues

IN THIS CHAPTER YOU WILL LEARN

- The difference between marketing and sales
- Why marketing is an essential business task
- What is unique about how exhibitions contribute to marketing a product or service
- Ways exhibitions are marketed

INTRODUCTION

What are exhibitions? The essence of the definition is captured in just five words: exhibitions are events that bring buyers and sellers together. Everything else there is to learn about them consists of "whys" and "hows." Buying, selling, interacting, promotion, and synergy are topics of discussion that all relate in some way to the concept of marketing. In order to see how exhibitions fit within both the context and concept of marketing, it is helpful to briefly review some Marketing 101.

CONTRIBUTOR

Stephen Schuldenfrei, President, Tradeshow Exhibitors Association

Defining Marketing

Because marketing and sales are so intertwined, the terms are often used interchangeably – and incorrectly. What exactly is marketing and how is it different from sales? Although an all-inclusive definition of marketing is difficult to nail down, this text relies on the following definition as it relates to the exhibition industry: *"Marketing is a process of identifying human wants and needs, and developing a plan to meet those wants and needs. Refers to everything involved with convincing an attendee to come to the event. Also refers to providing information to support the exhibit sales function."*

©2003 Convention Industry Council (www.conventionindustry.org)

Marketing involves a large set of activities designed to:
- Get the prospect's attention
- Create interest in the product or service
- Convince prospects that the product or service fills a need they have
- Motivate a desire within prospects to make a purchase decision
- Consummate the sale.

- As for the difference between marketing and sales, there is an ongoing debate. Both "marketing" and "sales" are used to describe revenue-generating activities. While they are very interdependent functions, sales is only one part of the marketing activity.

The American Marketing Association defines sales as *"any of a number of activities designed to promote customer purchase of a product or service. Sales can be done in person or over the phone, through email or other communication media. The process generally includes stages such as assessing customer needs, presenting product features and benefits to address those needs and negotiation on price, delivery and other elements."*

© 2006 MarketingPower, Inc. (www.marketingpower.com)

MARKETING

"A process of identifying human wants and needs, and developing a plan to meet those wants and needs. Refers to everything involved with convincing an attendee to come to the event. Also refers to providing information to support the exhibit sales function."

©2003 Convention Industry Council (www.conventionindustry.org)

Mark Smock, President of the Business Buyer Directory, points out that there are many marketing responsibilities that do not involve sales: For example, says Smock, marketing responsibilities also include:

- Establishing and justifying the company's best competitive position within a market
- Developing and sustaining customer relationships
- Locating and profiling potential markets and key participants within those markets
- Generating quality sales leads
- Developing effective selling tools
- Analyzing and tracking competitors' business strategies and tactics
- Defining, prioritizing and justifying new product/service improvements and developments
- Promoting an certain company product or service image
- Facilitating information transfer from customers to the rest of the company
- Simplifying the customer's product or service procurement process

©2004 by Business Buyer Directory. Reprinted with permission.

Just as sales is an integral part of marketing, exhibiting is a major part of marketing. Both have key roles in something called the marketing mix. The idea of a "marketing mix" was first presented over forty years ago by Neil Bordon of the Harvard School of Business. According to Michael Baker, author of *Marketing, An Introductory Text*, the term rests on the concept that there are a *"limited number of ingredients...[that] can [be] combined into an almost limitless number of combinations."*

A marketing mix is defined as the combination of product offerings used to reach a target market for the organization. The marketing mix comprises the Product (what the actual offering comprises), Price (the value exchanged for that offering), Promotion (the means of communicating that offering to the target audience, promotional mix) and distribution (also known as Place; the means of having the product offering available to the target audience). The marketing mix is also known as the Four Ps.

©CAPCO Marketing, Inc. (www. capcomarketing.com)

SALES

Any of a number of activities designed to promote customer purchase of a product or service. Sales can be done in person or over the phone, through email or other communication media. The process generally includes stages such as assessing customer needs, presenting product features and benefits to address those needs and negotiation on price, delivery and other elements."

© 2006 MarketingPower, Inc. (www. marketingpower.com)

What ingredients a marketing manager puts into his marketing "blender," spins around and pours out is his or her company's specific marketing strategy. With a nearly limitless number of permutations and combinations, finding identical mixes is about as likely as matching snowflakes. Some of the more important ingredients in the marketing mix are:

- Branding
- Pricing
- Distribution Channels
- Direct Sales (Outside & Inside Sales)
- Advertising
- Promotions
- Packaging

- Research
- Internet
- Exhibits
- Direct Mail
- Web sites
- Blogs, podcasts and RSS feeds

MARKETING MIX

A Marketing Mix is the combination of product offerings used to reach a target market for the organization. The marketing mix comprises the Product (what the actual offering comprises), Price (the value exchanged for that offering), Promotion (the means of communicating that offering to the target audience, promotional mix) and distribution (also known as Place, the means of having the product offering available to the target audience). The marketing mix is also known as the four Ps.

©CAPCO Marketing, Inc. (www. capcomarketing.com)

Where Exhibitions Fit

The funding to participate as an exhibitor in a tradeshow generally comes from the marketing budget. In many cases, the marketing budget has a separate line item allocation for the annual exhibits schedule. In other cases, the budget allocation to exhibit is not fully developed at the start of the fiscal year. This leaves the option to add or delete tradeshow participation as the year unfolds.

In other cases, the funding for exhibits is not separated out within the marketing budget. Rather, it is kept in a general budget category titled "Media and Promotions," and is allocated during the year on a case-by-case basis. Also, in some cases, the exhibiting budget is kept by the Sales Department.

Tradeshows earn their income by selling booth space to exhibitors. They also sell sponsorship programs to exhibitors and educational seminars to attendees. Potential exhibitors use their budgets and their marketing goals and objectives to decide which tradeshows to participate in, and how much money to spend in each tradeshow.

Why Exhibitions Work

In keeping with the responsibility of bringing buyers and sellers together, exhibitions have a key role to play in the marketing mix. Since human beings are gregarious by nature, most purchase decisions take place in face-to-face interactions. Print advertising, television and the Internet have not changed that to any large degree, despite thousands of efforts and millions of dollars spent. To paraphrase Corbin Ball, CMP, MS – an international speaker, consultant and writer on the worldwide use of technology – the Internet will replace face-to-face marketing only when we can taste a virtual beer.

Another major function of exhibitions in the marketing mix is the ability of face-to-face events in finding new customers. Exhibitions are much like retail mall stores where new prospects see a display and wander in – and unlike stores and shops, show attendees *pay for the privilege* of finding and buying new products!

Some marketing objectives are achieved as well by exhibitions. Exhibitions are a very personal activity. You can't reach the millions of persons that a TV ad does. Events will never win the CPM (Cost per Thousands) race against magazines. Face-to-face marketing just isn't a mass marketing tool. It is an excellent way to try a product and close a sale, however. Therefore, used as part of the marketing mix, exhibitions are very valuable activities.

Sales Cycles

Every sale – regardless of the product or the industry – goes through a sequence of phases known as the Sales Cycle.

1. First, the customer perceives a need for a new product or service.
2. Next, he or she begins to formulate how the product or service might be of use, or how it may solve a problem. At this stage, the consumer is shopping for the "right" product among many.
3. The third step is "conviction." Now the buyer has narrowed choices down to a few products.
4. Then the "desire" step is reached. "I've GOT to have this!" the customer thinks.
5. Finally, a sale is consummated. This is the final step and called The Close.

Graphically, the process is:

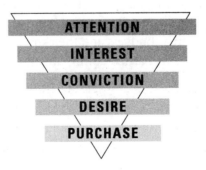

ATTENTION
INTEREST
CONVICTION
DESIRE
PURCHASE

Parallel to the buyer's viewpoint of attention, interest, conviction, desire and purchase is the marketing continuum. Marketing has come a long way over the centuries, but the process has not changed. The process runs from introduction of a product or service to the ultimate sale.

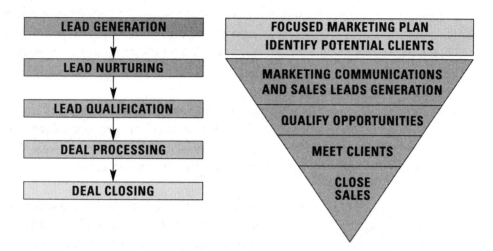

The very first step in selling a product is the Identification stage. Marketers answer the question "Who is my customer?" By identifying the "prospect", the huge universe is brought down to a manageable size. Everyone needs water, for example, but the universe for a municipal water system is identified by geographical boundaries. The bottled water marketer further classifies his prospect list by income or buying habits.

Once the customer is identified, the next stage is Introduction. Again if the universe is very large, mass media is more effective. MP3 players, for example, are a mass market product. However, the actual sales target for a manufacturer is the much smaller retail community. Therefore, a retail store chain which sells the MP3 player to the consumers is the actual customer. Consequently, the Consumer Electronics Show (CES) which includes thousands of retail buyers (but no consumers) might be an excellent match as a marketing tool for the manufacturers of MP3 players.

Prospecting

Prospecting is the process of sellers identifying potential buyers. Sales is the process of turning them into buyers. The best targets are prospects and suspects who:

- Have the need for the product or service.
- Have the buying authority to purchase the product or service.
- Have the money to spend on the product or service.

Exhibitions are very efficient at finding potential new buyers (called lead generation) from the limited universe of an exhibition's attendees. For more mass market lead generation, other forms of marketing may be more cost effective, although they have very high waste. A great direct mail campaign is one that generates 5 percent results. That means 95 percent of the effort and budget is worthless.

Where face-to-face media begin to overtake other forms of selling is in the Features & Benefits and Overcoming Objections stages. Why? Because these forms of engagement allow the marketer to talk with the prospect, answer their questions, read their body language and verbal inflections, and react to them. This results in high quality sales time. From this point forward, the most effective selling is done this way. New car sales are almost impossible to be done in any other way. Dealers and manufacturers all have very sophisticated Web sites, but few actual sales are made that way. The vast majority of sales are done in the showroom, or at least on the telephone.

Selling

The final step is, of course, the sale. CEIR research indicates that exhibition leads are 38 percent less expensive to close than a personal sales call. Exhibition sales average only 1.6 calls to close, and leads are 31 percent less expensive to contact. Sales generated from any other means require an average of 3.7 sales calls. In fact, some traditional sales advice is that 80 percent of all sales are made after the prospect has been contacted at least seven times. According to Adam Urbanski of The Marketing Mentors, however, the typical business person gives up after just one or two follow up contacts.

Exhibitions account for one to three of the seven necessary contacts by making contact via the pre-show promotion, the booth structure (as an ad), and, most importantly, the face-to-face opportunities to qualify and demonstrate the products and services.

SEE FIGURE 1

The Exhibition Triangle

There are three parties to every show: exhibitors, attendees/visitors and organizers. Each has a different agenda, but each depends on all the others.
- Exhibitors come to tradeshows to do many things:
- Generate sales leads from existing customers
- Generate sales leads from new (and often unknown) prospects
- Educate customers about products and services
- Show dealers and distributors how to sell effectively
- Promote awareness of company and capabilities
- Introduce new products and services

FIGURE 1

HOW MUCH DOES IT COST TO CLOSE A SALE?

$1,117 vs. $625

TOTAL COST:
• No Exhibition Lead
• Field Sales Call Follow-Up

Cost Includes:
• $302 (cost of contacting
    a prospect in the field)
• x 3.7 (average number of sales
    calls to close a sale)

TOTAL COST:
• Lead Exhibition Lead
• Lead Field Sales Call Follow-Up

Cost Includes:
• $302 (cost of contacting
    a prospect in the field)
• x1.3 (average number of sales
    calls to close a sale)
• +$233 (cost per contact
    at an exhibition)

Source: Center for Exhibition Industry Research, Data & Strategies Group, Framingham, MA.

• Accumulate competitive information
• Gain publicity and press
• Identify new customers
• Conduct business with other exhibitors
• Reach high-quality prospects
• Meet key customers
• Enter new markets (both geographic and product).

Attendees come to tradeshows also to accomplish a number of goals:
• Discover what's new
• Identify future suppliers
• Buy products and services
• Meet key suppliers
• Comparison shop
• Network with fellow industry people
• Solve problems.

Organizers produce shows to:
• Bring buyers and sellers together
• Expand their product line (multi media)
• Earn valuable revenue

An exhibition is often described as a magazine in three dimensions. It's a live version of a paper product. Here's how the three components of a magazine might compare to equivalent components of an exhibition:
• The magazine reader is … the attendee or buyer at an exhibition.
• The advertiser is … the exhibitor
• The editorial content is … the conference program

Because of this basic relationship, it is no wonder that so many publishing companies are also major producers of shows and events. They already have frequent access to the audience (their subscription lists), exhibitors (their advertising and prospect base) and sources for the program (their writers). In addition, publishers usually have or can easily enhance their overhead and human resources capabilities with very small additional cost. This makes the event division of publishers usually the most profitable part of their business model.

SUMMARY

Creating a marketing plan for an exhibition begins with understanding how exhibitions work as a marketing vehicle, how they fit in the marketing mix of potential exhibitors, and how to close a sale. When marketing to attendees, show organizers must decide what would most influence them, so that the best media can be chosen to get the message across to the targeted audiences.

QUESTIONS FOR DISCUSSION

① Which job is more important to the success of an exhibition: having a marketing plan or making sales?

② Define face-to-face marketing and discuss why this is a key part of the definition of an exhibitions.

③ Why do you think closing a sale is often the most difficult part of the sales cycle?

Chapter 2
Competitive Analysis

*"The key part of your brand is a quality product.
Creating exceptional content is the number one thing."*

– Rufus Griscom, *Building Buzz for
Your Web Project, SXSW 2006*

Section II: Business Issues

IN THIS CHAPTER YOU WILL LEARN
- How to do a Strategic Analysis
- How to do a Tactical Analysis
- How to use this information to position a tradeshow in the market

INTRODUCTION

Building the success of an exhibition is no different than building the success of any other product or major franchised service. It's a matter of building a successful brand, in large part by capitalizing on information about what competitors are doing. This chapter will give you the tools to gather that critical information.

CONTRIBUTOR

Francis Friedman, President, Time & Place Strategies

Call it face-to-face marketing, a tradeshow, an exhibition, exposition, or convention. Any of these events is – at its core – a brand-building undertaking whose success depends on selling a target audience on the merits of participation.

As a result of the expanded media and exhibition competition, each individual exhibition brand is seeking to convince potential exhibitors and sponsors that its exhibition should get the largest share of that exhibitor's budget. Exhibition sales teams and marketing programs are designed to work with potential exhibitor prospects to demonstrate how exhibiting in their particular exhibition will help that exhibitor meet his marketing and sales goals and objectives. Exhibition marketing and sales programs are designed to demonstrate the superiority of that exhibition compared to other exhibitions, events and media options. In short, the target audience is most likely to participate in an event whose sales team has thoroughly presented its merits and potential return on investment.

First and foremost, show organizers seek to build an exhibition that meets the needs of attendees. Participants must see the right exhibitors with the right mix of products and services, participate in the educational sessions that meet their continuing education needs, and network with their peers and industry experts. In addition, show organizers also seek to brand that exhibition so that it stands out against the competition and against all other event opportunities in which attendees can participate. Because of the limits of attendees' time and travel budgets, show organizers want to make their individual exhibition brand experience a compelling one so the attendees will stay "brand loyal" and return for the next edition of that exhibition.

Because a given exhibition will compete for exhibitor marketing budgets with other exhibitions and corporate/company events, it is necessary to be sure that the exhibition is competitive in the marketplace. Show organizers need to be able to defend their brand against other exhibitions, as well as be able to capitalize on market and program weaknesses in other exhibition brands. Show organizers must also be ready to take advantage of new opportunities that arise in the marketplace.

Market research of all types ensures that an exhibition is well targeted, highly relevant, and is moving ahead of competitive events. A thorough competitive analysis will permit show organizers to see where they might be able to take sales and market share away from another exhibition. Conversely, an analysis might reveal where a show is vulnerable to losing sales and market share, or discover additional market opportunities and new exhibition ideas.

All information that has been gathered about the competition an exhibition or event faces may be compiled in a Competitive Analysis Report. The final report usually has an Executive Summary at the beginning that recaps all the findings, as well as the conclusions reached. It could also include a summary of recommendations. There may also be a different section for each exhibition studied. Many organizations plan for periodic updating of this research.

Types of Competitive Analysis

There are two fundamental types of competitive analyses: Strategic Analysis and Tactical Analysis. The Strategic Analysis is an overview of an industry or market segment that focuses on analyzing an exhibition's positioning in that market. Tactical Analysis is much more detailed, and can include such things as lists of exhibitors, size of the booth space taken by individual exhibitors, booth space for the whole show organized by size of booth, sponsorship programs, and advertising and promotional spending. It is focused on gathering in-depth information about each competitive exhibition, and comparing that information to the show being studied.

Strategic Analysis

Strategic Analysis looks at the larger competitive picture in a given market or market segment. It analyzes the different exhibitions in that market space to determine the focus, relative strength in the market, exhibitor and attendee appeal, and vulnerability to other shows. It is designed to evaluate how well an exhibition is positioned in the market that it serves – in other words, where does it "fit in" in terms of uniqueness, desirability or appeal. A show organizer does not want to produce an exhibition that is just like its competition. There is no advantage to this in the marketplace, as it creates confusion and indecision among potential exhibitors and attendees. Rather, each show organizer wants to produce an exhibition that is unique, has clear-cut market advantages, and is compelling to exhibitors and attendees in its own right.

Like any commercial product, exhibitions and events are created and marketed to be commercially viable in a competitive marketplace. Exhibitions and events must generate a paying audience, and make a profit, in order to stay in business. This is true for events produced by not-for-profit organizations like associations, as well as events produced by for-profit private exhibition producers.

The first stage is to understand what business or industry an exhibition or event serves. As a general rule, the tighter the focus of an exhibition on a given subject or industry, the more attractive the show becomes to a specific target audience. For example, consider an exhibition whose target audience is intended to be medical doctors. This is too broad a definition, because there are all kinds of medical specialties. A more effective exhibition would be produced for just one specialty – Internal Medicine, for example. Organizers of the most effective exhibition, however, would focus the event's content to suit the many smaller sub-specialties within Internal Medicine; for example, specialists who focus on the lungs, liver, or heart.

By narrowing the focus, show organizers can immediately answer the questions "What business are we in?" and "What market segments do we serve?" For purposes of discussion, this chapter will focus on producing a medical exhibition for Internal Medicine practitioners who specialize in the heart. Therefore, the exhibition can be defined as being in the business of "Medicine" serving professionals in "Cardiology."

Tools Used in Building a Strategic Analysis

A thorough job here will lead to an assessment of all exhibitions, conferences, and events related to the industry or market segment being researched. Some of the research tools which can be used include:

- Web searches for exhibitions, events and associations in that industry (Use common search engines and key words)
- Publications in that industry (use major online bookstores)
- Exhibition industry reference sources such as *Tradeshow Week Data Book*
- www.tsnn.com (Tradeshow News Network.com)
- American Society of Association Executives *Directory of Associations*, Published by Gale Research (www.asae.org)
- *Standard Rate & Data Service* (a traditional reference source for trade publications that accept advertising)
- Attending competitive exhibitions.

These tools and sources assist the show organizer in gathering data about the given market, and the existing exhibitions that serve that market. These sources also make it possible to assemble the types of competitive data that will be presented in the next segment of this chapter.

The most frequently gathered information in conducting a competitive analysis includes the following information for each exhibition studied:

1. Who owns the show? For each exhibition, it is important to record the following information:
   a. Formal name of the show and its Web site address
   b. Name, address, phone number, and Web site of the company who produces the show
   c. Name, address, phone number and Web site of the organization who owns the show (Note that some shows may be owned by an organization who subcontracts the production of it to another group.)

The assessments in Items 1-b and 1-c reveal if the show is produced by a not-for-profit organization such as an association, or if it is produced by a private for-profit organization. This information also reveals if the exhibition or event is being produced by an integrated media company that may have publications, Web sites, and other exhibitions and events serving various aspect of this market. Integrated media companies are a recent trend in the exhibition industry, resulting from the acquisition of exhibitions by magazine publishers in order to capture more advertising and exhibiting dollars while furthering their reach into the industry they serve.

2. What is the subject focus of the show as the exhibition organizer has presented it in the description of the show on their Web site, or in various reference sources?

3. Who are the target audiences for attendees and exhibitors? What are the attendees looking for, and what are the exhibitors selling?

4. How often is it produced? (Once a year, two or more times a year, every other year?)

5. Is it in a fixed location each time, or does it rotate from city to city?

6. What is the size of the show in terms of floor area and attendee count?

7. Is the exhibition or event considered a local, regional, national or international event? (Usually contained in the description of the show, or can be inferred from looking at various facts about the show related to its size and it usual location schedule.)

8. Is it a very narrowly-focused "vertical show" or is it more "horizontal" in its market focus? For example, the Car Wash show is a vertical show dealing strictly with car wash-related exhibitors and attendees. A show for gas stations however would be classified as horizontal, because modern gas stations also include repair services, sales of tires, oil and batteries, convenience stores, food service, car washes, oil changes and automotive repairs.

9. Who are the major exhibitors, and how much space does each one take? Many exhibition Web sites include a listing of exhibitors and the booths that they occupy. For the larger exhibitors, it is also necessary to not only get the company name but also the division within the company that the exhibitor represents. For a large multi-division company such as a Sony, IBM or United Technologies, the specific division of the company is important because different divisions often participate in different exhibitions. Which company division is involved, and how much space each takes in that particular show, is important information.

As this information is gathered for each exhibition and event in a given market, the breadth and depth of exhibition coverage in that market segment will become apparent. From among the largest leading exhibitions down to the smallest local shows, the dominant shows in that market segment will emerge, including who produces them and which shows are national, regional and local.

For example, in the cardiology field there are two major annual events that dominate this field. The American Heart Association (AHA) produces a convention in November each year called the Scientific Sessions. In March each year, the American College of Cardiology (ACC) also holds a Scientific Sessions. In this case, each of these two events is produced by a professional association serving overlapping but slightly different audiences. Cardiologists interested in clinical education attend the ACC show, and cardiologists and scientists interested in research attend the AHA show. So as not to conflict with each other, these events are held three to four months apart, always in different regions of the country.

Contrast these cardiology events with trade events for the gift industry. Exhibitions in the gift industry tend to be produced on a local market basis by a large number of different producers. In addition, gift shows tend to be produced twice a year in the same city in order to allow regional buyers to shop the shows for new merchandise for their stores. The New York Gift Show is the largest exhibition in the gift industry in terms of number of exhibitors, exhibit space utilized and number of attendees. Around the United States, there are other important gift shows in cities such as Atlanta, Miami, Chicago, Los Angeles and San Francisco. In Canada, there are important gift shows in Toronto, Montreal and Vancouver.

When a competitive analysis is completed, it should enable a show manager to adequately understand what events serve the industry in question, where each exhibition fits, and if there are any new opportunities within that industry.

STRATEGIC ANALYSIS SHOULD PROVIDE THE FOLLOWING BASIC INFORMATION:

1. Complete details for each exhibition or event
   a. Name of the exhibition
   b. Purpose, focus, or positioning of the exhibition
   c. Primary target audience it seeks to reach
      i. Attendees, and
      ii. Exhibitors
   d. Name of the show owner (along with address, phone number and Web site)
   e. Name of the organization that produces the exhibition (along with address, phone number and Web site)
   f. How often produced (Annually, semi-annually, bi-annually, or other.)
   g. Dates for the exhibition

h. Location of the exhibition
  i. Same city each year?
  ii. Different city each year?
  iii. Rotation between a set number of cities
i. Size of the show
  i. Number of exhibitors
  ii. Number of attendees
  iii. Size of the exhibition in terms of floor area
j. Scope of the exhibition
  i. Local market
  ii. Regional market
  iii. National
  iv. International

Ownership Characteristics

The character of the industry can be determined from its ownership composition. An industry dominated by privately-owned, for-profit companies has a different character than if dominated by not-for-profit associations or professional societies. Also, if there are a significant number of private shows or events produced by large companies or vendors, there are unique challenges for public exhibition producers who are competing for a share of that exhibiting budget.

Because of their organizational and legal structure, the decision-making process of associations is less independent than their for-profit counterparts. For example, non-profits typically require more input from committees and advisory bodies. This slows down the speed of decision making, and includes organizational considerations on top of the market and competitive influences. On the other hand, for-profit show organizers are able to make faster business decisions driven by the financial considerations of the marketplace.

The Strategic Analysis will provide information on the ownership characteristics of various exhibitions to see if they are:

a. Association-owned
b. Association-produced
c. Outsourced to a management company
d. Owned and produced by for-profit companies
e. Private or corporate event.

Time & Location Patterns

For many industries, when its shows are held is very important to the commercial practices of that industry. In other cases, certain dominant exhibitions have set the time patterns for the industry based on nothing more than precedent. The importance of this is that exhibitors often have a marketing plan – including a budget – built upon these already established time patterns. So, to consider launching a new event in a given market segment, a show manager must be very aware of the existing events and accepted time frames.

Launching a new event within these accepted time frames means facing the established competition. Launching a new exhibition outside of these time frames means convincing a portion of the industry that the new show has something new and special that is not available within the existing exhibitions. Just as importantly, the new event must work for the benefit of everyone involved.

The location where an exhibition is held is also critical information. For example, an exhibition may be held in the spring on the east coast, and in the fall on the west coast. Or, one exhibition producer may hold the spring exhibition on one coast, and a different exhibition producer may hold the fall exhibition on the opposite coast. These time and location patterns provide important information regarding the nature and extent of the existing competition in a market segment, as well as the potential for launching a new event.

For example, the potential for a new exhibition may arise when a competitive analysis reveals that there is a spring show on the west coast, but no fall show on the east coast. These time and date pattern discovery would lead to further research and investigation concerning the potential business rationale that could be made for launching a new exhibition on the east coast in the fall.

In addition, a large exhibition may rotate into a region or city once every several years. There may be an opportunity to launch a new smaller exhibition that will be held in that region or city in the years the first exhibition does not rotate into that region or city. Additional research would be needed to confirm that there was enough potential interest to justify the launch of a new exhibition to fill those dates in the alternate years.

In addition, looking at time and location patterns will show that the most generally identifiable patterns are as follows:
a. Spring / Fall competitive pattern
b. East Coast / West Coast competitive pattern
c. North / South competitive patterns
d. Fixed location / rotational patterns.

Analyzing these patterns helps the exhibition production team to assess its exhibition brand's timing and location compared to the competition. Also, these patterns can assist in uncovering potential new exhibition opportunities.

Market Positioning

Show organizers use competitive analysis to evaluate the strength of their exhibition's brand; in other words, to determine how their exhibition is positioned in relation to the competition. In addition to its relative strength against the competition, a well-done analysis will also reveal an exhibition's Unique Selling Proposition – basically, what one competitor has to offer that no one else does.

As the competitive analysis is being developed, and information is gathered on the exhibition brand and the competing brands, the following Competitive Market Positioning Assessments will emerge for each exhibition:

a. The business or segment that the exhibition serves

b. How each exhibition is positioned in that market

c. The Unique Selling Proposition (USP) for each exhibition

d. Is it a narrow, vertical show or a broadly-based horizontal show?

e. Is it a local, regional, national, international, or private event?

This Competitive Market Positioning Assessment will provide a quick snapshot of all exhibitions in the market or market segments under review, and where each show fits. It will quickly point out where there are existing exhibitions, and where potential opportunities may exist.

Overlapping Exhibition/Event Identification

During the course of the competitive analysis, it is possible to discover exhibitions that overlap in some way. Consider the example mentioned earlier in this chapter regarding gas station exhibitions. In investigating gas station exhibitions, a car wash exhibition might be discovered. The car wash exhibition would present a highly-attractive, competitive opportunity for the gas station event's exhibitors who provide car washing equipment and supplies to gas station owners and operators. Show organizers of the gas station exhibition would be very concerned about losing their car wash exhibitors to the car wash exhibition.

Overlapping exhibitions represent both a threat and an opportunity. They represent a threat, because they may offer a stronger opportunity to exhibitors and attendees who might only be interested in a specific segment of that industry and who will never be interested in other events. They also represent an opportunity, because exhibitors at the overlapping exhibitions might be interested in reaching a new and more diverse audience.

In the Competitive Analysis Report, these overlapping exhibitions would be recorded in a separate section. For each overlapping exhibition, a note would be made as to where and how each show overlaps another segment or another show.

Tactical Analysis

The Tactical Analysis is an in-depth comparison of the details of one exhibition to the details of another. The depth of the detail can be varied to suit the needs of each exhibition team.

After conducting a Strategic Analysis, many show organizers will determine that there are only one or two exhibitions that are truly competitive to its exhibition. Once this determination is made, show organizers pursue an in-depth Tactical Analysis of these competing exhibitions.

The first task that is performed is looking at booth space. This shows relative exhibition income, and is a measure of financial and market strength. A brief chart will illustrate how this research can be organized.

BOOTH SPACE ANALYSIS
SHOW BEING ANALYZED V. COMPETITORS #1 AND #2

Exhibitors	Show Being Analyzed Square Feet	Show #1 Square Feet	Show #2 Square Feet
Exhibitor A	200	100	200
Exhibitor B	100	200	400
Exhibitor C	600	None	600
Exhibitor D	400	400	None
Exhibitor E	400	None	None
Exhibitor F	100	200	400
Exhibitor G	200	None	None
Exhibitor H	300	200	600
Exhibitor I	100	100	100

The information for this chart is taken from the sales records of the show being studied, and from published information for the competition. Many exhibitions have booth sizes or booth numbers for the exhibitors in their shows on the Web site for the show.

By assuming that a "standard" exhibition booth measures 10 ft X 10 ft (or 100 square feet), the individual exhibitor's square feet of booth space can be estimated when the number of booths an exhibitor buys is known. This estimate is developed by seeing how many different booth numbers are listed for that exhibitor in an exhibition plan. Each booth number is then estimated to be a 100 square foot booth. Again, this is an estimate using certain assumptions based upon publicly-available information.

Estimating the financial investments of exhibitors and attendees in various exhibitions based on booth space purchased will not be as accurate as the information show organizers will have on their own exhibition. Because publicly-available sources on the competition will never be 100 percent accurate, show organizers must consider their results are merely estimates of their competition's activities. Even though the Tactical Analysis is only an estimate of what is taking place inside other shows, it is still very valuable as a basis for many business decisions.

BOOTH SPACE ANALYSIS
SHOW BEING ANALYZED V. COMPETITORS #1 AND #2
BY COST PER SQUARE FOOT

Exhibitors	Show Being Analyzed Square Feet	Our Show $ @ $10.00/ft	Show #1 Square Feet	Show #1 $ @ $9.75/ft	Show #2 Square Feet	Show #2 $ @ $10.50/ft
Exhibitor A	200	$2,000	100	$975	200	$2,100
Exhibitor B	100	1,000	200	1,950	400	4,200
Exhibitor C	600	6,000	None	—	600	6,300
Exhibitor D	400	4,000	400	3,900	None	—
Exhibitor E	400	4,000	None	—	None	—
Exhibitor F	100	1,000	200	1,950	400	4,200
Exhibitor G	200	2,000	None	—	None	—
Exhibitor H	300	3,000	200	1,950	600	6,300
Exhibitor I	100	1,000	100	975	100	1,050

In the chart above, it is evident what each exhibitor spent in each of the three competitive shows. For example, Exhibitor B is estimated to have spent four times as much money on Competitive Exhibition #2 as he did at the exhibition being studied. Exhibitor H is estimated to have spent twice as much money on Competitive Exhibition #2 as he did at the exhibition being studied.

Clearly, one action step would be to have the exhibition's sales team spend more time talking with Exhibitors B and H to better understand why they spend more money at Competitive Exhibition #2. In addition to a more in-depth understanding of the perceived advantages offered by the competition, these discussions could lead to advice as to what show organizers could do to increase the appeal of the exhibition, and ways to sell more booth space to exhibitors B and H.

This detailed comparison of booth space is only one of many different in-depth studies that can be made among exhibitions in a Tactical Analysis, and can serve as a model for many others. Some of these could be:

• Pricing of booth space

• Promotional brochures (Both promotional copy and frequency of mailing)

• Web site design and content

• Advertising copy and graphic design elements

• Educational programs

• Keynote speakers

• Exhibition city and rotation patterns.

Any information that the exhibition team feels represents a significant differential between each exhibition should be gathered. By studying the differences, the team will be able to take action to reduce its vulnerability, and to also increase its own competitive strength.

SUMMARY

Competitive analysis and market research enable show organizers to manage their exhibition businesses both offensively – by identifying and researching new opportunities – and defensively – by analyzing potential threats and eliminating vulnerabilities, which will add value and strengthen their own brand.

QUESTIONS FOR DISCUSSION

① When shopping for a new home, how would the techniques presented in this chapter be applicable?

② What are the advantages and disadvantages to exhibitors of having two annual exhibitions in the field of cardiology?

③ As a show organizer, what would you do if you discovered a new exhibition which duplicated yours in several ways?

Section II: Business Issues

Chapter 3
Marketing to Exhibitors

*"Originality is the ability to present facts and
ideas as nobody has before, even though
the facts and ideas are not in themselves new."*

– Ernest Jones

Section II: Business Issues

IN THIS CHAPTER YOU WILL LEARN
- Why the show organizer needs a marketing plan for booth sales
- What goes into an exhibitor prospectus
- Some of the best sales and marketing techniques
- Why the Web is an important tool for potential exhibitors

INTRODUCTION

Exhibitions are critical to the financial stability of many associations hosting tradeshows, and the "bottom line" is the sole reason for the existence of consumer shows. As rental of exhibit space is usually the largest single item on the revenue side of any type of exhibition budget, it is important in today's competitive marketplace for show organizers to develop exhibitor-focused marketing and communication strategies which will attract a continual stream of new exhibitors, and retain as many as possible of the existing ones.

CONTRIBUTOR

Amanda K. Cecil, PhD, CMP, Assistant Professor, Indiana University, Department of Tourism, Conventions, and Event Management

There are two major sales efforts for any given exhibition: the show organizer must sell booth space, and also deliver a sufficient number of attendees to the exhibitors. Exhibitor marketing is a complex process that requires a sound strategic plan, including a timeline for creation of an exhibitor prospectus, advertising, public relations, e-marketing, direct sales, and international marketing.

The Exhibitor Prospectus

An exhibitor prospectus is a promotional direct mail piece or electronic document sent to current and prospective exhibitors to promote the benefits of exhibiting in a specific show, and encourage participation. This critical marketing piece provides potential exhibitors with the information they need to determine if this exhibition fits their company's sales goals and objectives. It contains information about the association or organization hosting the show, logistical details, eligibility requirements to participate, cost of exhibition space, floorplan of the exhibition, show rules and regulations, statistics on the show's attendees or market survey results, sponsorship and advertising opportunities, travel and destination tips, and the application for participation. An exhibitor prospectus can vary from a 20-page, full-color book (as for medical shows), to a glossy foldout brochure (as for many privately owned tradeshows), to a one-page information piece (as for a local consumer show), depending on the norms and standards in each industry.

SEE FIGURE 1

Elements of the Exhibitor Prospectus

1. Information on the Show Host

   The exhibitor prospectus begins with an introductory letter or section inviting potential exhibitors to explore the opportunity of participating in the exhibition by contracting for or buying booth space. It typically describes the host association, the goals of the convention and the benefits of participation, sometimes listing specific reasons why this event is better for exhibitors than a competing event. This section must clearly demonstrate that attendees will be the exhibitor's clientele, and although many show organizers shy away from exact numbers, they often mention roughly how many attendees are expected.

2. Logistical Information

   In order to evaluate the show, exhibitors must review the overall convention schedule. They must assess the number and quality hours of exhibiting, and how much time they will have with attendees. Additionally, show managers should detail the move-in and move-out schedule, special events in the exhibit hall, and other conflicting events that may compete with the exhibition for the attendees' attention.

FIGURE 1

This section also details the location of the exhibit hall, usually with a floorplan, and promotes the destination of the show as a place that both attendees and exhibitors will enjoy visiting. This information may be important to an exhibitor in terms of prioritizing this show against other exhibiting opportunities in terms of budget and location.

3. Eligibility Requirements to Participate

For many reasons, including complex taxation issues for non-profits who generate a large portion of their revenue from their conventions, not every exhibition will sell booth space to any company that wants to exhibit. Eligibility to participate in an exhibition hosted by a non-profit association is usually reserved for vendors whose products or services match the attendees, and whose products in some way contribute to the continuing education of those attendees. Some associations and other types of show organizers will reserve the right to deny any exhibitor who does not meet their requirements. This issue has been challenged legally, and can be complicated, so adequate consultation with legal experts is recommended with regard to "unrelated business income tax" liability.

Associations and organizations must also be careful not to exclude exhibitors in a way that would violate anti-trust laws. Anti-trust laws were created to prevent monopolies and unfair business practices. This issue usually arises either when one or sometimes two major shows dominate an industry, and/or when denying an exhibitor the ability to exhibit is seen as locking that company out of the marketplace. Again, this is an issue that requires specific legal review.

4. Cost to Exhibit

Exhibit cost is expressed in terms of square footage or types of booths. For example, the show may list a number of booth types, such as an island space for $2,500, or $6.25 per square foot. Some show managers opt to charge an additional amount for prime space or corner booths on the theory that better visibility should cost more. It is also important to include in the pricing exactly what the exhibitor space includes, such as whether pipe and drape, booth carpet, and utilities such as electrical service are provided, what kind of identification sign (if any) is included, and how many people can register for each booth without additional charge.

Exhibits may be sold as part of a sponsorship package. Many sponsorship packages include exhibit space and advertising. Vendors sponsoring meal functions, special events, educational sessions, and convention products (such as badge lanyards or bags) are important sources of revenue for show managers.

5. Floorplan

The floorplan of the show gives a visual depiction of the types of booths, number of booths, show entrances and other areas, such as food services, activities, or merchandise sales. Exhibitors will use this layout to ask for preferred booth locations when they contract for booth space. If space allows, exhibitors appreciate viewing the location of the exhibit hall in relation to educational breakout sessions, entrances to the overall building itself, and how traffic flow in and out of the exhibit hall relates to any other convention activities.

6. Show Rules and Regulations

This section is the "fine print" that allows the show manager to disclose any and all show rules and regulations before the exhibitor makes a purchase decision. Specific clauses regarding proper execution of the contract should be clearly described in this portion of the prospectus, including those which determine how exhibit space will be reserved, allocated and assigned, payment requirements and deadlines (including cancellation and no show policies), subletting space restrictions, display construction and limitation expectations, exhibitor representatives limitations and fees, selling and taking orders, facility rules and regulations, and liability and insurance. Obviously, this section can be complicated and may need legal review.

Many show organizers will also include the International Association of Exhibit Managers Display Specifications showing the correct physical layout of a standard (inline and perimeter), peninsula, and island space and limit exhibitors to these configurations only.

7. Attendee Demographics and Psychographics

Potential exhibitors closely analyze and review show statistics and market research, especially when faced with more than one show from which to choose. Participating in exhibitions can be costly, and companies closely review attendee demographics and psychographics to ensure that their target market will be attending this event. Therefore, show organizers often include extensive attendee demographics in terms of industry segment, level of management and level of financial or budgetary authority, along with information on the percentage of previous exhibitors who reported taking orders at the show.

8. Travel and Destination Information

Most exhibitors also review all travel and destination information when selecting a show, and take the cost of travel into consideration when making a decision. Group discounts for airfare and other transportation, and the system that the show organizer will use for reserving and allocating hotel rooms among exhibitors and attendees (especially the highly desirable ones) should be described, as this is an important issue for many exhibitors at high demand shows. Availability of opportunities to entertain clients in hotel suites and other locations, and also restrictions on entertaining attendees, should be made clear. Although it is easy to do research by visiting local Web sites, some indication of the variety of restaurants, cultural and sporting events available in the host city are still important.

9. Application for Participation
   Whether the form is included inside a print prospectus, posted online or provided at a later date, procedures for where to find and how to submit an application for booth space should be made clear. This document should be concise but complete, providing all the necessary information for both the exhibitor and the show organizer.

10. Other Information
    Additional information in the prospectus may include a comprehensive or sample list of exhibitors from the previous year (as an enticement to join competitors), an exhibitor checklist outlining the important deadlines and exhibitor responsibilities (to show what will be involved in exhibiting), testimonies from satisfied exhibitors (always effective), and in some cases, more "fine print" such as the need for exhibitors to comply with the Americans With Disabilities Act.

SEE FIGURE 2

Database Management for Marketing

Without a customized data management system, organizing and planning for marketing campaigns to potential exhibitors, and communicating with exhibitors and vendors would be extremely difficult. There are several major "contact management" software packages on the market that can be adapted to use as sales tools for selling exhibit space, and many organizations customize existing databases to accomplish the same purpose.

Cutting corners in database management is a waste of money, time and resources. Understanding the capabilities of a database system requires a commitment from the host organization and exhibit management team members. It is imperative to have up-to-date information on all potential prospects for booth sales, and then to communicate with the right contact from the moment the booth is sold until the show is over.

The Sales Process

Sales management involves the planning, implementation and control of a larger, organized sales effort. The first priority in managing sales is to detail where, how and

FIGURE 2: IAEM Exhibitor Prospectus Example

EXPO! EXPO! WEDNESDAY, 29 NOVEMBER 2006, 11:00 a.m. — 5:00 p.m.
SAN DIEGO CONVENTION CENTER, SAN DIEGO, CALIFORNIA

Times are tough, budgets are tight, and you need sales. In an ideal world, customers would come to you. At Expo! Expo! 2006 the ideal is real. Save time and money by networking with hundreds of qualified decision makers under one roof. Whatever kind of solution you sell, Expo! Expo! is the one place where you can introduce your products and services, maintain exposure, educate the industry, establish partnerships, connect with customers, and generate revenue.

Who attends Expo! Expo!?

Exhibition and meeting organizers from around the globe gather with suppliers in the exhibition industry to look for strategic industry partners to maximize their budgets and increase their efficiencies. They are searching for new and innovative technology, creative destinations, and dynamic contractors to assist them in reaching their goals. Click here to see who the attendees were in 2005. Click here to view all organizations that are currently represented within the IAEM membership.

Here's what 2005 exhibitors had to say:

"We were very pleased with the traffic on the floor and within 30 days were under contract with a new customer we met at the show!"
Alan Johnson, President, EPIC

"I can't tell you how happy we were as exhibitors, Our booth was busy the entire hours of the show. There were times when the 3 of us working were speaking and there were still people waiting to hear about our products." Ray Giovine, Vice President, NGN

"The show went really well. There were no problems/issues. The exhibit time is great - one day - wouldn't want it any other way. We had great traffic." Neil Williams, Director of Marketing, Ungerboeck Systems International

What are the attendee demographics?

See buyers that you want to see.

Over 55% of attendees in 2005 were show organizers!

* Association Show Organizer
* Consumer Show Organizer
* Independent Show Organizer
* Corporate Show Organizer
* Non-Exhibiting Supplier
* Exhibiting Supplier

Meet active buyers with purchasing authority and immediate needs.

* Senior Executive
* Vice President
* Director
* Manager
* Coordinator
* Support Staff, Administration
* General Management
* Show Organizing
* Operations
* Communications
* Sales/Marketing

2005 Attendee Quick Facts

* 24% were first-time attendees.
* Nearly 2,000 attended Expo! Expo! 2005.
* Over 7% of attendees represented 25 foreign countries.
* 71% of attendees spent 3-5½ hours on the show floor.
* 279 exhibitors reserved over 40,000 sq ft of exhibit space
* 20% were first time exhibitors; 35% exhibited 10 years or more.
* 86% of exhibitors rated the show Excellent-Very Good-Good
* 83% exhibitors met their exhibiting objectives.
* 91% of exhibitors plan to exhibit at a future Expo! Expo!
* 100% felt that they received effective exhibitor communication prior to Expo! Expo!

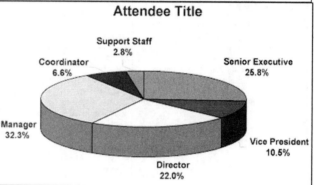

Attendee Categories

Non-Exhibiting Supplier 8.6%
Association Show Organizer 28.8%
Consumer Show Organizer 2.3%
Independent Show Organizer 18.2%
Corporate Show Organizer 5.8%
Exhibiting Supplier 31.2%

Attendee Title

Support Staff 2.8%
Senior Executive 25.8%
Coordinator 6.6%
Vice President 10.5%
Manager 32.3%
Director 22.0%

Who should exhibit?

If you offer any of the following categories of products and services for the exhibition industry, **RESERVE YOUR SPACE TODAY!** Join the growing list of respected exhibitors. Click here to view last year's Expo! Expo! 2005 Exhibitors.

A/V Equip./Rentals/Production	Facility-Public Expo	Message System
Advertising/Promotional Services	Facility-World Trade Center	Personnel (Temporary)
Airline	Floor Manager	Photography
Association	Florist/Plant Rental	Plumbing Contractor
Business Services: Shipping/ Financial/Accounting	Freight-Air	Premiums/Promotions
Catering Services	Freight-Common Carrier	Product Locators/Message Centers
Cleaning/Janitorial Services	Freight-Van Line	Publications/Dailies
Communication Equipment	Furniture Rental/Booth Furnishings	Registration Services/ Badging System
Computer Rentals	Graphics/Printing	Registration Supplies
Computer Software: Exhibition/ Event	Hostesses/Modeling Services/ Entertainment/Talent Service	Security Services
Consultant	Hotel-Exhibit Space < 30,000 square feet	Service Contractor-General
Convention Bureau	Hotel-Exhibit Space > 30,000 square feet	Service Contractor-I&D
Customs Broker	Housing/Travel Services	Show Management
Destination Management	Insurance	Signage
Education/Training	International Exhibitor Services	Special Events/Tour Operations
Electrical Contractor	Internet/Web Services/Webcasting/ System	Surveys/Audience Response System
Electronic Information Centers	Design/Software	Telecommunications
Exhibit Designer/Builder	Lead Retrieval/Management Systems	Theme Park
Facility-Arena/ Auditorium/ Stadium	Literature Displays/Kiosks	Translation Services
Facility-Convention Center	Marketing Services/Research/ Traffic Builders	Transportation/Shuttle Services
Facility-Fairground		

"We were very happy with the show this year (our first) and looking forward to the next."
Candis Roby, Marketing Manager, Veris Consulting, LLC

"I think this past Expo was the best yet. I know it was for us." Richard Einhorn, President, Production Transport, Inc.

What are the benefits of exhibiting at Expo! Expo!?

- Have cost effective access to more than 90 percent of the Tradeshow Week 200 trade show organizers.
- Contact new prospects and generate leads.
- Promote your organization's image and maximize its market exposure.
- Discuss the needs of your customers face-to-face and demonstrate solutions.
- Research the competition and develop ways to distinguish your products and services.
- Test or launch new products and services at the customer level.
- Develop your database to strengthen your overall sales and marketing programs.
- Network and build relationships with decision makers and influencers.
- Introduce your company to IAEM members.
- Up-sell existing clients.

What does a booth cost, and what does it include?
Cost:
$2,500 per 10'x10' space (member rate)

Includes:

* Pipe and Drape – 8' draped back wall and 3' draped side rails
* 7" x 44" Identification Sign
* 3 "Expo! Expo! Only" exhibit hall badges per 100 square feet for your exhibit staff
* 3 Opening Reception tickets per 100 square feet
* 3 Opening General Session Tickets
* 1 lead retrieval unit (at exhibitor's request)
* 1 pre-meeting attendee registration list (at exhibitor's request)
* 6 exclusive, non-competing, exhibit hours – Wednesday, 29 November 11:00 a.m. – 5:00 p.m.
* Complimentary lunch and dessert served in the exhibition hall for exhibitors and attendees
* Unlimited VIP "Expo! Expo! Only" passes good for free exhibit hall admission for your preferred customers not planning to attend Expo! Expo! IAEM's Annual Meeting & Exhibition as an attendee
* Use of the Expo! Expo! Exhibitor Logo for marketing purposes
* Virtual booth which includes contact information and description, product and services category selections for search purposes and company URL.
* Listing in exhibitor section of the on-site program
* Listing in the on-site map
* Access to the on-site Press Room where you can place your media kits and press releases for distribution to the attending press
* Standard booth cleaning (pre-show)
* Tips and Templates for pre-show exhibitor promotion and marketing

How do I reserve a booth?

Click here to download the 2006 Application and Contract for Exhibition Space. Click here to view the 2006 online Floor Plan. Complete the contract and fax it to Julie Anderson at +1 (972) 458-8119 with a 50% deposit. There is limited space available. Don't be left out! **Reserve your exhibit space today.**

Questions? Contact Julie Anderson, CEM, Director of Exhibitions, at janderson@iaem.org, or +1 (972) 687-9206.

What advertising and sponsorship opportunities are available?

Increase your ROI with exciting sponsorship and advertising opportunities that will enhance your visibility at Expo! Expo! Choose from a variety of advertising and sponsorship options. If you are interested in sponsorship opportunities for Expo! Expo! 2006, please email mailto:cbreden@iaem.org.

> *"IAEM has launched added value this year in matching exhibitors with customer needs. IAEM's service is a partnership and a leading organization in my opinion."* Brant Henkel, National Sales Manager, Charlotte, Visit Charlotte
>
> *"This was a great show – heard nothing but great comments from other exhibitors & attendees."* Lew Hoff, President, Bartizan Connects

at what cost sales must be made in order to meet the organization's exhibit sales goals. In order to measure sales success, revenue goals and objectives must be clearly outlined in the marketing plan.

Although it is a very expensive and time-consuming method, direct sales, also called personal selling, is a focused, effective approach to contacting potential and returning exhibitors. Customers crave a personal, continuing relationship with organizations with which they do business; therefore, a show's sales force must recognize the power of this medium.

Although the Sales Cycle is the same regardless of the product or the industry, there are some particular steps to go through when selling booth space to potential exhibitors:

- Prospecting – Identifying and qualifying potential exhibitors through referrals, advertising, direct mail, telemarketing, and other avenues. Identifying the key contact who makes decisions on exhibitions is critical.

- Pre-approach – Researching the prospect's background, and identifying the needs of that particular prospect, will allow the sales manager to focus on the show benefits that match that prospect's needs.

- Presentation – Establishing rapport with the prospect, building trust, determining needs, illustrating benefits through specific examples, and explaining and translating the features of the show.

- Handling Objections – Overcoming sales resistance or unwillingness to make a decision by providing more information and addressing specific concerns.

- Closing – Obtaining a commitment by asking for the order; Getting the "yes."

- Follow Up – Keeping the customer informed and confirming satisfaction, informing customers of new services or changes, handling complaints, and selling or cross-selling additional services.

Telemarketing

A major support tool for personal selling is outbound telemarketing, utilizing a customized database of prospects. Telemarketing is the most personalized mass marketing medium available, and offers an ideal way to enhance a direct mail campaign.

There are positives and negatives to using telemarketing as a campaign strategy. First, telemarketing can be very effective. The response rate produced by telemarketing campaigns are on average 2.5 to 10 times higher than those produced by direct mail. Notably, a telemarketing campaign can be started and stopped very quickly based on its effectiveness in the marketplace.

On the other hand, a telemarketing effort's costs are high compared to direct mail and some forms of advertising. A single call can average between $5-10. Before dedicating dollars and resources to an extensive telemarketing campaign, consider the following:

- Exhibit space sales may or may not be an appropriate goal for telemarketing. Typically, exhibitors are solicited through alternative means, and by a sales team member.

- Telemarketing should only be handled by experienced, qualified individuals. This is not a task for part-time employees or students. Work closely with the telemarketing team to ensure they are trained and familiar with the event, the offer, the attendees, and the industry. Consider working with a service bureau using a formal script to execute this strategy.

- Telemarketing works best with a combination of direct mail. Timing is critical. Calling prospects following a direct mail campaign can help reinforce personal contact. This is especially important in terms of exhibit sales.
- Expect and demand cumulative results throughout the campaign: hours spent, contacts made, bad information, sales completed, refusals, and interested leads.
- Follow-up with a telemarketing program is essential. Programs can easily miss out on potential sales opportunities if someone does not follow-up. A sales representation should contact the interested party within 24 hours from the initial contact.

Web site Design

Promoting an exhibition on the Internet is now a common practice, and exhibitors are becoming more accustomed to researching shows via the Web. Show managers must focus on providing updated content, compelling graphics and pictures, and a site that exhibitors find persuasive and informative. Exhibitors also expect to find links to official service providers as well, particularly the general contractor and housing provider.

Equally important, exhibit prospects must be able to find and access the Web site when researching shows. With millions of Web sites now in existence, most search engines routinely return thousands of "hits." Therefore, identifying the appropriate key words for the show, and working to make the show's link appear on the top of the list, is a goal a professional Web developer can assist with. Adding the show's Web address to appropriate search engines, indices and subject directories can ensure that a particular show's potential attendees and exhibitors can easily find your Web site.

When marketing an exhibition through the Internet, trouble-free access for the end user should be the main objective. In addition to being compatible with multiple types of Web browsers, content should be condensed to fit the time and attention span of today's busy Web user. Spell check all documents and text, and routinely test Web site links, adjusting any internal or external links that may not be working. Finally, consider how the text will appear in another language, especially if the show has an international market.

Advertising

Advertising is a powerful, persuasive medium that can assist in creating awareness among prospective exhibitors, and reinforce a connection with returning exhibitors. A show's advertising should accomplish three goals:

- Increase awareness among key decision makers who approve exhibition choices.

- Increase preference for your show.
- Generate inquires from those fitting the exhibitor criteria.

As with every marketing medium, research and planning for advertisement placement needs to take place. A clear understanding of the show's booth sales objectives needs to be mapped out and communicated in a detailed plan. It is critical that the advertising expenditures to which sufficient budgets have been allocated be included in the marketing plan.

Developing and executing a sound creative strategy is considered the most critical part of advertising. Advertising tends to get lost in the clutter and noise of the millions of advertising messages that are available today. To crash through these barriers, the appropriate vehicle within the categories of print, Internet, broadcast, or outdoor must be selected. A good strategy will utilize the right levels of saturation and the right timing for the appearance of the ads. These are commonly referred to as scheduling, "reach," and "frequency."

Reach is the number of different potential customers exposed to a media message within a given time period. It is expressed as a percentage, and takes into account duplicated audiences. Frequency is the average number of times individuals are exposed to an advertiser within a given time period. When combined, reach and frequency are used to analyze and compare alternative media schedules using the same budget.

The scheduling of advertisements can make or break a campaign. The media plan must delineate "flighting" versus "continuous" advertising. Flighting refers to periodic waves of coverage interspersed with periods of no activity. Continuous advertising is a schedule with little or no variations in pressure. On the other hand, "pulsing" refers to a combination of the two concepts – a continuous base of support augmented by intermittent bursts of pressure.

Other key advertising strategies include:
- **Dominate the Dominant Media**
  Select only the top magazines or publications for the targeted industry and advertise in them heavily.
- **Front-loading the Message**
  For event promotion, it is important to get the message out early in order to set the stage and allow exhibitors to research and budget for show.
- **Opportunity Buys**
  Take advantage of special issues, discounts or volume deals offered by selected media.

International Marketing

In today's economy, show organizers are dealing with ever-changing global markets while international trade continues to be a lucrative business. It is no secret that many "American-owned" companies are now operated in other countries. Overseas marketing efforts require extensive research, focused sales promotion, direct selling through local channels, and thoughtful customer cultivation and service.

To target specific overseas markets, exploring trade data and statistics will assist the show organizer in selecting regional markets that have a high volume of export products suitable for the show, high rates of growth, favorable trading conditions, and other key factors governing international trade. The United States & Foreign Commercial Service, a division of the US Department of Commerce, is staffed to offer direction in international trade issues.

Researching overseas markets and using government sources to compile export statistics is a vital first step. Partnering with trade associations, overseas trade magazine publishers, US and foreign government offices that promote trade in the region, and mailing list compilers and brokers may be the best approaches to accessing prospective exhibiting companies' contact information. It is important to note that the availability and quality of the lists may vary a great deal, and a show organizer may need to seek the services of a computer bureau specializing in direct mail. Additionally, language, business practices, culture, and laws and regulations regarding direct mail differ between countries and even within countries. In order to avoid doing something illegal or unethical inadvertently, consulting with a local expert is imperative.

According to many show organizers, the best way to persuade overseas companies to exhibit is to demonstrate that the show is much greater than the sum of its attendees. The opportunity to exhibit at a US show will allow them to develop relationships with American distributors and manufacturers, while selling their product or service to attendees and other exhibitors. There is great potential to establish long-term partnership or agents agreements with other vendors.

Direct mail can be a cost-effective and targeted method of international marketing, garnering a lot of attention by overseas companies. This process should be measurable, assuming the markets and customer types are coded and tracked.

In terms of advertising to an international market, the show manager should attempt to "dominate the dominant media." Because production of a translated or bilingual ad can be costly, the show organizer should research publications with the largest target audience. Since many international journals tend to be customer versus industry oriented, the organizer should also inquire about the demographics of the publication's audience. Show organizers should also strive for good placement – such as the inside or outside cover – and request at least three appearances in the publication to emphasize frequency. If possible, listing a local contact for the international reader can be beneficial. This person should be able to answer questions in the native language, and be available in the country's time zone.

SUMMARY

Marketing to exhibitors is a series of promotional tasks beginning with the preparation of an attractive prospectus to create "buzz" among potential exhibitors and encourage them to participate in the exhibition. Other ways to reach potential exhibitors include telemarketing, personal selling, advertising and creating a Web site that is easy to find and use. Each show will benefit from a customized mix of these techniques.

QUESTIONS FOR DISCUSSION

① Is it more important to spend money on marketing to exhibitors or marketing to attendees?

② What's the best "bang for the buck" in marketing dollars?

③ How would you define "buzz"?

Chapter 4
Marketing to Attendees/Visitors

*"No computer network with pretty graphics can ever replace
the salespeople that make our society work."*

– Clifford Stoll, Silicon Snake Oil, 1995

Section II: Business Issues

IN THIS CHAPTER YOU WILL LEARN
- What you need to know about exhibition attendees
- How trade and consumer events differ in marketing needs
- How to create a marketing strategy to attract attendees
- Distinct benefits of campaigns in different media

INTRODUCTION

Attendee demographics – where the attendees come from and who they are – is important in developing an attendee marketing campaign. For example, an exhibition which draws a national or international audience will be marketed very differently from those with a regional, state or local scope. In addition, trade or industry exhibitions, and consumer exhibitions are marketed very differently from each other. Attendees are very different in terms of motivation, expectations and needs. Show organizers must address these differences when developing marketing strategies.

CONTRIBUTOR

Amanda K. Cecil, PhD, CMP, Assistant Professor, Indiana University, Department of Tourism, Conventions, and Event Management

Understanding the Exhibition's Attendees/Visitors

Note: It is important to note that outside of North America, attendees are generally referred to as "visitors."

An exhibition attendee can be described as "an individual registered for or participating in an event" (CIC, 2006). They are professionals from organizations that utilize the products, services or equipment displayed at exhibitions. Show organizers tend to classify exhibition attendees into three categories: (1) buyer (2) purchasing agent or (3) research and development specialist. A buyer selects which types and brands of products to buy and makes final decisions. A purchasing agent may also make decisions, but tends to order and re-buy products already in use within the company. The research and development specialist, often an engineer or scientist, has the technical skills and knowledge necessary for product development, but often only recommends to others in his or her organization what products to buy. All of these categories of attendees are important contacts for the exhibitor.

Attendees at Tradeshows

Attendance at private industry exhibitions, often called tradeshows, is limited to members of that industry only, and usually requires pre-certification or proof of membership such as a relevant business card. Trade associations who often sponsor this type of event may offer a variety of levels for the attendee to choose from when registering, such as full-conference fee, a multiple registrant rate, a one-day pass, a companion pass, or an early bird discounted rate. Associations may also offer a non-member rate, which tends to be substantially more expensive than the membership conference rate.

Most tradeshows or exhibitions are part of a larger educational program, commonly referred to as a convention. The success of an industry convention depends on the show organizer's ability to present potential attendees with the right combination of valuable educational programming, networking and problem-solving opportunities, and new ideas to take back to their jobs. Attendees also want to be guaranteed that the vendors they are seeking will be participating in the exhibition portion of the event, and that the educational programs are relevant to their needs. Documenting the success of previous exhibitions (sometimes with testimonials from past attendees) helps to convince those who did not attend that they missed an opportunity to gain some professional development skills, and assist their companies in reviewing new products and services. Coming up with these types of success stories is challenging for a new exhibition launch, and can also be difficult for an industry event in distress.

Marketing the dates and locations of industry exhibition attendees should be an ongoing and year-round process, and not just included in pre-event publications and announcements. Often, as soon as one convention is concluded, marketing for the next immediately begins, sometimes waiting in the background to hit the Web site immediately after the current show closes. In addition, many trade associations secure locations and dates for future conventions three to ten years in advance, so this information is readily available for publication as soon as definitely confirmed. Industry professionals and association members who eagerly anticipate and regularly attend certain conventions often want to reserve the appropriate block of time on their calendars far in advance. Therefore, it's a marketing benefit to many association and event Web sites to keep future dates posted as far out as possible.

Consumer Exhibitions

Contrary to trade events, consumer exhibitions are open to the general public, and attendees are the end users of the products or services. Attendees are either enthusiasts of the exhibition's focus, or participants in the activity as a hobby or craft. Attendees live in the surrounding area, and their motivation for coming to the exhibition is not professional development or purchases, but may range from seeking specific products or service information to just window shopping.

Consumer exhibition organizers charge an admission fee or sell tickets to the event. Although advance registration is not required, pre-sold tickets are usually discounted in some way. Group ticket sales are popular for some consumer events, and show organizers tend to target local and regional organizations, such as sporting clubs, that may have an interest in the event. In addition, it is not uncommon that a small portion of a consumer show's proceeds support a local or regional charity or community effort.

Consumer shows sometimes offer seminars or demonstrations of interest to attendees, such as cooking demonstrations, golf swing clinics, and musical performances, as well as discounted merchandise priced significantly below retail (also known as "show specials"), and promotional activities such as raffles and drawings for free trips and cash prizes. Celebrity or notable icons appearing at the exhibition, either paid for by the show organizer or individual exhibitors, tend to drive attendance and media interest in the event.

Marketing for customer exhibitions typically starts earlier than for tradeshows, usually six to eight months prior to the event, with an aggressive marketing blitz utilizing local media starting only four to six weeks out. Major marketing efforts may center on new special programming additions, or the release of discount programs. Annual events have to emphasize that there will be something past attendees have never seen before to keep generating repeat attendance.

Attendee Marketing Strategies for Show Organizers

According to an article entitled "Attendee Marketing: What Works Now" in the April 2006 edition of *EXPO Magazine*, nearly 49 percent of shows increased their marketing budgets in 2005, up from 39 percent of shows in 2004. In addition, positive or steady trends in attendance, growth and budget stability were reported. Therefore, it seems clear that show organizers are finding it necessary to dedicate more and more of their budgets to promoting their events.

There are several different marketing mediums used by show organizers to attract attendees to exhibitions, including direct mail, e-marketing, advertising and media.

Direct Mail Marketing

Direct mail, or any form of communication that is transmitted though the mail, is commonly used for promoting both industry and consumer exhibitions and according to the article "Marketwatch: Attendee Marketing" in the May 2006 edition of *EXPO Magazine*, organizers spend 41 percent of their budgets on direct mail efforts. This can include creating and mailing brochures and postcards, and the relevant printing and postage costs. Even though show organizers currently rank direct mail as the most effective marketing tool, they project using it less in the coming years (*Expo Magazine*, April 2006), presumably in anticipation of more electronic means.

However, most show managers still believe that an eye-catching piece that provides essential information is critical to helping potential attendees decide whether or not the event looks interesting. The best direct mail pieces issue an immediate call to action for readers, usually a way to register for the event, either by mail on online.

In addition to a proven track record, there are several other advantages to launching a direct mail campaign for an exhibition. First, direct mail can be used to target specific industry markets and geographical areas by acquiring or purchasing lists that have been appropriately sorted by zip code or some common affiliation, such as memberships in relevant groups. In this case, direct mail can be an inexpensive medium for reaching only the people who are likely to be interested in the event. Direct mail can also be personalized, and may allow for creative options to be added. In addition, it is a marketing strategy which can be measured and tested for effectiveness by building in ways to track where a respondent received his or her promotional information. Return on investment for a direct mailing campaign is measured by response rate, and evaluation of each attempt is important in determining the best marketing methods for any specific event.

The fundamental guideline for creating an effective direct marketing package can be summarized in the "AIDA formula".

A Get the prospect's undivided **ATTENTION**.

I Create **INTEREST** by showing the prospect the benefits of attending this show.

D Create **DESIRE** in the prospect by proving the value of the event.

A Stimulate **ACTION** by the prospect to register and attend the show.

Although it may seem obvious, experts agree that mailing to only the right potential attendees is an important component for any direct mail campaign. Creating, managing and maintaining a targeted attendee mailing list is a challenging and necessary task for all show organizers. There are three options in regard to assembling a mailing list:

• Build a list using past sales or registration records, routine office correspondence, inquiries, referrals, lists from past direct mail campaigns, contest entrants, recommendations from others inside and outside the organization, directories, government sources, lists in trade magazines, and lists exchanged with other parties.

• Rent or purchase lists that are available through list compliers, list brokers, trade publications, and associations.

• Use a combination of the two options, utilizing rented lists for prospecting and in-house lists for delivering the message to the core audience.

Include the answers to the following questions in any direct mail piece designed for potential attendees:

• What type of exhibition is this? Is this a private or a public exhibition? Who is invited to attend?

• Who is hosting the exhibition? Who are the exhibition's organizers, supporters & sponsors? A short history of the exhibition and its organizers may be appropriate.

• When and where is it being held? List the exhibition's dates, location and exhibition hours. Travel information, such as parking, local hotel accommodations, airport access, and directions to the exhibition's venue need to be included.

• What type of exhibitors, or what companies, are exhibiting at the exhibition? List the committed exhibitors by company name or product or service type.

• What educational programs and other features will be offered in concert with the exhibition? Describe the educational program with a daily agenda of all industry speakers or recognizable names.

• What are the costs to attend?

• How do I register? Specifically detail attendee's fees, registration categories, special group, senior or child discounts, cut-off dates for early bird rates, and cancellation policies (applies only to industry exhibitions).

- Who benefits from the exhibition? Charities? Professional organizations? Students?
- Mention if monies from the exhibition will go to support local or national charities, professional development for industry segments, student scholarships or other initiatives.

Direct mail also has its drawbacks. Even with good contact information, direct mail historically yields a low response rate – 5 percent is an acceptable return for business-to-business direct mail efforts. Plus, it can be an extremely time-consuming venture, and error-prone. Compiling a good list of potential attendees, especially new prospects, is not only difficult but can be very costly. Rushing through the design or database creation process can increase the likelihood of problems, increasing costs, and compromising effectiveness. It is always important to have production and mailing timelines, to stick to them carefully, and to observe any postal restrictions which will ensure timely delivery of the piece. Any promotional piece that arrives too late for the attendee to make a decision to attend is wasted time and money for a show organizer.

E-Marketing

Exhibitions are increasingly relying on email, Web site advertising, and online registration and ticketing to market to potential exhibition attendees.

Email marketing can be used in many ways to manage attendee communication, from keeping in touch with registrants to promoting advance registration. While it may take six to eight weeks to receive a response from a direct mail piece, approximately 80 percent of email marketing campaigns receive responses within 48 hours (Jupiter Research in *EXPO Magazine*, 2006). When using email, resist the urge to email too often, since email overload is widespread. Purge lists of "bounce back" responses after each transmission so as to not continue to send to non-existent addresses. Also, many marketing experts believe that the best email campaigns are those that utilize only "opt-in" marketing; in other words, sending only to recipients who have agreed to have information sent to them. Another option is "opt-out" marketing, where an email is sent without permission, but allows the recipient to request that they be taken off the list. Even the major Web retailers utilize opt-out etiquette.

Email marketing is both cost effective and measurable. When comparing the cost of email with direct mail and telemarketing, email is clearly cheaper. In addition, email messages are often very effective because they are so much easier to personalize for each recipient. By including information about the recipient's buying preferences and other pertinent information, show organizers can maximize their return on investment. For a combination of these reasons, direct marketers are devoting a larger percentage of their budget to email use.

However, as more sophisticated spam and junk mail blocking software is introduced into the market, many messages may be lost even when using an opt-in system. Exhibition marketers need to be aware of all legislation regarding email spamming, and ensure compliance with the law's provisions. In particular, marketers should note the CAN-SPAM Act of 2003 which details penalties for violations of deceptive commercial email.

Average cost per opt-in, email message	$.20 each
Average cost per direct mail piece	$.75-$2
Average cost for telemarketing per person	$1-3

2001 eMarketer Report cited in Expo Magazine, *May 2006*

Web Marketing

Because the exhibition Web site is an important attendee marketing tool, show organizers should concentrate on innovative ways to enhance Web content. Conveying the marketing story of the exhibition will only help those interested in attending the exhibition, or who may still be undecided.

In addition to good content, both exhibitors and attendees must be easily able to navigate the exhibition Web site without spending much time or effort finding dates, times, locations, educational sessions and often a preview of the floorplan. Limiting the number of clicks through the Web site, and designing the site with the user in mind, will make the exhibition site most effective for all target audiences. It may be necessary to hire special Web design talent to keep up with the latest in Web design technology and strategy.

Accepting online show registrations, educational programming reservations or special event ticket orders for banquets of other optional entertainment events from the Web site is becoming a standard practice for most exhibitions. This option is cost-effective and convenient for both attendees and show organizers. Incentives for attendees include early-bird registration fees, discounts to register online, other special benefits such as eligibility for prize drawings, and value – added content and advance information. Show organizers are attracted to the time-saving features of instant confirmation, customized reporting, the elimination of manual data entry and the ability to combine the registration and ticketing functions.

Advertising

Although advertising efforts, timing, and media are very different for consumer exhibitions and tradeshows, all advertising campaigns targeted toward attendees need to do three things:

- Increase awareness of the event in question to individuals who can make the decision to attend, or with the power to approve the attendance of others
- Increase preference for the event in question over competitors
- Generate valid pre-registration from those qualified to attend, or pre-sale of group or individual tickets.

The key to a sound advertising campaign is research and planning. Advertising dollars spent without a clear objective in mind are almost always dollars wasted. The efforts and budget devoted to advertising must complement the overall marketing goals and objectives, and work in concert with other media directives. Examples of legitimate advertising objectives include:

- Develop awareness of the exhibition to new attendees
- Introduce new features and benefits of the exhibition
- Expand the exhibition's reach into new markets or geographical areas
- Reinforce marketing message to past attendees
- Generate sales leads.

Advertising Tradeshows to Attendees

Private show organizers use precisely targeted, niche advertising media to promote their exhibitions and educational programs. Industry and professional publications, newsletters, journals, magazines and banner ads on selected Web sites are the advertising media of choice for most trade exhibitions. Because attendees must either be pre-qualified, or meet minimum criteria to participate in the exhibition or convention, few show organizers advertise or market to the masses. Advertising campaigns for international or national events tend to run yearly, promoting next year's date and location immediately following that year's exhibition.

Because most of the larger trade exhibitions attract an international audience and promote a global focus, show organizers should not underestimate the importance of researching advertising opportunities overseas:

- Ensure the publication is a true trade magazine and is not consumer-oriented
- List the local contact for the international reader to contact with questions or to register
- Use a reputable translation firm and ask the publisher to double-check the translations for possible errors.

PROMOTIONAL TIMELINE FOR A CONSUMER SHOW

30 days out

Develop press releases to talk about special feature, celebrities, letting the media know what is in-store, etc. This will also give TV and radios the opportunity to explore special guests as to whether there is a personality that might be a good fit for their shows as well. As an example: One of your celebrities could be on-air the week preceding the show if that guest is out of town perhaps they could be on a morning show the opening day.

10-14 days out

Begin advertising and promotion campaign. Depending on the amount of coverage that is budgeted, the ad schedule should start slow and build to the maximum four or five days before the event.

4-5 days out

Period of time for the majority of paid advertising. The week prior should also be the time to utilize any celebrities on air talking about the event. Outdoor advertising should also begin the same time as well as Internet advertising. If outdoor advertising is purchased, often those buys will consist of a month. Try to purchase billboards by the day so that the message can be delivered the week of the event. The more concentrated the advertising effort on TV, Radio, Outdoor, Internet, Print, etc the better.

Print advertising needs to follow the same time frame, but an ad should appear in the paper every day of the event as well. Do not rely on print to drive traffic. Print advertising serves as a reference so when the attendee hears something on air or sees a billboard they can go to the paper to learn the what, when, where, costs, etc.

Advertising Consumer Exhibitions to Attendees

Using appropriate, targeted advertising channels can assist show organizers in justifying the perceived high costs of television, radio, newspaper, outdoor, Web site, or industry magazine or publications. By reaching a large number of people from new or established segments, advertising may actually be one of the most inexpensive ways to reach potential attendees and reinforce the event's positioning.

Advertising can be expensive, however, so consumer show organizers frequently pursue media partnerships and trades to reduce costs while increasing exposure to the exhibition. Since most make use of local and regional television, radio, newspaper and specialty publications, partnerships with local radio of TV stations or with local publishing companies is common. The show organizer might offer visibility at the event in return for a discount on expenditures. Determining the size, scope, and focus of the show will help dictate timing as well as which advertising media to use. For example, attendee demographics for a boat show might indicate usage of the local daily newspaper for advertising, while a skateboarding show might point more to a local rock station. Frequency may also be a decision factor since consumer exhibitions tend to use more frequent advertising closer to the exhibition date.

Public and Media Relations

Public relations, or PR, is one of the most inexpensive marketing communications tools an organization or exhibition sponsor can use. Often available to show organizers at no charge, the unique advantage of PR is that it is perceived by the audience as an impartial view. The readers of PR placements assume that it is the publisher's opinion that is being expressed, and the message gains instant credibility. However, show organizers have little to no control over how the message is ultimately constructed and presented by the media. Putting together a comprehensive plan with specific objectives can direct public relations efforts to their most favorable end.

Before launching any PR activities, the following issues should be addressed:
- What specific goals does the organization have for a PR campaign?
  - Increase awareness of a new exhibition location
  - Promote changes in dates of your exhibition
  - Increase attendance at your educational programs or demonstrations
  - Generate inquiries by professionals to receive copies of the exhibition's brochure
  - Combat rumors spread by the exhibition's competitors
- How can these objectives be accomplished?
  - Tools and techniques to meet the objectives
  - Timeline to complete PR efforts

- ◦ Involvement of an outside firm
- ◦ Media training for organization's spokesperson
- Who will control each element of the PR campaign?
  - ◦ Contact or spokesperson for the exhibition interacting with editors, reporters and writers
  - ◦ Technical review and policy review for all PR messages
- How much (if any) of the budget will be dedicated to PR efforts?
  - ◦ Outside services such as artwork, printing, mail services, photography, video production, travel and entertainment, mailing lists and subscriptions
  - ◦ Salaries and outside fees of targeted PR efforts
- What methods will be used to measure the PR campaign's success?
  - ◦ Collection of press and video clips
  - ◦ Evaluation methods of quality and quantity of placements
  - ◦ Tracking number of inquiries as a result of PR
  - ◦ Survey for changes in attitudes and awareness

Media relations refers to the establishment and maintenance of relationships with identified media reporters, editors, publishers, broadcast producers, radio and television owners and managers. When dealing with the media, show organizers must understand the nature of their roles, always observing a code of behavior. Stories that are not perceived as newsworthy – in other words, those that would interest a general audience – will quickly be dismissed by media representatives.

Here are some tips for generating media attention:
- Send the media a written proposal that clearly outlines the facts of the event. Do not use deceptive language or exaggerate the highlights of the exhibition
- Avoid favoring one reporter or news or radio station over another
- Write a tailored press release to match the audience's or readers' understanding of the subject or interest
- Follow up appropriately, but do not harass reporters, editors or station managers
- Provide media contacts with a press kit that details the background of the organization and exhibition. Include a recent press release, fact sheet, Q&A sheet, promotional brochures, photos and biographies of keynote speakers, celebrities or other notables, and camera-ready artwork
- Sponsor a press briefing, press conference, or press reception to get acquainted with the media and make major announcements
- Invite the media to the exhibition and treat them like VIPs. Offer guided tours of the exhibitions or arrange interviews with exhibition organizers, board members, or celebrities

- Use PR experts when appropriate. Hiring an individual who is an expert in working with the media may be worth every dollar, especially if the exhibition has major announcements, needs assistance in creating a newsworthy spin, or continues to get poor coverage.

SUMMARY

Since providing a sufficient number of attendees is critical to the success of any event, the show organizer must have a working knowledge of marketing. Whether considering direct mail, email or advertising to attract attendees/visitors, the show organizer must have a working knowledge of the pros and cons, costs and technical issues of each media, and continually evaluate results and re-allocate expenditures.

QUESTIONS FOR DISCUSSION

① Why does marketing to consumer show visitors generally begin later than marketing to tradeshow attendees?

② Why is newspaper advertising more effective for consumer shows than for trade only events?

③ Name at least three characteristics of an effective Web site.

Section II: Business Issues

Chapter 5
Partnership Marketing

"Glory is fleeting, but obscurity is forever."

–Napoleon Bonaparte

Section II: Business Issues

IN THIS CHAPTER YOU WILL LEARN

- The benefits of a partnership marketing program
- The steps in valuing sponsorships for an exhibition
- How to approach sales of sponsorships
- The elements of a good partnership agreement

INTRODUCTION

Exhibitions create a unique opportunity to help exhibitors achieve their sales and marketing goals. Show organizers work with exhibitors to create additional opportunities for exposure by offering sponsorship of various events, publications and services occurring at the exhibition through a process called Partnership (or Relationship) Marketing.

CONTRIBUTORS

Robert Dallmeyer, President, RD International; Jane Lorimer, CME, Managing Director, Lorimer Consulting Group; Cathy Breden, CAE, CMP, Chief Operating Officer, International Association for Exhibition Management

There is a natural synergy between a company purchasing exhibit space and a show organizer who can provide additional methods for exposure. Sponsorships provide another medium for companies to give their products visibility at an exhibition.

Providing a variety of ways to gain exposure with the target audience, including Partnership Marketing, has been proven beneficial to the exhibitor by research conducted by CEIR (*The Power of Exhibitions II. Maximizing the Role of Exhibitions in the Total Marketing Mix,* Jeff Tanner, Center for Exhibition Industry Research).

AVERAGE ATTRACTION EFFICIENCY

The percentage of the targeted audience the exhibitor or sponsor was able to attract increased by integrating these components:

Advertising	+46%
Sponsorships	+104%
Press conferences	+77%
Hospitality functions	+86%

Converting visitors to qualified leads increases when integrating these components:

Pre-show promotion	+50%
At-show hospitality	+62%
Staff training	+68%

Developing a Sponsorship and Advertising Program

Sponsorship is defined as an investment in cash or in-kind services or products, in return for access to exploitable business potential associated with an event or a highly publicized entity. Typically, sponsors are recognized in the exhibition's promotional collateral, on signage or in other creatively-visible applications.

Advertising includes information about an organization that the show organizer pays to have printed or announced in various forms of media and promotional collateral.

Show organizers naturally welcome additional income. However, when developing a partnership program, organizers should focus on adding value to an event, not just revenue. If the program and the event are viewed as valuable by exhibitors, and the exhibitors can substantiate their return on investment, then the revenue will naturally flow in.

Section II: Business Issues

The first step in developing a successful partnership marketing program for an exhibition or event is to summarize the event's value, having the following information readily available:

- What is the attendance at the event? Is the event audited by an outside independent party certified by the Exhibition and Event Industry Audit Commission?
- What is the ratio of buyers to sellers?
- What are the demographics of the event, including the level of buying influence of those who attend?
- How many exhibitions in the same industry or market are there currently? Are there multiple event opportunities, or just one or two?
- How many times does show management communicate with buyers throughout the year?
- What other competing events are in the marketing space, and where and when are those events held?

The next step is to create a spreadsheet and write down all opportunities for both sponsorships and advertising. Some opportunities might include:

Sponsorship
- Social functions such as opening night receptions and award or gala dinners
- General session entertainment
- Keynote speakers
- Hotel room amenities
- Grand prize drawings
- Lanyards with imprinted company logo
- Educational sessions
- Morning and afternoon breaks
- Bottled water with a company's logo and contact information on the label
- Special functions with the senior level decision makers
- Cyber Café where attendees can check their email
- Registration portfolios or bags
- Candy or refreshments at the registration area
- Conference writing pads
- Pens
- Educational session handouts
- Shuttle buses

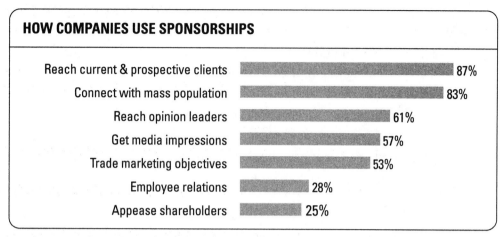

HOW COMPANIES USE SPONSORSHIPS

Reach current & prospective clients	87%
Connect with mass population	83%
Reach opinion leaders	61%
Get media impressions	57%
Trade marketing objectives	53%
Employee relations	28%
Appease shareholders	25%

Source: Sponsorship Marketing Global Report

Advertising

- Banner advertising on the event site
- Putting a wrap on a shuttle bus advertising the company
- Decals on the floor of the show
- Show directory advertising
- Advertising on video monitors
- Advertising on the map of the show floor
- Advertising in the on-line floor map
- Advertising on the outside wrap or in promotional brochures sent out by show management
- Advertising in the on-site guide
- Banner advertising on signs in a convention facility

The list of opportunities is limited only by one's imagination and knowledge of what exhibitors want and might find valuable. Often exhibitors are more creative at making suggestions for new opportunities than are show organizers, since exhibitors sometimes bring ideas from other shows in which they participate. Organizers can also conduct research through focus groups or surveys to determine what the event might bear if it is a new sponsorship or advertising program.

Show organizers should also look at what other exhibitions – both competing and non-competing – are doing, and what they are charging for sponsorship and advertising. Assign estimated appropriate values for the offerings, taking into consideration what the true costs are to show management for the sponsorship. For each opportunity, take the number of attendees who are buying influencers, and divide that number by the value assigned to determine the cost per reach.

Section II: Business Issues

Pricing

Pricing sponsorships is an art. While it can be tempting to project unrealistic values for potential opportunities, careful pricing is crucial, and should be analyzed carefully. When assigning a price to a sponsorship opportunity, there are several scenarios that can be explored:

- A flat fee based on the value that has been placed on the sponsorship
- A flat fee based on covering some percentage of the costs
- A flat fee based on covering all the costs, plus an amount above the cost
- A fee based on the exclusivity of the sponsorship.

For instance, if a sponsorship for registration bags is valued at $40,000, and 7,000 attendees are expected, the cost per reach is $5.71 (40,000 divided by 7,000). In this example, the bags cost $5 each (a total of $35,000 for 7,000 bags), so in addition to covering cost of the bags, the organizer is charging an arbitrary fee ($5,000) to cover the anticipated costs of production, and for covering any additional expenses such as shipping or handling. Registration bags are typically attractive to exhibitors because attendees take them home and use them in their business and personal lives, making the reach of the branded bag higher.

An in-kind or" trade out" sponsorship is one that benefits both the sponsor and show management, and one where money generally does not change hands. For instance, a company might have a technology application that would help the exhibition. A trade out could be negotiated for the company to provide that technology at no charge. In return, show management would give the company complimentary booth space and/or complimentary registrations.

Many exhibitions will assign tiered pricing for sponsorship levels, identifying what a sponsor will receive in recognition for their sponsorship. See the sample below:

SAMPLE

All sponsors receive maximum exposure to the Widget Tool Expo audience before, during and after the event. A company may choose any combination of sponsorships to build the most effective traffic-building program possible. All sponsors must be exhibitors in the Widget Tool Expo, and will receive onsite signage recognition.

Platinum Sponsor $50,000+
- Platinum recognition sign to be displayed in booth
- Recognition in the on-site program
- Complimentary 10x10 exhibit space

- Link from the Widget Tool Expo event site to the sponsor's Web page
- 4 invitations to the Chairman's Private Reception
- 4 free meeting registration passes
- Name, logo and click-through in show issue of Widget Tools for Everyone Magazine

Gold Sponsor $20,000+

- Gold recognition sign to be displayed in booth
- Recognition in the on-site program
- Link from the Widget Tool event site to the sponsor's Web page
- 2 invitations to the Chairman's Private Reception
- 2 free meeting registration passes
- Name and click-through in show issue of Widget Tools for Everyone Magazine

Silver Sponsor $10,000+

- Silver recognition sign to be displayed in booth
- Recognition in the on-site program
- Link from the Widget Tool event site to the sponsor's Web page
- 1 invitation to the Chairman's Private Reception
- 1 free meeting registration pass

Bronze Sponsor $5,000+

- Bronze recognition sign to be displayed in booth
- Recognition in the on-site program
- Link from the Widget Tool event site to the sponsor's Web page

The Media Kit

A media kit contains basic information on an event, including statistical details on attendee demographics, and all sponsorship and advertising opportunities, including specifications, and deadlines.

Exhibitors and sponsors need to make their purchasing decisions based on empirical numbers rather than self-reported numbers from organizers. An independent third-party audit verifying the attendance of prior events is important in ensuring that exhibitors are confident that the attendance numbers and demographics being reported are accurate. The audit will also categorize job functions of buyers (for example, CEO, CFO, CMO, attorney, vice president.), based on information collected on the registration form. In addition, the audit may identify the number of employees in each company (if they originally registered as a company unit), geographic location, or any other demographic information that is valuable to the exhibition organizer in marketing that event.

All of this key information should be included in a professionally-designed media kit that can be printed and formatted for posting on the event's Web site, and made available to all exhibitors and other potentially interested parties.

Integrated Marketing

Integrated marketing is a good opportunity for exhibition organizers to engage in developing a partnership with the sponsor. Integrated marketing is a series of marketing activities with a common focus. The execution of each individual piece is consistent with, and supportive of, each of the other pieces of the marketing plan.

The best way for exhibition and sponsorship sales staffs to engage in partnership marketing is to learn what the sponsors' marketing objectives are, and to build packages that will help that sponsor achieve those objectives. For instance, a supplier is bringing a new product to market and wants to use an exhibition to introduce it to the marketplace. A savvy show management sales person will build a package to meet the needs of the company.

A major factor in a sponsor's success is the ability to measure the return on investment, and the sales staff for the exhibition needs to be able to assist the sponsor in this. A typical sponsorship package might include:
• Booth space
• Advertising in the promotional brochure and show directory
• A banner ad on the event's Web site
• Sponsorship of a general session including time at the microphone for the sponsor to say a few words
• Permission to put a brochure at each seat
• Permission to provide an amenity in each attendee's hotel room that evening to reinforce the message.

If the company were to purchase each of these separately, the cost for the opportunity might not be feasible, so one measure of value is the bundled price versus the *a la carte* pricing.

Sometimes, return on investment is just not measurable, and most companies understand this. However, an ideal outcome is for the sponsoring company to be able to measure at least a portion of the return by calculating cost per impression, media coverage gained and Web hits. Prior to the sale of the package, the organizer needs to understand what metrics they could supply in an event report that would support measurable results.

Figure 2 – Typical Sponsorship Success Measures

QUANTIFIABLE	QUALITATIVE
Actual 'people' counts • Full conference • Exhibits only • One-day	**Sponsor-specific surveys** • Recall, impression of company, etc.
Audited numbers • Professional attendees • Exhibitor personnel • Media/analysts. • Advertising • Where, when, reach	**Access to clients, VIPs** • One trip, one expense **Purchase intent** • Sales conversion, leads, increased booth visits • Willingness to consider brands
Cost per impression • Each point of impact	**Signage** • Placement, exposure
Advertising • Where, when, reach	**Media coverage** • Before, during, after
Cost per impression • Each point of impact	

Source: Lorimer Consulting Group, Denver, Colorado

Partnership Marketing Sales

There is no "one size fits all" when it comes to the sales staff who are responsible for selling sponsorships, advertising and partnership marketing. Some organizations may have a full-time sales staff that focuses on sales to potential exhibitors, advertisers and sponsors, while others may have a person who works in several departments.

Salespeople need to be trained in overcoming the objections they will surely receive from companies who want to purchase a minimal presence at an exhibition. In addition to having a good product to sell, they also need to clearly understand how to present a business case, and have mastery of valid statistics. Natural sales personalities are always motivated by compensation, and sponsorship sales compensation usually includes bonus and commission programs tied to revenue and budget. In addition to all of the above, the most successful sales staffs are usually empowered to broker deals with companies who want to get their message out to the exhibition's audience.

Some exhibition organizers have a requirement that in order to sponsor or advertise in an exhibition-related event, the sponsor must be an exhibitor, while others will permit a sponsorship or advertising entry without exhibiting, as long as the price of the sponsorship is at a certain level. When organizers limit sponsorships to only those who exhibit, it's because they believe that too many companies coming in as sponsors and not purchasing space on the show floor may dilute the value of the exhibition itself. An experienced show organizer will understand their market and what is appropriate to offer.

Researching the Prospect

The first step in the sales cycle for sponsorships, just as in the sales cycle for any product or for booth sales, is to learn as much as possible about the prospect and to be well educated about the event being represented. The Internet is an excellent way to research companies, their products and brands, as well as what some of their challenges might be in increasing profits. Talking with vendors in the industry, and monitoring industry publications for trends, will give salespeople unique insight and the ability to converse effectively with current and prospective partners.

Maintaining a contact management database is important for scheduling calls and emails, tracking sales and inventory, and keeping track of discussions and what might have been promised to a company.

Making the Calls

Once the sales staff has been trained, acquired the tools for overcoming objections, been empowered to close business, provided with a list of frequently-asked questions, prospect lists, and a sales plan, it is time to find sponsorship dollars. A major challenge that the sales staff might encounter is finding out who the decision-maker is within a company, since often many people are involved in taking the company's product to an exhibition, but only one or two people have the authority to made decisions about expenditures. Perseverance and asking the right questions will eventually lead to clarification and the right contact.

Sales staffs must be experienced in communicating the value proposition to the potential sponsor, practicing from scripts until the words flow naturally. The value proposition statement clearly summarizes the differentiation of the exhibition from other marketing channels, including competing events and outlines the return on investment. Briefly, a template for creating a value proposition is provided below. The first portion of the value proposition asserts the value of the offering, and the second sentence asserts the positioning of that value. Here's an example of a script that might be used:

> We'd like to present to your company the opportunity to be the sole sponsor of our opening reception at our exhibition, which would put your company name prominently in front of 5,000 potential buyers for two hours. Unlike

other shows in our industry, we invite our buyers to attend this gala event free, and for many, this kickoff event is the high point of their visit to our show.

Here's an example of how to put together a Value Proposition Template, inserting the specific information relevant to any exhibition:

First Sentence: For (ABC Company) who (is trying to reach DEF buyers), the (Annual XYZ Show) is the (only exhibition in this field) that (provides access to thousands of buyers who meet exactly those criteria).

Second Sentence: Unlike (the 123 Show) our exhibition (occurs at the best possible time of the year – or insert other positive selling proposition).

Putting everything in writing

Many organizers will negotiate on sponsorship pricing, depending on a variety of factors including:

• A new event that has not yet been proven in the marketplace

• Revenue needs of the exhibition

• Timing of the event. Perhaps there are a couple of breaks that have not sold and the event is in three weeks. The organizer would like to have some of those costs covered. The sponsor would not have had the benefit of being included in pre-show promotional collateral. In this instance, a discounted price on the sponsorship is appropriate.

• Partial sponsorships to cover some of the costs of a sponsorship. For instance, a high profile keynote speaker may cost $50,000. The organizer might be willing to cover a portion of the cost of the keynote, knowing that the high profile person will be a big draw for attendance. The organizer might negotiate that the sponsor pay $35,000 and the organizer will cover the other $15,000.

If possible, to close a deal on a sponsorship, the organizer needs to be flexible, with the ability to include value added items that do not have any real costs.

To ensure that there are no misunderstandings, a written agreement should be developed, outlining the expectations of both the sponsor and the organizer. Include the sponsor objectives; in other words, what does the sponsoring company wants to achieve by participating? If those expectations can be quantified, include those specifics. For example, an objective might be to increase awareness of the brand, or to identify new customers, which could be measured by documenting exposure, demographics, media and actual sales leads.

Outline specifically what each party to the agreement is going to do to meet those expectations. For the sponsor, it might be to exhibit at the event with a 20' x 20' island booth, with a pre-show promotion incentive mailer to buyers encouraging them to stop by the booth and win a prize, attend the opening reception, or a networking luncheon to socialize and meet buyers in a more relaxed atmosphere.

Also include what level and label of sponsorship the partner will be, and how the company will be described in the collateral materials. (Sponsor, vendor, partner, platinum, bronze, gold, or some other designation.)

Include in the agreement exactly what the sponsor will receive or what the rights are for the sponsorship. Will advertisements be included in the deal, and if so, by what date should material be received? How many complimentary registrations will the sponsor receive? How and where will the sponsor be recognized? Does the sponsor receive any special seating at a dinner or access to an event they would not normally be allowed to access? Is the sponsor able to distribute printed material?

The agreement should include what fees are to be paid and by what date. Many organizers will require a 50 percent payment to reserve the sponsorship, with the other 50 percent due prior to the event. To be safe, the final payment might be required 90-120 days prior to the event, so that if the sponsor backs out of the sponsorship, it can be re-sold. It also gives the organizer's staff enough time to delete the sponsor out of any printed material.

Clearly defining all expectations will help to eliminate any disputes; however, it is important to include in the agreement how such disputes as may arise will be handled. Rather than a termination clause that might allow the sponsor to terminate without prior notice, include a process by which the disputing party would notify the other party about a problem in writing. Sometimes, disputes cannot be resolved, and it is important to put a clause in the agreement stating that disputes will be resolved through arbitration rather than litigation, and to include penalties for cancellation within a specified time frame of the event.

Any information or material that the sponsor needs to provide the organizer, along with specific deadlines should be included, as well as any special shipping details and deadlines in the agreement.

Finally, include in the agreement any information on subsequent year event sponsorships or advertising. Will the sponsor have first right of refusal for the sponsorship, and if so, by what date should the sponsor inform show management and by what method – a telephone call, email, or written letter? If the sponsorship is a multiple year agreement, how will subsequent year pricing be determined?

Many large exhibitions are able to sell multiple year agreements, so including information on how the sponsorship will be valued for future years is important. The pricing increase may be determined by some measure of the Consumer Price Index (CPI), growth in attendance, or an increase in the value of the sponsorship. If the schedule permits, consider holding a Partner VIP Reception at or near the conclusion of the event as a way to sign sponsors up for the following year's event.

Care and Feeding of Partnership Marketing

The sale has been closed and the agreement signed, but the work is not yet done. It is important to remember that it costs six times more to acquire a new customer than it does to retain an existing one. This holds true in partnership marketing as well. Now that the sale has been closed, a large part of the responsibility for ensuring success of that partnership falls to the exhibition organizer. There are steps that can and should be taken leading up to and following the exhibition.

- Contact the sponsor regularly to make sure they are following through on their pre-show promotion, reminding the sponsor of upcoming deadlines and asking if they need assistance. Basically, keep in touch with the customer.
- Recognition, recognition, recognition! Be sure to recognize the sponsor in pre-show, on-site and post event collateral.
- Be sure that correct signage is strategically placed on site.
- Follow-up with the sponsor personally. Distribute a post-event survey to gather valuable information on what was successful and what might need to be changed.

The reality is that some companies will not be pleased with their sponsorship participation, for a variety of reasons. These companies usually fall into one of these categories:

- Companies who jump from one event to another, changing their sponsorships every year. Typically, there is no forethought given to goals or objectives.
- Prior supporters who eliminate all sponsorships because they may have had a bad experience. These companies usually do not know why the sponsorship did not generate any results, and seldom take the time to find out.
- Some companies will agree to a sponsorship because they get caught up in the excitement and perceived payoffs, or because a competitor is there. These companies have no goals or expectations.

Negative outcomes stem primarily from three things:

1. Idealistic or unrealistic expectations on the part of the sponsor.
2. Poor selection on the part of the sponsor. The company did not do enough research on the event to understand whether it was the best place to meet their marketing objectives.
3. Inadequate execution on the part of either the sponsor or the organizer.

It is important to understand these elements when working with prospective sponsors or those sponsors who have decided not to participate at a future event.

SUMMARY

An effective partnership marketing program not only contributes to the success of the exhibition overall, but also provides additional ways for sponsors and advertisers to reach their key marketing objectives. If careful consideration is given to developing a program where all parties are partners in the equation, success is ensured.

QUESTIONS FOR DISCUSSION

① If you were an exhibitor with a large booth at a trade association show but wanted to have more visibility, what sponsorship opportunities would appeal to you the most?

② Why do radio stations make good marketing partners for consumer shows?

③ Name some of the sponsors of recent Olympic Games (or future ones) and discuss why they are memorable.

Chapter 6
Legal Considerations

"A good and faithful judge prefers what is right to what is expedient."

– Horace

Section II: Business Issues

IN THIS CHAPTER YOU WILL LEARN
- How to begin the negotiation and contracting processes
- What makes a binding contract
- Understanding the basic components of contracts
- Unique provisions in hotel and facility contracts
- Additional common contract clauses
- Checklist for exhibitor contracts

INTRODUCTION

Facility and service provider contracts in the meetings and tradeshow industry are becoming increasingly complex. Today's contracts require a greater commitment on behalf of organizations than in the past. This has brought with it an increased potential for liability to organizations because of the strict enforcement of contractual provisions, especially attrition / performance and cancellation / liquidated damages clauses. Therefore, it is essential that meeting planners and show managers be prepared before negotiating hotel contracts.

CONTRIBUTOR

Mark Roysner, Attorney at Law, Law Office of Mark Roysner / Roysner and Associates

The Negotiation Process

The negotiation process should be thought of as something akin to the courtship before the marriage ceremony. It almost always starts off warm and friendly, with each of the parties exchanging pleasantries, and giving their "sales pitches" about what makes each of them special. Immediately thereafter, it can go in one of two directions. This burgeoning relationship can either continue to flourish and prosper, or it can become as tumultuous as a roller coaster ride. However, if a successful relationship is what each party actually wants, then from the very beginning each must realize they are in it together for the long haul. Each party must show a willingness to compromise when necessary. This way, the parties can achieve their mutually beneficial goals, and provide the best services possible to their respective clients and customers.

Show managers can negotiate a great number of items in a contract, but it takes thoughtful and direct communication to satisfy both their objectives and the other party's. The days of "my word is my bond" and the "handshake deal" are gone forever. In today's litigious atmosphere, all contractual issues must be addressed in writing. If you require special concessions, carefully choose those which will positively impact your budget or that are critical to your event. Always allow yourself enough time to carefully and thoughtfully negotiate the deal you are contemplating. Most of the costliest mistakes are due either to rushing into the deal, or not allowing adequate time to clearly and concisely address everything in the contract before it is finalized.

So remember, if a successful event is what the parties really want, be up front with each other from the very start. Show managers must know what they want, and what they can live without. Then, they must find out if these same goals hold true for the other party. If both parties can negotiate with integrity, and be forthright and honest with each other from the outset, then the bonds forged during this negotiation process will make for an enduring and productive partnership.

Thus, what is true about any long lasting relationship holds true for contracts in the meeting and tradeshow industry: the best contracts are built on a solid foundation of mutual respect and trust. However, if this cannot be achieved during the negotiation process, maybe it never can be achieved. Therefore, one should strongly consider walking away from the deal before any real damage can be done. Dissolution of a contract, like that of a marriage, can be quite unpleasant, and costly for everyone involved. Nevertheless, when a contract can be negotiated with the utmost honesty and integrity, it is truly a valuable accomplishment. Negotiating a contract that is **_mutually fair and reasonable_** in its written terms and conditions, and – even more significant, to the parties involved – in its interpretation and implementation is a very satisfying achievement.

Beginning the Process

Doing your homework in advance goes a long way towards ensuring an efficient and productive negotiation. To begin on the right foot and avoid confusion down the road, submit a detailed request for proposal (RFP) to each facility or service provider under consideration. The RFP should clearly identify all needs, dates of required service, and past event history, if applicable. Alternative dates should also be included.

The show manager should inform facilities as to the plan for using the required meeting space, such as whether the function will involve general sessions, educational sessions, food and beverage functions, show offices, or exhibits. Potential service providers should also be informed of the approximate times for the various functions that will be held and include room configurations. This will assist the facility or service contractor in determining if they can satisfactorily accommodate the event. While producing an RFP may seem cumbersome, it will become a great time saver when dealing with other service providers, since it provides the same information to each service provider under consideration.

Nevertheless, remember to keep "pie in the sky" projections about future potential to an absolute minimum. Overly inflated projections, if not realized, can be very costly to an organization. Furthermore, if a contract dispute arises, the potential exists that a court may interpret such erroneous projections as material misrepresentations. Finally, the show manager must specify that he or she need a written response to the RFP by a specific date, and indicate when a final decision will be made.

Determining Authority

A number of organizations are now enlisting the services of third-party companies to assist with their selection of facilities and, in some cases, having them function as the primary negotiators in the organization's contract formation process. While these emerging practices may benefit both organizations, it still remains the responsibility of the show organizer to make absolutely sure that the final contract presented for signature accurately reflects terms and conditions that are fully acceptable to the organization.

Signing the Final Version

The contract should only be confirmed on a definite basis after the final version has been thoroughly reviewed line by line. This final version should have incorporated into it all of the modifications the parties agreed upon during the negotiation process. If a final clean signature edition, incorporating all of the agreed-upon modifications is not prepared, then any modification made on the original contract should be acknowledged and initialed by both parties. This can help avoid potential problems and ambiguities in the future, such as forgetting to incorporate a critical modification or clause, or having one of the parties claim they did not agree to a specific term or condition in the contract prior to signing.

A show manager must never state in writing or orally that his or her organization has accepted the contract on a definite basis, unless the intention is to sign the contract in its present form. Otherwise, a show manager may find that he or she may have just entered into, however mistakenly, a legally binding contract

What Makes a Binding Contract

Once a list has been determined of the company or companies that meet the organization's facility or service requirements, either through the RFP process or direct contact, the actual negotiation process can begin. At this time, if a tentative proposal has not already been received, ask for an initial proposal, incorporating all of the information supplied. This initial proposal will provide an excellent starting point to begin the process, since the show manager will be signing a finalized version of this document to confirm the terms or conditions of the deal on a definite basis.

The executed (signed) contract is a legally binding agreement, which identifies the parties, and expresses their mutual intention to enter the terms and conditions contained within it. In legal jargon, these contractual elements are "offer, acceptance, consideration, and mutuality." They identify the parties to be bound, and the subject matter of the contract. Additionally, for a contract to be enforceable, the parties signing it must be legally competent, and it must meet the requirements of the Statute of Frauds.

Legal competency, in terms of contract law, requires that the signing parties be of legal age (18 or more years of age). Furthermore, when the contract was executed, the parties must have been without mental disability or incapacity (suffering from mental illness or under the influence of a mind-altering or intoxicating substance).

The Statute of Frauds, as it pertains to contracts for the procurement of goods, states that no lawsuit or action can be maintained, unless there is a written memorandum (written contract). Additionally, it must be signed by the party to be charged, or by an authorized agent (the party in breach of the contract), unless by its own terms, the contract can be performed within a year. In essence, if a show manager entered into an oral contract for services, it may be valid and legally binding, if the terms agreed to can be performed within one year from the date it was entered into.

Goods contracts, such as for the purchase of merchandise, products, commodities, supplies, or food and beverages, usually fall within the provisions of the Uniform Commercial Code (UCC § 2-201), which addresses the sale of goods. According to

Black's Law Dictionary, the Code provides that a contract for the sale of goods for the price of $500 or more is not enforceable, by way of action or defense, unless there is some form of writing sufficient to show that a contract has been made between the parties, and signed by the party against whom enforcement is sought, or his authorized agent.

In addition to the most familiar contract clauses, such as those addressing guest room blocks, room rates, and function space in hotel contracts, most contracts also contain what is commonly referred to as boilerplate language (commonly referred to as "Boilerplate" or "Legalese"). These legal clauses have captions such as Performance, Liquated Damages, Attrition, Indemnification, Arbitration, Compliance or Performance, Jurisdiction, and *Force Majeure*, to name a few. They usually contain the so-called "fine print" nobody really wants to read and usually does not bother to read until a disagreement between the parties arises. There is an old saying in contract law, "the large print giveth and the small print taketh away." While this is a bit caustic, there is some wisdom in the saying. A typical contract contains a number of clauses that are commonly viewed as "boilerplate" or "just the standard language." However, before dismissing these clauses as "just that same old legal stuff," a show manager should review them with as much or more thoroughness as the clauses which address the actual meeting details. If a problematic situation arises, these "legalese" clauses can create liability that will impact the way both parties will do business. Therefore, the best way to prevent potential pitfalls, or at least minimize their potentially disastrous results, is to be prepared for the unexpected or the remotely possible in advance.

Contracts are comprised of Terms, Covenants, and Conditions clauses. This means that upon executing the final version of the contract, the show manager will not only have negotiated the types of facilities and /or services to be provided, rates and costs, dates of service, and other commonly reviewed provisions, but will have also accepted all of the legal (boilerplate) provisions and restrictions in their totality.

Before signing a final version of the contract, the show manager needs to understand the differences between breaching and defaulting on a contract, and cancellation or termination of a contract.

A breach is the failure to perform any term, condition, or promise that forms the entire or part of a contract, and there is no legal excuse to do so. If the breach is partial, as to one part of the contract or less significant than a material breach, the non-breaching or aggrieved party generally does not have the right to walk away from their contractual obligations. However, the non-breaching party has the right to seek damages, for the harm caused by the breaching party. On the other hand, if the breach is material, one that is substantial and significant as to its effect on the overall contract, this usually excuses further performance of the contract by the non-breaching party. Moreover, it affords them the right to seek legal remedies, such as filing a lawsuit for damages.

For purposes of this discussion, default is similar to a breach. It occurs when a party to a contract fails, either by omission or failure, to perform a legal or contractual duty under the contract. Furthermore, on occasion, courts have found one party to be in default when they perform a dishonest or wrongful act pertaining to the terms of the contract.

Termination means ending or discharging the entire contract. Usually this occurs before the end of the anticipated duration of the contract. When a contract is terminated by mutual agreement of all parties, in most cases it is done so without any further legal recourse or remedies to each other. This form of termination generally occurs due to unforeseeable events caused by external forces, making performance of the contract impossible or impracticable for its intended purpose. These types of events are most commonly known as Acts of God, *Force Majeure*, or Excused Non-performance.

Often the word "termination" is used synonymously with cancellation. In this instance, it is used by the non-breaching party as one of its remedies, due to the default of the other party. The cancellation occurs when either party puts an end (releases them from their obligations) to the contract for breach by the other. Its effect is the same as a "termination," except that the canceling or non-breaching party still retains any legal remedy for breach of the whole contract or any unperformed balance.

Since default or breach of contract can be a two-way street, show managers must take care not to get caught signing a one-way contract. Make sure to take the time to clearly define what will constitute a breach, and the remedies available to both the parties. Make sure these triggering events are both reasonable and justifiable.

The most important thing is to carefully read every line in the contract – and most importantly, understand its long-term ramifications – before signing it. It is usually the performance/attrition and boilerplate clauses that trigger very costly legal disputes. A thorough review of these clauses prior to finalizing and signing a contract can be the most beneficial and cost-saving measure show managers can take to ensure their organizations' profitability. A lawyer well-versed in complex meeting and tradeshow industry contracts can help guide the process, but the show organizer has the final responsibility.

Remember that despite the subtle complexity of contracts they can, in fact, be opportunities to create a win-win situation between two parties. The following pages will help to make sense of the common components of meeting and tradeshow industry type contracts, as well as the typical legal clauses. Finally, we have included some typical pitfalls that should be avoided.

Understanding the Basic Components

The Contracting Parties

Use the full legal name and place of business address in identifying all of the parties to be bound by the contract. This simple step is very important because the parties to the contract will ultimately be held responsible for any rights, privileges, obligations, and liability created under the final signed contract.

Because more companies are managing properties instead of owning them outright, make sure that the facility's management company (ABC Company) is referred to as "agent for XYZ Company (Owner)." This helps to preserve the validity of the contract in case the hotel's management company is replaced by another company before the event, or in case the hotel's owners sell the facility. Otherwise, although a contract with the management company could still be valid, and action might still be able to be brought against them for breach, it may be unenforceable with the actual owner. Also consider adding a provision that would give the option to either re-negotiate or terminate the contract should the management company or facility change ownership after the contract is finalized.

Subject Matter of the Contract

When contracting with another party, identify the type of services or facilities to be provided with some level of specificity. For events at facilities, use only the actual event name. If the event is primarily known by its generic name, add the year to the name to avoid any ambiguity about which event the contract pertains to.

Double Checking Dates

The dates and pattern of the event are frequently overlooked or taken for granted. Always make it a habit to double check the dates entered on all contracts to make sure they are correct. Also, in hotel and facility contracts, outline the entire arrival/departure pattern and, if applicable, the guest room block per night, including suites and the total number of room nights to be utilized.

More major problems arise because of improperly-held dates in facility contracts than for almost any other reason. All too often, one party or another transposes the dates or mistakenly alters the function space commitment. If caught too late, this simple mistake can be the most difficult and costly to correct. Take care to carefully check and match the dates and arrival/departure patterns held with the days and year of the event. In addition, check whether any major holidays fall within the pattern. Remember, Easter, Passover, Rosh Hashanah, and Yom Kippur do not fall on the same date or even in the same month every year.

Determining Costs

When negotiating and confirming rates and costs, make sure to get them in writing. If rates are to be confirmed after the contract has been signed, make sure a formula is in place to determine how the rates and other costs will be calculated. Using an example of how a rate will be calculated in the future is always a good way to avoid problems and misunderstandings down the road.

Never agree to pay for unspecified charges that will be "determined later by the service provider or facility." However, if such fees are foreseeable, but unable to be determined in advance, make sure to add a clause into the contract spelling out exactly how and when these charges will be determined. At the very least, a clause should be added stating something to the effect that: "If anything occurs that materially affects either party's commitment, financial or otherwise, to each other, any charges related to these changes must be reasonable and must be agreed to by mutual written consent."

Like the discounts that suppliers offer for early payment, it is worthwhile to try to negotiate language into a contract that calls for a discount on fees if the final bill is paid early. On the other hand, certainly do not compromise the ability to fully review charges for the sake of a discount. Additionally, ask if a percentage discount off of the standard pricing for services (such as electric, utilities, telephone, and graphics) can be extended if the order is placed early.

Service Fees and Surcharges

Because more and more hotels are adding Resort/Hotel Fees, surcharges and mandatory service fees on top of the guest's confirmed guest room rate, provisions should be added into the contract stating that that no hotel or resort fees or surcharges will be added for services already provided by the hotel on a complimentary basis at the time the contract is signed. Note also that all gratuities and service charges will be at the guest's discretion except for in-room food service, or as otherwise provided in the contract.

One should also add similar clauses to the service provider contracts to address issues such as fuel surcharges, transportation fees, overages, and handling charges. This clause should either restrict the addition of any such charges or, at the very least, clearly and concisely state under what set of specific circumstances a surcharge or cost increase can be applied, and exactly how that surcharge or cost increase will be calculated and applied.

Periodic Reviews

Whenever a contract contains a review clause based on an evaluation of an organization's past performance or future expectations, make sure that the other party does not have the right to unilaterally adjust the amount of space or services to be provided without the organization's prior, written consent. This is important because if the other party does adjust the amount of goods or services to be provided, or the amount of function space or guest rooms to be blocked based on the organization's prior history or future projections, the organization could still be held liable for performance/attrition fees if the predetermined percentage of the original contracted quantity is not fulfilled. To prevent this potential problem, other provisions in the contract should specifically spell out the organization's liability for preference/attrition fees if the original minimum usage requirements are not fulfilled or are adjusted at a later date.

Because of more stringent enforcement of guest room block performance clauses in hotel contracts, it is always wise to add a clause providing for periodic review and modification of the organization's guest room block needs without liability to the organization. Otherwise, performance clauses can and often do assess monetary damages to the organization if the actual guest room pick-up, or the organization's revenues, fall below the hotel's projections. At the very least, include a clause that allows adjustments to the guest room needs only if there is the mutual written consent of the parties, and that states that all modifications will be made without *any* liability to either party. This should be done because sometimes an organization's past guest room pick-up history at a similar hotel may have been due to numerous factors that affected the prior year's attendance, but under the current conditions are no longer relevant to the upcoming event.

Commissions and Rebates

When a show manager is to receive a commission or rebate for an organization or third-party company based on revenue generated by the event or guest room utilization, the commission payment clause must be crafted carefully, spelling out exactly how it is to be calculated and who will receive it.

Specify in the contract what is and what is not commissionable. Will commissions and/or rebates be paid on all revenue generated, or on a pre-determined portion of revenue generated? Also, make sure the agreement states when the commission is to be paid. Will it be permissible for the paying party to hold off paying the commission until the master account is settled?

In the case of commissions and rebates related to hotel room usage, the following questions must be answered. Who receives the commission from the hotel? Will it be the organization, or a third-party management company or meeting brokerage firm? What types of organization guest rooms will be commissionable? Does the commission payment include all revenue- producing rooms, or just certain types of rooms within the overall guest room block, such as speaker and staff rooms? Does it include pre- and post-stay revenue? What about commissions for revenue received by the hotel due to no-shows, early departure fees, and non-refundable deposits? How is payment to be made: as a cash payment or as a credit to the master account?

In order to avoid being accused of unfair or deceptive business practices, some companies (predominantly hotels) routinely require an organization receiving these rebates to fully disclose the amount of the rebate and their intended purpose. This is most often accomplished by requiring the organization to publish this rebate/add-on information, including the actual dollar amount, in all their promotional material, and on all of the organization's guest room reservation forms.

Damages for Breach of Contract

Know up front how damages for a breach of performance (that is, each party's contractual obligations and duties as set forth in the contract, such as attrition clauses in hotel contracts) and cancellation will be assessed, and when they will be due and payable. Always spell out in the contract whether these fees will be based on actual damages suffered by the non-breaching party, or liquidated damages. Actual damages are the real, substantial and just damages awarded to a non-breaching party as compensation for the actual damages and real loss suffered due to the breaching party. Actual damages can take the form of compensatory damages (to restore the non-breaching party to the position they were in prior to the breach), expectancy damages (to place the non-breaching party in the position they would have been in had the contract been performed) and incidental damages (out of pocket expenses) resulting from the breach. Liquidated damages, on the other hand, are contractually pre-determined damages that one party agrees to pay to the other party if they breach some provision of the contract. Liquidated damages are to be arrived at by a good faith effort to estimate the actual damage that will probably arise from the breach. Regardless of which type of damage provision the parties ultimately negotiate, show organizers must make sure to limit their organization's exposure to any potential damages in the case of cancellation or termination not of their making.

To protect against the facility breaching the contract that results in the lack of an easily-definable and enforceable remedy, always add a Construction, Refurbishment, and Remodeling Clause, as well as a Double Booking Policy Clause to hotel and facility contracts. How many times have veteran show organizers heard "No, we're not planning any type of construction or remodeling that would have an effect on your show that I know of" or, "Of course the space is yours"? Knowing and addressing these potential pitfalls up front can help avoid them altogether, saving a great deal of aggravation and money in the long run.

Cancellation and Attrition Charges

Before finalizing any contract, read the cancellation and performance clauses regarding the potential financial liability very carefully. If the clause as presently stated is not acceptable, re-negotiate it until the parties have jointly drafted a mutually acceptable provision. If that is not possible, strongly consider walking away from the deal.

Cancellation and Performance clauses are not consistent from one contract to another, or from one facility to another, even if they are managed by the same company. The timing and conditions of these clauses can vary, and be quite demanding. To draft the most favorable clause, and avoid as many potential pitfalls as possible, first define what type of events will trigger a termination (Acts of God, or unforeseeable events making it impossible or highly impracticable to perform) as opposed to the kinds of events that will cause cancellation (termination by the non-breaching party due to a material breach by the other party) of the entire contract. Second, plainly establish what will constitute a partial breach (partial non-performance such as attrition). In addition, incorporate formulas or examples into these types of clauses to distinctly illustrate when cancellation or attrition fees are to be applied, and how they are to be calculated. Also specify the refund policy relative to the cancellation clauses, especially if the prepaid deposits could be in excess of a potential cancellation fee.

Additionally, the contract needs to address when monetary damages available under the contract will be paid to the non-breaching party. Furthermore, prior to paying *actual* monetary damages to a hotel, reserve the right to determine if the hotel has fulfilled its legal duty to mitigate the actual damages incurred by the cancellation through reasonable commercial efforts to book alternative business over the dates released. Liquidated damages (pre-determined fees) must be structured so that they will not be considered a penalty for cancellation, something known as "unjust enrichment." Nevertheless, a show manager should try to negotiate these clauses based on the event, its objectives and other issues of importance to the organization.

Another point to consider in hotel contracts is that more and more hotels are trying to recover, as part of their liquidated damages, their "projected" or "anticipated" gross revenue from sleeping rooms, function space, food and beverage events, and ancillary services such as restaurant outlets, telephone, room services, and recreational facilities. Before a show organizer agrees to this type of provision, carefully determine how the hotel plans to calculate these "anticipated revenues," since every group has a somewhat different usage of in-house facilities. Remind the hotel that liquidated damages are never to be assessed as penalties. Therefore, at the very most, the actual damages or pre-determined liquidated damages should only be based on net revenues (that is, actual loss of anticipated profits). Damages should never be based on gross revenue (unjust enrichment), since the hotel will not have experienced any additional out–of-pocket expenses for supplies and labor except the sales effort if the event is not going to take place to begin with, or they know well enough in advance about the organization's room pick-up or food or beverage function expenditures.

Cancellation/Performance/Attrition fees should, in most cases, constitute the non-breaching party's sole and exclusive remedy for any and all damages, costs or expenses it may have suffered or incurred as a result of cancellation of the entire contract, or any form of performance attrition under the contract. In most cases, the parties should also stipulate that except for the damages expressly stated in the contract, both parties will not be liable for consequential or incidental damages of any nature for any reason whatsoever.

> **TIP**
> Remember to adjust any cancellation fee formula to take into consideration the maximum allowable reduction for attrition as outlined in the Hotel Agreement. For example, if the organization will only be responsible for paying an attrition fee if the guest room usage falls below 80 percent of the revenue-producing portion of the guest room block, factor out the additional 20 percent from being incorporated into a cancellation fee.

Force Majeure

Since there are various factors beyond anyone's control (also known as "Acts of God") which could make it impossible to hold an event as originally intended, standard clauses for excused non-performance should be written to allow the termination of the agreement without liability. These are called "*Force Majeure*" clauses and are bilateral provisions that protect both parties. Never allow the other party to remove itself from any liability arising out of forces beyond its reasonable control, or "Acts of God," without providing the same protection for the other organization.

> **TIP**
> Remember that a termination of a facility or hotel contract due to a Force Majeure event can also have tremendous impact on service provider contracts. Be sure that there are Force Majeure provisions in all service provider agreements which link together the right to terminate those contracts if the hotel or facility contract is terminated due to a Force Majeure occurrence. (In other words, hotel contracts must relate to availability of the convention center.)

Property Damage

More and more companies have expressly incorporated a property damage provision into their contracts. It is proper and legally enforceable that an organization takes responsibility for the damage caused to property or premises by them or their employees, agents, and representatives acting directly on behalf of the organization, or when acting within the scope of employment. However, one should not agree to any contractual provision that makes an organization liable for damages caused by an attendee or their guests – or any one else for that matter – that is outside of the show organizer's reasonable control, and acting outside the scope of their employment.

Simply stated, *"If you break it, you fix it."* That is fair, and show organizers should definitely carry appropriate liability insurance for such occurrences. However, make sure if such a clause exists, that it specifies the time frame (for example, within 48 hours after final event move-out date) and the method the parties will use for documenting and reporting any damage that one of the parties may be liable for causing. This can easily be accomplished by the use of time-stamped photographs, or videotape of the facility or property damaged. Don't be caught in a situation where a company or facility calls months after the event, having concluded that an organization owes them for some damage they just discovered

Conversely, should a service provider, a facility's personnel or their authorized contractors, destroy or damage property belonging to the organization or its contractors, or lose property while it was under their control due to their own negligence, they should be held responsible for its replacement or repair.

Master Accounts

The event manager should make arrangements with the other party to review charges to the master account on a daily basis, or at least very carefully review the figures before the end of the event if at all possible. This is the best time to do so, because memories are fresh concerning the various functions and possible charges, making final approval and payment of the bill much easier.

Some companies specify that all master accounts must be paid within 30 days of the event's conclusion or late fees may be assessed for late payment. Others require an advance deposit on the projected total charges to the organization's master account, or a partial payment prior to the end of the event. To avoid potential disputes concerning unapproved charges, both parties need to:

• Determine who is authorized to charge to the master account
• State what charges are allowed on the master account, and that the organization will not be responsible for charges that have not been authorized in writing by the official signatory for the organization
• State when the master account will be reviewed
• Set a deadline date by which time the other party has to submit all final charges, invoices and fees

- Explain what type of supporting documents the hotel needs to provide before an invoice will be paid
- Decide when payment is due
- Agree on a procedure for handling disputed charges.

If all of these issues are not addressed in advance, it is almost certain that one or more of them will crop up after the event.

Deposits and Refunds

A deposit is a cash payment in advance for a service or facility. Such payment obligates the accepting party to provide the space or service contracted for as stated in the contract. The show organizer should be sure that the actual deposit and payment schedule is spelled out completely in the contract.

Whether refunds are due the organization or an individual attendee, spell out when any refunds will be made to the appropriate party. Also add a provision that guest room deposits will be refunded, or that early departure fees will be waived, if an individual must cancel their guaranteed guest room reservation prior to arrival or during their stay due to an emergency.

Late Payments

What constitutes a late payment? Identify all items subject to late payment in the contract. Establish a schedule that defines "lateness," as well as what, if any, late fees will be incurred. It must be a time frame that can reasonably be met. For example, if the other party's billing procedures are such that it takes extra time to process a payment, or they do not supply billing documentation, a late payment fee should not be required.

The show manager must keep a watchful eye out for any late fee (penalty) clauses or provisions whereby the other party can accelerate the entire payment or deposit schedule, or terminate the entire contract (or in some cases all future events also under contract with that party) and hold the organization liable for all damages, if an installment of final payment is not paid by its due date or shortly thereafter without providing reasonable notice and an opportunity to cure the default. If the other party adds a clause about interest rate charges on the outstanding amount, modify it, so that the interest to be charged is not greater than the maximum amount allowable under that state's laws.

Considerations and Concessions

There are a number of areas that an event manager can negotiate into their contracts with facilities and service providers. These areas are usually referred to as "Special Concessions," also known as the client's "Wish List."

TIP

The term "Special Concession" as used in the negotiation process is somewhat misleading as to what is actually taking place. Concession means to give in, surrender, sacrifice or concede to a demand or claim. In this instance, the term concession tends to give the wrong impression, namely, that one party is giving in or giving something of value without receiving a benefit in its place from the other party. In reality, concessions are simply an ordinary part of the "give and take" that goes into getting the parties to achieve a meeting of the minds and to consummate the deal. The term consideration would be better suited to describe this negotiating function.

TIP

When one party presents a "Wish List" to the other party, he or she should have a fairly good idea of what is actually acceptable when all is said and done. Take into account the fact that a great deal of what the other party is willing to offer, and finally agree to, will depend on market conditions at the time of contract formation. To be as realistic as possible, consider the following factors:

- The amount of net revenue the contract represents to the other party, including ancillary events such as exhibitor functions

- The time of year of the event (whether it is scheduled to take place over the off-season, shoulder or peak seasons)

- The time between the contract signing date and the actual event

- The other party's potential to contract with another group with higher revenue-producing potential during the same time frame

- The actual cost to the other party's bottom line by granting the concession

- Whether the denial of some of the requested "Considerations" will cause the organization to contract with some other third party.

Considerations can be anything the parties agree to. What the organization actually receives will always be determined by the value of its business to the other party.

Be sure that any considerations or other special arrangements agreed to during the negotiations are clearly spelled out in the final contract, regardless of how minor they may seem. Always include how many of a particular concession will be offered, and if applicable, the dates over which the concession will be provided. No previously agreed-to terms, regardless if they were in writing or orally stated, will be enforceable if the signed contract has an "Entirety of the Agreement" provision.

Option Dates

An option date clause is an agreement that grants the organization the right (an option) to accept the contract, at the exclusion of other offers, at the agreed-upon price and terms within a specified time frame. In essence, they are separate contracts of first refusal. Although a modified form of option clause is commonly used in the industry under contract law for the lease of space, they are not legally enforceable unless there is separate consideration (independent of the consideration paid for the contract itself) paid to make the offer exclusive. This means that unless consideration is paid to the facility in exchange for holding the option open for exercise at a future date, and at the exclusion of all others, the facility is not under any legal obligation to honor the option. In essence, want of consideration renders an option a gratuitous offer.

In the context of hotel contracts, option clauses are offered as a courtesy, and for the most part, hotels have been very good about honoring them. First, the parties mutually agree to a date by when contract negotiations will conclude and a final contract needs to be executed, and that in the interim, the hotel will notify the show organizer (preferably in writing) that another organization has expressed a desire to immediately confirm the dates currently being held by the organization on a tentative basis. After this notification, the facility usually allows a certain number of days to either exercise the option to confirm the dates, or release the space.

Unique Hotel and Convention Center Issues

Guest Room Rates

Hotels, like airlines, usually have a wide range of rates they offer to individuals and groups. Guest room rates are usually based on a variety of factors. They include the type of occupancy (single or double, and extra person), guest room category (standard, deluxe, executive), and location of the floor in the hotel (executive club floor, view from room, floor number). Other times, guest room rates are solely based on the demand for guest rooms over the time frame being requested.

Unless expressed otherwise in the Agreement, and regardless of the types of guest room rates offered, the guest room rates quoted will be "net rates," that is, the rates exclude all taxes, commissions, and rebates. Therefore, if rates include a commission, taxes or rebates, modify any rate provision in writing to avoid confusion.

Published Rates

Published rates or, as they are commonly called, "rack rates," are a hotel's published rates. Typically, these rack rates are posted in the guest rooms, either on the back of the door, or in the closet. Rack rates are the rates for single and double occupancy that the hotel would offer an individual who has walked in off the street. They are rates offered to people who call the hotel's reservation center directly, or who want to book a room that is not in connection with a meeting or a corporate rate program. While this may seem insignificant, rack rates are very important since these are the rates a hotel typically uses as the benchmark from which the actual meeting rate negotiations begin. More often than not, a hotel's proposal will state that the hotel will confirm guest room rates as a percentage off their published or rack rates.

Guest Room Plans

Although it may seem unnecessary, a good practice when starting the rate negotiation phase is to determine which of the following rate plans will be applicable to your group: Full American, Modified American or the Continental Plan. With the exception of boutique hotels and specialty resorts, the meeting or convention rates quoted will be based on a European Plan, which means no meals are included as part of the room rate. This is the industry standard in the United States today. Under a Full American Plan, three full meals are included each day in the room rate. The Modified American Plan includes breakfast and dinner, and the Continental Plan includes breakfast each morning, from which has stemmed the cottage industry known as Bed and Breakfast Inns.

Types of Convention Rates

A group's confirmed guest room rates are usually based on some negotiated variation of the hotel's published rack rates structure as they exist about one year prior to the actual meeting dates. Traditionally, these rates are based on a predetermined (negotiated) percentage off the rack rates in one or more guest room categories, with each guest room category having a specific number of guest rooms or room types allotted to a specific rate. When working within a multiple rate structure, it is good practice to contractually determine the number of guest rooms the hotel will provide in each rate category. Also, how the confirmed rate will be offered will need to be defined. Will the guest room rates be based on a flat rate, run of the house rates, or a series of single and double rates?

A show organizer needs to be aware that the term "flat rates" can have two significantly different meanings: as one separate confirmed rate for all single and a different confirmed rate for all double occupancy guest rooms, or as the same confirmed rate regardless of whether the guest room is used for single or double occupancy. Additionally, since flat rates may only apply to a specific number and/or type of guest rooms, try to negotiate a "run of the house" rate. A run of the house rate is a flat single/double rate, or a single and double rate that is applicable for all available rooms in the hotel's inventory regardless of room type and location, except suites and sometimes guest rooms on the concierge or club level floors.

In addition to negotiating favorable guest room rates for attendees, a show organizer must remember to add a provision into the contract providing special guest room rates for speakers and staff rooms not covered by the complimentary guest room allotment.

Complimentary Rooms

Securing complimentary rooms during a meeting can be quite important in maintaining the organization's budget. Furthermore, because hotels have a tendency to use their own distinctive methods for determining the number of complimentary rooms or units a group receives, there must be a clear understanding between the parties of the terms and methods used to determine a group's complimentary allotment. The best way to accomplish this is through mutually agreed-upon definitions and illustrations in the contract itself.

Moreover, for allotment purposes, complimentary rooms are normally calculated on a per unit basis. For example, one unit normally equals one room; two units equals a one bedroom plus parlor suite, or an executive room might even be two units, depending on the size or luxury of a room. To avoid any misunderstanding, include a detailed breakdown of the number of units to be assigned for each type of suite in the hotel's inventory.

Cut-off Dates

This is the designated date after which the client must release or add to the commitment for their guest room block. After this time, the hotel will sell its rooms to any potential customer. Depending on the type of attrition clause negotiated, the hotel may still hold the group liable for guest rooms not picked up. The standard cut-off is 30 days prior to the official meeting dates, or first day of arrival (define this in the agreement), but it can vary from as much as 60 days to as little as seven days, depending on the hotel, and what is negotiated.

Specify in the contract whether the group's confirmed rates will be applicable after the cut-off date. Otherwise, in most cases, the hotel will offer their published rates to guests trying to make reservations after the cut-off, regardless of their hotel availability and the guest room pick-up to date. Furthermore, determine if guest rooms reserved after the cut-off will be "subject to space and rate availability," or "subject to availability," both of which allow the hotel to unilaterally decide what "availability" means in a particular instance. Therefore, to avoid this potential pitfall, consider using the phrase, "if any guest rooms are available in the hotel." The difference between one use and the other of these phrases can have a significant impact on the overall guest room pick-up.

Substitution of Names

Always try to add a provision in the contract that the hotel agrees to the substitution of guest names after the cut-off date for similar guest rooms previously reserved but later cancelled. This will allow canceled guests to be replaced with new guests into the existing room block at the group's confirmed rates. This type of provision will help minimize exposure to attrition fees by allowing the hotel to backfill into your contracted guest room block.

Relocation of Guests

A clear policy specifying how dishonored reservations (commonly called "walked" guests) will be handled should be established and included in the contract. The industry standard has been that a hotel will relocate the displaced guest to another nearby hotel. Make sure it is a "comparable" hotel, and define the term "nearby" as a measure of miles (radius) from the hotel. Have the hotel agree to pay for the guest's lodging for at least the first night they are displaced, or – if possible – all the nights they are displaced. Additionally, have the hotel agree to cover the cost of any rate differential between the guest's rate at the hotel and the rate being charged at the alternative property for the duration of their stay. The hotel should agree to transport the guest to and from one hotel to the other throughout the meeting. Also, get the hotel to agree to pay the group for the commission they would have received had the guest not been walked, since a walk constitutes a breach of contract. They should also be willing to pay for a phone call or two by the guest to advise those needing to know his or her new location. The hotel should also commit to returning the guest to the original hotel as soon as possible.

> **TIP**
> Make sure that the organization is credited for maximum guest room utilization, and if commissions are involved, add a provision stating that the hotel agrees to credit the group for all of the room nights the guests are displaced, and pay commissions based on the guest's confirmed rate, for each night the guest is displaced.

Change in Quality of a Facility

Because many events are booked with hotels, convention centers and other types of event and exposition facilities years in advance of their actual dates, it is a good practice to include a clause in the contract that includes "walk away rights" should the physical condition and appearance deteriorate significantly from when the facility was booked. This should be done in tandem with a periodic site re-inspection schedule.

Event and exposition facilities are like ships – they are in a constant state of repair, refurbishment, or remodeling. Any sufficient variances in the physical structure or appearance of the hotel or exhibition facility could dramatically impact an event. Any construction project can affect guest rooms and function space availability and access, noise levels, parking, ingress and egress from the facility, traffic around the facility, and the facility's general appearance. Therefore, determine not only whether there may be any physical alteration of the facility just prior to or during the event, but also what will be the foreseeable impact that such alterations will or could have on the event's success.

Usually, facilities are willing to work their restoration efforts around an event schedule if possible. However, this may not always be the case. To protect the integrity of the event, always have a provision that obligates advanced notification of any physical alterations planned for one or two years prior to, and continuing through the conclusion of the event, regardless of how perceptively minor the alterations are – with the exception of ordinarily-scheduled routine maintenance. Be very specific about how and when notification of any planned or ongoing physical changes to the property should be given. Make sure this notification allows enough lead time to make alternative arrangements if the facility's plans go off schedule, or if the proposed changes will have a detrimental impact on the event or the guests. Also, carefully draft a provision spelling out when and how the contract can be terminated without liability, also known as "walk-away rights," if the facility's operations will compromise the event to guard against being locked into a very unfavorable situation. Consider adding a clause providing for re-negotiating certain terms of the contract if relocating the event is either not possible, or the host organization opts not to do so.

Co-Dependency

Whenever an organization is utilizing multiple hotels, a co-headquarters hotel, and/or a convention center facility, it is always wise to add an "essential facility clause" into the contract. An essential facility clause allows for the termination of the contract without liability, or at the very least, re-negotiation and waiver of performance-related damages, if one or more of the essential facilities becomes unavailable for the organization's intended usage as stated in the contract. This clause helps protect the show organizer if the other hotels or the convention center necessary to satisfy the guest room block or the event's space requirements remains or becomes unavailable.

Additionally, a variation of this type of clause should be used when booking an event into a particular city and hotel when their availability is contingent upon a planned center expansion project, still to be completed (or started), or the "to be announced any day now" mega hotel project the city has been trying to develop does not materialize, or will not be completed in time for your event.

Concurrent Meetings

A show organizer has the right to specify that a facility is not to be shared with a competitive event, or "incompatible event," as well as to ask for a specified window of time in which a competitive event cannot be scheduled. A contract should also specify that show organizers be notified by the hotel or convention center about potential bookings of competitive events after the contract has been signed. In addition, show organizers have some responsibility to be diligent towards managing this, and periodically monitor the situation. Inquire before booking an event in a facility as to what other groups are meeting there at or around the same time frame. Also, make sure to clearly define what constitutes an "incompatible" or "conflicting" group.

Function Space
Function space is usually a designated area in a facility specifically designed and equipped to be used for events such as exhibits, general sessions, seminars, workshops, committee meetings, board meetings, and food and beverage functions. Generally, this space is referred to as "function" or "meeting space." Regardless of what name is used, this is space which an organization or individual has contracted for with the facility, to be used by them for a predetermined time frame, to the exclusion of others.

When initially contracting a facility, inquire whether the function space actually available and being offered is adequate to fully accommodate the function space requirements. As discussed earlier, submit a detailed RFP to the facility outlining the show's needs. It is the show organizer's obligation to know how much space is needed and within what time frame. Generally, this information is based on the host organization's past performance, and realistic growth projections. In the case of first-time events, it should be carefully based on the best estimate from a careful analysis of available information.

The facility's obligation is to know the quantity, size, shape, physical limitations and availability of all space. It is the mutual obligation of the organization and the facility to determine if there is a satisfactory match between requirements.

Facilities may or may not charge the organization for function space use, depending on a number of factors. Most facilities have rates established for the rental of function space based on the length of time the space is needed. Ask for a rate sheet. Also, facilities may have separate rates for seating, tables, risers, head tables, microphones and other audio- visual equipment and special power. A few of the factors that affect function space rental rates are:
- Overall guest room night usage booth citywide and in a specific hotel
- Ratio of guest rooms to meeting space required in a specific hotel
- Overall number and type of food and beverage functions
- If the function space room is being used for a meeting, food function or exhibits

- Number of ancillary food and beverage functions to be hosted by affiliate groups
- Revenue produced by food and beverage in the suites and restaurants.

Future estimates and interaction between the show organizer and facility representative are very important. Always be realistic, erring on the side of conservatism, since any estimates and projections provided to a facility may be used in the future to determine lost revenue for the purpose of calculating performance/ attrition fees.

Function Space Charges

Sometimes, hotel contract formulas are used to establish the basis for function space charges based on an organization's guest room pick-up, separate and apart from the organization's guest room attrition clause. A show organizer must be very careful when reviewing and entering into these types of provisions, as they may allow the hotel to assess the group two separate attrition fees: one for lost guest room revenue, and a second fee for meeting charges. Both fees are based upon guest room night use.

In some instances, function space charges may be waived, even if a group occupies a small number of sleeping rooms, if there are food and beverage functions involved with the meeting, or if the group guarantees to the facility an overall minimum revenue for scheduled food and beverage functions. The waiver can also be dependent upon the number of people involved, the scope of the event other groups have in the facility at the same time, and whether the group has been with the facility in the past or plans to return in the future.

Meeting Room Charges

Function space set-ups that go beyond the established minimum standard almost always result in set-up charges. Facility and organization representatives must agree on a definition for this "norm." In many cases, it will be theater, U-shape, hollow square, or conference style set-ups, along with a head table and a podium. However, this varies enough to warrant a discussion between the show organizer and facility representatives to define the norm. If there are charges, ask for a written breakdown. Are they are based on per room, per chair set or per man-hour? Are there are any minimum costs involved? Also, find out how total equipment inventory will be divided among all groups meeting in the facility at a given time.

Occasionally, in addition charging meeting room rental fees, a facility will consider an organization's requirements for an early move-in or late move-out to set up a function room for staging, rigging, wiring a computer workroom, storage facilities or – in some cases, even offices and press rooms – as chargeable special set-ups. To avoid any unnecessary surprises on move-in day, be sure to add a question to the site evaluation checklist asking how the facility determines whether there will be charges for early move-in or set-up. If so, determine what alternate arrangements are available during the move-in or move-out at no charge.

Move-In and Move-Out

This is the time needed by the facility and outside contractors or working volunteers to prepare (move in or set-up) a meeting room for a scheduled event, and to remove (move out or tear down) furniture and equipment after the event's conclusion. These time requirements should be addressed and provided for in the schedule of events provided to the facility. Also make sure to define whether any additional charges will be applied for set-up and tear-down time, or if it is part of the overall function space rental charges.

Function Space Programs

Without question, in order to protect the integrity of the event, always make it a mandatory practice to attach a schedule of events (preliminary program) to the signed contract. Make sure the schedule of events contains a detailed list of the function space being held under contract. Preferably, list the space by room names, dates, and overall estimated times. However, if a facility is unable, or unwilling to commit to this for any host of reasons, at least get them to commit to the s pace being held, based on dates, overall times, and function room dimensions and square footage.

This helps to ensure that the contracted function space is not accidentally released to another group prior to the submission of the tentative function program. This will help determine if the facility breached the Agreement should a dispute arise regarding the allocation of function space.

Furthermore, make sure to have a clause in the Agreement that states that, prior to the release by the facility of any function space listed, the organization's preliminary, tentative or final programs are submitted in writing to the event manager, and must be approved in writing by the event manager before any release can actually take place.

Exclusive Services

As facilities look to expand their profit centers, this issue is becoming bigger every day. The show organizer must be aware of what services a facility considers exclusive presently, or plans to make exclusive in the future.

Know exactly what services the facility provides on an exclusive basis, and the cost for those services. Get a commitment on how far in advance the facility will confirm rates for those services. Additionally, strongly consider adding a clause to the contract that allows the show organizer to retain the right to contract with third party providers for any current, non-exclusive services without any additional fees (surcharges) being levied on the used group, or its service provider of such services.

> **TIP**
> Pertaining to non-exclusive services, some facilities try to stipulate the hiring of their personnel, or an approved outsider service provider, for various functions that are "non-exclusive." Either eliminate this from the contract, or negotiate a specific financial or service benefit if their staff is employed instead of an independent security, paramedic or cleaning service.

Food and Beverage Functions

In general the following food and beverage information should be included in the agreement with the facility:

- Final Prices: Have the facility agree to a specific date when they will provide the group with confirmed food and beverage prices. Ask the facility to guarantee that the rates being quoted will not be greater than the menu prices in effect at the time the prices are confirmed. This can be an advantage if confirmed rates are being obtained a year in advance, or right before a price change. Facilities tend to quote food and beverage prices three to six months in advance, but sometimes it is possible to confirm these costs earlier than that.

- Gratuities and Service Charges: The show organizer should determine the facility's gratuity and service charges policy, since they are no longer one and the same. Normally, gratuities are added to the food and beverage costs, either before or after the taxes are added. Sometimes, however, gratuities can be a part of the labor agreement. Both parties should understand how such charges will be applied to basic food and beverage costs. Moreover, it is important to understand how these service charges and gratuities are distributed between the facility and the service staff. Also, organizations should make their tax-exempt status known to the facility early in their discussions. This may eliminate incorrect billing for sales taxes.

- Corkage Charges: These are charges that may be placed on food and beverages brought in for use at an event scheduled for the group. Rarely are these types of charges seen in standard documents, because almost every facility has a strict policy about not allowing food or beverages to be brought into the facility by outside vendors or other sources. However, the issue may still arise when a sponsor or exhibitor brings their own line of food or beverage products into the facility for distribution and/or on-site consumption. If you know at the time of contracting that this type of situation may arise, be sure to address it in the contract. This can potentially preserve the relationship with major exhibitors, therefore safeguarding their participation in future events.

Guarantees and Food and Beverage Attrition

Almost without exception, meetings and exhibitions have scheduled food and beverage functions. The cost of these can be paid directly by the organization, by the organization's participation at cash bar functions, or at cash-and-carry food service stands specifically set up for the organization in a designated function space area versus public space, or by sponsors or affiliate organizations.

Regardless of the source of payment for these food and beverage functions, if the contract contains a minimum food and beverage revenue guarantee, make absolutely sure the organization is credited for any and all revenue generated by the organization's overall event taking place at the hotel, including the exhibitors' and affiliates' hospitality suites and catered functions whenever possible.

Any food and beverage attrition fee agreed to, if separate and apart from the guest room attrition and/or function space attrition, should be based on the lost profits (net revenue) from such sales due to attrition, not the gross revenue. The reason is simple. Most hotel and convention centers require an attendee cover guarantee deadline date, usually well in advance of the actual function. By this deadline, they must be provided with the minimum number of guaranteed covers (attendance figures) the show organizer will be responsible for paying, regardless of whether the actual attendance is below this figure.

Therefore, if any attrition occurs before this deadline date, the hotel or center will have only incurred damages in the way of lost profits. They will not have incurred additional damages from out of pocket expenses, because they will not have to pay for additional labor or food, beverages or other supplies. And, for any attrition that they incur after the deadline date, they will be duly compensated under the minimum guarantee.

Exhibit Space Rental Rates

Like meeting space, exhibit space may be provided with or without charge. A lot depends on the guest room usage and food and beverage revenue, as well as the other factors. The bottom line will always be, "How much does the facility want the business?"

Alternatively, the facility may want exhibit rental but agree to waive the meeting room rental, or vice versa. Inquire exactly how the exhibit rental rate is to be calculated for the function where the exhibits will be housed. They may be based on:

- Net square feet of exhibit space per day, or for the duration of the event
- A flat rate for the entire exposition hall per day or for the duration of the event
- A per booth per day or for the duration of the event.

Additionally, determine what, if any, additional charges there will be for move-in and move-out days, whether air-conditioning and heating is included on all rental days, and what rental charges, if any, will be applied to non-commercial (non revenue producing), educational, or public service exhibits.

Move-in and Move-out

It is standard for a group to receive a pre-determined number of complimentary move-in and move-out days at most publicly-owned convention center facilities. However, not all facilities provide the same arrangements, so do not assume this is automatic. On the other hand, most hotels and private convention center facilities do not, as a matter of standard policy, provide any complimentary move- in or move-out days; therefore, this must be negotiated into the contract. It is the show organizer's responsibility to make sure that any move-in and move-out arrangements are fully articulated in the contract. If more than the complimentary allotment of move-in and move-out time is necessary, try to negotiate a special rate for the additional number of days needed. Usually, a facility will try to accommodate if they really want the event's business, so this request is reasonable under the circumstances. Additionally, never get "boxed in" to an unreasonable number of move-in or move-out days for the show, and do not overbook these days either.

Exhibit Hall Services

The show organizer should always list in the facility contract the services or items that are included in the rental rates, as well as the services for which there will be additional charges. The following items may or may not be included in the exhibit rental rates, depending on the type of facility being utilized and what has been negotiated into the contract:

• General hall cleaning, general lighting, air conditioning and heating during show hours
• Storage and office space
• Electricity, gas, plumbing, water, and necessary signage
• Telephone service & Internet access
• Cost of hall cleaning
• A specified level of security.

Also, the facility should provide information concerning the percent (or amount) of any sales taxes, excise taxes and/or royalty fees on rental charges, space sales, exhibitors' sales activities or ticket sales, and to whom and when these levies must be paid.

Licenses and Permits

It is the show manager's responsibility to obtain all licenses or permits required by state and local ordinances, and to determine applicable fees, and whether the organization or the exhibitor is responsible for payment of such fees for each permit or license required. Some cities charge a fee for the approval of exhibition plans by a fire marshal, or require a fire marshal to be on the premises during the exposition, so plan for this in the budget.

Security
When security is provided, clarify with the facility if their in-house security service must be utilized, or if in the organization can bring in its own security contractor. If the facility security must be used, determine the hours and cost involved, as well as who will be liable for the security officer's actions and omissions.

Special Limitations
Every exhibition facility has special limitations, such as floor load limits, dock space, doors to the facility, truck-marshaling areas, empty storage space and trash removal. The show manager should determine the effect and to what extent such limitations will have on move-in, the show itself, and move-out

Union Jurisdiction
If applicable, the show organizer needs to understand how the labor union situation in the chosen city might differ from those the organization may have used in the past. Union work rules can significantly affect the actual move-in and move-out schedule, and its associated costs. Check out the work rules of the union with jurisdiction in the facility. Sometimes, it's better to pay for more move-in and out days to save on labor costs, and sometimes it is not. Remember, "How it has always worked in the past" is not necessarily relevant to the present situation or city.

Ask the facility which unions have jurisdiction: teamsters, electricians, riggers, carpenters, decorators, and stagehands, among others. The show manager needs to find out the expiration dates of union contracts, as well as if the facility requires the hiring of union labor for all available positions (guards, ticket sellers, and other event staff).

Utilities
Lights, air conditioning and heat is included for the show days, but not necessarily during the move-in and move-out days. Depending on when the event is scheduled, this can be a costly issue if not negotiated and resolved up front. Furthermore, 24-hour electrical service to exhibit booths is not a given, so be sure to clarify any related concerns.

Trash Disposal and Abandoned Property
It is common for a facility to charge for trash removal, especially if they need special equipment or extra personnel to do the job. Although these charges do exist and are

warranted, try to negotiate for one or more trash hauling bins to be provided and emptied by the facility at no cost.

Also, if the facility provides trashcans in the exhibit area (as opposed to hauling bins), determine which party is responsible for their placement, emptying during the show, and final return to their original storage location, and any costs involved.

If something is to be left behind, the show manager should assign responsibility and liability to someone, and plan ahead for this with the contractor to determine the best means of removing unwanted material. Do not take for granted that this "trash" will simply be thrown away by the building without additional cost. Recycling programs are also an option.

Signs and Displays

Facility or convention centers are rightfully concerned about the overall appearance and condition of their facilities, especially their public and function space areas. It is not uncommon for a facility to insert a paragraph into the contract pertaining to the posting of signs and displays. Although these clauses usually are not problematic to a group, review them carefully to ensure that they will not be in conflict with the exhibition's requirements; if they are, adjust them accordingly. Find out who is authorized to hang signage, and what, if any, are the charges associated with the hanging of signs, banner, and displays.

Control of Concession Sales

Even if no "concession" type activity is planned – such as souvenir sales, or other types of items generally accompanying public events like concerts – this clause should either be removed or clarified as to exactly what is covered by this clause. If the facility has a gift shop, pro shop, or business center, a concession clause has the potential to affect any ancillary activities, such as literature kiosks, book and sundry sales, as well as exhibitor promotional activities. Therefore, either remove the concession clause completely, or make sure it is articulated thoroughly.

Access to the Event

Sometimes, it is important for the facility sales staff and other employees to escort their guests and prospective organizations through and around the event. However, the show manager has the right to control this activity, and certainly has the right of approval within any function and exhibit space being utilized by the event. For example, a contract may stipulate that the facility's sales staff may not show the organization's competitors through the show without the manager's knowledge or approval during a site visit. Show management also has the right to restrict or ban the taking of still or video pictures of the event by anyone, including facility staff, for any reason.

Additional Common Contract Clauses
Indemnification and Hold Harmless

This clause secures one party against loss or damage caused by another. It makes the Indemnitor (the party who is contractually bound to indemnify or protect the other party) responsible for reimbursing the Indemnitee (the other party) against the losses it incurred. While these losses may somehow be connected to the actions of the Indemnitor or its agents, at the same time, these were not the fault of the Indemnitee. Usually, the Indemnitor ends up reimbursing the Indemnitee for any costs it incurred to defend itself in an action brought against it by a third party, and to pay any judgments (settlements or monetary damages) already paid out by the indemnity to a third party.

Try to make indemnification clauses a bilateral provision when it is in the best interest of the organization to do so, such as in the case of service providers and facility contracts. This means that each party agrees to indemnify, defend and hold the other party harmless, unless one of the parties is negligent for its actions or omissions or intentional misconduct. Sometimes the parties will specify the actual level of negligence, which is not covered by the indemnification provision, such as sole or gross negligence.

When it comes to outside service providers, the organization should always be indemnified by the service provider (or contractor). The organization's willingness to agree to indemnify a service provider should be carefully evaluated. The final determination to do so should be based on the specific type and scope of the services to be provided, and how much direct involvement the organization will have pertaining to those services that are delivered to its members and event attendees.

Liquor Liability

Liquor liability continues to be a growing concern for the meetings and tradeshow industry whenever an organization sponsors any type of event where liquor is served. This is especially true for the "social host," an individual or organization, which provides a hosted bar paid for by the sponsor of the event where alcoholic beverages are to be served to the guests, as opposed to a "commercial host," who is usually a bar, restaurant, or a cash bar arrangement at a function where the entity is actually selling the liquor directly to the guests.

State laws which place liability on social hosts for property and personal damages suffered by a third party who is injured by an individual who becomes intoxicated while at a sponsored or meeting-related event differ greatly from state to state. Since the law in this area is still evolving, the show organizer may want to protect his or her organization right from the start by purchasing liquor liability insurance as part of the event's overall insurance coverage. At a minimum, check with the Alcohol

Beverage Control Board in the state where the event will be held to get the latest information regarding social and commercial host liability, since both are likely to occur during the planned event.

Americans with Disabilities Act

Title III of the Americans with Disabilities Act defines what types of facilities are considered public entities under the Act. Moreover, it addresses how the owners and organizations which utilize them need to ensure that the facilities to be used are accessible to persons with disabilities. Section 302 states:

> *"No individual shall be discriminated against on the basis of disability in the full and equal enjoyment of the goods, services, facilities, privileges, advantages, or accommodations by any person who owns, leases (or leases to), or operates a place of public accommodations."*

Therefore, because hotels and convention centers are deemed places of public accommodation, under the ADA, it is the organization's responsibility to make sure the facilities where the event is held, as well as the actual event, are accessible to individuals with disabilities. In most instances, the facility will accept responsibility for ADA compliance in their function space, public space, common areas and guest rooms to remove barriers, and make them accessible. In turn, they require the organization to take responsibility, and pay for auxiliary aids and services, which pertain directly to the program – such as audible signals, Braille signage for event functions, large print materials, computers, and sign language interpreters. Be sure to determine the extent of the organization's responsibility for ADA compliance, since under the law, the show manager is fully responsible for the organization's ADA compliance requirements regardless of what the contract says.

Fire, Health and Safety

Because our society is becoming ever more litigious, it is important for organizations to review and understand their potential liability exposure from third parties due to the contracts they enter into. According to statutory and case law, the Doctrine of Negligence (Duty of Reasonable Care) rests on the duty of every person to exercise due care in his or her conduct toward others from which injury may result. In negligence cases, a person or entity can be found liable if there is a failure to use such care as a reasonably prudent and careful person would have used under similar circumstances. Therefore, an organization could be found negligent (liable for damages), if they did not reasonably investigate whether the facility they selected to host their event was up to current fire, safety and health codes, and an attendee was harmed as a result of this failure to conduct a reasonable inquiry. So to help limit the organization's liability exposure from an accident to an individual or their property, always include a provision in all service and facility contracts which states that the facility and/or service provider is in compliance with current federal, state and local fire, safety and health codes and regulations, and will remain in compliance over the duration of the contract. This clause also goes a long way in showing that due care was taken to protect the attendees' well being, and that the company and/or facilities chosen were, or claimed to be, reasonably safe when the contract was signed.

Confidential Information

It is important to protect the organization's trademarks, logos, trade secrets and other intellectual property. Therefore, always consider adding a confidentiality and/or nondisclosure provision into the services provider agreement, whenever the organization is providing it with confidential and proprietary information.

Assignment of the Contract

Assignment is an act of transferring to another all or part of one's property, interest, or rights. If a contract contains a provision permitting its transfer by either party, or if the contract is silent as to the parties' right to transfer their interests, it may be transferred. On the other hand, if the contract states it is either not assignable, or only could be assigned by mutual consent, either party could, depending on the circumstances, lose its right to transfer the contract to a third party unless the non-transferring party agrees to do so at its sole discretion.

This issue of assignability becomes important if the organization is considering selling the event or show to a third party in the future, if the entire organization is being acquired by another entity through a merger or a buy-out, and/or if the facility or service provider's management or owner changes. Even if there is a remote possibility of a sale or merger affecting the event or organization, the show organizer should either add an assignment clause, or modify the current clause, to allow assignment under these circumstances. While the invalidity of such non-assignment clauses may prevail in court, these kinds of costly battles can easily be avoided by using a little foresight in the negotiation. If the facility's or service provider's company management changes, or is sold by its owner prior to the event, this change could severely impact the enforceability of the organization's agreement. Therefore, it is important to address both of these possibilities up front.

Also, if assignment is permitted under the contract, make sure that the contract as written will remain binding upon the respective successors, assigns, and personal representatives of the parties.

Arbitration

An arbitration clause is a voluntary clause allowing for compulsory arbitration in case of a dispute as to the rights, obligations or liabilities provided for in the contract. It is used as an alternative to litigation. This type of alternative dispute resolution involves the selection of a neutral third party (arbitrator) that renders a binding or non-binding decision after a hearing at which both parties have an opportunity to present their cases.

Although arbitration is often an excellent alternative to litigation, it can have its drawbacks. When show organizers agree to binding arbitration, they waive their legal rights to "have their day in court." Therefore, keep in mind that if the case is lost in binding arbitration, the decision is final and without further recourse.

There are two standard types of arbitration: 1) Binding – the arbitrator's decision is final, and judgment rendered can be entered in any court having jurisdiction, and 2) Non- binding, where a party, if it so chooses, can appeal the arbitrator's decision to a court having jurisdiction.

Notification

Whenever a contract necessitates any interaction between the parties, or requires performance by specified dates, it should contain a notice provision. This clause enables the parties to address how notice will be provided, such as by regular mail, certified mail, fax or some other way. This type of clause further identifies the parties to be notified for a particular purpose, outlines the rules for determining when notice is deemed to have been received, and what procedures are required when a party changes address.

Neutral Drafting

If a dispute arises revolving around the interpretation of a term or condition of an agreement, the court will strictly construe the agreement against the party that drafted the agreement. Therefore, if an organization's representatives plan on offering their own contract to the other party, or jointly negotiating the contract between the parties, a Joint Drafting and Neutral Construction provision should be added. It allows the court to dispense with having to strictly interpret the provision in question against the party who originally drafted it, and allows the court or arbitrator to consider the meaning and intent of the provision from a neutral position.

Authorization

Make sure that the person listed as signatory on the contract has the authority – that is, the power – to enter into the Agreement, and that it is within the scope of their job related duties to sign it on behalf of the organization reserving hotel guest room and function space. Additionally, make sure that the hotel's representative who will be counter- signing the contract on the hotel's behalf has the same authority to do so.

The individual or individuals who will be signing the contract on behalf of their respective organizations should always use their full names and official titles when signing any agreement. Furthermore, if third-party representatives are authorized to sign the contract on another organization's behalf, they should use the following format: ABC Representative Company (that is, the third-party representative) *as agent for* "XXX Organization" (that is, the association or company who will be actually responsible for performance under the contract). Otherwise, the third party representative can be held personally liable for performance under the terms of the contract.

> **TIP**
>
> Never fill in the effective date until the Agreement has been finalized in its entirety.
>
> Also, if a facsimile bearing the signature of the parties is to be considered an enforceable original in place of or until the parties exchange the actual signed original, and/or for any future documents related to the performance of the Agreement, have a Facsimile clause placed into the contract.

Exhibitor Contract Example

San Diego, California   28 - 30 November

Expo! Expo! Exhibition
Wednesday, 29 November 2006
San Diego Convention Center
San Diego, CA
Halls E, F & G
11:00 a.m. – 5:00 p.m.

Application and Contract for Exhibition Space

Please complete the **2-PAGE** form and return it to IAEM. Page 3 is for your reference.

Administrative Contact (receives all information):_____Title_____

Administrative Contact Phone: _____FAX:_____ Email Address: _____

SALES Contact (company contact person):_____Title_____

SALES Contact Phone: _____FAX:_____ Email Address: _____

SECTION 1: Basic Company Information – Print Information EXACTLY as it should appear in the Onsite Program and on the website.	
Company Name:	Member Number:
Company Address:	
City: State/Province: Zip Code/ Postal Code: Country:	
Phone: Fax:	
E-mail: Website:	

SECTION 2: Company Description – Print Information EXACTLY as it should appear on the website.
Please provide a 20-word description of your company's background or specialty. Text in excess of 20 words will be edited.
Information Submitted by: Telephone:

SECTION: 3 Products and Services Listing for Onsite Program and website

Please indicate no more than 6 product(s) or services that your company provides. Lists in excess of 6 will be edited.

_____1. A/V Equip./Rentals/Production
_____2. Advertising/Promotional Services
_____3. Airline
_____4. Association
_____5. Business Services:
     Shipping/Financial/Accounting
_____6. Catering Services
_____7. Cleaning/Janitorial Services
_____8. Communication Equipment
_____9. Computer Rentals
_____10. Computer Software:
     Exhibition/Event, Floor plan Mgmt
_____11. Consultant
_____12. Convention Bureau
_____13. Customs Broker
_____14. Destination Management
_____15. Education/Training
_____16. Electrical Contractor
_____17. Electronic Information Centers
_____18. Exhibit Designer/Builder
_____19. Facility-Arena/Auditorium/Stadium
_____20. Facility-Convention Center
_____21. Facility-Fairground

_____22. Facility-Public Expo
_____23. Facility-World Trade Center
_____24. Floor Manager
_____25. Florist/Plant Rental
_____26. Freight-Air
_____27. Freight-Common Carrier
_____28. Freight-Van Line
_____29. Furniture Rental/Booth Furnishings
_____30. Graphics/Printing
_____31. Hostesses/Modeling Services/
     Entertainment/Talent Service
_____32. Hotel-Exhibit Space < 30,000 sq. ft.
_____33. Hotel-Exhibit Space > 30,000 sq. ft.
_____34. Housing/Travel Services
_____35. Insurance
_____36. International Exhibitor Services
_____37. Internet/Web Services/Webcasting/
     System Design/Software
_____38. Lead Retrieval/Management Systems
_____39. Literature Displays/Kiosks
_____40. Marketing Services/Research/ Traffic
     Builders

_____41. Message System
_____42. Personnel (Temporary)
_____43. Photography
_____44. Plumbing Contractor
_____45. Premiums/Promotions
_____46. Product Locators/Message Centers
_____47. Publications/Dailies
_____48. Registration Services/Badging Sys.
_____49. Registration Supplies
_____50. Security Services
_____51. Service Contractor-General
_____52. Service Contractor-I&D
_____53. Show Management
_____54. Signage
_____55. Special Events/Tour Operations
_____56. Surveys/Audience Response Sys.
_____57. Telecommunications
_____58. Theme Park
_____59. Translation Services
_____60. Transportation/Shuttle Services

Please select 4 exhibit space choices 1)_____ 2)_____ 3)_____ 4)_____
List maximum of 4 companies you DO NOT want to be near: 1)_____ 2)_____ 3)_____ 4)_____

SECTION 4: Fees: Exhibit Space & Additional Listing Opportunities

Exhibit Space Includes: Pipe and Drape; ID sign; 3 "Expo Only" registrations per 100 sq ft: each reg. includes show floor access, Opening General Session & Opening Reception; lead retrieval unit; 1 pre-meeting attendee registration list; standard booth cleaning (pre-show); STANDARD online virtual booth: includes company address & email address, 20-word description online and in the onsite program, listing of 6 products & services, link to company web site, one contact name w/email address and promotion of 1 product.

Exhibit Space

Booth Space	Regular Member Rate *IAEM Member in good standing*	Non-Member Rate	Corner	Totals
100 square feet	$2,500	$3,500	+ $100 per corner	
200 square feet	$5,000	$7,000	+ $100 per corner	
300 square feet	$7,500	$10,500	+ $100 per corner	
400 square feet	$10,000	$14,000	+ $100 per corner	

Additional Listing Opportunities

STANDARD online virtual booth: includes company address & email address, **20**-word description online and in the onsite program, listing of **6** products & services, link to company web site, **1** contact name w/email address, promotion of **1** product.	$0 (included in booth fee)	$0
PREMIUM online virtual booth: includes company address & email address, **50**-word description online and in the onsite program, listing of **6** products & services, link to company web site, **2** contact names w/email address, promotion of **2** products; coupon; press release; company logo online and in onsite program; list **2** special events; brochure – PDF.	$450	
Ultimate online virtual booth: includes company address & email address, **100**-word description online and in the onsite program, listing of **6** products & services, link to company web site, **4** contact names w/email address, promotion of **5** products; coupon; press release; company logo online and in onsite program; list **4** special events; brochure – PDF; audio/video webcast.	$550	
50 Word description on line and in the Onsite Program	$150	
Black and White Logo online and in the Onsite Program	$150	
Total Exhibit Space and Listing Fees		
50% Deposit (After 9/1/06, 100% payment required)		

SECTION 5: Payment

50% deposit is due with the contract if submitted on or before 1 September 2006. Contracts submitted after 1 September, 2006 require 100% payment. Balance is due no later than 1 September 2006.

❑   Check Enclosed – Check Number_____in the amount of $_____**payable to IAEM**

❑   Charge $_____ to the following credit card: ❑ MasterCard   ❑ VISA   ❑ American Express   ❑ Discover

    Card # _____Expiration Date _____

    Name on Card: _____Signature _____

Agreed to____ Date________________________

Company Authorized Signature

Print Name____ Title________________________

Accepted by_______________________________________ Date________________________

IAEM Authorized Signature

Please return signed contract along with payment to:

IAEM
Attention: Julie Anderson, CEM, Director of Show Development
8111 LBJ Freeway, Suite 750
Dallas, TX 75251
PH: +1 (972) 687-9206 FAX: +1 (972) 458-8119
EMAIL: janderson@iaem.org

For Expo! Expo! Management Use Only:

Date Received____________ Date Assigned____________
Exhibit Space(s) Assigned ____________
Total Square Footage ________ sq. ft.
Total Space Fee $____________
Deposit Received $____________
___Member Number # ____________
___Non-Member
Name of Salesperson ____________

Rules Governing Expo! Expo! San Diego, CA 29 November, 2006

1. Defined Terms: The term Exhibition means Expo! Expo! currently scheduled to be held in San Diego, CA on 29 November 2006 at the San Diego Convention Center. The Exhibition is sponsored by the International Association for Exhibition Management (IAEM), its officers, directors, agents, affiliates, representatives, employees, or assigns, unless the context requires otherwise. The term "Exhibitor" means the company or person or any of its officers, directors, shareholders, employees, contractors, agents, or representatives that applied for exhibit space rental and agreed to enter into this contract.

2. Contract Acceptance: The Contract shall become effective when it has been signed by a duly authorized representative of the exhibiting company and counter-signed by a duly authorized representative of IAEM.

3. Qualification of Exhibitors: IAEM reserves the right to determine eligibility of exhibitor for inclusion in the Exhibition prior to, or after, execution of the Agreement. Products and services displayed must be exhibition industry related; and that are intended for and generally used in a manner that conform to State, Federal, or other applicable laws or regulations. No other products can be displayed. No exhibitor shall display any product or display or distribute advertisements for a product which infringes upon the registered trademark, copyright or patent of another company, as has been determined by a court of competent jurisdiction. Product comparisons using product or written materials of companys other than the contracted exhibitor are prohibited.

IAEM, in its sole judgment, will determine the appropriateness of products exhibited, and reserves the right to prohibit display or advertisement of products which are in violation of these Exhibition Rules or do not meet the Exhibition's objectives.

4. Space Assignment and Attendees: Although IAEM will attempt to accommodate Exhibitor requests for specific booths, no guarantees can be made that the Exhibitor will be assigned the specific booth(s) requested. Exhibitor acknowledges that he/she is not contracting for a specific booth(s), but rather for the right to participate as an Exhibitor in Expo! Expo! 2006. IAEM makes no representations or warranties with respect to the demographic nature and/or number of exhibitors and/or attendees. The method of determining space assignment shall be established by IAEM and may be changed from time to time without notice to exhibitors in order to accommodate what IAEM perceives as the best interest of the Exhibition. No rights or privileges are created for any exhibitor as a result of previous space assignments or years of participation in the Exhibition or other exhibitions produced by IAEM.

5. Use of Space: Exhibitor shall not assign, sell its rights, sublet, share, or apportion the whole or any part of the space allotted, or have representatives, products, equipment, signs or printed materials from other than its own company in the said exhibit space without the written consent of IAEM. Sharing of a 10'x10' exhibit space is permitted only by a CVB and one 'publicly' owned facility.

6. Cancellation of Participation: Cancellation of all or a portion of any exhibit space must be in writing via certified mail (return receipt requested). IAEM shall withhold 10% of total booth cost as an administrative fee for any cancellation of confirmed exhibit space, on or before 30 June 2006.

After 30 June 2006, this refund schedule will be strictly followed. Written notification received:

-1 July 2006 to 2 August 2006, Exhibitor shall be liable for 50% of total rental cost of each space canceled as liquidated damages.

-3 August 2006 to 1 September 2006, Exhibitor shall be liable for 75% of rental cost of each space canceled as liquidated damages.

-After 1 September 2006 Exhibitor shall be liable for 100% of the rental cost of each space canceled as liquidated damages. A 100% cancellation fee will be charged after 1 September 2006 for any reason whatsoever. Refunds and liquidated damages are based on full exhibit space rental cost, and not the deposit. IAEM shall not be liable for interest on any amount refunded.

7. Downsizing by Exhibitor: An Exhibitor may be required to move to a new location if the Exhibitor requests a downsizing of space. A fee of 50% of the difference between the cost of the original total exhibition fee and the downsized exhibition fee, at the current rate, will be charged on any IAEM approved downsizing on or before 15 June, 2006. The fee increases to 100% after 15 June, 2006. The above downsizing fees shall be in addition to the actual cost of the downsized exhibition fee.

8. Exhibit Space Occupancy: Any Exhibitor failing to occupy its assigned space one hour prior to the Exhibition's opening, or who leaves his or her space unattended during the Exhibit hours, forfeits their rights to the space. All exhibits must be open for business during the Exhibition hours. Exhibitors may not dismantle their display until the official closing time or until the Exhibition is officially closed by IAEM.

9. Exhibitor Breach: Cancellation of Exhibit Space: If an Exhibitor fails to make required payments as described in the exhibit space contract, or any other material breach, IAEM may terminate the Exhibitor's participation in the Exhibition without further notice and without obligation to refund moneys previously paid. Exhibitors may not move-in until full payment is received.

10. Cancellation of the Exhibition: If IAEM cancels the Exhibition due to circumstances beyond the reasonable control of IAEM (such as Acts of "God," Act of War, governmental emergency, labor strike or unavailability of the exhibit facility), IAEM shall refund to each Exhibitor its exhibit space rental payment previously paid, minus a share of costs and expenses incurred in full satisfaction of all liabilities.

11. Exhibit Design and Inclusions: Exhibitor agrees to abide by exhibit display and construction guidelines published by IAEM and included in the Exhibitor Service Manual. All Exhibitors must remain within the confines of their own space, and no Exhibitor will be permitted to erect signs or display products in such a manner as to obstruct the view, occasion injury, or disadvantageously affect the display of other Exhibitors.

12. Character of Displays; Use of Aisles and Common Areas: Distribution of samples and printed matter of any kind, and any promotional material, is restricted to the exhibit booth. Each Exhibitor agrees to exhibit only products which it represents. All exhibits shall display products or services in a tasteful manner. The aisles, passageways, and overhead space remain strictly under the control of IAEM and no signs, decorations, banners, advertising material or special exhibit will be permitted in the aisles. Employees must remain within the booth occupied by their employers. Any and all advertising distribution must be made from the Exhibitor's booth space. Stickers are prohibited in the exhibit area. (Handouts with gummed backing that adhere or cause adhesion are considered stickers.)

13. Listing and Promotional Materials: By exhibiting at the Exhibition, Exhibitors grant IAEM a fully-paid, perpetual non-exclusive license to use, display and reproduce the name of Exhibitors in any directory listing the exhibiting companys at the Exhibition and to use such names in promotional materials. IAEM shall not be liable for any errors in any listing or descriptions or for omitting any Exhibitor from the directory or other lists or materials. Exhibitors may not use the IAEM corporate logo but, with permission, may use the show logos.

14. Copyrighted Materials: Exhibitors shall not play or permit the playing or performance of, or distribution of any copyrighted materials at the Exhibition unless it has obtained all necessary rights and paid all required royalties, fees or other payment.

15. Safety, Fire and Health: Federal, State and City laws must be strictly observed. A full listing of these fire and safety regulations will be found in the Exhibitor Service Manual.

16. Sound Devices: The use of devices for mechanical reproduction of sound or music is permitted, but must be controlled. Sound of any kind must not be projected outside of the exhibit booth. Exhibitors are specifically prohibited from employing any carnival-type attraction, animal or human, or from operating such noise-creating devices as bells, horns, or megaphones.

17. Contractor Services: IAEM has contracted with official contractors to provide both exclusive and non-exclusive services at Expo! Expo! While exhibitors may utilize exhibitor-appointed contractors (EAC) for non-exclusive services at Expo! Expo! within certain guidelines, exhibitors other than official contractors may not solicit exhibitors to provide products or services at Expo! Expo! A complete listing of official exclusive and non-exclusive contractors and EAC guidelines will be provided in the Exhibitor Services Manual.

18. Exhibitor Representatives: Exhibitor reps are limited to personnel employed by the Exhibitor listed on the contract and its named participants who have been deemed appropriate and representative of the exhibiting company. The purchase of each (10'x10') exhibit space includes three (3) Expo! Expo! only exhibitor representative registrations.

19. Care of Exhibit Facility: Exhibitor shall promptly pay for any and all damage to the Exhibit Facility or associated facilities, booth equipment or the property of others caused by the Exhibitor or any of its employees, agents, contractors, or representatives.

20. Taxes and Licenses: Exhibitor shall be solely responsible for obtaining any licenses, permits, or approvals under Federal, State, or local law applicable to its activities at the Exhibition. Exhibitor shall be solely responsible for obtaining any necessary tax identification numbers and permits and for paying all taxes, license fees, use fees, or other fees, charges or penalties that become due to any governmental authority in connection with its activities at the Exhibition. It is understood and agreed that this Contract constitutes a non-assignable license and privilege only ad is not, under any circumstances, intended to constitute a lease or any other conveyance of real property a partnership, employment agreement or joint venture between the parties.

21. Observance of Laws: Exhibitor shall abide by and observe all Federal, State, and local laws, codes, ordinances, rules and regulations of the Exhibit Facility (including any union labor work rules). Without limiting the forgoing, Exhibitor shall construct its exhibits to comply with the Americans with Disabilities Act.

22. Assumption of Risks: General Liability Insurance - Mandatory: Expo! Expo! Each Exhibitor **MUST** provide a Certificate of Insurance evidencing Commercial General Liability insurance. Certificates must be sent to, and received by, IAEM by 1 November 2006. Not providing a Certificate of Insurance will exclude the exhibiting company from participating in Expo! Expo! Please note that Commercial General Liability Certificates of Insurance must show the following: Combined Single Limit of liability in the amounts of $1,000,000 per occurrence/$2,000,000 general aggregate. The Additional Insureds should be listed as IAEM and the San Diego Convention Center. Exhibitor expressly assumes all risk associated with, resulting from or arising in connection with Exhibitor's participation or presence at the Exhibition, including, without limitation, all risks of theft, loss, harm or injury to the person (including death), property, business or profits of Exhibitor, whether caused by negligence, intentional act, accident, Act of God or otherwise. Exhibitor has sole responsibility for its property or any theft, damage or other loss to such property (whether or not stored in any courtesy storage areas), including any subrogation claims by its insurer. The exhibitor agrees to carry appropriate insurance to cover these risks. Neither IAEM nor the San Diego Convention Center Facility accepts responsibility, nor is a bailment created, for property delivered by or to the Exhibitor. Neither IAEM nor the Exhibit Facility, nor any of their respective officers, directors, shareholders, agents, employees, representatives or assigns, shall be liable for, and Exhibitor hereby releases all of them from, and covenants not to sue any of them with respect to, any and all risks, damages and liabilities described in this paragraph.

23. Exhibitor Service Manual: Approximately 90 days before the Exhibition, a link to the electronic Exhibitor Service Manual will be sent to the "Administrative Contact" listed on the contract. The Exhibitor Service Manual will include information integral to your company's participation at the Exhibition, including but not limited to: additional Exhibitor Rules and Regulations, official contractor order forms, registration, shipping and drayage, utilities and building services, decorator, audio/visual, exhibitor display rules and move-in/move-out schedules, and insurance information.

24. Incorporation of Rules and Regulations: Any and all matters pertaining to the Exhibition not specifically covered by this Contract and the rules and regulations as described in the Exhibitor Service Manual, shall be subject to determination by IAEM. IAEM may adopt rules or regulations from time to time governing such matters, and may amend or revoke them at any time, upon reasonable notice to the Exhibitor.

25. Right To Offset: IAEM shall have the right to offset the amount of any obligation due and owing to IAEM from the Exhibitor whether under this agreement or any other agreement between IAEM and the Exhibitor. IAEM may cancel this contract in the event that the Exhibitor is past due on any amounts due to IAEM for any reason.

26. Interest and Collection Fees: Any exhibitor that does not meet all financial obligations when due will be responsible for all outstanding debts, interest at one and one-half percent (1.5%) per month, and any fees (including attorney's fees and/or collection fees of not less than 25% of the remaining balance due IAEM incurs to recover the debt. There will be a $25 charge for all returned checks. If the above interest amount, attorney's fees and/or collection fees, and returned check fees exceed the limits allowed by applicable laws, then the maximum interest and such fees as allowed by such laws shall be paid to IAEM by the Exhibitor.

A contract between the show organizer and an exhibitor for rental of the exhibit space can vary from a minimal to a complex, and may or may not incorporate other binding documents (such as Rules and Regulations). Some of the essential items in an exhibitor contract include:

> ✓ Identifying information on both parties
>
> ✓ Signatures from both parties
>
> ✓ Agreement to abide by the exposition's rules, regulations and official floorplan, and whether this information is included in the contract or is a separate document
>
> ✓ Requirements for payment of exhibit fees
>
> ✓ Exhibit hours and completed installation date and time
>
> ✓ Height and sign limitations
>
> ✓ Restrictions on space sharing
>
> ✓ Regulations re operation of sound and lighting equipment
>
> ✓ Hold Harmless clause for the sponsoring organization and facility
>
> ✓ Security service details
>
> ✓ Union requirements
>
> ✓ Move-in and Move-out dates and times
>
> ✓ Safety and fire regulations (or reference additional documents)
>
> ✓ Trash removal services and options
>
> ✓ Storage regulations and options

IAEM's *Exhibitor Rules & Regulations* should also be incorporated into the show rules.

SUMMARY

The legalities surrounding hotel and facility contracts are some of the most complex skills a show organizer will be required to master. A working knowledge of the art of negotiation and the basic components of a contract are essential to a show organizer.

But it is also important to understand when to bring in professional legal assistance, although each organization will vary in its assessment of the need for legal advice.

QUESTIONS FOR DISCUSSION

① How much of the contracting process should be done by the exhibit manager and how much by legal counsel?

② How would you explain the phrase "a win-win situation" relative to hotel contract negotiations?

③ What is usually at the top of your "wish list" when negotiating contracts for exhibit facilities?

Chapter 7
Risk Management

"Here lie the bones of Ranger Jones. He failed to plan so he planned to fail."

– Sergeant, US Army Ranger School, Ft. Benning, GA

Section II: Business Issues

IN THIS CHAPTER YOU WILL LEARN:

- Options in managing risk
- Common types of insurance coverage
- Which parties carry which types of insurance
- How and when to buy insurance for your event.

INTRODUCTION

Show management is the art of planning for the unexpected. It relies on the show organizer's ability to build in the degree of flexibility necessary to accommodate all the inevitable, ever-changing external factors beyond anyone's control. Bottom line: show organizers are in the business of managing risks.

CONTRIBUTOR

Jack Buttine, President, John Buttine Exhibition Insurance

Risk Management

Closely related to on-site crisis and emergency planning management, risk management involves elements of both finance and resource management. This chapter details how careful preemptive planning may serve to reduce financial liability.

The term crisis is defined as an imminent critical situation with an inherent element that may jeopardize the safety and wellbeing of one or more event attendees. It is important to create a crisis management plan that is grounded in the four concepts: preparedness, mitigation, response and recovery. Development of a crisis management plan needs to start in the initial planning stages of the event. The show organizer needs to closely examine the areas that tend to be central to potential emergencies, and plan accordingly.

With regard to insurance coverage, there are three principles of risk that can assist show organizers in developing a crisis management plan:

- Risk Avoidance: Avoidance of programs and activities that are potentially dangerous, or could justify a potential insurance claim. This principle reduces risks in order to minimize their potential impact.
- Risk Retention: Assuming a portion of the liability and expense for perils for the event. This is accomplished by agreeing to a deductible payment and, in turn, receiving a reduced premium charge for the cost of the coverage provided by the insurance company.
- Risk Transfer: One of the most important clauses of a Certificate of Insurance is the indemnification clause. These clauses state that the management is **not** responsible, and indemnify management from any accidents caused by exhibitors or their employees.

In order to protect their employers' and clients' assets in an increasingly litigious society, show organizers must understand what types of insurance are available, which types should be purchased and when, and how to control their costs. For example, show organizers typically buy commercial general, exhibitor liability, property and crime insurance. A final program that is included in property insurance is a special form of business income insurance knows as event cancellation insurance.

Property Insurance

Property insurance provides coverage against loss of owned property that show organizers bring to the event, property of others that the show organizer is responsible for – such as coat checkroom and overnight storage – and property the show organizers rent – such as furniture and computers.

Property insurance should cover the replacement value of the insured items. Replacement value means "new for old with no deduction for depreciation."

An insurance policy protects on what is referred to as an "all risk" basis. "All risk" is not exactly accurate, as most "all risk" policies are subject to a number of standard exclusions. For example, typical exclusions may include perils that cannot be insured, such as war, nuclear disaster and civil uprising, or perils whose coverage requires an additional charge either on the existing policy, or on a different type altogether, such as earthquake, loss of power or water damage.

Property policies can also have sub-limits that apply to certain types of property. These sub-limits usually apply to items valued at $5,000 or less which can be easily pilfered and disposed of, such as jewelry and cash. These items can be insured on a special policy.

Deductibles are included in property policies. Common deductible amounts are generally $10,000 or less. A deductible is the part of the loss that is paid by the "insured." The deductible must be satisfied before the insurance company pays anything. Deductibles are applied on a per loss basis; that is, each loss has a separate deductible.

When discussing responsibility for the property of others, show organizers will want to use a vendor whenever possible. For example, when a vendor operates the coat checkroom, it is ultimately the vendor who is responsible for any loss. Because coat checking is their business, the vendor provides the primary insurance. However, if the show organizer who selected this vendor is also found partially responsible for any property loss, the show organizer's insurance will pay after the coat check vendor's insurance is exhausted.

Commercial General Liability Insurance

Commercial General Liability (CGL) is a policy bought by all show organizers. CGL protects the show organizer from liability claims due to bodily injury or property damage arising from a show or special event. The CGL policy's standard limit is $1,000,000 per occurrence and $2,000,000 annual aggregate. This policy will meet most of the insurance requirements of the event venue.

There are two types of CGL insurance policies: occurrences and claims-made. Because the claims-made policy only covers instances reported within a specific time frame, and because a claims-made policy must be in force when the claim is reported, show organizers are typically more interested in the occurrences policy. An occurrence-based policy will pay a covered claim regardless of when the claim is reported.

Additional Insured status is conferred on the CGL policy. An Additional Insured is a person or entity that is protected by another insurance policy. Additional Insured status gives the additionally insured's party rights to legal defense and settlement costs for acts that are done either by the Named Insured, or by the Named Insured and the Additional Insured. It generally does not cover the additionally insured party for acts that are of the sole negligence of the additional party.

There are times when a show will be outsourced to a management company who will buy the CGL policy, and extend coverage to the show owner or sponsor as an Additional Insured. A point to know about Additional Insured status is that the additionally insured entity receives coverage for its vicarious liability arising from the additionally insured's relationship to the Named Insured. However the additionally insured entity should always have its own insurance. Show organizers should use care when drafting contracts requiring Additional Insured status so that their insurance will pay in excess of the amount available to that which is available to them as Additional Insured.

Typical limits of the CGL policy are shown below.

Each Occurrence	$1,000,000
Annual Aggregate	$2,000,000
Personal & Advertising Injury	$1,000,000
Fire Damage Legal Liability	$300,000
Medical Payments to Others	$5,000

The CGL policy also contains endorsements. Two critical endorsements to remember are:

- Blanket Additional Insured Endorsement: This automatically confers Additional Insured status on all parties whom show organizers are required by contract to name as Additional Insureds. Examples of such are show sponsors and show venues, including their ownership interests.
- Per-event Aggregate Endorsement: This endorsement states that each event has a separate annual aggregate limit. CGL policies have an Annual Aggregate amount. The per-event aggregate endorsement amends the policy so that each event has a separate aggregate limit. This is helpful because without the per-event aggregate endorsement, a large claim in the beginning of the year could erode the show organizer's limits of insurance for later in the year. In a year where there are many claims at an event, show organizers could even find that their CGL limit is exhausted before the end of the policy period.

The CGL limits are usually supplemented by umbrella liability policies. An umbrella policy is a special form of liability insurance that is designed to protect the insured for unknown contingencies over and above the normal coverages. Umbrella limits range from as low as $1,000,000 to as high as $50,000,000 and more.

The umbrella liability policy will provide additional limits, not only to the CGL, but also to the auto liability and employers liability policies. (The employers liability policy is part of the workers compensation policy.) The minimum umbrella liability coverage a show organizer should have is $5,000,000. This is also the minimum limit each vendor should carry.

How much liability insurance is needed? There is no formula to help make this determination. However, premiums tend to be based on assessed risk, such as how many booths there are, the estimated attendance, the nature of the show, products being displayed, the asset size and the limits of liability required by a venue or lease agreement.

Exhibitors Liability Insurance

Exhibitors liability insurance protects the show manager's insurance costs from increasing due to claims filed by exhibitors. Exhibitor's liability is also helpful to the exhibitors who do not buy insurance, or whose insurance does not pay claims brought in US courts. Exhibitors in certain types of events, such as art and antique fairs and small manufacturing shows, frequently do not have insurance. Foreign exhibitors who have insurance in their countries will find that their coverage applies worldwide, but only if the claim is brought in their home jurisdiction.

Show managers have two options in obtaining this coverage. They can contract with an insurance company for a blanket policy to cover all exhibitors, or they can place applications in the event's set-up manual for exhibitors to complete and send directly to the insurance broker. In the latter case, the broker can give the show manager a report prior to the event stating all exhibitors who purchased insurance.

Crime Insurance

Crime or fidelity insurance is necessary at shows where cash is collected. Crime insurance will cover door receipts or other cash. The crime coverage limit should be based on how much cash there will be on hand. Most show managers will know the estimated daily collection amount, and choose to select that as their crime insurance limit. This policy has a deductible that is the same size as the property insurance deductible. Crime deductibles apply on a per-loss basis.

Transporting cash to the bank can present problems depending on how much cash is collected. A common technique is to hire an armored guard company to pick up cash on a daily basis. As with all vendors, there should be a Certificate of Insurance from the armored guard company.

The security company you select for the show often carries crime insurance for your benefit. This policy is called a Third Party Fidelity Bond. This policy protects your exhibitors from theft of their goods by the security company's employees.

Event Cancellation Insurance

In addition to general liability insurance, show managers often purchase event cancellation insurance. Many show organizers consider this type of insurance a form of customer service. In the event a product cannot be delivered to buyers or attendees on the show floor, customers will expect a refund of their fees, which will be covered by event cancellation insurance.

Event cancellation insurance is a type of business interruption policy that is unique to the exhibition and special event industries. It protects the show manager's financial investment in the event. Often referred to as *sleep insurance,* it allows show managers to keep their anticipated profits, pay expenses incurred up to the time of the loss, and return exhibit, attendance and sponsorship fees, as well as the costs of education seminars.

Sponsorship fees and education seminar costs are an increasingly large part of an event's income. Both can be insured by a cancellation policy. Should a loss occur, the question at hand will be how much of the sponsorship benefit was received up to the time of the loss, or how much of the education session was completed. The answer will determine the claim amount.

Cancellation insurance covers a number of perils including cancellation, postponement, abandonment, interruption, failure to move out on time and reduction in attendance. The policy is a form of "all risk" insurance in the coverage, and is defined by its exclusions. Insurance vendors often say that everything is covered except what is excluded. Standard exclusions exist either because it is impossible to insure against the peril, or the peril is better insured by a different type of policy. Common exclusions include loss due to:

- Circumstances that existed prior to the purchase of the policy, or management's failure to make adequate preparations
- Teleconferencing or non-appearance of a key speaker, unless specially added to the policy
- Adverse weather in outdoor events or events held in temporary structures, unless added to the policy
- Types of income that were not declared to the insurance company at the time of purchase, or that were added later by endorsement
- Construction, renovation or expansion of the venue
- Reduction in attendance that is not due to any event-related issue, such as a poor business environment or lack of buyer interest

- Criminal activity on part of show management
- Pollution and nuclear, chemical or biological disasters
- Terrorism. (Most policies provide a limited form of terrorism coverage or give options to "buy back" this exclusion).

Periodically, insurance companies will add exclusions to insurance policies based on changes in laws or conditions that can affect the coverage that they offer. For example, SARS and avian flu are relatively new perils, and not much is known about them. What insurers cannot understand or quantify they will either charge extra for or exclude from coverage.

Several years ago, terrorism in the US was excluded from all event cancellation policies. Over time, insurance companies are becoming aware of the threat of terrorism, and are now offering a variety of ways to obtain terrorism insurance.

Certificates of Insurance

As mentioned, liability insurance protects show managers from claims brought against them for injuries caused to others. There are actually very few things a show manager could do that are likely to cause a claim. However, vendors and other partners can cause many types of claims at a show or event for which the show manager can be sued. That is why evidence of CGL and other insurance must be required from all vendors. Certificates of Insurance should be kept for at least five years. Show managers should have a system to gather and maintain a file containing all vendor certificates. In the event of a claim, having these readily available will be very valuable to show management and the event's insurer.

SEE FIGURE 1

When to Buy Event Cancellation Insurance

Although insurance is often bought on an annual basis, cancellation insurance policies should be bought as soon as a show organizer has a financial interest in an event. Simply put, once the show organizer signs a lease or begins to sell space for an event, cancellation insurance should be purchased to protect the financial interest.

Consider a manager who heads up one event per year. As soon as the lease is signed, coverage should be bought; as soon as the event concludes and next year's event is planned, coverage should be renewed. The cost is the same regardless of when coverage is bought. The earlier insurance is purchased, the longer the show manager will be covered. When a show organizer is in charge of many events, the same principles apply. The idea is to keep events covered for 12 months at a time, all the time. In order to do so, it may be necessary to obtain coverage either quarterly, or at whatever interval is necessary in order to maintain insurance for all the events.

FIGURE 1

ACORD™ CERTIFICATE OF LIABILITY INSURANCE

OP ID BL 9IAEM01

DATE (MM/DD/YYYY) 03/21/06

PRODUCER	THIS CERTIFICATE IS ISSUED AS A MATTER OF INFORMATION ONLY AND CONFERS NO RIGHTS UPON THE CERTIFICATE HOLDER. THIS CERTIFICATE DOES NOT AMEND, EXTEND OR ALTER THE COVERAGE AFFORDED BY THE POLICIES BELOW.	
John Buttine, Inc 125 Park Avenue, 3rd Floor New York NY 10017-5613 Phone: 212-697-1010 Fax: 212-986-2822	INSURERS AFFORDING COVERAGE	NAIC #
INSURED	INSURER A: ABC Company	
	INSURER B:	
VENDOR NAME 123 Main Street Anytown NY 10000	INSURER C:	
	INSURER D:	
	INSURER E:	

COVERAGES

THE POLICIES OF INSURANCE LISTED BELOW HAVE BEEN ISSUED TO THE INSURED NAMED ABOVE FOR THE POLICY PERIOD INDICATED. NOTWITHSTANDING ANY REQUIREMENT, TERM OR CONDITION OF ANY CONTRACT OR OTHER DOCUMENT WITH RESPECT TO WHICH THIS CERTIFICATE MAY BE ISSUED OR MAY PERTAIN, THE INSURANCE AFFORDED BY THE POLICIES DESCRIBED HEREIN IS SUBJECT TO ALL THE TERMS, EXCLUSIONS AND CONDITIONS OF SUCH POLICIES. AGGREGATE LIMITS SHOWN MAY HAVE BEEN REDUCED BY PAID CLAIMS.

INSR LTR	ADD'L INSRD	TYPE OF INSURANCE	POLICY NUMBER	POLICY EFFECTIVE DATE (MM/DD/YY)	POLICY EXPIRATION DATE (MM/DD/YY)	LIMITS	
A	X X	GENERAL LIABILITY X COMMERCIAL GENERAL LIABILITY CLAIMS MADE X OCCUR	123456789	01/01/06	01/01/07	EACH OCCURRENCE	$ 1,000,000
						DAMAGE TO RENTED PREMISES (Ea occurrence)	$ 50,000
						MED EXP (Any one person)	$ 5,000
						PERSONAL & ADV INJURY	$ 1,000,000
		GEN'L AGGREGATE LIMIT APPLIES PER: X POLICY PRO-JECT LOC				GENERAL AGGREGATE	$ 2,000,000
						PRODUCTS - COMP/OP AGG	$ 1,000,000
A		AUTOMOBILE LIABILITY ANY AUTO X ALL OWNED AUTOS SCHEDULED AUTOS X HIRED AUTOS X NON-OWNED AUTOS	456789123	01/01/06	01/01/07	COMBINED SINGLE LIMIT (Ea accident)	$ 1,000,000
						BODILY INJURY (Per person)	$
						BODILY INJURY (Per accident)	$
						PROPERTY DAMAGE (Per accident)	$
A		GARAGE LIABILITY ANY AUTO				AUTO ONLY - EA ACCIDENT	$
						OTHER THAN AUTO ONLY: EA ACC AGG	$ $
A		EXCESS/UMBRELLA LIABILITY X OCCUR CLAIMS MADE DEDUCTIBLE RETENTION $	789123456	01/01/06	01/01/07	EACH OCCURRENCE	$ 4,000,000
						AGGREGATE	$ 4,000,000
							$
							$
A		WORKERS COMPENSATION AND EMPLOYERS' LIABILITY ANY PROPRIETOR/PARTNER/EXECUTIVE OFFICER/MEMBER EXCLUDED? If yes, describe under SPECIAL PROVISIONS below	987654321	01/01/06	01/01/07	X WC STATU-TORY LIMITS OTH-ER	
						E.L. EACH ACCIDENT	$ 500,000
						E.L. DISEASE - EA EMPLOYEE	$ 500,000
						E.L. DISEASE - POLICY LIMIT	$ 500,000
A		OTHER Liquor Liability	152434356	01/01/06	01/01/07	Limit	1,000,000

DESCRIPTION OF OPERATIONS / LOCATIONS / VEHICLES / EXCLUSIONS ADDED BY ENDORSEMENT / SPECIAL PROVISIONS

(Fill in name of Event Organizer), its affiliated companies, and their officers and employees are listed as Additional Insureds as respects operations performed by the named insured.

CERTIFICATE HOLDER	CANCELLATION
IAEM006 NAME OF EVENT ORGANIZER 321 Park Lane Anytown NY 10000	SHOULD ANY OF THE ABOVE DESCRIBED POLICIES BE CANCELLED BEFORE THE EXPIRATION DATE THEREOF, THE ISSUING INSURER WILL ENDEAVOR TO MAIL __30__ DAYS WRITTEN NOTICE TO THE CERTIFICATE HOLDER NAMED TO THE LEFT, BUT FAILURE TO DO SO SHALL IMPOSE NO OBLIGATION OR LIABILITY OF ANY KIND UPON THE INSURER, ITS AGENTS OR REPRESENTATIVES. AUTHORIZED REPRESENTATIVE

ACORD 25 (2001/08) © ACORD CORPORATION 1988

Cost Factors

Cost of cancellation policies are based on several factors. There is always a basic cancellation insurance rate to which insurance companies may add additional charges based on where and when the event occurs. For example, events that are in areas prone to earthquakes receive an additional cost due to the threat earthquake damage. The same applies to events held in areas that are affected by hurricanes or winter weather. Additional charges apply.

Another cost factor is an event's loss history. Managers of events that have sustained losses will often pay more because their events are seen as prone to loss, due to either their location or the time of the year in which they occur.

Much of the cost of this insurance, like all insurance, is based on either the insurance industry's claim experience, or investment returns of the insurance company. Adverse weather has a dramatic impact on all property insurance, including cancellation insurance.

Insurance companies frequently buy insurance called reinsurance. The reinsurance increases as losses occur. Over an eighteen month period between 2004 and 2005, seven of the largest storms ever to strike North America occurred. The losses to insurers and reinsurers were in excess of $40 billion. This will continue to impact cancellation insurance rates for a long time.

How to Buy Cancellation Insurance

Event cancellation insurance is expensive because it is a specialty type of coverage. Group purchase of any form of insurance is always an advantage for the buyer. There are several buying programs from established insurance brokers and agents, which are often sponsored by either IAEM or ASAE.

The show manager's relationship with a cancellation insurance broker, and the broker's experience in helping to settle claims, are both important. If the broker does not understand the coverage or the exhibition industry, problems are more likely to result when a claim occurs. To learn who the brokers are, call trade associations, consult colleagues, and look for ads on the Internet or in the trade press.

Insurance Claim Reporting

The basic rule is to report claims as promptly as possible. Late notice impedes the insurance company's ability to react, and may cause a claim to be denied. To aid in claim reporting, always bring the following to the show site:

- Blank liability claim reporting forms. Be sure the policy number and name of the insurance company are on each form
- Camera for taking photos of any damaged property
- Name and 24/7 telephone number of the insurance broker, and the insurance company's "800" claim-reporting hotline telephone numbers.

As mentioned, property losses occur when property is stolen, lost or damaged. When the matter is reported to the insurer or broker, be ready to provide:

- Date and time of the loss
- Cause of loss
- Location of loss
- Full description of the property involved
- Estimate of the value of the loss
- Name of person most knowledgeable of the loss

After the loss, safeguard the property from further damage if possible. Prepare an inventory of the damaged items. Before discarding anything, always try to get the insurance company's approval, or take photos of the goods prior to discarding them. Save copies of local newspapers if they have information on your claim. This is especially valuable for weather-related event cancellation claims

Liability claims at an exhibition or special event can present a unique claim-handling situation for the insurer. If a large number of exhibitors or attendees are involved, make sure the insurance company reacts quickly, and sends representatives to gather information and statements. Remember, when the show is over, everyone departs, and information will be much harder to obtain.

Always:
- Note the name of a responding police department or ambulance
- Take statements, names and telephone numbers from any injured parties or witnesses.
- Include just the facts in statements: who, what, when and where. No opinions or extra information is necessary.
- Never admit liability in any situation. An opinion or statement is seldom necessary at the time of an incident.

Event cancellation claims require special handling by all show personnel. At the first hint of a pending problem involving the venue, or anything else affecting the event – such as a strike or adverse weather event – report it to the insurer or broker.

Time is always of the essence. Experience has shown that exhibitors and attendees have the same concerns as show managers, and they want to know the status of the event. If possible, know the cell phone numbers and locations of as many of the event's exhibitors and attendees as possible, and know how to contact all the show staff. For example, when a snowstorm is forecast during an event, show managers have used their contact information to inform exhibitors and attendees of changes in show hours or other pertinent details.

Section II: Business Issues

SUMMARY

The show organizer can approach risk management in several ways: by working to avoid or reduce exposure to risk, by recognizing risks and planning for them, or by transferring the responsibility for a risk to another party. Show organizers should do a complete risk assessment for an exhibition to determine the types and amounts of insurance that should be carried in order to limit potential losses. All approaches benefit from a partnership with a knowledgeable insurance broker.

QUESTIONS FOR DISCUSSION

① In what ways can an exhibitor seek reimbursement for expenses incurred when a show cancels?
② Do you think all exhibitors in all types of shows – no exceptions – should be required to purchase liability insurance?
③ What kinds of insurance do you carry in your personal life?

Chapter 1
Site Selection

"It is our choices that show what we really are, far more than our abilities."
– J.K. Rowling Harry Potter and the Chamber of Secrets, 1999

Section III: Venues

IN THIS CHAPTER YOU WILL LEARN

- What four factors go into assessing a site for a future event
- What role economic impact can play in site selection
- What an exhibition manager looks for in a site inspection
- What a meeting manager looks for in a site inspection
- What an official services contractor looks for in a site inspection

INTRODUCTION

Selecting the proper site for an exhibition is crucial to its overall success. Choosing an appropriate exhibition site is not a matter of just looking for a "large, empty box." Choosing the perfect building in the wrong location can do irreparable damage, and vice versa. Making the right decision in site selection requires gathering and analyzing a large amount of input from all stakeholders.

CONTRIBUTORS

Stuart Aizenberg, CEM, Director of Tradeshows, National Automatic Merchandising Association; Paul Cunniffe, Director of National Accounts, GES Exposition Services; Cindy Ferguson, CEM, Director of Marketing, Association of Professional Rental Organizations; John Plescia, CMP, CEM, Event Operations Manager, Orange County Convention Center

There are a series of factors that must be taken into consideration when assessing the feasibility of using a facility or a city as the site for an event. These factors include:

- Attendance marketing (Can this site be marketed?)
- Basic facility requirements (Does it meet the event requirements?)
- Value of the event to the community (Is this event the right match?)
- The site visit (Does this location meet all criteria?)

A comprehensive review of each of these factors will enable the organizer to make an informed decision as to the best site for the next exhibition.

Attendance Marketing Factors

Because attendance is one of the keys to an event's success, exhibition managers must look at several attendance marketing factors that could impact site selection choices this year, next year, or five years or more down the road.

Event Objective: Will the rationale for the event remain static? Are planning and future growth initiatives for the exhibition going to require revision? Will there be an overall shift in focus that may have a direct bearing on the site choice?

Geographic Location: Geographic location is probably the single most significant determinant of site selection. In determining the criteria used for site selection for any particular exhibition, management, owners, and sponsors need to carefully define their target markets. What is attractive and accessible depends upon the type of show. In the case of a consumer exhibition, accessible may mean close and convenient. Consumer exhibitions tend to draw from more localized markets; since attendees are "day-trippers," the efficiency of the area's highway systems is very important.

Tradeshows, which are primarily business-to-business in nature, may use access to public transportation, especially airports, as one of their primary determinants of location choice. A site may also be attractive because of the variety of entertainment and tourism options, or because it is in the middle of a rich business environment. On average, these shows last more than one day. Therefore, the adequacy of local housing is also quite important when making the final decision. Obviously, these sites are usually close to large population centers.

Policies, politics and practicalities also play a role in geographic selection. Some groups may be restricted technically or practically from meeting in certain areas. For example, state associations usually must meet within their own state. An association representing the liquor industry would most likely not meet in a city with restrictions and attitudes on alcoholic beverages. A sailing exhibition in a city with no bodies of water might seem out of place, even though the city has good accessibility, housing and exhibition space.

Exhibitions are sometimes rotated among a limited number of cities that meet all the show's criteria and have high tourism appeal. For example, an association might meet in Atlanta one year, Chicago the next year, San Francisco the following year, and then Atlanta again the year after that. This provides for easy planning by the exhibitors, since these choices are published well in advance of the convention. It also does two other things. First, the added appeal of major tourism cities helps maximize attendance. Business people want to go to such places, as well as attend the exhibition. Some attendees may bring guests along for leisure activities. This helps the exhibition's attendance, and usually its reputation since it becomes an enjoyable learning experience Second, the geographic rotation puts the show within easy and affordable reach of the local markets every few years. Since air travel and long hotel stays can be an expensive proposition for smaller companies and individuals, attending every year may not be feasible for some attendees. But with the exhibition rotated to major population and business centers, regional attendance becomes attractive for this market segment.

Demographics: Are the demographics of the region relatively stable? Has there been a population decline or increase? Has there been a significant shift of categories within the demographic base? What are the projected social demographic trends for the region? Is the audience going to undergo a fundamental change in age, gender or values?

Needs Analysis: Will the exhibition's present audience want or need to attend the exhibition next year or five years from now? Is it possible to accurately predict the profile of a typical attendee and accurately assess attendees' future needs and wants?

Competition: How many other major events are scheduled in the market channel? What kind of public events are scheduled? Is a major sports franchise housed in the immediate vicinity or in the facility you are considering? What municipal government and convention and visitors bureau (CVB) policies govern the facility regarding date protection and like events sharing the venue?

Transportation Access: What is the interstate highway system like into the area? Is it good enough that distance will not be a factor in drawing out-of-area attendees? What is the public transportation system like? Does it provide service to the facility's front door, or one or two blocks away? Does it provide convenient access to the local airport and train terminals? Are the access roads to the facility paved and in good repair? Is the facility easy to find?

What is the parking situation in the immediate area and within a 10-block radius of the facility? In the case of consumer shows, a much higher percentage of exhibitors and sometimes a sizable majority of attendees will arrive via automobile. In either case, those attendees and exhibitors who drive in or rent cars locally will need some amount of parking space.

Past event statistics and knowledge of the traffic patterns in a particular geographical area can help determine how many parking spaces will be needed. Many exhibition centers include parking areas. In addition to whatever interior parking is available, the areas surrounding most convention centers usually have surface lots or multistory parking garages that can be utilized. Proximity to the facility, auto and pedestrian security, and cost are all factors to consider in transportation planning.

Are there changes planned for the transportation system? Will construction affect facility access next year or in five years time?
- After assessing local transportation, exhibition managers need to look at regional and national transportation links.
- Does the local airport serve as a hub for a major airline?
- Does the airport service regional carriers?
- Does the airport have daily flights from key markets?
- What is the cost of air travel relative to other destinations?
- What are the transportation links from the airport to the exhibition site? This is a prime consideration, especially if the airport services a sprawling metropolitan area and is more than 20 miles from the downtown corridor or the exhibition site. Is the city serviced by a rapid transit system linking smaller communities by commuter trains?

Transportation costs for out-of-town delegates and exhibitors can be costly, and may affect their decision to attend. These factors should be given careful consideration during the final site selection process.

Ancillary Services: If a convention center is being used, do hotels in the area fall into a variety of price ranges? Are restaurants, shopping and points of interest within a 10-block radius? These are drawing cards for out-of-area attendees and exhibitors.

Basic Facility Requirements

Convention centers are used most commonly for exhibitions because they offer most of the services necessary for the successful staging of an exhibition under one roof. There are other types of exhibition space as well, including multi-purpose facilities and hotel exhibit halls and ballrooms. Convention centers offer exhibition managers six basic capacities:
- They provide the physical essentials for hosting an exhibition, such as flat, open space that is generally serviced by utility connections and food preparation areas.
- They provide meeting space and break-out rooms.
- They can usually accommodate auditorium or theater set-ups for large audiences.

- They often have arena space with auditorium or forum-style fixed seating for large public events.
- Most feature on-site catering and the space to feed large groups.
- Many have the latest in communication technology systems.

Value of Event

Another factor that may affect site selections is the actual or perceived value of an event to the community. Even though a hall may have everything needed to ensure a successful event, it may prove out of reach due to policies in place that preclude leasing space to "low impact" events, such as consumer shows or events that do not use a large number of hotel rooms. Every exhibition manager should have documented proof as to the total economic impact the event has upon the community. This information is a vital negotiating tool that can be used to procure good dates and well-equipped halls for well-planned trade or consumer shows next year, or five years hence. Spending by attendees at exhibitions and events has a considerable impact on local economies. Convention and event attendees stimulate spending in a wide spectrum of travel industry sectors, as well as other areas such as retail, entertainment, recreation, and transportation. These expenditures advance an area's growth and prosperity by supporting a significant number of local jobs, and providing a source of local tax revenues.

The Destination Marketing Association International (formerly International Association of Convention & Visitors Bureaus) assists its members by providing a database called the Meeting Information Network (MINT). This valuable tool can be used not only for prospecting future business, but also for finding out the value of an event. Some of the metrics used by destinations to value an event, and therefore making it important for the organizer to document, include:

- Number of attendees
- Demographics of attendees
- Hotel room nights
- Attrition rates
- Number of food and beverage events
- Off-site events
- Exhibition space fees
- Meeting room expenses
- Equipment rentals
- Technology service fees
- Food and beverage expenses of attendees
- Services hired
- Promotional expenditures within event city
- Local transportation within city

The Site Visit

The final factor that will affect the site selection is the site visit. If possible, it is best to make at least two site visits prior to a decision. The first is an official visit with facility representatives to explain details and point out special features. The second visit should be done unaccompanied by facility staff, either during a "down day" or during another event. While a show is in progress it can be interesting to observe areas such as the trash disposal area, back loading docks and service corridors, and notice whether they are clean and well-maintained. A show manager can also talk to other show managers who have hosted an event in the hall and ask whether there are specific areas of concern that need to be addressed in this facility.

Site selection is a time-consuming process that requires attention to detail, planning and teamwork. It takes the coordinated efforts of the show manager, the official services contractor and a meeting manager to find a facility that adequately meets the requirements for all aspects of an exhibition.

Site Visits from Different Perspectives

Because an event's success is also contingent upon having all of the players on the exhibition manager's team working together, it is a good exercise to look at site selection from three different points of view: the exhibition manager's, the official services contractor's, and the meeting manager's (if meetings will be a part of the program). Each person has a different perception of the environment in which he or she will need to operate.

It is wise for the official services contractor to be present at the initial site inspection. If a contractor has not been selected prior to the initial site inspection, revisit the site with the contractor, the exhibition manager and the meeting manager.

Site Selection from the Exhibition Manager's Perspective

After determining which type of facility is suited to a particular event, the show organizer must have a clear understanding of the physical attributes of the building. Here are some key areas to tour in a site inspection, and information to gather:

1. Exhibit Hall

a. **Gross square footage**: Is the space divisible? Are there adjacent halls for future exhibit expansion should the exhibition grow more rapidly than predicted?

b. **Ceiling height**: Is it uniform throughout? What is the minimum height? Do fixtures, catwalks, etc. impede full floor-to-ceiling capacity? While modern centers and hotels have been designed to host exhibits and their accompanying functions, many older halls and ballrooms may present some physical challenges. Most convention centers have over 20 feet of clearance below the duct and support structures. Some have rooms with as much as 50 feet of clearance. Modern hotel exhibit space often has from 20-35 feet of clearance. However, older facilities may have lowered ceilings, duct work, chandeliers, or light fixtures that could interfere with taller exhibits.

c. **Floor load capacity**: Is it uniform throughout the building? If the exhibit hall is located on a second floor, has the floor-load capacity been certified by a structural engineer? Most modern floor-load factors are 300 pounds per square foot or higher. Upper floors are usually built to handle a minimum dead weight of no greater than 50 pound per square foot. Floor composition is usually reinforced concrete, but may be covered with other materials such as carpet – especially on the upper floors. If the event being planned has heavy machinery or other high dead-weight components, a floor-load analysis should be performed by the show manager and facility manager before determining the layout. While carpet may provide attendee comfort and help reduce ambient noise, it also limits color scheme choices, and may restrict the kind of traffic that can pass over it.

d. **Obstructions**: Are there columns or utility ports that prevent clear access to all floor areas? Are they shown on the facility floorplan?

e. **Doors**: pedestrian and freight. What is the size of the actual opening? Are there restrictions as to use? Are all man doors equipped with panic hardware?

f. **Loading docks**: Are there drive-in bays? Are load-leveling docks available? How many are there? Are all docks common use, or are some reserved for facility operations use, with the balance assigned for events according to the number of halls booked? What is the off-street access to the loading area? Will traffic be a factor during set-up or tear-down? Is there a parking lot or separate area for trailer storage? Are there accommodations for personally owned vehicles (POVs) to unload and load, such as vans and box trucks belonging to smaller exhibitors? Will Exhibitor Appointed Contractors (EACs) have a location to stage their equipment without interfering with the official services contractor's operation?

g. **Storage/Waste Removal**: Are there on-site facilities for crate storage and contractor equipment? Are there restrictions as to the type of materials stored? Are there special regulations regarding the handling of stored materials, such as boxes broken down, or shrink-wrapped on a pallet? What is the capacity for waste removal? For example, how many open-top dumpsters and trash compactors are available, and what is the capacity of each? Is there a recycling program in place? If so, how is it implemented? What materials are being recycled – paper, cardboard, wood, carpet, padding, or plastic?

h. **Ventilation System**: Is the hall air-conditioned? Is the entire building on a single control system, or does each hall have its own climate control? Are there special exhaust system tie-ins or specialty areas, such as for cooking demonstrations?

i. **Utilities**: What is the type and intensity of the lighting? Does the hall have water and gas service lines and hookups? Is there access to compressed air or flexible water service and drains? Where are they located? What is the maximum electrical power available to the hall? Can the site accommodate special electrical and lighting hookups for entertainment stages? Most centers have reading-level lighting in the 70-110 foot candles range, but will special fixtures, coloration, or controls be necessary?

j. **Communications**: Is telephone and Internet service available to exhibitors in the hall? Is there a public address system? Is this system facility-wide, or can it be isolated in one hall? Is the facility wired for sound? For example, will it handle sound and audio systems from outside suppliers? Does the facility have the capacity to accommodate new information technology systems such as facility-wide computer links and networks? Are wireless data services available? What is the overall Internet capacity of the facility's infrastructure?

k. **Show Services Available**: Does the facility provide specialty show services such as banner hanging, forklifts, cherry pickers, furniture rental, staging, risers, or turnstiles?

l. **Advertising**: What are the opportunities for event signage and advertising sponsorships such as banners, window clings, and floor graphics? Does the facility charge an advertising fee? Are rigging (suspension) services available or exclusive? Does the venue rent cherry pickers or other lift equipment?

Private facilities may have exclusive contracts with the companies that supply services not available from facility personnel. Larger facilities typically do not use exclusive contractors. The local convention and visitors bureau can usually provide a list of members, detailing what services are available. Particular needs will determine which suppliers will be used and to what extent. If not already handled by the facility as part of the rental, outside suppliers will be needed for utility hookups, carpentry, plumbing, decorating, security, maintenance, food and beverage, materials handling, housekeeping, and any other services that might be required. By further comparing the show's needs to the equipment and services available from these suppliers, any shortfalls can be detected early and appropriate action taken.

If a show is a national group that either meets in several cities each year, or annually rotates among major cities, it may be wise to choose one national contractor rather than a local one in each location. Larger contractors usually have offices in most major convention cities. Because of their shared databases and familiarity with a particular show, they can service an account from any of their offices. Obviously, repetition and familiarity are two of the cornerstones of service efficiency.

m. **Regulations and Restrictions**: What are the facility's policies regarding exclusives in the areas of ticket sellers, ticket takers, catering, telecommunications, utilities, security, and service contractors? How do national, state and municipal fire and building codes affect activities held in the facility? What are the municipal and state insurance, tax and licensing regulations with respect to the facility?

n. **Does the facility meet the minimum requirements for people with disabilities?**: Generally in the United States, facilities are legally responsible for seeing to it that building features are compliant with the Americans with Disabilities Act (ADA), while shows are responsible for their event elements. Liability can be passed or shared with exhibitors for access issues to their individual booths. Regardless of where the event is held, an extensive site inspection of a facility will go a long way toward providing equal access and opportunity for physically-disabled attendees.

SITE INSPECTION CHECKLIST

Whether you visit one destination or several, using a site inspection checklist helps ensure that you do not overlook important features and services during your visit. At a minimum, your checklist should include the following:

THE DESTINATION

Accessibility
✓ Ease and cost
✓ Proximity to airport
✓ Accessible to people with disabilities
✓ Adequate taxi/limousine service (cost)
✓ Sufficient parking space (cost)
✓ Availability and cost of shuttle service
✓ Adequate airport assistance
✓ Adequate number of flights into destination
✓ Seasonality of destination (peak season versus off-season)

Environment
✓ Availability of local attractions
✓ Shopping

✓ Recreation

✓ Restaurants

✓ Business services

✓ Weather conditions

✓ Appearance

✓ Safety of destination

✓ Impact of local ordinances on your organization (e.g., smoking laws, gaming laws, liquor service)

✓ Economic health of community

✓ Reputation of area/facility for hosting meetings

✓ Support and services available from local convention bureau

✓ Availability of experienced suppliers, such as A/V firms, exhibit service contractors, temporary help, and security

HOTEL ACCOMMODATIONS

Accessibility

✓ Registration desk easy to find; sufficient space and personnel in relation to guest rooms; ability to handle peak check-in/check-out times for major groups; efficient front desk personnel

✓ Modern elevators and escalators in sufficient number to serve guests when the facility is full

✓ Accessible, fully staffed message and information desk; rapid response to telephone calls; quick delivery of messages

✓ Availability of guest services; e.g., business center, drug stores, banks, emergency services, gift shop, concierge, safety deposit boxes, and so on

✓ Availability of beverage and ice machines on each floor

✓ Service elevator accessibility

✓ Rooms equipped for people with disabilities

✓ Availability of executive floor offering special guest services

Environment

✓ Efficient, friendly doormen and bellmen

✓ Attractive, clean lobby

✓ Comfortable clean rooms: furniture in good condition, modern bathroom fixtures, adequate lighting, adequate closet space and hangers, iron/ironing board, coffee maker, refrigerator and/or mini bar, work desk with Internet and telephone

✓ Smoke detectors in all public areas, audio and visual fire alarms, sprinkling system in all public areas and guest rooms, and fire exit information clearly posted

✓ Adequate lighting and cleanliness of hallways

✓ Size of standard room versus deluxe room

✓ Number and types of suites and availability of suite floor plans

✓ Reservations procedures and policies

✓ Room category classifications (floor number, nonsmoking, ocean view, and so on) and number available in each category

✓ Number of rooms available for early arrivals and late departures (luggage storage for early arrivals)

✓ Current convention rate and rack rate for individual guests (not part of the group)

✓ Date hotel will provide firm rates (confirm 1 year out or more if possible)

✓ Best rate guarantee policy including Internet reservation providers

✓ Guarantee and deposit requirements

✓ Check-in and check-out hours

✓ Cut-off date for the room block

✓ Check-cashing policies and types of credit cards accepted

✓ Refund policy for cancellations

✓ Number of nonsmoking floors (standard and concierge)

✓ Dates of any planned renovations

✓ Any change in hotel ownership being discussed

✓ Availability of a health club, hours, and cost

✓ Telephone access charges (long distance, local, and calling card)

✓ High-speed wireless Internet accessibility in guest rooms (Is there a fee?)

✓ Card or key system for guest rooms

✓ Adequate parking space (free or for a fee?)

✓ Hotel emergency plan (meeting manager should review)

✓ Hotel emergency exits clearly marked

✓ Comparison of king-bed versus double-bed room categories

✓ Additional room fees, if applicable (resort fees, room occupancy taxes, and so on)

✓ Charges for early departures

✓ Room service and hours of operation

✓ Ability of hotel to accept Internet reservations either through hotel's web site and/or CVBs

✓ Competing meeting currently booked into the facility

✓ Willingness to work with third-party planner, destination management company, and so on

✓ Hotel's union status (is all or part of the hotel unionized?)

✓ Hotel handling fee for incoming organization's shipments (excludes exhibit drayage)

MEETING SPACE

Accessibility

✓ Accessibility for people with disabilities

✓ Proximity of space for refreshment breaks

✓ Restrooms in proximity to meeting space

Environment

✓ General suitability of meeting rooms for designated uses (current floor plans)

✓ Number of meeting rooms adequate for requirements

✓ Size of rooms (prepare scale diagrams; incorporate all equipment, staging, and decorations; and calculate the desired square footage per person for required setup)

✓ Ability to accommodate required setup: theater, classroom, conference, or banquet style

✓ Capacity of each room compared to expected attendance at session

✓ High ceilings (10 feet is considered minimum) and no columns or obstructions for A/V presentations

✓ Adequacy of lighting: adjustable controls, brightness

✓ High-speed wireless Internet accessibility (is there a fee?)

✓ Meeting rooms available for committee and business meetings or ancillary group functions

✓ Pre-meeting and post-meeting space available for affiliated ancillary groups

✓ In-house sound and A/V company available

✓ Electronic signage outside each meeting room (or will manual signs be required?)

FOOD AND BEVERAGE SERVICE

Public Outlets

✓ Availability of food and beverage outlets, types, and hours of operation

✓ Appearance and cleanliness

✓ Cleanliness of food preparation areas

✓ Adequate staffing at peak times

✓ Attitude of personnel

✓ Prompt and efficient service

✓ Variety of menus

✓ Cost range

✓ Reservations policy

✓ Feasibility of setting up additional food outlets for continental breakfast and quick luncheon service, if necessary

✓ Feasibility of using public food outlets for group functions during non-peak hours

Group Functions

✓ Quality and service

✓ Diversity of menus

✓ Costs: tax and gratuities; projected price increases by the time of the meeting; extra labor charges for small-group functions (set menu pricing 1 year out)

✓ Liquor laws (restricted times)

✓ Cash bar policies: bartender cost and minimum hours, cashier charges, drink prices

✓ Current banquet menus

✓ Guarantee policies: when a guarantee is required, number set and prepared for beyond guarantee

✓ Special services: tailored menus, theme parties, unique refreshment breaks, food substitutions available, table decorations, dance floor

✓ Size and inventory of banquet rounds (60-inch rounds, 72-inch rounds, and standard seating capacity 8 or 10 people)

✓ Room service: diversity of menu, prompt and efficient telephone manner, prompt delivery, quality, hours of operation

EXHIBIT SPACE

✓ Number of loading docks and proximity to exhibit area

✓ Truck marshalling area

✓ Availability and location of freight receiving area

✓ Location of utilities (type, location, and number)

✓ Maximum floor load
✓ Security of area (officers required?)
✓ Location of fire exits
✓ Proximity to food service areas, restrooms, and telephones
✓ Availability of sufficient time for move-in and move-out
✓ Reputation of facility regarding union relations
✓ Decorations to enhance facility appearance
✓ Availability of supplemental lighting
✓ High-speed wireless Internet accessibility
✓ Proximity of exhibit hall to other portions of the meeting
✓ First aid station
✓ Availability of office space for exposition manager, service contractors, and suppliers
✓ Crate storage areas and policies
✓ Fire marshal regulations
✓ Air conditioning, heating, and lighting restrictions during set-up and take-down
✓ Floor plans of convention center including ceiling heights
✓ Exclusive services, i.e., security, food and beverage, hall cleaning
✓ Aisle signage, banners, hanging weight restrictions, and so on

OFFICES AND OTHER SERVICES

✓ Is designated group registration area out of general public/high traffic area?
✓ Sufficient space for furniture and equipment necessary to perform the business at hand
✓ Good lighting
✓ Easy for attendees to locate
✓ Adequate electrical outlets
✓ Availability of house telephones or telephone jacks
✓ Ability to secure space after hours
✓ Flexibility regarding tentative agenda versus meeting space locked in by a signed contract
✓ Accessibility for people with disabilities

EQUIPMENT

✓ Inventory sufficient to meet set-up requirements for simultaneous functions
✓ Tables: number and condition of each type (6-foot long, 8-foot long, 30-inch wide, 18-inch wide, 60-inch round, 72-inch round, half rounds, and high-top cocktail tables)
✓ Chairs: types and sizes
✓ Riser sections, stages

2. Public Service Areas

a. Washrooms: How many restrooms are available for the location and number available for the event? Are they handicapped accessible? Who is responsible for cleaning and maintenance during the event?

b. Ticket Booths & Registration Areas: Where are the locations and how many are available for the event? Are there secure coat check facilities available? Are all these areas handicapped accessible?

c. Food Service Outlets: Are seating areas available? Who is responsible for cleaning and trash removal? Is there flexibility in the menu selections?

d. Ancillary Services: Are there medical services or a first aid office on site? How are they staffed? Are there ATMs on site? Are there childcare facilities? What are the policies regarding staffing and insurance?

3. Administrative Area

a. Facility Policies: What is the published policy regarding date protection and security threats such as bomb threats or fire? What is the emergency plan? What are the rules regarding signs and outdoor advertising?

b. Labor: Is it a union or a right-to-work facility? What are the rates per hour, regular time, weekend, holidays and overtime? What unions, if any, have jurisdiction in the facility? What are the specific areas assigned to each union? What is the length of union contracts with the facility? Will any expire during or near to the event dates?

c. Insurance Requirements: What are the policies regarding liability insurance and workers compensation clearances in the hall?

d. Licensing Requirements: Are there special licenses required to hold an event in the chosen facility? Are the exhibitors, especially those from outside the area, required to have special business licenses? Are there special tax assessments on consumer events, or sales made at consumer events?

Site Selection from the Meeting Planner's Perspective

When choosing an event site, most exhibition managers focus on the physical environment required for the exhibition. Obviously, every site will have different features and limitations. However, when an education program is superimposed upon the exhibition's requirements, often the site's very best selling features can become limitations. To the meeting manager, site selection often involves an entirely different set of requirements.

For example, there is the question of distance. How far is the exhibition floor from the meeting area? Is it on the same level, or even in the same building? Room layouts, corridors and sound proofing will all have to be examined in the context of the educational program to see whether the site is suitable for the entire event. The following checklist will help determine whether the proposed site will meet the education and general program needs for the event.

Ceilings: Ceiling height and hanging obstructions are two factors that need to be examined. If a ceiling is too low, it restricts the size of the projection screen that can be used. Low ceilings may cause reverberation in a long room. Secondly, the facility floorplan may indicate a 20-foot ceiling. However, if there are chandeliers or other lighting fixtures that have an extended drop, typically four to eight feet, the usable ceiling height has effectively been reduced by that amount. In addition, consider the texture of the ceiling. Acoustical tile is usually better than exposed beams, as it provides better sound dispersal for the room.

Photo courtesy of Orange County Convention Center

Walls: Most major convention facilities have meeting rooms that can be reconfigured by the use of movable or temporary walls. Partition systems can sometimes be a serious problem for meeting privacy and presentation effectiveness. Sound can "bleed" from one meeting room to another. While many centers claim their wall systems are soundproof, the sound control of these types of partitions (and permanent walls) should be tested during the site inspection.

Floors: Carpeted floors are usually better for meetings than uncarpeted, wooden, or concrete floors. Aside from the scraping of chairs, the harder surface can reflect a "fracture" sound. Since carpets absorb sound, even the noise from a full room can be eased somewhat because of carpeted flooring.

Columns: Many older facilities and some newer ones still use vertical support columns as a part of the building's overall infrastructure. Columns of any kind usually present problems for meetings. The room should be inspected to make sure that every angle of the room that will be used has a good view of the speaker or presentation area. Poorly placed columns can effectively reduce a room to 50 percent or less of its usable capacity.

Windows: Windows are a source of ambient light and sometimes distracting sound. If there are windows in the room, make sure they can be covered completely to produce a good viewing area for slides, overheads and other projected images. Windows that face busy streets or construction areas can be particularly troublesome. A peaceful exterior environment during a weekend pre-conference inspection may be filled with noise and other distractions if the meeting is held during the week or at rush hour. Conversely, if day-long, intense education sessions are planned, windows and natural light help keep attendees awake. Windowed rooms often present interesting challenges for meeting planners.

Lighting: Check the kind of lighting being used in the meeting rooms. Mercury lights take time to come to full capacity. Because incandescent lights can be dimmed, they are preferred over fluorescent lights for meeting rooms. Slowly dimming the lights allows the eyes to adjust, and promotes uninterrupted visibility. If the room is divisible, does each portioned segment have an independent user-friendly lighting control panel? In general, the lighting should be adequate for the size of the room. Finally, the lights in larger rooms should be divided into stations so that the lights can be dimmed over the screen, but still provide adequate brightness for note taking.

Mirrors: Mirrors may pose a problem. First, they reflect projection equipment and make it difficult to use. Second, attendees may see themselves in the mirror and be distracted from the presentation.

Doors: Doors can diminish the amount of available meeting space in a sectioned room. They are also openings through which sound enters a meeting room. Service doors are sometimes a particular problem, because sound from the kitchen or service corridors will enter the room. Squeaky doors, or doors that bang when opened or shut, will also be distracting. Also, many meeting facilities have peepholes in the doors so people can look into the room without opening the door and possibly interrupting an important moment in the program.

Doors should provide easy egress in emergency situations. This factor is often overlooked when checking out large meeting rooms during a site inspection. In several facilities, partitioning larger rooms into smaller meeting rooms produces a maze effect that may leave attendees confused as to the actual exit out of the area. Ensure that all exit doors are marked, and lead to larger, clearly marked public corridors.

Electrical: Some facilities may not have adequate electrical capabilities for the program. Ask the facility manager for information about watts and power capabilities, and compare these to your requirements. Outlets should be plentiful and convenient. This can be a concern in rooms that are divisible by partitions.

Exits: National and state fire codes require an unobstructed view and access to all exits. This can sometimes limit the flexibility of how a room can be used.

Sound Systems: Most facilities have an in-house, hard-wired sound system. In most cases, such systems are adequate. Many venues charge patch fees to allow audio-visual contractors for plugging into the house audio systems. Some facilities may exclusively provide microphones and audio support. Multimedia presentations may require additional equipment. If considering a multimedia presentation, ensure there is ample space in the room for the type of equipment needed. Is there a permanent stage with theatrical lighting and sound, or will portable equipment be needed? What is the nature of the overall communication system? Will it be affected if a presentation must be plugged into the house system? Is there a permanent sound/projection room?

Lighting for multimedia presentations raise additional concerns. Do the lights have individual controls that allow dimming and blackout? Is a lighting remote control available? Is the system capable of providing follow spots? If there is a stage, are there any lighting restrictions? In case of an emergency, are auxiliary power units available?

Other considerations: The meeting manager will also have other concerns that will need to be addressed during the site inspection. Adequate equipment in the form of tables and chairs, easy access to catering facilities, adequate labor and support staff for meeting room set-ups and catered functions should be added to the site inspection checklist. Facility policies regarding union labor, costs for room set-ups and changes must be taken into consideration. Additionally, many facilities have exclusive agreements with audio-visual and catering contractors.

CONVENTION CENTER SITE INSPECTION CHECKLIST

Many considerations factor into the decision to select an event destination. Among them is accessibility, hotel availability, the appeal of local restaurants and attractions, and, of course, the cost/value equation. But for groups that stage exhibits, the search always begins with a detailed workup of the destination's major Convention Center. Can it accommodate a particular event? What services are provided? What are the labor rules? Which special local ordinances apply? What are the costs? The number of details can be overwhelming. The following checklist, developed in conjunction with SMG, serves as a road map for any Convention Center site inspection.

SPECIFICATIONS

✓ Is the Center publicly or privately owned and managed?

✓ Are there any special city or state ordinances?

✓ What permits are required?

✓ What is the total square footage or exhibit space? Meeting space?

✓ How is the space configured? Are there columns in the exhibit halls?

✓ What is the maximum floor load in the exhibit halls?

✓ Is there a minimum net square footage required in every exhibit hall?

✓ Where is exhibit space located relative to registration areas? Is the registration area included in the rental?

✓ What is the number and size of meeting rooms? How many meeting rooms are included with rental of the hall?

✓ What type of security does the building provide?

✓ Are all areas of the Center ADA-approved?

✓ What emergency procedures are in effect at the Center? Are there EMT services on the premises?

✓ Does the Center offer wireless Internet? Is the building wired to run a signal to all meeting rooms?

✓ Are there hanging points throughout the building? Are there any restrictions on where signage can be placed? Ask for a diagram.

✓ Is there sufficient parking close to the Center? Does the Center offer daily in and out parking privileges? Is there complimentary parking for show management and/or vendors?

✓ Are there any anticipated construction projects?

   • Obtain a copy of the Convention Center's standard license agreement, and have an attorney review it.

FEES

✓ Is the Convention Center rental based on a daily rate? Or an event rate?

✓ Does the rental include move-in, move-out days? If not, are these charged at the same rate as event days?

✓ Is there heat or air conditioning during move-in, move-out days? What is the charge for use?

✓ Is there a charge for trash removal?

✓ What are the deposit and full payment requirements?

✓ What are the insurance requirements?

✓ Is there a charge for HVAC services?

✓ Is there a charge for keys to meeting rooms or offices? What is the cost of a lost key?

SERVICES

✓ Which services are exclusive? Ask for a list of the specific service providers.

✓ Which services are complimentary? Request cost schedules for all others.

✓ Is there a patch fee for using an A-V company not affiliated with the Center?

✓ Can items be taped to the wall? Is special tape required?

✓ Does the Center have an in-house floor plan designer?

✓ Does the Center have a business center?

✓ Is there a concierge/information desk within the Center?

✓ What is included in the standard room setup? What additional services/equipment will be charged for? Ask for a price list.

✓ Does the Center charge for room set changes?

✓ Is water service complimentary?

✓ What types of reader boards and/or electronic boards are available? Is there a charge?

✓ Can the Center provide ticket takers, sellers and cashiers, ushers and security personnel? Ask for a fee schedule.

LABOR & SHIPPING

✓ Is the building a union facility? What are the labor rules? When do the contracts expire?

✓ Can the group handle its own rigging?

✓ Are there union regulations specific to certain meeting rooms or other space?

✓ Is there a marshaling area for trucks?

✓ How many docks does the Center have? What are the dimensions of the largest dock?

✓ What is the load limit?

✓ Does the facility have forklifts or must the decorator provide them? What are the rental fees?

✓ Are there dollies or push carts available? Ask for a fee schedule.

✓ Does the equipment require a Center employee to operate? What is the charge?

✓ Can materials be shipped to the Center? Can materials be stored prior to the start of the event?

✓ Is there security at the docks…or will the group need to provide it?

FOOD & BEVERAGE

✓ Who is the food service provider at the Convention Center?

✓ Are there additional food outlets within the facility? Do they require a guarantee to remain open? What are the hours?

✓ Is there an option of a food & beverage waiver to cover rental at the Center?

✓ Can food or beverage be brought into the Center?

✓ Does the caterer offer "sampling" of food that will be served?

MISCELLANEOUS

✓ Will there be other groups in the building at the same time? If so, who are they?

✓ Are there restrictions on automobile displays? Is a permit or fire marshal approval required?

✓ Are doors locked at a certain time? Is there a charge for working after hours?

HOUSING REQUIREMENTS

✓ How many hotels are connected to the Center?

✓ How many hotels are within walking distance?

✓ What would be the room block commitment of the headquarters hotel?

✓ What is the total committable room block in the downtown area?

✓ Is free shuttle service provided for hotels that are not within walking distance of the Center? Do the bureau and/or hotels offer a rebate to cover the cost of shuttles?

✓ Will hotels and the Convention Center sign contracts at the same time?

Site Selection from the Official Services Contractor's Perspective

Often there are certain physical characteristics of the facility that an official services contractor would like the show organizer to be aware of before making a decision. The contractor is less concerned with the attractiveness of a facility than with its practicality. These are concerns that, if addressed at the outset, will save both the show organizer and the exhibitors time and money.

Dock space: As a rule, convention centers have loading docks that can accommodate most trucks, vans, and private vehicles that will be arriving with exhibitor freight. The more loading docks that are available in close proximity to the exhibit hall, the faster move-in and move-out will be. This will help control costs. Some convention centers are able to allow trucks direct access to drive right onto the show floor. Again, this allows for faster freight movement which will save exhibitors money.

If an exhibition is going to be in a hotel, in most cases the dock access will be more difficult. The same loading docks that the official services contractor uses are sometimes also used for the delivery of the hotel's daily supplies. If so, it is necessary to determine if an elevator can be blocked for exclusive use during the exhibition's move-in and move-out times.

Infrastructure: Once inside the hall, the service contractor will look at the facility differently than the casual observer. While the observer may notice the nice artwork on the walls, the contractor is looking at columns, ceiling heights, electrical ports, floor load capacities, hanging points, and attendee access routes to the hall. Columns are common in many exhibit halls. When the show manager works with the official services contractor to design the floorplan, the columns will affect booth frontage, as well as aisle space.

Electrical: Service contractors want to know where the electrical ports are, and how their locations will impact the exhibitors. Electrical ports are usually placed in the floor but can also be in the ceiling, which can detract from the look of the show, and in some instances, can interfere with an exhibitor's booth arrangements.

Floor load: Both convention center and hotel exhibit halls measure their floor load by pounds per square foot. A carpeted floor will save the expense of having to carpet the aisles and save exhibitors from having to carpet their booths, but there may be restrictions on running forklifts or other heavy equipment over the carpet and facility concerns about wear and tear due to booths and exhibit traffic.

Rigging: Looking upward, the contractor will look for potential hanging points where aisle, directional and sponsorship signs can be hung. Signage can define the look of an exhibition. If the hall is easily accessed, then the amount of money spent on signage can be lessened. Working together, the organizer and contractor can make a show look good in almost any location.

SUMMARY

Site selection requires detailed planning, since many exhibition managers must choose event venues three to five – and in some cases, up to ten – years in advance. This means careful consideration of all perspectives and all factors that could impact the event in the future. Many an exhibition manager has been caught in the situation of having to contain too large a show in too small a space, and vice versa. Similarly a show's attendee base or the make up of exhibitors can also change. The best show organizers review as many data points as possible and then make the best decision possible.

QUESTIONS FOR DISCUSSION

① List three of the features your home city uses to attract visitors, whether or not there is an exhibition facility there. What types of events would appreciate these features most?

② Would it be better to book too large or too small an exhibit hall?

③ What would be the appropriate steps to take when it turns out that the facility chosen far in advance is no longer the best choice for an event?

Chapter 2
Facilities

"Drive thy business or it will drive thee."
– Benjamin Franklin

Section III: Venues

IN THIS CHAPTER YOU WILL LEARN
- The different types of facilities that host exhibitions
- How facilities calculate rental charges
- Why some venues give priority to certain types of events
- How event venues are different outside the US

INTRODUCTION

A show organizer's understanding of the type of facility under consideration could be the difference between a profitable and successful tradeshow, and one that is not. Knowing the purpose of the facility and how it is managed are important first steps in selecting a venue. A convention center built for the purpose of increasing visitors, compared to a center designed to serve the local community, will likely have differences in booking policies, pricing, and possibly the ability to properly service the show. This chapter examines the various types of facilities where trade and consumer shows are held. Perhaps the most important thing to remember is that all convention and trade centers are somehow unique; show organizers who understand this principle and use it to their advantage are typically very successful.

CONTRIBUTOR

Brian Monroe, Director of Sales & Marketing, Myrtle Beach Convention Center

Chapter 2 — Facilities

Convention Centers

To understand today's convention center, one must step back about thirty or forty years and consider how some venues began with a completely different purpose. Today, the term municipal or civic center is not widely used; however, many of today's convention centers began as civic centers designed to serve the local community. Yesterday's civic centers attracted consumer and community events, and typically included a large multi-purpose hall capable of housing anything from a local banquet to the traveling circus. Some civic centers may have had an auditorium or arena attached, but most didn't have the quality meeting space and amenities required of today's tradeshows and conventions. As the exhibition and meeting industry grew, city leaders began to realize the economic benefit of bringing events to their communities. Some facilities simply changed their names from "civic center" to "convention center". Others began convention center building initiatives that improved facility standards and increased customer expectations tremendously.

The majority of convention centers in the United States today have been built either by the city, county or state, and their purpose is to create economic impact for the overall community. Consider these varieties of convention centers and how each works to create economic impact:

City, County, or State Government Owned and Operated Convention Centers

These venues have been funded with tax revenues, some from the local citizenry, but most by state and local hotel and amenity taxes charged to the visitor. Marketing of these facilities emphasizes selling the convention center space to the convention or exhibition that will create the most economic impact. Economic impact is best calculated by multiplying the number of **hotel room nights** (contracted by the show manager) times an amount the attendee is expected to spend during the show.

> **Example 1:** Show A requires 100,000 gross square feet of exhibit space, and 3,000 hotel rooms have been contracted. The attendee occupying the hotel room is expected to spend $250 per day on accommodations, food and other charges. The minimum economic impact of this show is 3,000 room nights times $250, which equals $750,000.

> **Example 2:** Show B requires 250,000 gross square feet of exhibit space, and 750 hotel rooms have been contracted. The minimum economic impact of this show is 750 room nights times $250, which equals $187,500.

While this formula is used by most facilities and local bureaus, and touches the key issues, there are also other factors that contribute to economic impact, such as sales tax revenue, exhibitor spending on show services and hospitality, entertainment and restaurant revenue, local transportation usage, and many others. Producers of consumer shows often point to these other economic impact factors as evidence of their value to the local economy, and as an argument for higher priority in obtaining prime dates at a facility.

When the mission is to generate the greatest economic benefit to the community, based on these examples, the facility would be more likely to solicit Show A, even though Show B uses more exhibit space. The successful show manager will know the economic impact his or her show represents, and will use that information to negotiate date availability and rental rates at these publicly-owned convention centers.

Another consideration of publicly-owned convention centers is how the center is administered or managed. Some centers are administered as a department of the city, county or state owning the venue. Show organizers may find challenges negotiating with local governments. Reducing the facility rental could require a vote of the city council.

Myrtle Beach Convention Center, Myrtle Beach, South Carolina, USA

A governing body known as a convention center authority may manage other publicly-owned venues. City leaders are appointed to serve, and the authority resembles a board of directors that guides the daily operations of the convention center. Show organizers may find this management style favorable, as it typically results in an operation that looks more like a business and less like a government agency.

Some publicly-owned venues have management agreements with third-party companies that operate the facilities for the owners. Contracting with a third-party management company often reduces the financial risk for the owner. The management company staffs the organization, and may guarantee the owner a return on the investment made in the center. Show organizers may see benefits like improved service. However, as there is a desire to create profitability for the owners as well as the third-party management group, negotiation of rates and services in these convention centers may prove challenging.

How a convention center is managed should not necessarily be a factor in venue selection; however, understanding that facility's goals and objectives should be considered. Successful exhibitions require a sense of partnership between show management and the convention center. Understanding a convention center's mission and how it is managed could assist the show manager's planning and budgeting process. It is important to understand that each venue is as unique as the area in which it is located, and that laws and restrictions vary considerably. Almost every convention center has a rules and regulations booklet that is considered part of the agreement between the center and show management. During the site selection process, show managers should ask for and carefully review the facility's rules and regulations to make certain there isn't some restriction that could diminish the exhibition's effectiveness. (Many of these restrictions will have to be built into the exhibitor contract for booth rental.)

Convention centers also have a different ways of charging for exhibit halls and meeting space. Here are some examples of how facility rental may be proposed:

Daily Rental of the Exhibit Hall
This is typically a daily charge that includes the use of the exhibit hall. Some venues charge the full rental on days that the show is open, and half rental on move-in and move-out days.

Exhibit Hall Rental based on the amount of net square feet of booth space sold
Some convention centers charge a fee for each net square foot sold by the show. The agreement with a center may quote rent at $8,000 or $.40 cents per net square foot used or sold, whichever is greater. The $8,000 represents a minimum fee. Should the exhibit booths sold exceed the minimum, the rent would increase accordingly. (Ex. $8,000 / $.40 cents = 20,000 net square feet minimum. Should 25,000 net square feet be sold, the rent would increase by $2000. 5,000 extra feet multiplied by $.40 cents = $2,000.)

Some centers will charge a net square rental fee that includes all move-in, move- out and show days. Some centers will charge net square rental on a per day basis. The following example shows similar net square footage rental fees, yet one is quoted as a daily fee and the other includes all the days required.

Convention Center A

$8,000 or $.40 cents per net square foot used, whichever is greater. This quote includes up to four show days and one complimentary move-in or move-out day for each paid show day.

Convention Center B

$2,000 per show day or $.10 cents per net square foot used per day, whichever is greater. Move-in and move-out days will be charged at $1,000 per day or $.05 cents per net square foot used, whichever is greater.

A show manager is planning a three day show that will require two move-in days and one move-out day, and expects to sell 28,000 net square feet of exhibit booth space. Based on these specifications, consider the following price comparison between convention centers A & B noted above:

Convention Center A

28,000 nsf x $.40 cents = $11,200 and includes all six days required.

Convention Center B

28,000 nsf x $.10 cents = $2,800 x 3 show days = $8400
28,000 nsf x $.05 cents = $1,400 x 3 move in and move-out days = $4200
Total rent for convention center B = $12,600

This example shows how pricing between the two centers initially appeared very different, but became very similar once calculations were made based on the needs of the show. It is interesting to note that the center that looked the least expensive was in reality more expensive once all the charges were totaled.

Rental of meeting and ballroom space in convention centers is normally assessed on a per day fee. Some facilities may include a proportionate amount of meeting space along with the rental of the exhibit hall. Others centers may consider reducing meeting room rental based on the food and beverage revenues associated with the event, or perhaps even based on the number of hotel rooms being used in the city.

Exhibit hall rental usually only includes the use of the hall itself. Electrical, plumbing and communication services are almost always in addition to the rent, although often passed on to the exhibiting company. Most of the other elements such as pipe and drape; carpeting, and signage are provided by service contractors. Meeting and ballroom fees generally include one set-up for the duration of the show; changes to that set-up could result in additional fees.

Major convention center facility, San Diego Convention Center, San Diego, California, USA

Privately-owned Convention Centers

Profitability may be the bottom line for a privately-owned convention center operation, yet that doesn't necessarily mean the show manager will pay more for services in these facilities. Because they are competing with centers that are heavily subsidized, private facilities may leverage efficient staffing, booking policies and value-added services to minimize their costs and maximize revenues. Less than ten percent of convention centers and exhibit halls are privately owned and operated. Each example of a privately-owned center could differ considerably as to the reason why they exist. One reason could be to fill hotel rooms owned by the same entity. With over a million square feet of exhibit floor and meeting space, the Sands Expo & Convention Center in Las Vegas is the largest privately-owned and operated convention center in the United States. Connected to the Center is the 4,100 room Venetian Resort Hotel and Casino. Although Las Vegas is in a league of its own as a convention destination, the Sands exists to help fill those 4,100 rooms.

Gambling revenues generated in the casino also enter the equation. In this instance, show managers may find pricing of exhibit hall rental and services at this type of facility to be less than those found in a publicly-owned facility, in an effort to attract more business into the owner's other ventures.

Conference Centers

The term conference center could mean many things to many people. A conference center may be a rustic mountain retreat, or a luxurious resort by the sea. Using the term conference center, however, denotes that the facility includes meeting space.

Many corporations own conference centers that they operate for their own use in addition to marketing to events outside of the company. Religious and social organizations own and operate conference centers that facilitate both religious and secular events.

Although conference centers may be able to house small exhibitions, typically they don't have an exhibit hall or the amenities necessary to host larger exhibitions. Exhibit booth services such as electricity and plumbing may be limited. Appropriately sized loading docks and ramps to facilitate exhibitor move-in may be limited, or even none existent. A conference center may include sleeping accommodations, or may simply offer meeting space. Conference centers generally rent space for a flat daily fee.

Hotels with Conference Centers

As reviewed above, a conference center is a multi-dimensional term. Facilities marketed as hotel and conference centers are likely to be as varied as conference centers; however, adding the two words "hotel and" instantly tells buyers that sleeping accommodations are conveniently located near the facility. Most hotel and conference center facilities have sleeping rooms either within or attached to the conference center, and while others may not be physically connected, the hotel will be within walking distance from the conference center. Event planners often seek out facilities that can accommodate the event under one roof, minimizing an attendee's movement from hotel room to meeting room.

The varieties of hotel and conference center facilities available are as broad as facilities simply labeled conference centers. Hotel and conference centers, however, most often cater primarily to meetings and conventions. Although the meeting and ballroom space in a hotel and conference center may be used as exhibition space, rarely does this type of facility have adequate exhibit hall space, or the amenities necessary to successfully host a larger exhibition.

The meeting and ballroom space in a hotel and conference center is typically rented daily. If considering this type of facility, it is likely that hotel accommodations will be required. If this is the case, depending on seasonal demand, meeting and ballroom rental may be reduced or waived altogether if potential sleeping room or catering revenues warrant a discount. If using meeting or ballroom space for exhibits, it is likely that the daily rental fee would apply versus traditional exhibit hall or convention center pricing structures.

A hotel and conference center will be a successful venue as long as the event planner has matched the facility with the physical needs and objectives of the show. As there are many varieties of hotels and conference centers, the show organizer must examine the goals and objectives of the show, and select a hotel and conference center if this type of facility meets those objectives.

International Convention Centers

Convention centers are built throughout the world for similar reasons as communities in the United States have invested in these facilities. Economic development is the top priority. Physical differences are minimal when comparing convention centers wherever the location. Exhibit hall space, loading docks and exhibitor services are similar both domestically and abroad. In an international convention center, the meeting and ballroom space may not be in proportion to the amount of exhibit space available. While international trade and consumer shows seem to focus on promoting commerce and trade, their American counterparts emphasize the educational events offered along with tradeshows.

As with domestic facilities, show managers should research and understand how international convention centers are owned and operated. Where convention centers in America are primarily publicly owned and operated as "loss leaders," meaning that they are under-priced with the expectation that income from related businesses (primarily local hotels and restaurants) will provide the missing revenue to the city or other owner. Exhibition facilities in other countries are more often privately owned and operated profitably on their own.

Pricing of exhibit space internationally is similar to convention centers in the United States. Options include either a daily flat rate rental fee, or a per net square meter fee, since exhibit space is advertised and sold according to the metric system. Exhibitors are charged for services such as electrical access similar to how they would be charged in the United States. Convention centers in the United States may discount exhibit hall rental, but rarely advertise their willingness to do so. However a large convention and exhibition center located in Asia actually promotes a twenty to forty percent discount of rental fees to exhibition organizers who lease exhibit space during low demand periods, or who commit to multiple years.

Some international convention centers actually own and produce the tradeshows happening in that facility. Typically, tradeshows owned by convention centers promote the community's primary industries and business interests. In Europe specifically, the term "fair" is often used to describe an exhibition. Emphasis on commerce and business-to-business selling through the exhibition or fair is strong. In January 1992, 13 centers (or centres) formed the European Major Exhibition Centre Association (EMECA), an organization dedicated to professionalism in servicing exhibition organizers, exhibitors, buyers and visitors. The EMECA also collects economic impact data associated with European fairs and exhibitions. Simultaneous interpretation capabilities are standard, particularly in facilities designed to host meetings as well as exhibitions.

Messe Frankfurt, Frankfurt Germany, Over 3.4 million square feet of exhibit space

Organizations like the EMECA, IAEM and others have succeeded in creating industry standards and best practices for servicing exhibitions. These international standards of convention center management make most facilities appear to be very similar in design and functionality despite the location.

Fairgrounds and Expo Centers

In the United States, many states and local municipalities own a fairground. Fairgrounds developed from county, regional and state fairs emphasizing agricultural expositions and entertainment each fall. Many of these annual events bring a huge boost to the local economy. Over time, these communities have built permanent exposition facilities to house the exhibits each year.

A fairground exposition hall may be little more than a large barn-like structure designed to display livestock and heavy equipment. Other buildings at a fairground may include meeting rooms, banquet space, and kitchens. Since fairgrounds rarely get used for a fair more than once a year, some cities rent the buildings located on the fairgrounds, primarily to consumer shows and local community events. Rental fees are typically assessed daily according to the size of room or space occupied. On-site vehicle parking or public transportation is typically very accessible and affordable at fairgrounds. Hotel rooms may not be nearby.

As noted earlier in the chapter, some international centers refer to exhibitions as fairs, and one may find the term fairground used with reference to a convention center. As the word "fair" may mean different things to different cultures, the condition, appearance and purpose of fairgrounds are quite varied. The selection process should warrant a site inspection of the venue to ensure it will meet the needs of the event being planned.

The term "Expo Center" is typically used to describe a facility that primarily hosts consumer shows or community events. An Expo center may be either privately owned, or owned by a public or private partnership formed to spur economic development. Expo centers may have meeting space and hotel accommodations nearby, but may not offer the quality and services provided as standards in other convention centers. As with fairgrounds, Expo centers should be accessible to public transportation or have ample parking and access to local expressways. Fees for the exhibit space are typically charged on a per day basis.

SUMMARY

Selecting the right convention center to house an exhibit may seem like a daunting task, but it doesn't need to be. The show organizer's success depends on understanding as much as possible about the demographics of the attendees and exhibitors. How attendees and exhibitors will respond to a destination should always be the first priority. There must be a partnership between the show manager, convention center and the destination in order for a successful show to be created. Beyond the physical attributes of a convention center, doing business in an environment with people who perform, and with whom show organizers can have a good, working relationship is key.

Section III: Venues

① What are the pros and cons of working in a large convention center vs. a small conference center?

② Why do you think a city would choose to outsource management of its own convention center?

③ How does having a casino under the same roof make the cost of the exhibit hall cheaper?

Chapter 3
Convention & Visitor Bureaus

"Convention and Visitor Bureaus (CVB) are not-for-profit organizations charged with representing a specific destination and helping the long-term development of communities through a travel and tourism strategy. Convention and visitor bureaus are usually membership organizations bringing together businesses that rely on tourism and meetings for revenue."

– Destination Marketing Association International

Section III: Venues

IN THIS CHAPTER YOU WILL LEARN TO:

- Recognize the role of convention and visitor bureaus in the marketing and solicitation of meetings and conventions.
- Identify the benefits to meeting planners to engage the services of the convention and visitor bureau.
- Understand the organization and funding mechanisms that provide resources to convention and visitor bureaus

INTRODUCTION

Marketing a city destination, venue or meeting site is unquestionably the most important task of any hospitality business or organization engaged in meetings and conventions. Typically, all of the "major players" in the meetings and convention industry will engage in the sales and marketing process to influence where show organizers choose to hold their events. Some have a greater stake in this activity than others.

CONTRIBUTOR

John Smith, CFE, Adjunct Faculty, Georgia State University

A Competitive Environment

Competition is fierce among all the major first and second tier meetings and convention cities. The show organizer will have many good choices, and will be solicited by all the "players" in the meetings and convention industry with both hard and soft sales approaches. The host cities as well as the convention centers must consider meetings and conventions as "perishable products," much like a hotel room that goes unsold. For them, marketing their products to show organizers and producers is vitally important. Accordingly, substantial monies are spent on staffing sales and marketing departments, and on creating effective advertising, marketing and promotions programs.

Moreover, for many of the contractors, suppliers and lodging corporations who operate nationwide, the actual site of the event will not be as important as actually securing the contracts for these services. Nevertheless, these companies also have their "preferred" sites with which to do business and perhaps maximize their profit margins. Access to equipment and inventory, labor contracts, travel and transportation all have an influence on a supplier's preferences.

Hotel chains, depending on actual ownership of the local properties, may have a stake in an event's decision to choose one location over another. In gaming environments, the potential revenue generated from meetings and conventions will add another factor into the sales and marketing considerations of the host property.

Purpose of the Convention and Visitor Bureau

Convention and visitor bureaus serve one major purpose: to attract visitors to the host city. They can also be considered as the "marketing department" for a city's tourism industry. Accordingly, the convention and visitor bureau will create strategic plans, goals and objectives to attract visitors from state, regional, national and international origins. In this age of "metrics," the convention and visitor bureau's performance is easily measured by counting "heads on beds!"

2005 EXPACT NATIONAL SPENDING FIGURES, a Study Funded by the DMAI Foundation on events held in the United States:

- Delegates spend an average of US$1,036 per event or US$290 per day. The average length of stay is 3.56 nights.
- 77% of all delegate spending is accounted for by lodging (47%) and food & beverage (28%).
- Per delegate spending by organizers averages US$101 per event or US$24 per day. Food and beverage accounts for the largest share of their expenditures.
- Tradeshows and conventions all have an exhibition component, which contributes additional spending to the local economy. The average event lasts approximately 3.8 days with total exhibiting company expenditures averaging US$375 per delegate, or US$100 per day.

- Over 65% of exhibitor spending in the host city is attributed to staff lodging, meals and transportation.
- Consistent with previous studies, events held in larger destinations tend to produce more spending. Larger destinations also tend to host events that are broader in scope (e.g., drawing a regional, national or international audience), which also translates into additional spending.
- Just over 80% of all delegates stay in hotels. 12% commute daily to the event from home and 7% stay with friends or relatives.

Most convention and visitor bureaus will divide their tasks into specific market segments: Group Meetings, Business Traveler, Leisure Group Travel, and Individual Vacation Traveler. Of these, group meetings generally command the most marketing dollars in cities who compete for major conventions and tradeshows. However, the most successful cities are those who not only have a good market share of meetings and conventions, but are also an attractive destination for individual tourist and group vacations. These two market segments go hand-in-hand, and are the reason convention and visitor bureaus were created.

Another correlating purpose of a convention and visitor bureau is to coordinate the marketing efforts of the city's hotel, convention and other meetings industry players when soliciting events. These organizations join the convention and visitor bureau as members to further promote and coordinate this process. In addition to these organizations, the convention and visitor bureau provides a liaison with city and state tourism departments, all in an effort to enhance the effectiveness of these common goals.

For the meeting planner, the convention and visitor bureau provides a single source of contact for all the services needed to conduct a meeting or convention in the host city. Even though more than half of all meetings involve less than 200 people, a convention and visitor bureau considers these meetings as strategically important as major city-wide events because they all help grow the hospitality industry in the host city.

Organization and Ownership of the Convention and Visitor Bureau

Most convention and visitor bureaus in the United States are created as not-for-profit, tax exempt organizations. A board of directors is the governing body that selects the management staff and approves budgets, major contracts, strategic plans and other governance duties.

The convention and visitor bureau will generally enter into an agreement with a government entity in order to provide a mechanism whereby transient occupancy (hotel/motel) and other tax revenues may be provided to offset the expenses of operation. The governing board generally has strong representation from the local lodging industry, whose success is directly related to the success of the convention and visitor bureau in attracting group meetings and leisure travelers to the city.

Although most convention and visitor bureaus are not part of city or state government, they are very close to such government entities, and the two must work closely together to achieve success.

Membership in a convention and visitor bureau is open to any organization or business with an interest in meetings, conventions, travel and tourism. Hospitality companies who operate in multiple locations may hold memberships in multiple bureaus. Membership includes companies who provide services and supplies to the meetings industry, as well as show organizers and event management companies.

Convention and visitor bureaus conduct formal annual meetings to report on strategic plans, budgets and governance. They also conduct periodic membership meetings to meet members' needs in networking, education and professional development. At major industry events and periodically throughout the year, the convention and visitor bureau will host special promotional events, familiarization tours and other marketing opportunities to match bureau members with potential customers and solicit future business.

In 1914, a group of convention and visitor bureaus created the International Association of Convention and Visitor Bureaus to promote sound professional practices in the solicitation and serving of meetings, conventions and tourism. Today, this professional association known as Destination Marketing Association International, continues to provide educational resources and networking opportunities to its members, and information on the convention and visitor bureau sector of the hospitality industry.

Funding

As a general rule, convention and visitor bureaus operate as entities separate but closely affiliated with local and state governments, and most derive a majority of their operating revenues from one or more tax revenue sources. Typically, a portion of the transient occupancy tax (TOT) – also referred to as hotel/motel tax – is the primary source of funding for a city's convention and visitor bureau. Other tax sources could include rental car tax, restaurant and entertainment tax. As the convention and visitor bureau's primary mission is to attract conventions and visitors to the city, it naturally follows that these groups would be the source of taxing to support the cost of these marketing efforts – a popular response from the voters who seek someone to share their tax burden.

As discussed later in this chapter, there are risks associated with local governments extending this tax burden to transient visitors, many of whom are going to be a convention's attendees. For the individual business traveler or the family on a vacation, the amount of additional taxes attached to a hotel room, taxi fare, or rental car fee will probably go unnoticed, and is certainly never considered when making those travel plans. However, for a convention with thousands of attendees and exhibitors, such additional tax burdens are significant, and should be considered along with other costs in making final site selection decisions.

The second major source of revenue for a convention and visitor bureau is derived from the private sector. Private sector funding consists of membership dues, profits from convention and visitor bureau programs and sponsored events, and contributed services. Revenues from these private sector sources is generally less than 40 percent of the income budget of most bureaus, as the major source of funding is from transient occupancy taxes. Hospitality companies and organizations engaged in the meetings and convention industry maintain memberships at least in their local, and perhaps in multiple city convention and visitor bureaus. In addition to supporting the vitality of the industry, particularly in their home city, their return on investment is access to lead information on future meeting and convention events.

Although transient occupancy taxes and membership dues provide adequate funding for most bureaus, in highly competitive markets additional funding resources are needed for advertising and promotional campaigns and special incentive programs to attract or retain meetings and convention business.

Even though convention and visitor bureaus are private not-of-profit corporations, because they operate on a portion of public tax revenues, they are subject to most open record laws of local government. Accordingly, these organizations are held to very high standards as to accountability and dispensation of funds for marketing and promotion.

Convention and visitor bureaus are often facilitators of special incentive and discount contribution programs offered by local hotels, convention centers, and other major players in the local meetings and convention business. Because of the nature of their corporate organization, tax regulations and budgetary constraints, however, these arrangements generally do not include the convention and visitor bureau actually handling any of the funds, or being contractually responsible for the performance of these special incentive programs.

Services Provided to Meeting Planners and Show Organizers

Convention and visitor bureaus are the meeting planner's advocate. Because their business is to attract visitors to their cities, the meetings and conventions market segment is where they capture their highest return on investment on their marketing and promotional dollars.

Exhibitor and attendee needs, traffic flow, facility features and specialty booth requirements can be skillfully combined to create an effective, efficient and attractive floor plan.

Photos courtesy Freeman, Dallas, TX.

Promoting Tourism

Destination appeal is critically important for the meeting or convention to realize its full attendance potential. The convention and visitor bureau can be vitally important to the meeting planner by offering plans, proposals and suggestions on how meeting attendees can enjoy their stay in the host city, and hopefully bring along a family member to spend an extra day or two. Attractions, without distractions from the focus of the meeting, is a goal shared by both meeting planner and bureau. Developing spouse programs, recommending destination management companies, providing ideas on tourism opportunities – not only in the host city but in the state region – are all essential functions and services provided by convention and visitor bureaus.

Servicing the Client

Many in the hospitality Industry refer to the modern environment as the "Experience Economy." In other words, just providing good service is simply not good enough. Consumers demand "something extra" in addition to good service. Growing companies who are attracting the largest market share – like Starbucks, Carnival Cruise Lines, and Southwest Airlines – have built their attraction on their understanding of the experience economy.

Convention and visitor bureaus are no different. The Internet has been the great equalizer in providing the consumer with information about products, services, costs and availability. Every city has a dynamic Web site, with links to every potential product and service that could possibly be required by the meeting planner. The most successful convention and visitor bureaus have figured out the best ways to differentiate their product from that of their competitors.

Convention and visitor bureaus have naturally moved towards providing expert services to meeting planners, and making their "experience" with planning and conducting an event in their city the very best it can be. This is how convention and visitor bureaus can, and do, entice meeting planners to choose their city for their future events.

Convention and visitor bureaus strive to enhance the pre-show planning and on-site execution of your event with the objective to make this a smooth, efficient and accurate process. Almost all convention and visitor bureaus publish some type of "meeting planners guide," providing the show organizer with information on all of the city's services, including lodging accommodations, event facilities, service contractors and suppliers, attractions, transportation companies and other hospitality services.

Bureaus also work very closely with departments of public safety, transportation, parks and recreation. This is a very important service to meeting planners when any type of special accommodation may be required, or if there is another event happening which may require coordination. For example, a city may plan a public festival or parade with streets closed which may adversely affect an exhibition's shuttle bus plan, or a show may have need for the city to close a portion of a street to accommodate a special shuttle bus plan. In either case, having an advocate in the bureau working for the show's interests is important.

In the political arena, the convention and visitor bureau maintains very close relationships with mayors, county commissioners, governors and other political dignitaries. They will provide letters of welcome for show programs, assist in arrangements for personal appearances at ribbon cuttings, opening sessions and other high profile elements of your meeting or convention. Government officials also welcome this opportunity, and if the press is following, the event can receive some additional (and free) publicity.

Soliciting Business

Convention and visitor bureaus also maintain attractive and comprehensive Web sites. Most will provide an automated request for proposal (RFP) service, but to receive that personal service customary with planning a major meeting or convention, one should make personal contact with the bureau. Once this personal contact is made – either by phone, e-mail or the automated RFP method – the convention and visitor bureau will provide the services of a sales professional to help the meeting planner with the information requested for the proposed future event.

Most of the larger convention and visitor bureaus have a dedicated sales staff for the meetings and convention market segment. They will be eager to provide information about meeting space, convention center and hotel availability, as well as arrange possible site inspections. Their expertise lies in their ability to match the meeting planner's needs with local hospitality contractors and suppliers.

If the convention center or major hotels are committed to other events, either on a tentative or confirmed basis, the convention and visitor bureau is in the best position to research and explore alternate spaces and dates, including the ability to potentially negotiate the movement of previously-committed events. This is a dynamic and flexible industry. With many major first tier cities booking events far into the future, the meeting planner's needs may change as space requirements shrink or grow. Again, this is where the convention and visitor bureau's sales professionals can provide invaluable services to meeting planners in knowing where opportunities may lie in the busy meeting and convention calendar, and to offer solutions to what may seem to be an impossible scenario.

Facilitating the Housing Program

During the proposal stage of a major event, the show organizer may either look to the convention and visitor bureau to play the lead role in assembling the room blocks at local hotels, or delegate this task to a third party housing provider. In larger cities, this can be a very challenging process. With long move-in and move-out periods associated with most major conventions, hotels must aggressively seek opportunities for smaller meetings and conventions, corporate travel, and leisure travel business to meet revenue goals. Hotels that are part of other enterprises such as casinos or resorts have other booking priorities which may compete with traditional meetings and convention business.

The convention and visitor bureau or third party housing provider provides a crucial role in negotiating these room block arrangements with local hotels, and accommodating the meeting planner's special requests for VIP arrangements, designation of the headquarters hotel and similar functions. Additionally, the convention and visitor bureau is prepared to recommend a variety of hotel properties in different price ranges, which may also be an important requirement for the Small Meetings in the Educational, Religious, Fraternal (SMERF) market sector or similar groups. A goal of every meeting planner is to consolidate the room block to the smallest number possible of quality convention hotels in closest proximity to the meeting site. Not only does this increased density assist in creating a positive "vibe," it also impacts the event logistically and economically by reducing shuttle bus costs, saving travel time between hotels and the meeting site and helping to ward off the potential loss of attendees to other attractions.

Meeting and convention planners have many desires regarding a hotel property's booking policies for events which may be competitive or distracting to its purposes. Moreover, in major meetings and conventions, the threat of ambush marketing practices is ever-present (generally, this means situations such as competitive events piggy-backing in the same city or exhibitors who utilize hotel space without paying for exhibit space inside the exhibit hall). On the other hand, hotel properties, many of whom are owned by private investors, sometimes are more concerned about profitability than with the ultimate wishes of the meeting and convention industry. It is here that the convention and visitor bureau in each city is not only the meeting planner's advocate, but a watchdog in encouraging booking and business practices that favor these interests. Granted, major conventions and tradeshows command tremendous purchasing power when considering a future host city, but the assistance and contributions of the local convention and visitor bureau can and should be utilized for maximum effectiveness.

Promoting the Event

Creating favorable advertising campaigns and promotions for the host city is another major service of the convention and visitor bureau. In addition to the Bureau's responsibilities to increase the amount of meetings and conventions, the leisure tourism market is another major goal. The advertising programs and products created to attract the individual or group tourist market are equally effective with assisting show organizers to increase attendance at major meetings and tradeshows. Moreover, the convention and visitor bureau has important knowledge and contacts with local and state tourism offices, and links to their promotional materials and services.

Building show attendance is a top priority with most meeting planners. The convention and visitor bureau can partner with the show organizer to maximize these efforts. Important links may also be available with local and state Chambers of Commerce. Although Chambers of Commerce are typically more focused on permanent business development and relocations, they possess valuable information on potential companies in the region who could possibly bring additional attendees or exhibitors to exhibitions and conventions. Again, the convention and visitor bureau can provide access to these organizations, all of whom share the objective of assisting show organizers with increasing show attendance.

Other Special Services
Additionally, the convention and visitor bureau offers other customized services, including:
- Provision of marketing and promotional materials to assist the meeting planner in attracting maximum attendance and providing the most positive guest experience
- Staff for registration services and other show logistics
- Development of guest activities and access to area special events
- Assistance with access to local academic faculty and to local educational facilities pertaining to the objectives of the meeting
- Assistance with booking local speakers and celebrities

Research and Data Collection
The Meeting Information Network (MINT) is a database operated by the Destination Marketing Association International, the professional association for convention and visitor bureaus. Available to member bureaus and meeting planners, the MINT system is a shared repository of information and history about association and corporate meetings. Members gain access to the demographics, preferences and histories of those meetings. The criteria for meetings registered on the MINT system are:
- Meetings that use 50 or more rooms on a peak night
- Meetings that are held on a regularly-scheduled basis
- Meetings that rotate within at least one state.

MINT has profiles on more than 27,000 meetings from over 14,000 organizations and 150 convention and visitor bureaus. MINT provides countless research opportunities for convention and visitor bureaus to launch feasibility studies and track trends, as well as generate profiles of potential business leads.

MINT can be used by meeting planners as a negotiating tool. Having an accurate meeting history report provides a powerful basis for negotiating with your future meeting destination. Information contained in the MINT database has usually been reviewed already by the host city's convention and visitor bureau and hotels prior to the first face-to-face meetings on future events. Through the bureau's research and use of the MINT database, all parties are aware of the business potential offered by the meeting or convention.

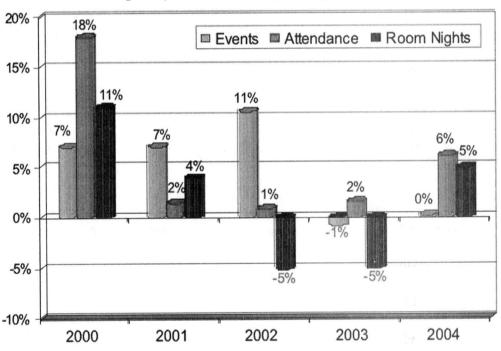

Annual Growth in MINT Events, Attendance and Room Nights (Consistent Reporting Set of Bureaus)

Graph provided courtesy of DMA/MINT and Conventions, Sports & Leisure International (SCL)

Services Provided to Attendees, Visitors and Tourists

In most cities, the convention and visitor bureau's other main purpose is to promote tourism to the host city. Just as the doorman greets the customers and welcomes them to a hotel or restaurant, the convention and visitor bureau is that one special organization that welcomes visitors to the city. In today's information age, the services provided to visitors by the local convention and visitor bureau are now best communicated by the Internet. On most convention and visitor bureau's Web sites, the visitor can find an array of information and services to meet every need.

Convention and visitor bureau Web sites serve as the official home of information for visitors and meeting planners. With links to every major player in the hospitality industry, these Web sites are generally subdivided into customized menus for tourists, meeting planners, tour and travel group organizers, and people moving to the city.

For the visitor who may be an individual tourist or an attendee coming to a major meeting or convention, the convention and visitor bureau will provide expert information on lodging and accommodations, dining, things to see and do, sports, arts and culture, shopping and other activities of interest to visitors and a calendar of events. The bureau will also publish and distribute maps and information on transportation, attractions within local neighborhoods and unique events.

The convention and visitor bureau is also a great resource for special guest packages that incorporate lodging, dining and event activities, many of which are sponsored in part by the bureau's member partners.

In addition to providing access to this information through its Web site, convention and visitor bureaus also host visitor centers in airports, major hotels and within the central business district. Most large bureaus will publish guest information for distribution in hotel rooms and restaurants.

Convention and visitor bureaus work in coordination with city and state departments of travel and tourism to provide visitors with information on expanding their stay, not only in the city but also in the surrounding region. Again, for the attendee coming to a major meeting or convention, the convention and visitor bureau is an excellent resource to meeting planners trying to make this a rewarding experience for their attendees.

Services Provided to Local Members of the Convention and Visitor Bureau

The members of a convention and visitor bureau consist of individuals, companies, organizations, major corporations, governments and advocacy groups who are involved in the development, operation and growth of the hospitality industry. The majority of members in most bureaus are small businesses who are directly engaged in providing services to the tourism, meetings and convention industry.

By becoming a member of the convention and visitor bureau, these companies gain a distinct competitive advantage. Access to future business opportunities, market research, cooperative marketing opportunities, future meeting and convention calendars, and contact names are just a few of the benefits such membership provides.

For small businesses engaged in meetings and convention services, having access to future confirmed bookings is vital. This information may not be "confidential" *per se*, but it is difficult to obtain at the local level. Having access to "members only" information listing confirmed events for the future, size, dates, and services customarily required is of strategic importance to these smaller companies.

The convention and visitor bureau also provides valuable information to its members in the form of market research studies and strategic planning. Programs are conducted periodically with members on a variety of subjects, such as improving customer service and market share.

Networking always ranks high as a benefit to joining professional associations and business organizations. The convention and visitor bureau is no different; in fact, the organization depends heavily on networking among its members to promote the overall goals and objectives of its city's hospitality industry. Creating and building excellent customer relations is a key to growth in the hospitality industry. The convention and visitor bureau provides this opportunity for members to network together, meet customers and prospective new employees, and grow their businesses.

Coordination with Other City and State Tourism Organizations

Few convention and visitor bureaus will publicly state that they have sufficient budgets to operate effectively in today's competitive environment. It is also short-sighted to think that a local convention and visitor bureau can succeed in attracting tourists, meetings and conventions without the broader influence of the region's attractions and appeal. Accordingly, convention and visitor bureaus will develop and continually enhance positive collaboration with the government-sponsored agencies and departments charged with economic development, travel and tourism. Governments know very well the benefits of this industry, and the tremendous tax revenue generated through visitor spending, creation of jobs (and subsequent personal income tax revenues) and the enhancement of quality of life for all local citizens (also beneficial at election time).

The convention and visitor bureau must capitalize on these collaborative benefits to maximize its effectiveness in attracting visitors to the host city. In more successful cities, the bureau – working in conjunction with state and local offices of tourism – will have developed common marketing schemes, trademarks and logos. Advertising professionals will attest to the fact such coordination will help these cities to brand their product, and subsequently and substantially increase their image in the marketplace. Unfortunately, not all cities will have a song written about it like "New York, New York" or "I Left My Heart in San Francisco." Regardless, cities have to coordinate their marketing and promotional programs for maximum exposure and effectiveness. The convention and visitor bureau plays a lead role in coordinating this branding effort.

For the meeting planner, having access to city and state tourism programs and opportunities for the benefit of the attendees is a critical element of show promotion. The convention and visitor bureau, again acting as the direct contact with the meeting planner, can provide this information directly.

Advocates for the Industry

In addition to pointing show organizers to local services, convention and visitor bureaus are often the convention and meetings industry's principal advocate on the municipal and state level, working in conjunction with other industry organizations and advocacy groups. Issues may include political approval to expand a convention center, reducing crime in the central business district, addressing problems with panhandling, and how transient occupancy taxes are to be used.

Show organizers may wonder why they should be concerned about any one city's problems with local government. The answer is twofold. First, many meetings and conventions need to be in specific cities for their markets, and it is important for these cities to maintain an attractive and successful meeting environment. Second, mayors, councilpersons, county commissioners and governors all have their own organizations, and frequently look to each other for solutions to governance problems. What happens in one city may soon spread throughout the nation.

An example may be the use of the transient occupancy (hotel/motel) tax. Unfortunately, some cities have used transient occupancy and related taxes on visitors for purposes not related to the promotion of travel and tourism, or for enhancing the visitors' experiences. "Taxation without representation" was a battle cry of the founding fathers of the United States, and has a familiar "ring" when cities use transient occupancy taxes to supplement general operating funds and other non-visitor related programs.

As an advocate of the meetings and convention industry, the convention and visitor bureau plays an important and expressive role in lobbying city and state legislatures on the proper and limited use of such taxes. Additionally, the bureau is the primary "lobby" for effective programs on the care of the homeless, drug and alcohol rehabilitation, clean streets and sidewalks, safety and security, transportation improvements, and any other government or private development program that enhances the attractiveness of the host city to visitors.

In performing these roles as an advocate of the industry, convention and visitor bureaus collaborates with other industry organizations involved in restaurants, lodging, meeting and conventions. When these organizations join together, leaders of government, the people and the business community listen. Travel and tourism are tremendous economic engines, contributing more than $545 billion annually to the nation's economy and generating more than $94 billion in tax revenues. Convention and visitor bureaus are the principle drivers, and people listen!

International Markets

"The world is shrinking" is a tired and dated expression from the 1960s, but the reality of this statement is most relevant today. In any major meeting or convention, a growing percentage of both exhibitors and attendees will come from international destinations.

The role of the convention and visitor bureau in this demanding environment is simple: adapt to the expanding international markets and special needs of international attendees to remain competitive. The Destination Marketing Association International sponsors an event called IMEX, a worldwide exhibition for incentive travel, meetings and events. Such events bring together national and regional tourist offices, major hotel groups, airlines, destination management companies, service providers, trade associations and other companies and organizations from the national and international hospitality industry.

Regardless of whether the host city is an "international gateway" or simply a favorable regional meeting site, convention and visitor bureaus can take a leadership role in communities to ensure international guests are welcomed and accommodated. For major meetings and conventions, bureaus can assist show organizers in qualifying for the U.S. Department of Commerce's International Buyer Program. Under the International Buyer Program, the department's United States Commercial Service recruits foreign buyer delegations from U.S. embassies abroad, and brings them to exhibitions in the United States to facilitate matchmaking with American businesses exhibiting at the show. The International Buyer Program provides United States companies interested in exporting with an excellent opportunity to meet with potential sales representatives and strategic partners without ever leaving the country.

The International Buyer Program is executed in more than 70 countries representing America's major trading partners, and also in U.S. embassies in countries where the Commercial Service does not maintain offices. Meeting planners should recognize the potential for using resources like the Commercial Service to expand their event's international presence, and provide a valuable service to exhibiting companies who seek to expand in international markets.

SUMMARY

Convention and visitor bureaus play a major in the local city's tourism and hospitality industry. They serve as the centerpiece of the city's marketing efforts to attract both meeting groups and leisure travelers. Convention and visitor bureaus provide valuable services to meeting planners. They act as advocates and industry partners, providing access to ideas, services and suppliers. Convention and visitor bureaus provide these services at little or no charge to both the meeting planners and their host constituents. Their objectives are to ensure the success of the events and the growth of the hospitality industry in their host city.

QUESTIONS FOR DISCUSSION

① What is the exact name of the destination marketing agency in your home town – or in the largest nearby city that has one?

② What is more important, promoting a destination to tourists or to convention attendees?

③ What are the pros and cons of convention and visitor bureaus being funded by tax revenues?

Section III: Venues

Chapter 1
Project Management

"*Make no little plans; for they have no magic to stir people's blood and will probably not be realized. Instead, make big plans; aim high in hope and work, remembering that a noble, logical diagram once recorded will not die.*"

– Daniel H. Burnham

Section IV: Show Planning

IN THIS CHAPTER YOU WILL LEARN

- Why project management is important to exhibition management
- Why planning, organizing, directing and controlling are the essential elements
- How to use the Gantt chart diagram method
- How to collect and review feedback from all phases of the event

INTRODUCTION

Project management may be the number one skill required of show organizers. Without a plan of action leading right up to opening day, the success or failure of booth sales doesn't matter, the best contract negotiations in the world mean nothing, and marketing and promotion of the event are useless. Fortunately, there are ways to learn how to do project management, and how to adapt these techniques easily to the exhibition industry.

CONTRIBUTOR

Christine Fletcher, CEM, Producer, Encore Event Management

Ancient Beginnings

The discipline of project planning to achieve long-term, large scale goals has been a human endeavor from the beginning of time. The ancient Egyptians, for example, employed rather simple control and resource techniques including brute force to motivate the workforce in building the Pyramids. While their means are considered primitive and inhumane by modern management standards, the Egyptians' project planning efforts in 2550 B.C. resulted in the only remaining Wonder of the Ancient World, the Great Pyramid at Giza. Comprised of 2,300,000 blocks of stone – each weighing between two and 70 tons – and completed within a specific time frame (prior to the end of a Pharaoh's lifespan), the Pyramids were constructed long before Egyptian project managers benefited from the advent of modern machines or technology.

Fast forward to World War I, when Henry Gantt (1861–1919), an American engineer and social scientist, studied the complex process and time-intensive labor involved with US Navy ship construction. During his studies, Henry Gantt developed production charts, designed with horizontal task bars and milestone markers, as a means to graphically depict a project schedule. His gift to the world – now referred to as Gantt chart diagrams – help plan, coordinate, and track specific tasks in a multifarious, large-scale project by outlining the sequence and duration of all tasks within each phase of a project's process. Gantt chart diagrams have proven to be such a powerful management tool that they have remained virtually unchanged for nearly one hundred years. Gantt chart diagrams were utilized in planning the invasion of Normandy, the construction of the Interstate Highway System and Hoover Dam, a Wonder of the Modern World.

Developing a Gantt chart to guide show organizers throughout the four phases of the exposition lifespan – planning, promotion, production, and post-analysis – is still the best way to ensure success in producing an event.

Project Management for Exhibition Management

Project management is a multifaceted, global topic. Therefore, to make our discussion specific to exhibitions, we will use a consumer show case study to explore each element of the project management process. At the end of the chapter, these elements will culminate into a comprehensive Gantt chart suitable for practical application.

To begin, a *project* is a significant undertaking which (i) encompasses a set of tasks and (ii) requires a concerted team effort to (iii) achieve the desired result within pre-determined time, quality and budget parameters. Some projects are a unique, one-time endeavor, while others may involve similar, repetitive components. For example, an event management firm may produce different types of exhibitions, such as tradeshows, consumer shows and association shows. The nature of the events themselves may be quite different, but the request for proposal (RFP) and site selection process is very similar.

Planning a successful exhibition in today's dynamic, global economy requires show organizers to work smarter by refining their management skills, streamlining communications, developing and enforcing timelines and budgets, and establishing accountability. A comprehensive project plan is the most efficient method for simultaneously managing these multiple projects. Much like a roadmap, the project plan provides clear directions to team members, enabling them to achieve the intended results within pre-determined time, resources, and quality guidelines.

In addition to a thorough project plan, equally effective management skills are also a critical element of the project management process. A roadmap without a skilled navigator is as ineffective as a project plan without a project manager. In similar fashion, a clear, concise, comprehensive project plan executed with effective project management skills ensures that a carefully planned and organized team effort will achieve a common goal: the flawless execution of your exhibition.

The discipline of project management involves four fundamental components:
• *Planning*
• *Organizing*
• *Directing*
• *Controlling*

Planning

Because they involve the project plan, the first two components – planning and organizing – are the technical aspects of project management. On the other hand, the directing and controlling efforts are the human elements of project management, involving the management of the exhibition's team. An effective project manager must be able to manage the project as well as the people. Because it requires a delicate balance between technical skills and people skills, project management is more art than science. A charismatic leader without a comprehensive plan is as ineffective as a great planner who lacks the ability to lead.

Planning involves:
• Defining the tasks to be accomplished
• Computing the resources required to complete the tasks
• Calculating the timeline in which the tasks should be completed

Similar to other strategic planning processes, the project management procedure for producing an exhibition includes the identification of a series of tasks and smaller action items or activities that need to be completed on time and on budget in order to launch the show – on time and on budget

The sequence of time and budget sensitive tasks and activities is called the critical path. The critical path is the "longest path through a project that determines the earliest date on which work can be completed" (Lewis, 1995, P.53). It is the duration of the project plan in its entirety, from beginning to end.

The approximate lifespan and lead time required to plan and prepare for the launch of a new show in a new market is 12-15 months. This timeline is only a guideline, and can fluctuate by a few months based upon the scope of the show, the size of the team, and the budget. For example, a repeat show in a repeat market will not require as much advance research and development, a team of 20 can accomplish more in less time than a team of 10, and a healthy budget can absorb rush charges for printing and shipping.

Assuming the average 12-15 month timeframe, the critical path for the first three lifespan phases of our consumer expo case study would appear like this:

> (A critical path can vary based on who the host organization is, staffing, time constraints and personal management styles. The following is one recommendation.)

LIFESPAN PHASE 1: PLANNING

Research & Development: 15 months – 1 year out

- Research show concept
- Research and gather demographics, statistics, trends
- Identify potential sponsors, exhibitors, attendees
- Develop budgets and forecasts
- Create business plan
- Identify potential markets appealing to your sponsors and attendees
- Identify best-suited facilities within target market
- Conduct site visits
- Develop marketing and promotion plan
- Develop crisis management plan
- Select insurance company
- Request for Proposals for official services contractor
- Develop and launch Web site

LIFESPAN PHASE 1: PROMOTION

Sponsor Campaign: 10 months – 6 months

- Purchase and create contact/mailing list for potential sponsors

- Develop sponsor levels and contracts
- Design sponsor marketing campaign
- Print sponsor marketing campaign
- Mail sponsor marketing campaign
- Repeat direct mailing 3-5 times
- Follow up with emails, phone calls, newsletters, updates, and personal visits between mailings
- Update Web site & floorplan with sponsor logos as they confirm
- Re-evaluate and adjust budget as sponsor funding is secured

Exhibitor Campaign: 6 months – 3 months

- Final sponsor payments due
- Purchase and create contact/mailing list for potential exhibitors
- Develop exhibitor contract
- Develop exhibitor kit & marketing campaign
- Print exhibitor kit & marketing campaign
- Mail exhibitor kit & marketing campaign
- Repeat direct mailing 3-5 times, up to 1 month prior to show date
- Follow up with emails, newsletters & updates between mailings
- Update Web site & floorplan with exhibitor list as they confirm

Consumer Campaign: 3 months – 1 month

- Final exhibitor payments due
- Contract time/space for TV, radio, print & highway billboards
- Purchase consumer mailing list
- Design print ads and direct mail piece
- Design billboard vinyls
- Submit graphic designs to sponsors for approval
- Produce TV commercial
- Draft radio script
- Run monthly magazine ad
- Billboards go up
- Send press release to media
- Mail consumer postcard
- Radio and TV ads start
- Design & print posters, flyers, admission coupons

LIFESPAN PHASE 1: PRODUCTION

Service Contracts: 2 months – 6 weeks

- Contract security service
- Contract licensed and bonded ticket sellers (unless facility provides)
- Contract emergency services provider (EMT or other) and confirm move-in, show hours & move-out

- Contract audio-visual, electric, Internet, ancillary services
- Apply for city permits for public signage & banners
- Send final round of press releases to media
- Ship posters, flyers, & admission coupons to sponsors & exhibitors
- Arrange travel & hotel plans for show staff

Confirmations: 1 month – 2 weeks

- Finalize floorplan
- Confirm move-in schedule and rules with sponsors & exhibitors
- Confirm travel & hotel arrangements for staff
- Confirm on-site media personalities, interviews and coverage
- Confirm on-site staff positions & responsibilities
- Ship materials to show site
- Print exhibitor badges
- Begin admission ticket pre-sales

On Site: 72 hours – 48 hours

- Pre-con meeting with facility, security, emergency services, labor, staff
- Official services contractor (OSC) tapes floor
- Electric, phone and Internet services installed
- OSC lays carpet, constructs stages, pavilion and demo areas
- OSC sets up home base for itself and show management
- OSC sets up pipe and drape, moves in tables, chairs

Sponsor Move-In: 48 hours – 24 hours

- Sponsors and larger exhibitors move in
- Test audio-visual, electric, phone, and Internet connections
- Dry run with staff, security, and paramedics or first-aid station staff
- Review crisis plan and exit strategy

Exhibitor Move-In: 24 hours – 8 hours

- Exhibitor move-in
- Host exhibitor education seminar
- Fire marshal walk-through

The critical path in our consumer expo case study is a skeleton outline, and many items can vary from show to show, and from show organizer to show organizer. The various tasks involved with a tradeshow or association show would also vary somewhat, and might include housing, transportation, and registration efforts.

Regardless of the size, nature and scope of the show, it is recommended that more time-consuming, complex tasks listed in the critical path be broken down into smaller, more manageable action items. This process is called the work breakdown structure (WBS). The WBS examines each task along the critical path, and reduces it into smaller action items. It then specifies how each activity will be achieved, who is assigned to each action item, the budgets associated with each phase, and the timeline for completion.

There is a distinct difference between a task and an action item (or activity) in the WBS. A task is a piece of assigned work within the overall project which can be assigned to a small task force or, in some cases, an individual. An action item or activity is a piece of assigned work within a task that can be accomplished by an individual in a relatively short period of time. In our case study above, for example, one task is listed as "Develop exhibitor kit;" therefore, the action items within that task in the WBS will appear as:

WORK BREAKDOWN STRUCTURE:

Task: Develop exhibitor marketing kit
Timeline: 3 weeks
Start: 1/3
Deadline: 1/24

Action Item	Timeline	Start	Deadline
Gather sponsor logos in EPS format	2 days	1/3	1/5
Design folder and envelope	3 days	1/3	1/6
Write content for compelling, marketing brochure	3 days	1/3	1/6
Purchase mailing list database	1 day	1/4	1/5
Develop exhibitor agreement	2 days	1/6	1/8
Add graphics to marketing brochure	3 days	1/6	1/9
Review folder design, approve or make edits	2 days	1/6	1/8
Print folder and envelope	7 days	1/8	1/15
Print Exhibitor Agreement	2 days	1/8	1/10
Request floorplan from OSC	1 day	1/9	1/10
Review marketing brochure, approve or edit	2 days	1/9	1/11
Email mailing list database to fulfillment house	1 day	1/9	1/10
Print marketing brochure	7 days	1/11	1/18
Compile brochure, exhibitor agreement and floorplan in folder; stuff envelopes	1 day	1/19	1/20
Ship exhibitor marketing kits to fulfillment house for mailing	3 days	1/21	1/24

The degree to which the tasks in the WBS are reduced is not an exact science. However, a good rule of thumb is to avoid listing action items that take less than an hour turnaround time. Conversely, tasks that are estimated to consume more than one week – or require more than one person to complete – might merit further reduction.

In comparing the WBS example to the critical path shown earlier in the chapter, consider how one task, which initially appears to be a relatively simple assignment, can adopt a new level of significance once the action items related to the task are taken into account.

Successful show organizers utilize a WBS within a project plan framework to effectively communicate the pre-determined course of action to their teams. Without this structure in place, the team might interpret the smaller activities as a series of unrelated tasks with no clear path toward the ultimate goal. Eventually, they may view their work as irrelevant, become increasingly frustrated, and unwittingly place the outcome of the entire project at risk. However, when the team fully grasps the concept of how the individual tasks fit together to achieve an understood goal, they benefit from a sense of advancement throughout various stages of the project.

Organizing

Organizing, the second aspect of the technical side of project management, is the act of transforming the documented plans into physical action; in other words, setting the wheels in motion. The first step in organizing is to assign the responsibilities for major tasks to the key players on the team. A show organizer's primes (or key players) are those individuals who lead smaller task forces on a particular phase or component within the project.

When assigning tasks and action items to individuals on the team, it is important to remember that this is not a decision to be taken lightly. It is essential to mold the activity to fit the team member, not vice versa. Creative, big-picture leaders might excel in developing marketing campaigns, but might not necessarily be able to manage the budget. A naturally cautious, worse-case-scenario type personality might develop a thorough crisis management plan, but not achieve the best results with sponsorship sales.

Once again, referring to the case study, the WBS evolves to include the prime assigned to the exhibitor kit development task, the team members assigned to each action item within that task, and the budget figures allotted for each activity. Note that an action as quick and simple as sending an email is still assigned a dollar figure. This helps offset indirect expenses like electricity to run the computer, and Internet Service Provider fees to power email. And even though an email may only take two minutes to type and send, it is still necessary to pay that team member for their time (wages, health insurance, employment taxes, and retirement plan benefits).

WBS WITH PRIME & BUDGET ASSIGNMENTS:

Task: Develop Exhibitor Kit
Prime: Reed
Timeline: 3 weeks
Start: 1/3
Deadline: 1/24
Budget: $7,500

Action Item	Prime	Timeline	Start	Deadline	Budget
Gather Sponsor logos in EPS format	Smith	2 days	1/3	1/5	$25
Design folder and envelope	Harris	3 days	1/3	1/6	$350
Write content for compelling, marketing brochure	Jones	3 days	1/3	1/6	$200
Purchase mailing list database	Smith	1 day	1/4	1/5	$1,500
Develop exhibitor agreement	Jones	2 days	1/6	1/8	$250
Add graphics to marketing brochure	Harris	3 days	1/6	1/9	$350
Review folder design, approve or make edits	Reed	2 days	1/6	1/8	$250
Print folder and envelope	Moore	7 days	1/8	1/15	$2,000
Print exhibitor agreement	Moore	2 days	1/8	1/10	$30
Request floorplan from OSC	Smith	1 day	1/9	1/10	$25
Review marketing brochure, approve or edit	Reed	2 days	1/9	1/11	$250
Email mailing list database to fulfillment house	Smith	1 day	1/9	1/10	$25
Print marketing brochure	Moore	7 days	1/11	1/18	$2,000
Compile brochure, exhibitor agreement & floorplan in folder; stuff envelopes	Interns	1 day	1/19	1/20	$150
Ship exhibitor kits to fulfillment house for mailing	Interns	3 days	1/21	1/24	$50

Directing

Now that the planning and organizing phases are complete, the "doing" phase begins. This is when the human elements of project management come into play. Directing can be defined as guiding and leading the efforts of the team and its key players. Once a team obtains specific direction toward a common goal, a project can quickly build momentum. If the show manager can accept the reality that his or her project will take on a life of its very own, and prepare for it, the roller-coaster that is certain to follow will be much more enjoyable.

Controlling

To retain control of this roller coaster, the show manager needs to monitor and influence the project's progress. Controlling involves overseeing the entire process to avoid deviations from the project plan, and taking corrective measures when necessary. Deviations or delays of any activity along the critical path will delay the entire project, unless other tasks can be accelerated. Acceleration is not always possible, however, because some tasks cannot begin until other tasks are complete. For instance, as described in the earlier example, the printing of a direct marketing piece cannot begin until the graphic designer completes the design. Likewise, the direct marketing piece cannot be mailed until the printer has completed its job.

The most effective method of controlling the project management process is by utilizing the Gantt chart diagram method mentioned earlier in this chapter (SEE FIGURE 1). By taking our case study example and converting the Excel spreadsheet into a horizontal bar chart, it becomes clear when each action item must begin, which items are dependent upon completion of other items, who is responsible, and when each deliverable is due.

FIGURE 1: Example of Gantt chart

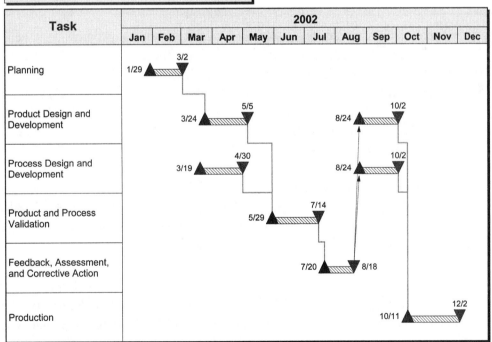

The delay that is created when tasks do not meet their intended deadline is referred to as slippage. Slippage is an early indication that a project is not progressing as planned. It is also the first warning sign that a crisis could occur during the show, if not before then. When shipments aren't sent on time, they aren't received on time, and this could launch a chain reaction of events from which show management may be unable to recover.

The simplest way to avoid slippage is to build in float time by over estimating time needed at the beginning of the process when you are estimating and establishing deadlines in the project plan. The show manager should recognize in advance and accept the fact that there will be unanticipated delays in every project. People fall ill, shipments get lost in transit and computer systems crash. Take these possible scenarios into consideration when estimating deadlines and timelines.

In addition to overestimating timelines, it is also wise to overestimate expenses. This will allow some breathing room in the budget for unexpected expenditures such as rush charges, postage increases and overtime.

There are two key elements to exercise control of a project
• Milestones (Clear, unambiguous targets of what deliverable is due and when)
• Consistent communication

For the project manager, milestones are a means to monitor progress. For the team however, they are tangible short-term goals offering more opportunity for immediate gratification than the distant completion of an entire project. Milestones maintain the team's momentum and encourage individual effort. They enable the team to measure their own progress, and to celebrate achievement throughout various phases of the project rather than just at its end.

Communication is the key to controlling the entire project. From gauging your team's progress and recognizing early indications of slippage, to promoting cooperation and continually motivating the team; all of these factors rely upon clear, consistent, communication. One way to facilitate communication is to establish a regular reporting structure.

First, provide the team the level of detail expected in each report including concrete, tangible facts, figures, and data. For example, the statement, "I called the printer to check on the status of the direct mail piece" is inadequate and useless. The information needed from the team should address the following questions:
• Did they speak to the printer or leave a voice mail?
• Did they follow up with an email?

- Did the printer send the order via UPS or FedEx?
- Was the shipment sent 2-day, ground, or priority overnight?
- What is the shipment tracking number?

Having the answers to the above questions will enable the show manager to closely follow the shipment, know when to expect its arrival, and allow some lead time to make alternate arrangements if the shipment is lost or delayed.

Second, set a specific time of the day and week for the team to meet or submit the status report. For example, a kick-off meeting on Monday mornings at 9:00 a.m. is a great jump start for the team each week. Depending on the size of the show and the size of the team, a second, mid-week status report may be needed. As the show date approaches, however, a daily meeting or status update might be in order.

Finally, insist on consistency. If progress reports are not submitted regularly and on time, it will be impossible to correct any deviations that occur along the critical path and will, therefore, encounter slippage. The true value of the communication process will become evident the first time it becomes evident that the plan is not progressing according to schedule.

Post Show Analysis

The final stage in the exhibition lifespan is the post-show analysis, which involves the review and evaluation of the completed event. Ironically, the post-show analysis actually begins long before the event fills the exhibit hall. As early as the promotion stage of the exhibition lifespan, show management can evaluate the results of the marketing campaign and identify more cost-effective, time-efficient methods to accomplish the tasks in the project plan.

In addition to surveying the team on how to improve internal processes, pre-event surveys of exhibitors and sponsors can assist with the event's success by helping gauge expectations prior to the show. Subsequently, post-event surveys are often conducted online (there are numerous products available to make this process quick and easy for the user) to gather comments and suggestions, and offer show management the benefits of tracking each evaluation.

SUMMARY

Project management is a critical function of the exhibition planning process which revolves around planning, organizing, directing and controlling – skills that are also useful in all areas of business management. Developing a Gantt chart diagram in the first lifespan phase of an exhibition can prove to be a helpful project management tool throughout the remaining life cycle of the event.

Section IV: Show Planning

QUESTIONS FOR DISCUSSION

① What is your current system for organizing tasks you need to do each day?

② If you have had training in other types of Project Management, what other methods or systems were you taught to use? Did they work for you?

③ Who do you think needs Project Management skills more: a chef, an accountant, a letter carrier, or an exhibition manager? Why?

Chapter 2
Floorplan Development

"It is often assumed that these complex [floor] plans adversely affect the performance of individual exhibits because of irregular traffic flow patterns ... average booth traffic scores indicate that location in a show is not a factor in booth traffic."

– Tradeshow Bureau Report (now CEIR)

Section IV: Show Planning

IN THIS CHAPTER YOU WILL LEARN
- The many separate factors that go into the design of a floorplan
- The importance of fire and safety codes and security and safety issues
- How different attendee and exhibitor profiles affect floorplan design
- How each facility's unique design impacts the floorplan
- Space assignment systems and how they affect the design
- Options for automation

INTRODUCTION

None of the many elements that are crucial to the success of an exhibition is as basic as the floorplan. A schematic drawing of the exhibit hall that includes the booths available for rental to the exhibitors, all obstructions, entrances, utility ports, and fixed services areas, the floorplan is the working drawing that becomes the exhibition marketplace. Without a workable floorplan that has been tailored to meet the needs of the exhibitors, and that functions within the physical parameters of the facility, the chances for a successful show are limited.

CONTRIBUTOR

Julia Smith, CEM, Vice President of Sales, GES Exposition Services

Strategic Planning

The floorplan is one of the most important elements to the success of an exhibition. Development of a strategic and accurate plan will provide access to all exhibitors and specialty areas, and will also impact the logistics of moving the show in and out of the facility. Ultimately, goals to consider when developing a floorplan are:

- Is it easy to read and navigate?
- Can contractors and exhibitors accomplish what they need to during move-in and move-out on deadline?
- Are all fire and safety codes being observed?
- Is there flexibility built into the plan if the layout needs to be expanded or reconfigured for any reason?
- Will it result in an attractive and functional show?
- Will exhibitors and sponsors be satisfied that they "got what they bought?"
- Does it incorporate feature areas that add value to the event?

This checklist and the elements discussed throughout this chapter will help drive a floorplan design that will meet the expectations of all the exhibition's audiences.

Developing a Floorplan

There are a number of elements that contribute to the creation of an effective floorplan, one that creates a positive selling environment for exhibitors and expedites the attendees' visit to the exhibit hall. Before diving in to the creation of a new floorplan, consider the following:

- Analysis of the strengths and weaknesses of existing plans
- Analysis of the strengths and weaknesses of the facility
- Exhibitor, industry and attendee demographics
- How space assignment or seniority systems will affect planning
- Aesthetic and visual appeal of various approaches
- Traffic flow patterns based on the layout as well as attendee behavior
- Security and safety restrictions and concerns.

Analysis of the Strengths and Weaknesses of Existing Plans

Sometimes, a show manager inherits an existing plan if he or she has changed jobs or assignments within the organization, or if the exhibition stays in the same facility year after year. It is easy to be complacent about an existing plan, particularly if it seems to be working. However, with the rapid change in business trends, and the changing buying habits of attendees, it is important to do a critical analysis of the show layout every year. A plan that never changes can become stale, and can result in attendees shopping in a pre-programmed pattern. It also may not meet the needs of an industry undergoing change, requiring consolidations or focus on "hot" new items. There are a number of ways to check the viability of an existing plan:

- Walk the show floor. Although there are many demands on a show manager's time at the show site, it is important to take the time to walk the show as an attendee would once the show is open. Make notes of areas with slow traffic, areas that are crowded, locations with line-of-sight challenges, and feature areas that are or are not drawing interest. Don't wait for exhibitors to come to the show office with complaints; ask them for their feedback. Look at how the exhibitors are using their space, and how that impacts the traffic patterns.

- Watch the show from above. Many convention centers have offices with windows on a level above the show floor, or a catwalk above the show, from which to view the traffic from overhead. Notice how traffic flows from the time attendees enter the hall until the time they depart. Do they break right when they enter the hall? Do they stop in island booths with open displays? Are they heading straight to food service areas for their morning coffee, then walking the floor from there? Are there areas of the floor that are not being visited at all?

- Conduct surveys of both exhibitors and attendees. While disgruntled exhibitors are usually forthcoming with unsolicited feedback, show managers may not hear directly from attendees about their show experience. As attendees trend toward shortening the length of their trips, they are looking for efficient ways to work the exhibition floor. Gather information about the types of products or services they are seeking, as well as information about whether they are there to research or to purchase.

- Visit the public areas. Analyze whether the registration layout, directional signs, entrance treatments and other areas are effective in driving traffic to the exhibit area, and where they distract from it.

Analysis of the Strengths and Weaknesses of Facility Features

A facility can be chosen for many different reasons, including a geographic rotation required by an association, costs, potential attendee draw or local base of potential attendees, size of space and/or hotel block needed, modes of transportation available, meeting room requirements or local host committee involvement.

Competing needs may result in an event being booked in a facility that draws quality attendees, but may pose some logistical challenges for an exhibition of a certain profile. Therefore, it is important to identify all of the features unique to the facility that will impact the event either positively or negatively. Then, the floorplan can be designed or altered to capitalize on the best features, and minimize any challenges. Ideally, these features will be identified through a site visit with key players. Walking the space twice – when it is empty, and when other events are in the facility – will give a visual understanding of the space.

Support team members can also give insight. Official services contractors with experience working in the facility are an excellent source of information, as well as the source for the original floorplan, revisions, and the final approved plan. The facility event coordinator and other support contractors can provide information based on their experiences in the exhibit space. Contact show managers of other events that have been held recently within the facility.

If a show organizer is unable to visit a facility prior to producing an exhibition within its space due to budget or timing issues, it is critical to use all of these resources. A one-dimensional floorplan tells only part of the story.

Many organizations have separate sales and operations teams. It is important that both teams be aligned with the goals of the plan, and that the sales team has sufficient operational understanding of the facility so that they do not place an exhibitor with special logistical needs or booth features in the wrong space. For instance, an exhibitor with a hanging sign needs to be in an area with sufficient ceiling height and rigging points; an exhibitor with a complex booth should not be placed in front of a freight door. Knowledge of the facility features gives the show manager an opportunity to maximize revenue, drive visual impact, manage logistics effectively, and drive greater interaction between exhibitors, attendees, sponsors, and the organization.

Exhibitor, Attendee and Industry Profiles

To create an effective floorplan, a working and current understanding of how the show's audience does business is critical. Assumptions must be continually updated based on changes in the industry, and the show's exhibitor and attendee bases.

The exhibition was created to meet the needs of a particular industry segment, but the event format can become obsolete almost overnight, particularly in technology fields or industries impacted by technology. Other trends that can impact a show's floorplan include industry consolidation (a merger of two companies can create a significant hole in an existing floorplan); new developments (invention of a surgical procedure or equipment can result in a pharmaceutical company needing expanded space); or market saturation and penetration.

Attendance at certain types of shows can even be driven by local and world events. After the events of 9/11, there was a trend towards "nesting," and many consumer events such as home and garden shows saw a surge in attendance. Interest rates and local disasters can impact building materials shows or servicing the home sales market.

The exhibitor prospectus and other marketing materials must reflect an understanding of the industry, and the show layout should be complimentary to the shopping habits of the attendees. In short, the successful show manager must determine how best to showcase the products and services that meet the needs of the show's designated market in a temporary exhibit environment.

Consider how exhibitors showcase their products, and how much time attendees have to spend on the show floor, based on the educational program, outside activities, and their average time in town for the meeting.

Whether a show is horizontal or vertical may impact design also. A horizontal show is one that is large in scope and includes many aspects of one industry; a vertical show strictly limits participation to a particular segment of the broader industry. For example, a horizontal show may need to be designed and sold in designated product zones so that attendees are not frustrated by a search through "miles of aisles" to comparison shop. Medical and scientific shows have unique requirements also. Professionals like doctors, nurses and scientists may need to attend an aggressive schedule of educational sessions, so mingling laboratory spaces, poster sessions, and other educational opportunities with the booth space on the show floor is common at these types of exhibitions. Having a current understanding of the show's exhibitors, attendees and the industries they represent will assist in the design of a flexible, contemporary and user-friendly floorplan.

Space Assignment Systems

Many established exhibitions use points or assignment systems when selling exhibit space. A priority points system may be based on the years an organization has participated in a show, the amount of space purchased, and other participation such as sponsorships and advertising dollars spent. When designing a plan to work within a points system, the floorplan must:

- Accommodate the space requirements of the established exhibitors who typically take the same amount of space each year
- Be able to meet the needs of new exhibitors, or established exhibitors who wish to grow their space
- Be flexible enough to adjust to the fluctuations of the market
- Be able to be adapted to different facilities or halls.

The model must be flexible enough to ensure that established exhibitors are satisfied, while allowing newer exhibitors an opportunity for good space and movement. The system must also allow for the ability to make changes for the good of the overall show, to drive traffic and keep a plan fresh and interesting. There are an infinite number of formulas that could be used to design space assignment systems. Regardless of which system is used, it should be consistently communicated and applied, easy to understand, and adaptable to the changing needs of the exhibition.

Aesthetic and Visual Appeal

Aesthetic and visual appeal within an exhibition layout relate to more than graphics and other décor. A floorplan should make attendees feel comfortable while they are moving throughout the floor without dodging obstacles or taking circuitous routes around large exhibits or other focal points. Designing a floorplan often involves working with a flat drawing on a desk or screen. Try to envision how the areas will be viewed when walking around them. Ask these questions when evaluating a potential floorplan design:

- Does the entrance to the exhibit hall invite attendees to explore the marketplace that has been created?
- Does traffic flow logically from the public space to the exhibit space to the feature areas?
- Are sponsorship elements and management décor items additions to the exhibit area, or do they actually impede flow?

Visual appeal should also include strategic placement of exhibitors on the floor. Even if a show organizer is working with a priority placement program, the placement of various sizes and types of displays must still be controlled. If all of the largest exhibitors are assigned spaces in the front of the hall, attendees may be met with a visual barrier when entering the hall, unless the exhibitors have open booth design. One solution is to design a setback in the front of the hall, but this may not be the most efficient use of space, particularly if there are space limitations.

Traffic Flow Patterns

Traffic flow refers to the manner in which people move from place to place within a defined area. Traffic flow can be impacted by the following:

- The number, type and size of exhibits, and their layouts
- The number of attendees, the exhibit hours and competing events, and the shopping habits of attendees
- The number and width of main aisles and cross aisles
- The type of activity within exhibit spaces – such as demonstrations or activities – that are stopping or diverting traffic
- The location of any activities within other areas on the exhibit floor, such as food service areas, and bookstores
- The placement and number of entrances and exits
- The location of registration, meeting rooms, and other key areas
- Directional signs, product locators, booth numbers and aisle signs.

Number and Size of Exhibit Spaces

Most exhibition floorplans in the United States are based on a 10' x 10' grid. A typical floorplan in a convention center would have aisles of 10' x 10' booths on either side of a 10' aisle.

One reason for the 10' x 10' grid is the placement of utility ports. If the utilities are accessed through floor ports, they are often placed on thirty-foot centers. This means that the ports would be located on the back wall line, rather than in the center of a booth or aisle. Ideally, columns are also placed to work within this grid.

SEE FIGURE 1

Booths can also be based on a grid that is 8' deep and 10' wide. This configuration is sometimes used in smaller areas such as hotel ballrooms to maximize the space, particularly if utility placement is not an issue, and aisles can be approved at 8' or 9'. However, it is important to keep the 10' width to accommodate pre-fabricated booth structures. Contractor equipment is also fabricated to work within these standard booth grids. The pipe used to suspend booth drape is adjustable to 8', 9' and 10' lengths, and standard aisle carpet is generally manufactured in 7'6", 9' and 10' widths.

Booths laid out in these 10' x 10' configurations are considered standard or linear booths. Linear booths have an aisle on one side (the front of the booth), with the exception of corner booths, which have aisles on two sides.

SEE FIGURE 2

Island booths are made by selling and configuring a minimum of four booths together in one exhibit space, with aisles on all four sides. Islands can have one or more levels of display, depending upon the show rules and the building regulations for double-decker, or multi-storied, booths. If island booths are created within a linear layout (such as in a 20' x 20' or 20' x 30'), the amount of saleable space decreases, as more cross aisles are created. If island booths are created by selling across existing aisles (following fire regulations for the building), they can actually add to the amount of saleable space.

SEE FIGURES 3 and 4

Peninsula booths should be a minimum of 20' x 20', but have aisles on just three sides.

SEE FIGURE 5

FIGURE 1: Floor plan showing location of utility grids on backwall line (and columns)

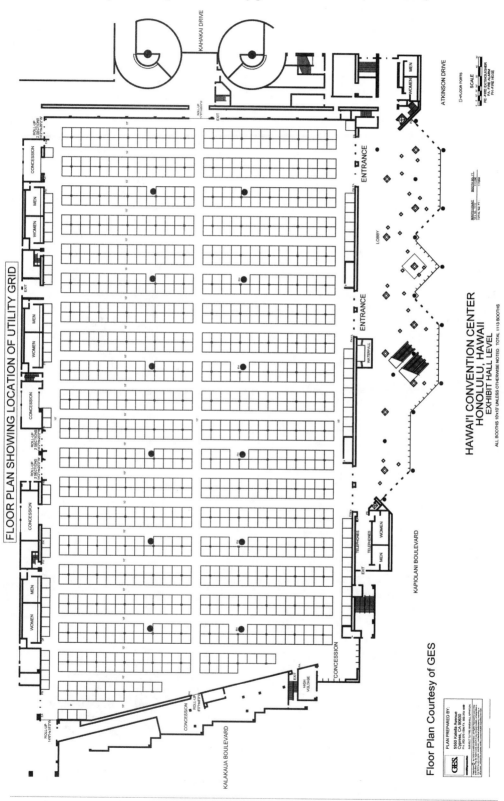

Floor Plan Courtesy of GES

FIGURE 2: Linear booth configuration (from IAEM)

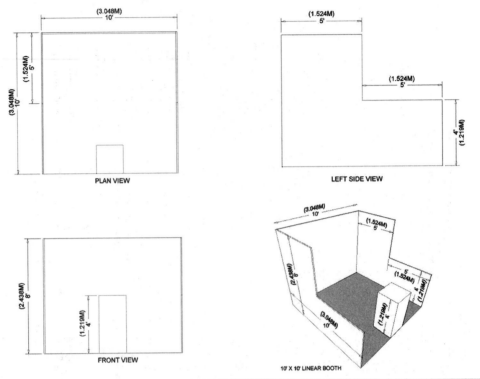

FIGURE 3: Island booth configuration (from IAEM)

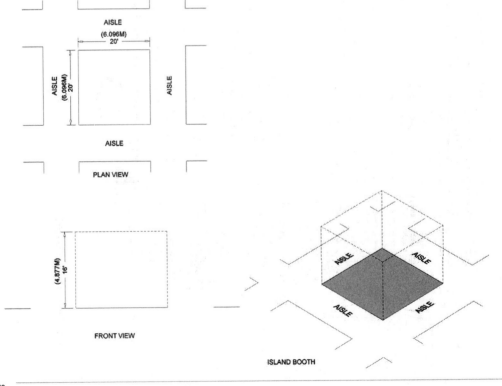

FIGURE 4: Floor plan with islands that are sold across aisles

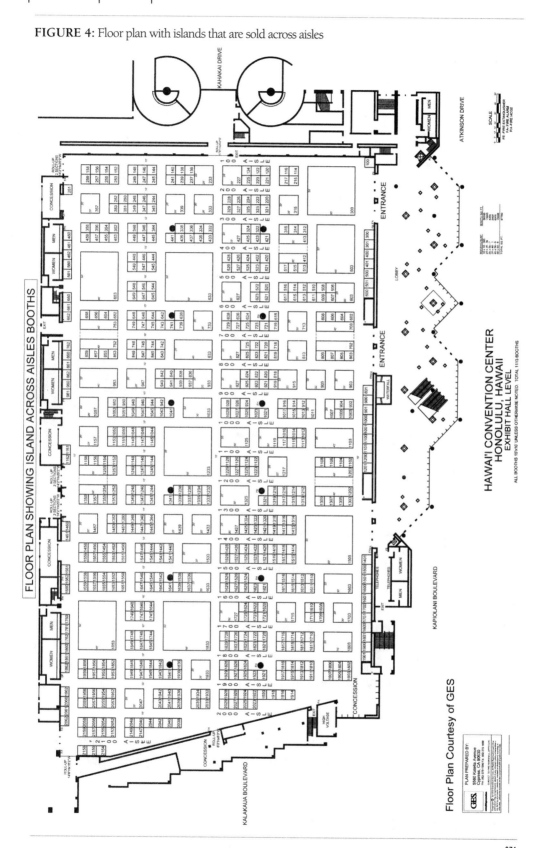

FIGURE 5: Peninsula booth configuration (from IAEM)

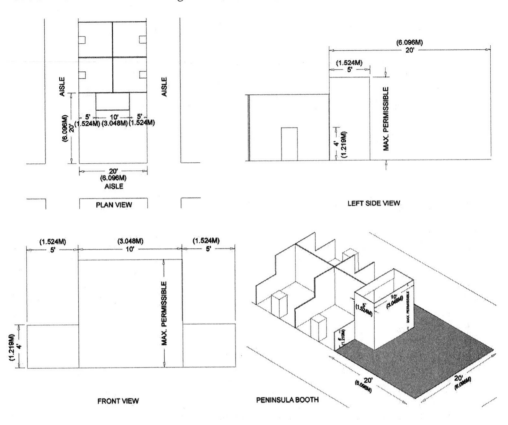

Occasionally, a show organizer will permit a 10' x 20' configuration to be sold as a peninsula. This is called an end cap. Generally, it is not advisable to sell booths in this configuration, because it is difficult to enforce the line of sight rules that apply.

Booth Numbering

The goal in numbering a floorplan is to devise a system that is logical, intuitive, and easy to follow. An attendee should be able to find a booth with a minimum of effort with a few aids, as the booth number is not always visible once booths and aisle carpet are installed. While convention center shows generally will have aisle signs, an exhibition in a hotel or facility with a low ceiling may not.

There are several numbering methods used for floorplans. The most common is street style numbering. Like buildings on a city street, even numbers are on one side of the aisle, with odd numbers on the other.

SEE FIGURE 6

FIGURE 6: Floor plan with street-style numbering

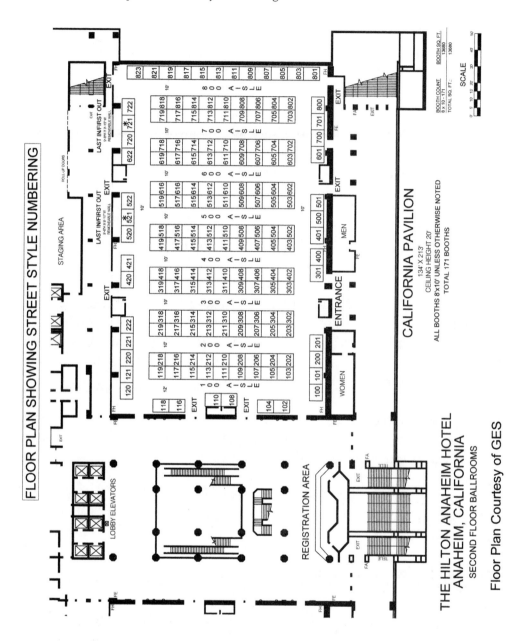

Sequential and/or serpentine numbering is typically used for smaller events such as those in hotel ballrooms. Sequential numbering may also be used in a particularly long aisle to avoid using four-digit booth numbers. In such a case, the 100 series could be on the left side of the aisle; the 200 series on the right. In serpentine numbering, the numbers wind up on side of an aisle and down the other. Some general tips about numbering:

- When numbering across a cross aisle, or other open area which could be used for exhibits, skip the next number(s) in sequence for that space. This allows for reconfiguration of the plan, without creating odd numbers such as 103a.
- When numbering a group of booths reconfigured into an island or peninsula, the lowest number in the booth grouping becomes the new number for the island or booth for consistency.
- Conversely, if island and peninsula spaces are included in the original plan, reserve all of the remaining numbers which would have identified the individual booths that made up the island. If the island or peninsula exhibitor cancels, the booth can be broken down and renumbered and sold as linear booths.

Aisle Sizes

Aisle widths may vary depending upon the applicable fire codes, the facility, and the show needs. Other factors that impact aisle width include anticipated attendance, special activities, move-in and move-out logistics, and aesthetics.

Local ordinances, fire codes, and facility rules may dictate not only the aisle width of a standard aisle, but may also set standards for total number of aisles, length and width of cross aisles, placement of aisles in conjunction with exits, and no-freight aisles. No freight aisles must be kept clear even during move-in and move-out, for access during emergencies and other safety reasons.

The volume and type of exhibit materials and freight in the show, the show schedule, and the type of equipment used in the set-up, such as fork lifts, boom or scissor lifts, or even cranes, can necessitate wider or additional aisles.

In general, an approved layout is essential before beginning to sell booth space. Make sure that any major reconfigurations impacting aisles are re-approved by the fire inspector and facility.

Feature and Presentation Areas

The show organizer may also choose to include feature and presentation areas on the show floor in addition to the traditional use of exhibit space. Features can draw traffic to the show floor and keep attendees on the show floor longer, but they can also create distractions that pull attendees away from the business being conducted by exhibitors. Feature areas may include:

- Cyber Cafes Computer-access stations)
- Food service stations/cafes/seating
- Association booths
- Bookstores
- Poster sessions

- Registration areas
- New product displays
- Product demonstration areas
- Cooking demonstrations
- Fashion shows
- Sports demonstrations or activities (like "hole in one" contests)
- Prize drawing/raffle areas

Strategic placement of feature areas can draw traffic to traditionally slow traffic areas. The availability of food and beverages – either sponsored or for purchase – can keep attendees from leaving the exhibition for meals or coffee.

Although prize drawings and new products can create tie-ins that draw interest to participating exhibitors, care must be taken that the noise and other activities do not interfere with the business environment on the floor.

Entrances and Exits

The location of entrances and exits are key drivers to the traffic patterns in the hall, and the designation of prime space. Entrances should be clearly indicated on the floorplan used in the exhibitor prospectus and on any other selling tools, such as an online plan. At the show site, entrances should be indicated by the appropriate combinations of directional signs, banners and other entrance treatments, which will be specific to the facility and the show. Within the hall, all exits should be easily located, and all illuminated exit signs must be uncovered and visible for both safety and traffic purposes.

Security and Safety

A show manager is responsible for ensuring that a floorplan meets all applicable safety and fire codes. From the initial plan design through all phases of reconfiguration, the goal is a workable plan that will be approved by the local fire inspector. The facility event coordinator, the convention bureau staff, and the show's local service contractors can provide information and guidance in these areas. Different rules apply in different cities and even facilities for fire marshal approval of the plan.

In addition to starting the sales process with a plan that is approvable, a show manager will need to know when the plan must be submitted for approval, and what types of changes necessitate that the plan be re-submitted. While the show's official services contractor can be of assistance in this process, the show manager must make sure there is a final, stamped and approved plan, and that it is on show site from the first day of move-in. On-site, the show manager is responsible for understanding and enforcing codes and regulations that may be as diverse as:

- How working machinery can be operated
- If food can be prepared in a booth
- Whether live animals can be displayed
- How vehicles must be prepared for display
- The number of attendees that can be in the hall at once
- Providing access to fire extinguishers, alarms and hoses.

In general, if items such as booths or feature areas are being removed from a plan, it will not need to be resubmitted. If items are being added or being changed significantly, the plan may need to be resubmitted. The more detailed the plan, the less likely that there will be issues at the show site, as there will be no surprises for the fire marshal.

A detailed floorplan will also help contractors and the facility set up the areas accurately, as it can be attached to work orders as a visual aid. Failure to observe applicable rules, or to obtain and follow an approved plan, can result in fines for both the show manager and individual exhibitors; it could even cause the show to be closed.

SEE FIGURE 7

Working with the Contractor

The official services contractor (OSC) is an excellent resource for what works in a particular facility or hall, and preparing the plan is typically a part of the contractual agreement with the OSC. The contractor can also provide an initial maxed out plan (a standard plan for the exhibit space that shows the maximum number of booths available for sale). Most show organizers start the floorplan design for a new location using a maxed out plan, or have the contractor apply the configurations from the most recent plan to the new space. If there is an in-house system for doing so, the show organizer can either maintain his or her own plan from this starting point, or have the contractor maintain all updates.

Automation and Floorplan Design

Floorplans produced by the official services contractor are generally maintained using AutoCAD (automated computer aided design) software. There are many software systems available now to assist show managers in maintaining and updating their own floorplans. Many show managers offer exhibitors the opportunity to select their space online, reconfiguring the space as the sales are made.

If a show manager maintains his or her own plan, regular updates should be provided to the contractor so that both parties are working from the same plan, particularly if the contractor is obtaining fire and safety approvals. Some of the available systems allow show managers to build in show-specific rules, so that these

FIGURE 7: Sample registration diagram

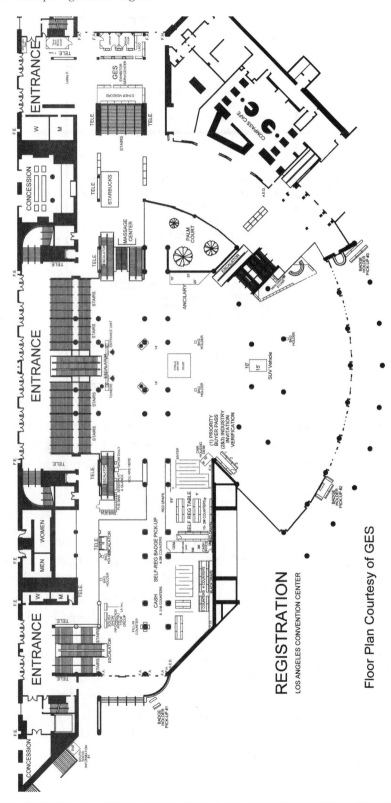

FIGURE 8: Sample legend

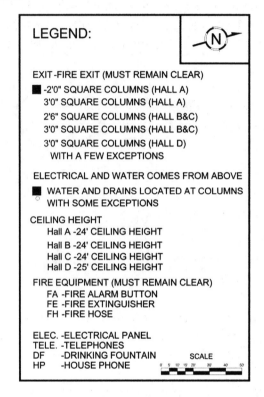

parameters are automatically considered and errors are not made when changes are made. The OSC is generally knowledgeable about what changes can create problems. In general, the systems maintained by OSCs are more robust than the systems used by show managers, and contain more detailed information, such as alternate views showing rigging and utility grids.

Whether the team is selling by way of a printed plan or a virtual plan (some shows post the floorplan online and update as commitments for specific booth locations are received), the show manager must ensure that all important elements are visible. Columns should be clearly marked with dimensions. Booth dimensions should be obvious. Entrances and exits should have arrows. There should be a legible legend (a key to abbreviations and symbols) with information on utility access, aisle widths and definitions of any abbreviations noted on the plan as well as an indication of the scale used (how the size of the plan relates to actual feet). The OSC also needs a regularly updated exhibitor list with booth dimensions to cross-reference with the floorplan. The data is used not only for mailings, order entry and to manage incoming calls for information, but also to ensure that exhibitor materials and rental items are delivered correctly.

SEE FIGURE 8

Tips for Designing Floorplans

This chapter contains the basic premises used to design a working floorplan. Each show has needs that are unique, and they continue to change as exhibitors, attendees and industries evolve. When developing a floorplan for the next show, remember the following:

- Visit other events for ideas
- Stay apprised of industry developments
- Survey exhibitors and attendees
- Design with options for reconfiguration
- Review the traffic flow in the exhibit hall selected
- Research the security, safety, and other applicable codes
- Build in features to enhance traffic
- Work closely with your official services contractor
- Review your space assignment systems
- Include key details for the approval process.

Keeping these elements in mind will increase the show manager's chances for presenting a vibrant and successful temporary marketing environment.

SUMMARY

After a strategic plan is created based on the event's particular characteristics, its "details, details and more details" that create an optimal floorplan. After the show organizer and the official services contractor work closely together to develop the initial plan to begin booth sales, many changes often take place before the doors open on the first show day. Tracking these changes, monitoring the requirements of all parties, and keeping all parties informed is a formidable challenge.

QUESTIONS FOR DISCUSSION

① Who has the primary responsibility for making sure the floorplan is drawn correctly?

② What would you do if the large exhibitors at your show wanted to be located as close as possible to the main entrance?

③ What are some of the other most popular locations in an exhibit hall?

Section IV: Show Planning

Chapter 3
Educational Programming

"Gold has its price. Learning is priceless."
– Ancient Eastern proverb

Section IV: Show Planning

IN THIS CHAPTER YOU WILL LEARN
- Why exhibitions include educational sessions
- What you need to know about your audiences
- Options in formats for educational sessions
- How to create the best learning environment possible

INTRODUCTION

Providing educational programming is an increasingly vital component to the overall objective of trade, consumer and international exhibitions. For many industry professionals, attending seminars before, during or after an exhibition may be the only continuing adult education they receive. Most non-profit associations offer some type of educational programming during their annual conventions, regional events, and chapter meetings. For example, the International Association for Exposition Management (IAEM) hosts an annual convention and exhibition in the fall called Expo! Expo! This event provides attendees with dozens of educational seminars to help them stay on the cutting edge of the exhibition industry. IAEM also hosts a spring event called the Professional Development Conference and Supplier Showcase. Both provide a forum for the exchange of information, and allow attendees to share best practices. Programming is also available at regional chapter meetings and in online formats.

CONTRIBUTOR

Curtis Love, PhD, Assistant Professor, UNLV, College of Hotel Administration

The Purpose of Programming

Some organizations include programming as part of the overall registration package for their events. The availability of educational sessions is a value-added service that can be used to attract attendees, and is often free of charge. Other organizations use programming as a revenue stream, and either charge per session, or create registration packages that allow attendees to select a number of seminars to attend for a set price.

In addition, many industry associations are creating certification programs to assist members in career development, as well as to provide another revenue stream for the association. Attending a certain number of classes and receiving Continuing Education Units (CEUs) may be one of several requirements to pursue official certification to obtain a license to practice in a particular industry. One CEU is roughly equivalent to 10 hours of learning in a structured situation. Examples would include people practicing in the medical, social work or counseling fields. Certification programs can also make a statement about a person's professionalism or experience in a particular industry. In hospitality, for example, the Convention Industry Council (www.conventionindustry.org) administers the Certified Meeting Professional (CMP) designation – a widely-recognized certification program. Applicants must accrue a minimum number of points to apply to take the certification exam. Points are awarded based on employment and activity in the convention industry. Attending educational seminars can account for up to 15 points of the 90-point minimum required to sit for the exam.

The Program Plan

As with planning the logistics for an exhibition, program planning begins with setting clear objectives. Program objectives tend to deal with operational issues, and have a "bottom-line" focus. They are usually very broadly defined, and underscore the educational mandate of the association or organization hosting the program. An example of a program objective might be: "To develop 25 workshops for member education at the annual meeting."

On the other hand, learning objectives flow from the program objectives, and focus on the intended learning outcomes for the program. They are learner or attendee-centered. Learning objectives can impact the selection of the educational format, speakers, room sets, audio-visual needs and many other factors. An example of a learning objective would be: "To develop a 50-minute workshop on using Web site design to facilitate attendee registration."

Questions to answer when planning this particular workshop might include: Will this session require extensive audio-visual needs, such as a computer, projection equipment and wireless Internet connection? Will attendees need to be seated at tables to take notes? How many attendees are likely to attend? How extensive should the attendee's knowledge of Web design be prior to attending?

Once the program and learning objectives are established, it is important to ensure that the two sides of the event program – the exhibition and the education program – work together for the common welfare of the attendees and the sponsoring organization. If there are different people planning the exhibition and educational programming, communication between the two must be constant, clear, and concrete. It is absolutely critical that each party knows exactly what the other is doing. Scheduling conflicts must be avoided at all costs. Try to minimize or eliminate scheduling educational seminars during show hours to avoid creating a climate of competition for the attendees' time. Show hours should be reserved for attendees to network and do business with the exhibitors.

The timing of educational sessions should not overlap with show hours, causing attendees to leave the show floor. Likewise, educational sessions should be scheduled before or after show hours so attendees can focus on their education, not necessarily business. In addition, those planning the exhibition and those planning the programming should work together in the promotion of the event. It is far better to promote the combined value of an exhibition and an educational program than to promote the two as separate entities.

Program Attendee Profile

Before a show organizer can start planning the format and content of the educational program, he or she needs information regarding who the audience will be.

Demographic information such as gender, age, nationality, experience level and professional status can impact the topics, delivery method, and depth of the content. The typical attendee's position in an organizational hierarchy often has an impact on educational needs. For example, junior and mid-level managers may be looking for ways to increase their potentials for advancement. Senior-level personnel may be more interested in strategic planning, leadership or more global economic issues. Many organizations create education tracks by identifying audience groups – that is, buyers and exhibitors – and creating programming specifically for that group. Further refinement would entail creating programming at the beginning, intermediate, and advanced level. Attendees can then self-select what sessions are most appropriate for their personal needs and abilities.

The Adult Learner

The adult learner is a term used to describe anyone over the age of 17 no longer enrolled in formal education – such as high school or college – on a full time basis. Using this definition, most adults are lifelong learners. We continue to learn, in both formal and informal ways, new ideas and processes that have applications both inside and outside the workplace. In fact, in order to remain current with rapid technological change, lifelong learning is a necessity.

Industry-based exhibitions that offer educational programs that capitalize on the need for further education will have a prosperous future. Although the field of adult education is quite vast, a few simple principles will help the novice show manager plan effective educational programming:

- Adults tend to bring a more practical, problem-solving approach to learning. They tend to see information that will have immediate relevance to their work or personal lives.
- Adults tend to prefer interactive learning environments as opposed to passive lecture presentations.
- Adults bring a range of life experiences to the learning environment against which they assess, accept, reject, or interpret new information and knowledge.
- All students have different learning styles.
- A range of teaching techniques should be incorporated in the programming.
- Adults tend to be self-directed learners. They are motivated best by an internal drive to learn. Forced participation may not be productive.
- Life history, cultural and social experiences can influence how a person learns.
- Adults have a variety of obligations ranging from job responsibilities, home life, civic and social activities. Taking time out for education is usually done at the expense of some other activity. Therefore, the educational experience should be perceived to be of significant value.
- Adults need a safe environment in which to learn. They should not be afraid to ask questions, make mistakes, and stretch their imagination. Feedback from instructors and peers should be positive and constructive.

LEARNING STYLES

Because there are a variety of learning styles, it is important to communicate in the manner that is most easily accepted by the individual learner. An effective speaker can design educational content and delivery methods that will accommodate the differences between learners. Although there are four primary learning styles, it is important to note that, while most people have a dominant preference, most are a combination of the three types.

Auditory learners learn through hearing. They learn best through verbal lectures, discussions, "talking things through," and listening to what others have to say. Auditory learners interpret the underlying meanings of speech through listening to tone of voice, pitch, speed and other nuances. Written information may have little meaning until it is heard.

Tactile learners learn by touching. Tactile persons learn best through a hands-on approach, actively exploring the physical world around them. They may find it hard to sit still for long periods and may become distracted by their need for activity and exploration.

Visual learners learn through seeing. These learners prefer to watch the instructor carefully to fully grasp the educational content. They tend to prefer sitting at the front of meeting room to avoid visual obstructions such as people's heads. They may think in pictures and learn best from visual displays including: PowerPoint presentations, overhead transparencies, videos, flipcharts and handouts. During a lecture or classroom discussion, visual learners often prefer to take detailed notes to absorb the information.

Adapted from http://www.ldpride.net

Designing the Program

The learning objectives, expected number of attendees, capacity of the facility, prominence of the speaker and other factors will impact the type of session format that is selected. There are a variety of session formats in use. The following are adapted from the Professional Meeting Management Association, a major professional organization for people who plan, execute or supply services for meetings and events.

- General Sessions or Plenary Session
  A session that all meeting participants attend. Industry leaders or well-known speakers may address the audience. General Sessions are often used to motivate, inform, and entertain attendees.

- Workshops
  Small groups who join a subject matter expert for a presentation on a particular topic. May be in a lecture format, but will preferably involve discussion and activity within the group. Often led by industry peers of the attendees – someone who is has considerable knowledge of the subject matter.

- Break-out Sessions
  Small discussion groups that are formed to address a specific task

- Panel Discussions
  A number of subject area specialists who each give a short presentation on a given topic. The audience is then allowed to interact with panelists and further the discussion.

- Roundtable Discussions
  A number of tables set up with a key topic expert assigned to each table. Experts lead discussion with attendees who select to sit at their table.

- Hands-on Participation
  Some topics, products and services are best showcased by providing the attendees with actual experience. For example, demonstrating a new computer software program is easier if attendees can actually try it out.

- Poster Session
  Used frequently in academic meetings, the presenter literally creates a poster summarizing their research or topic of interest. At the appointed time, the presenter stands by their poster and interacts with interested attendees on a one-on-one basis.

HOW LONG SHOULD SESSIONS LAST?

The length of sessions differs with the objectives of the meeting, the size and dynamics of the group, and the size of the facility and proximity of meeting rooms. The availability of food outlets, restrooms, and other amenities may also be a factor in determining the length of sessions, as well as how much time to schedule between sessions. In today's world of cell phones, Web-connected personal communication devices, and wireless Internet connections, it is better to err on the side of planning for a little extra time between sessions rather than too little. Many people multi-task throughout the day, juggling emails, text messages, and phone calls while they are attending events. It is very disruptive if people enter sessions late because they did not have time to take care of personal business between programs. If the meeting rooms are far removed from the exhibition floor, allow sufficient time for attendees to arrive on time. The following time guidelines are suggested by Meetings Professional International:

- Workshops: 45-60 minutes with 15 minutes for questions and answers

- Lunch with speaker: 90 minutes to two hours

- Panel Discussions: 45 -60 minutes (10 to 15 minutes per panelists including 15 minutes of question and answers)

- Refreshment breaks: 20 minutes for groups of 50; 30 minutes for larger groups

- Dinner: 30 minutes per course

- Reception: (prior to dinner) 30 minutes to one hour

- Reception-style dinner: one to two hours

- Time allowed for movement between sessions located in the same area: 5-100 people, five minutes; 100-500 people, 10 minutes; and 500+ 15 minutes

Selecting Topics and Speakers

Different approaches are used in deciding which session topics to include in educational programming. Some organizations develop topics internally – within the association, or by show management – then, qualified speakers are sought to present at the appointed time. Other organizations, especially in the non-profit association market, establish a program committee, which may operate with a program chair and several sub-committees. Topics and speakers are approved by this committee, often with input from members.

Many associations query their members with a Call for Topics (or a Call for Presentations or Papers) that basically asks members to suggest topics, session objectives and potential speakers. Typically, the Call for Topics is announced at the current year's event for the following year's schedule. It may be a paper form distributed in the registration bag, an electronic kiosk at the show seeking input, or by an email invitation sent just after an event. It can take several months to solicit and review topics, find appropriate speakers, obtain session objectives and outcomes from the speakers.

Most organizations will ask speakers to sign a contract agreeing to the topic, time and date, program length, audio-visual requirements and restrictions, required room set-up, speaker fees, expenses and reimbursements, cancellation clause, dress code, permission to audio or video tape the presentation, and even the publishing rights (print or online) of the content of the presentation. Speaker Guidelines are typically provided to inform the speaker of everything he or she will need to know about presenting to a particular group. Speaker guidelines should include information such as the history of the organization, experience levels within the group, presentation guidelines, and expectations.

PRESENTATION SUBMISSION FOR ANNUAL MEETING

Challenge yourself and your colleagues!
ABC ASSOCIATION offers education and skills enhancement through workshops and seminars. If you would like to make a recommendation or participate in a future program as a facilitator, panelist or presenter, please complete this form and return to ABC ASSOCIATION at the address below.

Please type or print clearly.

Title of presentation: _____

Session Description (50 words or less):

Learner Outcomes/Course Objectives:
Please list all benefits for participants attending your session. (Minimum of three)

1. _____

2. _____

3. _____

4. _____

Suggested Length:
☐ Workshop (1.25 hours)
☐ Seminar (2.5 hours)

Target Audience: _____

Level of presentation
☐ Basic
☐ Intermediate
☐ Advanced

Suggested Format:
☐ Lecture
☐ Panel
☐ Other: _____

_____

Suggested speaker(s): If you plan on presenting or having someone present this topic with you, please list his or her name affiliation and phone number.

Name	Affiliation	Phone Number
1. _____	_____	_____
2. _____	_____	_____
3. _____	_____	_____

IMPORTANT: If ABC ASSOCIATION's Education Committee selects your proposal, you will be required to submit a handout to be distributed on site.

Your name: _____

Designations: _____ _____ Other: _____

Title: _____

Company: _____

Address: _____ City: _____

State/Province: _____ Postal Code: _____ Country: _____

Telephone: _____ Fax: _____

E-mail: _____

Please initial:_____ IF SELECTED AS A PRESENTER: I understand that I am responsible for paying all travel-related conference expenses and the required registration fees.

Signature_____ Date of Submission: _____

Return to: ABC ASSOCIATION

Selecting speakers involves several criteria. Non-profit associations may have dozens or even hundreds of individual sessions. They rely heavily on volunteers to share their areas of expertise. Although peer-to-peer learning can be exciting and beneficial to both presenters and the attendees, there are some concerns that volunteers may not be as gifted in their presentation capabilities. Even the most brilliant people will be quickly tuned out by the audience if their presentation skills are not up to the expectations of the group. This may result in people leaving the session early and negative evaluations of the session. Some organizations hold seminars specifically to train potential speakers for their events.

On the other hand, paid speakers should be knowledgeable and professional with exceptional presentation skills. There are numerous speakers bureaus easily found on the Internet that can provide the perfect speaker for your session by topic area, profession, and price point. Some speakers bureaus provide online streaming video of presenters to help organizations determine if a speaker is right for the group. Fees for professional speakers range from a few thousand dollars up to hundreds of thousands of dollars. Highly-paid speakers are often sponsored by key exhibitors or other organizations that seek the visibility and recognition this level of sponsorship can bring.

Another source for speakers is to contact the convention and visitors bureau in the host city. Most will have a list of local celebrities, university professors, and industry leaders who can speak to your group. Using locals is cost-effective in that there may not be a need to cover the costs of transportation or hotel accommodations.

The Learning Environment

Great topics and motivational speakers are not enough to ensure the success of a programming agenda. Attendee comfort is an increasingly important consideration in planning educational sessions. The physical environment in which education takes place can have a substantial impact on the attendee's ability to learn. Components of this environment that can impact the learning experience include room sets, seating, sound, food and beverage, audio-visual arrangements, décor and temperature. The better the learning environment, the more beneficial the program will be to the attendees.

Program Objectives

Understanding the attendee is very important. Why are the attendees there? What is the objective for the function? Is it a high profile board meeting for a major company? Is it an association meeting where people will attend training sessions that will impact how they do their jobs? Is it a training session for new exhibitors on how to maximize their experience at a show? Is it a forum for discussion about key industry trends? Knowing the objectives of the event will impact all the components that comprise the learning environment.

Selecting the Room Set-up

When selecting a meeting or function room and deciding on the room set-up, the primary goal is to provide the most comfortable arrangement that will promote open communication and interaction between attendees and presenters. In selecting the appropriate room set, ask a few questions:

• What is the objective of the function?
• Is this a formal or informal function?
• How much will participants interact with each other? Will attendees be separated into work groups or teams?
• What is the relationship between presenters and participants? Will the presenter want to interact closely with the attendees, or will it be a lecture format with little discussion?
• What activities are planned? Will extra space be required to do team work?

Once it has been determined why the attendees are at the function, it is easier to select an appropriate room set for them. A common rule is to provide three feet of space for each person if tables and chairs will be utilized. Therefore, only two people should be seated at a six foot table. There are many variations, but there are five basic room sets that are commonly used.

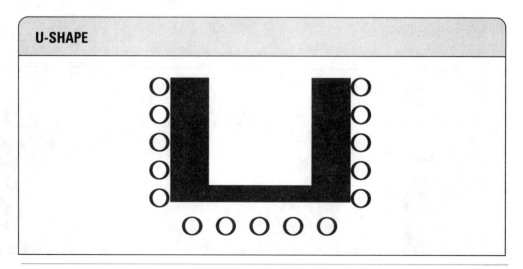

U-SHAPE

Generally used when:
- Sharing of information is the primary purpose of the meeting
- There is a need for clearly-defined leadership
- The facilitator needs access to the participants
- Training is the primary focus
- There is an emphasis on audio-visual presentations

Advantages
- Creates a feeling of connection and equity among participants
- Allows for eye and vocal contactffords participants a good view of activities going on at from of room, audio-visuals or presentations
- Allows participants to leave the room with minimal distraction
- Provides a writing surface

Disadvantages
- Setup takes up considerable space
- For maximum effectiveness, the size of the group not exceed 24 people

CLASSROOM (also called Schoolroom)

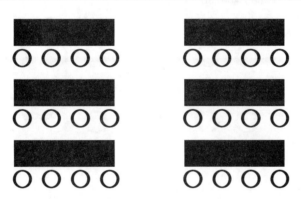

Generally used when:
- There is a need to accommodate large groups
- The meeting will be long (more than two hours)
- Considerable note-taking is required.

Advantages
- Accommodates large groups of people, up to 200 comfortably
- Provides everyone a good view of the front of the room
- Provides writing space (remember the three foot per person rule).

Disadvantages
- People in the back of the room may have difficulty seeing and hearing the presenter
- If set with a center aisle, the presenter may be looking down an aisle, not at the participants
- If set for a large group, may take require considerable space for set-up
- May be more expensive as a quantity of tables and linens may be required.

THEATRE (also called Auditorium Style)

Generally used when:
- There is a need to accommodate a large group of 200 or more
- Little interaction is expected between participants and speaker
- There is a short to moderate audio-visual or multimedia presentation

Advantages
- Maximizes seating capacity (Estimate room capacity by dividing the room dimensions by ten; so at 100' by 50' a room will hold 500 people.)
- Provides a strong central focus at the front of the room
- Most facilities have space to accommodate this setup

Disadvantages
- Note-taking is difficult
- Visual presentations may be difficult to see and hear in the back of the room
- No place to set coffee cups, plates, briefcases, laptops, and registration bags; attendees may use an adjoining empty seat for storage, thereby reducing your seating capacity

CONFERENCE STYLE (Refers to a wide variety of set-up configurations that are used for small meetings.)

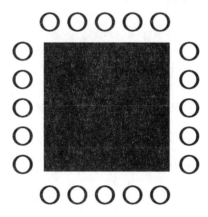

Generally used when:
- The size of the group is from five to 20 people
- Problem solving is the focus of the meeting
- A tightly controlled environment is needed
- There is a chair person facilitating the meeting.

Advantages
- It is easy for participants to interact
- Creates a sense of unity and connection among the group
- Creates a more formal atmosphere for serious work
- Allows facilitator to retain control of the meeting
- Ample writing space is available.

Disadvantages
- Seating arrangement around the table contributes to a "pecking order" mentality (boss at end of table)
- Difficult for all participants to see audio-visual presentations.

CRESCENT OR HALF-ROUNDS (Uses banquet round tables with no chairs on the table side closest to the presenter.)

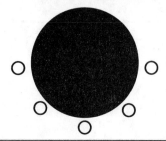

Generally used when:
- Participants are divided into groups for problem-solving
- Extensive use of workbooks, or handouts require more space
- A quick turnaround from a meal function to working in groups is needed.

Advantages
- Good set for group work (five seats at a 60" table, six seats at a 66"table, and seven at a 72" table)
- Allows for maximum comfort of attendees.

Disadvantages
- May require a lot of space, depending on the size of the group
- Sound bleed from other tables may occur.

Select Proper Seating

Banquet chairs, the standard seating accommodation in most facilities, are designed for convenient stacking and storage, not for the comfort of the meeting attendees. The average attendee may tolerate an uncomfortable chair for a few hours, but prolonged discomfort can lead to problems. Attendees will either be sore and unhappy, or they will consider leaving the meeting. If banquet chairs are the only option, allow ample room for comfort. As a rule, if using a classroom set-up, allow two chairs per six-foot table or three chairs per eight-foot table. Seat no more than eight people at a six-foot round table.

An ergonomically-designed chair with arm rests, adjustable height and proper support of the lower back is the best option if available. These are often called "eight-hour chairs," because they are comfortable for all-day meetings and events. If the facility doesn't own these types of chairs, try to rent them locally. It will make a big difference in the comfort and productivity of the meeting.

Enliven the Atmosphere

Music has an incredible impact on people. For early morning events, play upbeat instrumental music. Jazz or other quick-tempo music will stimulate attendees and prepare them for the day's activities. Use upbeat music during the day as attendees take breaks – especially after lunch when attendees begin to tire, or while doing group work. At the conclusion of the event, play softer music, such as classical or new age, to help attendees wind down and release stress. Avoid playing music with vocals, and be sure the volume is not too loud. Either the organization or the facility should be licensed to play the music so as to avoid serious legal complications.

Use Audio-Visual Wisely

Flip charts and overhead projectors are two of the most easily-tolerated forms of audio-visual (AV) equipment, and are common in most facilities. The use of PowerPoint and computer projection is also fairly common, but not all presenters are trained how to use them correctly. Most often, people try to put too much information on a single slide or page, making it difficult for anyone sitting further back than the first couple of rows to see what is written. A simple guideline is the 6 x 6 rule. There should be no more than six lines of text per slide and no more than six words in each line. Blue and black are the best colors for text. Slides should have a faint background color such as a light yellow or cream to make the text more visible. Avoid using dark backgrounds with light text as it may cause eye strain. Renting AV equipment can be a significant expense, so choose wisely and order only what is necessary.

Food and Beverage Selections

What attendees are offered to eat has a direct impact on how they function throughout the course of a meeting. Standard fare often includes breads and pastries for breakfast, pasta for lunch and perhaps cookies or other pastries for a mid-afternoon snack. All of these foods are loaded with carbohydrates and sugar, which tend to make people sleepy.

To keep attendees alert, add fresh fruits, juices and vegetables to the menu. Rather than put bowls of candy on tables, refresh and re-hydrate guests with chilled or frozen grapes or berries. Fruit "smoothies" (fresh fruit blended with ice or frozen yogurt) are always a big hit. Celery stuffed with cream cheese is another delicious and nutritious alternative. Protein-rich foods like cheese or egg dishes will also help keep attendees alert.

Create a Visual Impact

Most functions take place in multi-purpose rooms. These rooms are usually designed for flexibility, not as attractive places to gather. For example, the same room that holds a training workshop in the morning might hold a reception that evening. Even so, there are simple ways to make the décor of a room more inviting.

Plants and flowers are a great way to bring a bit of nature inside. Live foliage is best, but silk will also work. These give attendees an attractive focal point, and help disguise an otherwise plain room. Artwork on the walls will also help liven up a room. Contact local artists and allow them to display their work at your function. Consider using lightly scented candles to mask lingering food odors and refresh the stale air in many facilities. Sufficient lighting is also important. Natural light is best, but try to select meeting rooms that have adjustable lighting so you can adapt lighting needs throughout the day.

Optimizing Temperature

Temperature is one of the most common complaints of guests. Although finding a comfortable temperature for everyone is difficult, the optimal setting for a room is between 65° F and 70° F (18° C to 21° C). Too warm of an environment decreases concentration level and fosters daydreaming; too cold and attendees will be shivering.

The best way to gauge temperature is to know the show's attendees. Women and older adults typically prefer a warmer setting. Men generally prefer a cooler setting. If the group is mixed, consider setting the temperature in the cooler range, and hanging some inexpensive shawls or sweaters on a coat rack in the back of the room. People who are cold can cover up without having to adjust the room temperature. Consider selecting unattractive colors so attendees won't be tempted to "borrow" them permanently!

Feedback and Evaluation

In addition to selecting the right topics, choosing the appropriate speakers and the best delivery formats, creating the perfect room set-up, and enhancing the learning environment to maximize the learning potential of the attendees, there is still one very important component of the programming process remaining: evaluating the success of the programming.

Feedback from attendees is vital to provide quantifiable results of the programming's success, and to identify areas that need improvement. Results from session evaluations will be very helpful when selecting topics and speaker for the next year. For example, popular sessions may either be repeated, or grow from a workshop to a panel discussion. Evaluations can be paper-based and completed immediately after the session, or Internet-based and completed when convenient. Select the method that is most appropriate for the show's particular needs, and which will most likely be utilized by attendees and exhibitors.

SUMMARY

Attendees and exhibitors alike value the opportunity to learn from industry leaders, hired professional speakers, and from their peers. Planning educational programming for 10 or 10,000 requires focus on the overall objectives of event, and understanding of the adult learner, careful selection of topics and speakers, creating an effective learning environment, and thoughtful evaluation of the programming. Creating exciting and informative educational programming can greatly assist in providing a tangible value to exposition attendees.

QUESTIONS FOR DISCUSSION

① What kinds of exhibitions are least likely to have an educational component to them?

② Do you think it is better to sell tickets to individual educational sessions or to price registration to be all inclusive?

③ Is it the exhibition manager or the meeting planner who is responsible for determining how sessions rooms should be set up?

References

Connell, B., Chatfield-Taylor, C. and Collins, M. (2002) *Professional Convention Management* (4th ed.). Professional Convention Management: Chicago, IL

Meeting Professionals International (2002) Meetings and conventions: *A Planning Guide. Meeting Professionals International*: Dallas, TX

Section IV: Show Planning

Chapter 4
Food Functions & Special Events

"Sharing food with another human being is an intimate act that should not be indulged in lightly."

– MFK Fisher

Section IV: Show Planning

IN THIS CHAPTER YOU WILL LEARN

- Categories of special events, theme parties and off-site events
- The purpose and objectives of the event
- Styles of catering
- Types of meal functions, menu planning, menu design and pricing
- Types of beverage functions, beverage menu planning and pricing
- Liquor laws and third party liability
- Space requirements and room set-up

INTRODUCTION

The quality of the food, beverage and service levels can impact the overall impression of an event. While many attendees will simply regard food as fuel, for others it is an important component of the event experience. This is not an area to leave to chance, and one which requires a significant amount of specialized knowledge.

CONTRIBUTOR

Patti Shock, Professor, UNLV, College of Hotel Administration

Assessing Options for Food Service

Many planners outsource the planning and negotiation of catered events to third party planners or destination management companies. Many show managers are baffled as to what is negotiable, how event planners and caterers price, and where they will make concessions, but a working knowledge is necessary before a decision on how to manage the event is made. While it is much easier to transport a 20-member board of directors to a dinner at a local restaurant banquet room than to transport over a thousand attendees to an off-site location, show managers should expect that they may be required to do both – often at the same time.

Catering

Catered events generally have one host and one bill, and most attendees eat the same meal. An important consideration is the demographics of the group. For example, menu choices for a nurse's association would be different from a construction association. Always consider gender, age, ethnic background, and professions.

Catered events can be held in just about any location. On-premise catering is defined as being held in a facility that has its own permanent kitchens and function rooms, such as a hotel, restaurant or convention center. Off-premise catering transports food – either prepared, or to be prepared on site – to a location such as a tented area, museum, park or attraction.

Hotel and convention centers have their own catering departments which must be used. In a city-wide convention at which one hotel has been named the host hotel, most of the food functions and events are held there. Many meetings have at least one off-premise event, often the opening reception or closing gala or a themed event. Attendees want to experience some of the essence of the destination and they often get restless if they never leave the hotel.

Off-Premises Events

Two of the challenges with off-premises events (or not at the exhibition facility) are transportation and weather. Shuttle buses are an additional expense. Weather can spoil the best laid plans, so contingency measures must be arranged.

Many prominent and outstanding restaurants have banquet rooms, and larger restaurants have catering sales staff. The Internet has made it easy to research what local restaurants and special event facilities have to offer.

Just about every destination has some distinctive spaces for parties. For an off-premises event, first create a Request for Proposal (RFP) and send it to event managers or caterers in the area. After reviewing the proposals, if possible, schedule site inspections. Off-premises events are often outsourced to a Destination Management

Company (DMC). DMCs are familiar with the location, and have relationships established with the unique venues in the area. DMCs know the best caterers, decorators, shuttle companies, entertainment, and sources for any other product or service required. Although DMC services are an expense, they can often offset their costs through the discounted pricing they'll be quoted due to the volume they purchase throughout the year. Also, if there is a problem with the product or service, the DMC can usually get it resolved faster because of the amount of future business that would be jeopardized.

During the initial site inspections, ask for a copy of the facility's banquet menus and policies. Do they offer the type of menu items that would be appropriate for your group? Ask if they are prepared to handle custom menus if you decide not to use their printed offerings. When planning a custom menu, always check the skill level in the kitchen and the availability of special products.

QUESTIONS TO ASK
WHEN REQUESTING A FOOD SERVICE PROPOSAL

✓ When will I receive your written proposal?

✓ Who will I work with during the planning of the event?

✓ Who will my contact be on-site during the event?

✓ How many servers will be working the event?

✓ When is my final guarantee due?

✓ What are the chef's best menu items?

✓ What are your substitution policies for vegetarian plates and special meals?

✓ How many bartenders will be scheduled during the cocktail hour?

✓ Could you pass wine or champagne as guests arrive? Fee?

✓ Will wine be poured by the staff or placed on the tables? Extra fee?

✓ Are you ADA-compliant?

✓ What size tables do you have?

✓ What are the options for linen, chair covers, china, stemware, flatware, charger plates?

✓ What decorations do you provide for tables, buffets, and food stations?

✓ Do you provide table numbers?

✓ Can you provide a podium, mike and overhead projector?

✓ What is your policy regarding deposits and cancellations?

✓ When is the final payment due?

✓ Are there other charges for set-up, delivery, overtime, etc.?

✓ Do you take credit cards? Do you take personal checks?

✓ What percentage is overset above the guarantee?

✓ What is the sales tax?

✓ What are your gratuity/service charge policies?

✓ Are there any other fees or license requirements?

Convention Centers

Many show organizers opt to serve catered meals at the exhibition facility. Serving attendees all at once prevents strain on the restaurant outlets, keeps attendees from leaving the property, and assures that everyone will be back on time for sessions that follow.

Convention centers and stadiums usually have concession stands open. More and more tradeshows are holding the opening reception, or providing lunch on the show floor to attract attendees into the exhibits. As most convention centers are public entities, the food service is usually contracted out to companies such as ARAMARK or Sodexho. These contract food service companies have exclusive contracts, and other vendors or caterers are not allowed to work in the facility. Many convention centers have full service restaurants as well.

What to Serve

Meeting planners need to stay abreast of current food trends. For ideas on what is hot and what is not in meal planning and trends in food selection, many of the event and food trade publications are useful resources.

TYPES OF FUNCTIONS AND COMMON FOOD SELECTIONS:	
Continental Breakfast	Typically a bread or pastry, juice and coffee, although it can be upgraded with the addition of sliced fruit, yogurt and/or cold cereals.

Full Served Breakfast	Plated in the kitchen, and normally includes some type of egg dish such as scrambled eggs; a meat such as bacon or sausage, a potato item such as hashed browns, fruit and coffee.
Breakfast Buffet	A selection foods including fruits and fruit juices, egg dishes, meats, potatoes and breads
Refreshment Breaks	Often beverages only, but can include a snack such as brownies, chips or fruit.
Brunch	A late morning meal that includes both breakfast and lunch items.
Buffet Lunch	A hot or cold buffet with a variety of salads, vegetables, and meats. Deli buffets can include a make-your-own sandwich area.
Box Lunch	Packed to carry away from the hotel for a meal in a remote location. They can be eaten on a bus if there is a long ride to a destination or eaten at an off-site attraction or destination.
Full Served Lunch	A plated lunch, usually a three course hot meal, which typically includes a salad, a main course and a dessert. A one course cold meal is sometimes provided, such as a chicken salad served in a pineapple half.
Receptions	Networking events where people stand up and move around. Food is usually placed on tables around the room and/or waiters circulate with trays (sometimes called "butlered" service). There are often bars. Light receptions may only serve dry snacks and beverages and are often scheduled prior to a dinner. Heavy receptions would include hot and cold appetizers and possibly meat being carved, and are often planned instead of a dinner.
Dinner Buffet	A variety of salads, vegetables, meats, desserts and beverages. Often meats are carved and served by attendants.
Full Served Dinner	Usually a three to five course meal, including an appetizer, soup, salad, main course and a dessert. Food can be pre-plated in the kitchen (American Service), or served from trays to guests at the table (Banquet French Service).
Off-Site Event	Any event held away from the host hotel. It could be a reception at a famous landmark or a picnic at a local beach or park.
Theme Party	It can be a reception, buffet, served meal or even a refreshment break. Themes run the gamut; they can be based on the location of the event, such as a Gone with the Wind theme in Atlanta. The Internet is a great resource when looking for ideas.

Styles of Service:

There are many meal service styles, from buffets to white glove service. There is some disagreement on a few of the following definitions. This chapter follows US White House protocol. The White House publishes the *Green Book,* which explains how meals are to be served for presidential protocol. However, because of the confusion in this area, it is important to be sure that everyone involved agrees on what the service styles mean for the event.

Buffet: Tables have food attractively displayed. Guests serve themselves and take their full plates to a table to sit and eat. Beverages are most often served at the tables. Because there is no portion control, and surpluses must be built in to assure adequate quantities of each food item, buffets generally cost more than plated served meals, Allow adequate space around the table for lines to form. Provide one buffet line per 100 guests, with 120 being the break point.

Attended Buffet or **Attended Cafeteria**: Guests are served by chefs or attendants. This is more elegant and provides good portion control.

Combination Buffet: Inexpensive items, such as salads are presented buffet style, and guests serve themselves. Expensive items, such as meats, are served by an attendant for better portion control.

Plated Buffet: A selection of pre-plated foods set on a buffet table from which guests may select. This is also helpful for portion control.

Action Stations: Also called Performance Stations or Exhibition Cooking, Action stations are similar to an attended buffet, except food is being freshly prepared as guests wait and watch. Some common action stations include pastas, grilled meats or shrimp, omelets, crepes, sushi, flaming desserts, Caesar salad, Belgium waffles, and carved meats.

Reception: Light foods are served buffet style or passed on trays by servers, also known as butlered service. Guests usually stand and serve themselves, and do not usually sit down to eat. Receptions are often referred to as 'Walk and Talks." Plates can add as much as one-third to food costs, because people tend to heap food up on the plates. Some receptions serve only finger food.

Family Style or English: Guests are seated, and large serving platters and bowls of food are placed on the dining table by the servers. Guests pass the food around the table, and a waiter or food server will often carve the meat. This is an expensive style of service as surpluses must be built in.

Plated or "American Style": Guests are seated, and served food which has been pre-portioned and plated in the kitchen. Food is served from the left of the guest. The meat or entree is placed directly in front of the guest at the six o'clock position. Beverages are served from the right of the guest. When the guest has finished, both plates and glassware are removed from the right. American service is the most functional, most common, most economical, most controllable and most efficient type of service. This type of service usually has a server/guest ratio of 1:32, depending on the service level of the hotel or convention center.

Pre-Set: Some foods are already on the table when guests arrive. The most common items to preset are water, butter, bread, appetizer and/or salad. At luncheons, where time can be critical, the dessert is often preset as well. These are all cold items that hold up well.

Butlered: At receptions, butlering refers to having hors d'oeuvres passed on trays, where the guests help themselves. At dinner, butlering is an upscale type of service, with food often passed on silver trays. Guests use serving utensils to serve themselves at the table from a platter presented by the server. Butlering is similar to, and often confused with, Russian Service.

Russian: Guests are seated, and foods are cooked tableside on a *Rechaud* (portable cooking stove) that is on a *Gueridon* (a tableside cart with wheels). Servers place the food on platters (usually silver), then pass the platters at tableside. Guests help themselves from the platters. Service is from the left.

Banquet French: Guests are seated. Platters of food are assembled in the kitchen. Servers take the platters to the tables and serve from the left, placing the food on the guest's plate using two large silver forks or one fork and one spoon. Servers must be trained for this type of service.

Cart French: Less commonly used for banquets, except for small VIP functions, this style is most often used in upscale restaurants. Guests are seated and hot foods are prepared tableside using a *rechaud* on a *gueridon*. Cold foods, such as salads, are prepared only on the *gueridon*. Servers plate the finished foods directly on the guest plate, which is then placed in front of the guest from the right. Note that this is the only time food is served from the right.

Hand: Guests are seated. There is one server for every two guests. Servers wear white gloves. Foods are pre-plated. Each server carries two plates from the kitchen and stands behind the two guests assigned to him or her. At a signal from the room captain, all servings are set in front of all guests at the same time, synchronized. This procedure can be used for all courses, just the main course, or just the dessert. This is a very elegant and impressive style of service used mainly for VIP events, because the added labor is expensive.

Waiter Parade: White-gloved waiters march into the room and parade around the perimeter carrying food on trays, often to dramatic music with dimmed lights. This is especially effective with a Flaming Baked Alaska Dessert Parade. The row of flaming trays carried by the waiters slowly encircles the room. When the entire room is surrounded, the music stops and service starts. Guests are usually clapping at this point. The dessert is then brought to a side area, where it is sliced and served. Flaming dishes should never be in proximity to a guest.

The Wave: Servers are not assigned work stations or tables. All servers start at one end of the room and work straight across to the other end for both service and plate removal. All of the servers are on one team, and the whole room is the station. This is a "quick and dirty" form of service. It is not classy, but it is functional when you want fast service or the servers are inexperienced. Guests do not receive individualized attention. This is only appropriate with pre-plated foods.

Mixed Service Styles: Service styles may be changed or alternated within the meal. The whole meal does not have to conform to one type of service. For example, appetizers may be preset, the salads "Frenched" (dressing added after salads are placed on table) and the main course served American followed by a dessert buffet.

Creating a Menu

Years ago, menus rarely changed. Today, change is required to keep pace with the evolving tastes of the public. Most food trade journals feature annual opinion pieces on "What's In and What's Out," but here are some things that are generally always "in."

Seasonal Food	Locally grown produce, in-season. This is when food is at its peak flavor.
Ethnic Foods	Cuisines from ever-increasing areas of the world. The American palate has grown beyond the ethnic foods of the past – Italian, Chinese and Mexican – to include the foods of many Asian countries, the Middle East and South America.
High-Quality Ingredients	People may clip coupons for the grocery store, but when they eat out at a banquet, they want only the best. They don't want frozen, sweetened, strawberries; they prefer fresh Driscoll strawberries on their freshly- baked shortcake. They want huge, Idaho baked potatoes or Kobe beef.

Fresh Ingredients	The loss of flavor during preservation has made fresh food highly prized. Frozen, canned and dried foods are not appreciated.
New and Unusual Ingredients	Improved transportation in recent years brings new foods items that were formerly unknown to most Americans. These include cherimoyas, daikon, edamame, ugli fruit, star fruit, Yukon Gold potatoes, purple potatoes, and blood oranges. The Internet is a great source for exploring different types of exotic fruits and vegetables.
Safe Foods	Organic food consumption is increasing rapidly. Many people prefer foods free from pollution and pesticides.
Highly-Creative Presentations	Plate presentations are increasingly significant. We eat with our eyes before anything hits our taste buds.
Excellent Service	Food served promptly so that it is still hot, accompanied by gracious, polite service, adds significantly to the enjoyment of any meal.

Food Consumption Patterns

The history of the group is the most important factor when deciding how much food to order. A good determination can usually be made based on previous records. If this is a new event, or the history is not available, consider the demographics of the attendees.

General Guidelines

- Guests typically eat more during the first hour of the reception
- Guests will generally eat an average of seven *hors d' oeuvres* during the first hour
- A group that is predominately male will usually consumes more than a group that is predominantly female
- Older attendees usually eat less than their younger counterparts.

Type of Reception	Type of Eaters	# Hors d' Oeuvres per person
2 hours or less (dinner following)	Light Moderate Heavy	3-4 Pieces 5-7 Pieces 8+ Pieces
2 hours or less (no dinner)	Light Moderate Heavy	6-8 Pieces 10-12 Pieces 12+ Pieces
2-3 hours (no dinner)	Light Moderate Heavy	8-10 Pieces 10-12 Pieces 16+ Pieces

Consumption also depends on how many square feet are available for guests to move around in. In general, the tighter the quarters, the less food is consumed.

Service Timing

Fifteen minutes before you want to start service, dim the lights, ring chimes, start music, or open doors to get the guests to start moving to their tables.

The salad course should take from 20 to 30 minutes, depending on dressing or style of service. The main course should take from 30 to 50 minutes from serving to plate removal. Dessert service should take from 20 to 30 minutes.

A typical luncheon takes one hour and 15 minutes. A typical dinner takes two hours. To shorten times, consider having some items preset on the table, such as the appetizer course. For luncheons, have the dessert preset above the plate.

Menu Restrictions

Servers should know the preparation method and ingredients of every item on the menu. Many people have allergies or are restricted from eating certain items such as sugar or salt due to health concerns. While some people simply prefer not to eat red meat, others do not eat certain foods due to religious restrictions. There are several different types of vegetarians. Lacto-ovo vegetarians do not consume anything that has to be killed, but will eat animal by-products such as cheese, eggs and milk. On the other hand, vegans will not eat anything from any animal source, including dairy, butter, honey or even marshmallows. When preparing a vegetarian menu, if in doubt, opt for choices that are vegan-friendly.

Food and Beverage Attrition

Although attrition clauses are not popular with show organizers, they are beneficial because they set down legal obligations for both parties and establish liability limits. When a contract is signed, both parties want the food and beverage guarantee to be met. Caterers want to know firm numbers well in advance, while planners want to wait until the last minute to give the final guarantee. The planner usually agrees in the contract to buy a specific number of meals or to spend a specific amount of money on group food and beverage. If the guarantee is not met, the planner must pay the difference between the guarantee and the actual amount or an agreed upon percentage of the actual amount. This is called attrition.

The planner may also lose special considerations they have negotiated when facing attrition. Banquet space often is provided because of the revenue the group brings into the hotel through sleeping rooms and catered events. If the revenue is not realized, the hotel can charge for services that normally would have been complimentary, such as extra labor. The hotel could also reassign or reduce space being held for the event if minimums are not met.

Section IV: Show Planning

The catering manager's job is to maximize revenue per available room. They need a way to guarantee that money when booking a group. Show organizers should know how much revenue their event generates before negotiating an attrition clause. Caterers should determine how much money the group will be spending for the event, instead of focusing on a head count.

Beverage Events

Beverage events are popular, and include both refreshment breaks and receptions.

Refreshment breaks not only provide liquid refreshment and possibly a snack, but allow the attendee to move about, visit the rest room, return missed phone calls, and maybe move into another room for the next breakout session.

The following consumption table is provided by a meeting management company called Conferon.

HOW MUCH SHOULD YOU ORDER?			
For a Morning Break			
Drinks	All Male	All Female	50/50
Regular Coffee	Attendance x 60%	x 50%	x 55%
Decaf Coffee	Attendance x 20%	x 25%	x 25%
Tea	Attendance x 10%	x 15%	x 10%
Soda	Attendance x 25%	x 25%	x 25%
For an Afternoon Break			
Drinks	All Male	All Female	50/50
Regular Coffee	Attendance x 35%	x 30%	x 35%
Decaf Coffee	Attendance x 20%	x 20%	x 20%
Tea	Attendance x 10%	x 15%	x 10%
Soda	Attendance x 70%	x 70%	x 70%

How to use these charts: Locate the percentage associated with the makeup of your group and multiply that percentage by your overall attendance. Then divide the resulting number by 20 (six-ounce cups per gallon) to determine the number of gallons needed. Round each partial gallon up to the next highest half-gallon. For example, for a morning break at a conference that has an audience of 500 predominantly male attendees, the formula should be calculated as follows:

• Regular Coffee = 500 x 60% = 300 cups = 15 gallons
• Decaf Coffee = 500 x 20% = 100 cups = 5 gallons
• Tea = 500 x 10% = 50 cups = 2.5 gallons
• Soda = 500 x 25% = 125 sodas

Receptions are slightly different, because most provide alcoholic beverages and, most likely, a wider selection and quantity of food choices. Reasons for receptions include networking – looking for a job or business leads – and socializing, or as a way to "loosen guests up." It is far easier to sell to a relaxed potential buyer.

Categories of Liquor

The three categories of liquor are beer, wine and spirits. Beer and wine are considered soft liquor, and spirits are considered hard liquor. There are three categories of spirits:

Well Brands: Also called *house liquor*, they are less expensive liquor brands. Well brands are served when someone does not "call" a specific brand.

Call Brands: Priced in the mid-range, they are generally "called" for by name brand.

Premium Brands: These are high-quality, expensive liquors.

Beverages are typically sold:

By the Bottle: Common for *open bars* and poured wine at meal functions. The planner usually pays for all opened liquor bottles. Most hotels charge for each opened bottle, even if only one drink was poured out of it. A physical inventory is conducted at the start and finish of each event to establish the amount of liquor used. This method saves money, but can be a hassle to monitor and calculate. The show manager will not know the final cost until the end of the event. As a rule, group history will provide an indication of how much consumption to anticipate.

By the Drink: Typical for a cash bar. This method uses tickets or a cash register for control. Usually the price per drink is high enough to cover all related expenses, like lemon twists, lime wedges, olives and napkins. Drink prices are set to yield a standard beverage cost percentage set by the hotel. This is the amount of profit the hotel expects to make from the sale of the liquor. Percentages range from 12 to 18 percent for spirits, and usually around 25 percent for wine. The show manager will not know the final cost until the event has concluded.

Per Person: (Usually includes food). This is common for *open bars*. This method is more expensive for the planner, but less bother and effort. The planner chooses a plan, such as "Premium liquors for one hour," and tells the caterer how many people are coming. They agree on a price per person. (For example, $35 per person x 500 guests = $17,500.) Costs are known ahead of time, thereby avoiding any unpleasant surprises. Tickets are collected and the guarantee is monitored.

Charge per Hour: Similar to a "per person" fee structure, this method often includes a sliding scale, with higher costs for the first hour. This is because guests usually eat and drink more during the first hour, then level off. A firm guarantee must be provided before negotiating a per hour charge. Per person and per hour charges can also be combined. For example, a typical arrangement might look like this: $25 per person for the first hour, and $20 per person for the second hour. Therefore, hosting100 guests for a two-hour reception would cost $4500 ($25 x 100 =$2500 (+) $20 x 100 = $2000 (=) $4500). No consideration is given for those who arrive late or leave early; the fee is $45 per person, regardless.

Flat Rate Charge: Similar to price *per bottle*. The host pays one flat rate for the event, assuming that each guest will drink approximately two drinks during the first hour, and one drink per hour subsequently. (Confirm the history and demographics of your group.) Costs will vary based on the number of attendees, whether well, call or premium brands are used, and the type of food served.

Calculate total cost to determine the best option:
By the Bottle: If the hotel charges $80 for a bottle of Bourbon that yields 27 drinks, each drink costs the client $2.96. If guests are expected to drink two drinks per hour, for a one-hour reception for 1,000 people, purchasing by the bottle would cost $6,000. If purchased by the drink, at $4.50 per drink, the same group would cost $9,000. If purchased at $15 per person (no food), it would cost $15,000. Generally, the hotel makes more money selling per person.

Open Bar also called Host Bar: A host or sponsor pays for the event. Guests usually drink as much as they want of whatever they want. Liquor consumption is higher because someone else is paying.

Cash Bar also called No-Host Bar: Guests purchase their own drinks, usually purchasing tickets from a cashier to exchange with a bartender for a drink. At small events, the bartender may collect and serve, eliminating the cost of a cashier. Cashiers are usually charged as extra labor. Cashiers provide better control and speed up service. Bartenders do not have to handle dirty money, and then handle glassware

Combination Bar: Each attendee is given a certain number of drink tickets (usually two). If the guest wants a third drink, he or she must purchase it. Sometimes, the host pays for the first hour, and then it switches to a cash bar for the second hour. This method provides a certain number free drinks to guests, but maintains control over costs, and possible liability for providing unlimited drinks.

Limited Consumption Bar: This involves pricing by the drink, and usually a cash register is used. Hosts establish a dollar amount they are willing to spend. When the cash register reaches that amount, the bar is closed, although the bar may be reopened as a cash bar.

In all cases, extra charges are usually levied for bartenders and barbacks, cocktail servers, cashiers, security, and corkage. These items are negotiable, depending on the value of the business. For example, if a bar sells over $500 in liquor, the bartender charge may be waived. A barback is the bartender's helper, restocking liquor, and bringing fresh ice and glasses so the bartender will not have to leave the bar during service.

Show managers who wish to bring their own liquor into an establishment must check local laws. If allowed, be prepared to pay the establishment a per bottle "corkage" fee. Corkage is the fee added to liquor brought into the hotel but not purchased from the hotel. The hotel charges this fee to cover the cost of labor, use of the glasses (which must be delivered to the room, washed and placed back in storage), mixers, olives, and lemon peels.

Providing one bar/bartender per every 100 guests is normal. If all event guests are arriving at the same time, or you don't want your guests standing in long lines, you can request one bar/bartender for every 50 or 75 guests. Unless yours is very lucrative group, the hotel would most likely pass the labor charges on to you.

NUMBER OF DRINKS PER BOTTLE				
		1 ounce	1 1/4 ounce	1 1/2 ounce
Liter	33.8 ounces	33	27	22
5th - 750 ml	23.3 ounces	25	20	16

Liquor choices

Premium brands for spirits (also called hard liquor) are available in 750 ml and one-liter bottles. One 750 ml bottle equals 20 (1-1/4 ounce) servings. A one-liter bottle equals 27 (1-1/4 ounce) servings. Consumption will average three drinks per person during a normal reception period. Premium brands of wine are available in 750 ml bottles or 1.5 liters (magnums). One 750 ml bottle = five, 5-ounce servings. One 1.5 liter bottle = ten, 5-ounce servings. Consumption will usually average three glasses per person during a normal reception period, assuming that 50 percent of the people will order wine; Order thirty, 750 ml bottles for every 100 guests. Champagne should be served in a tall, narrow flute glass, instead of the classic *coupe*. Because there is less surface exposed to the air, the bubbles don't escape as fast, keeping the Champagne fresh and "bubbly."

Hospitality Suites

Hospitality suites are places for attendees to gather. Hospitality suites are typically held in a suite on a sleeping room floor in the US. They are usually sold by Catering, and handled by Room Service. Sometimes they are held in a public function room, and are both sold and serviced by Catering. Outside the US, exhibitors often provide hospitality services in the exhibit booth itself. Hospitality suites can be hosted by the sponsoring organization, a chapter of the organization, an exhibitor, a non-exhibiting corporation, an allied association or a person running for an office in the organization.

When located in hotels, they are normally open late in the evening, after 10:00 pm, but occasionally around the clock for continental breakfast in the morning, snacks and sodas in the afternoon and liquor and snacks in the evening. Some hospitality suites provide a full bar, while some only offer beer and wine. Some have an abundance of food; others have only dry snacks. Some offer desserts and specialty coffees. Consider ordering more food if the attendees have had an open evening and may not have had dinner.

Show organizers generally do not like to see "underground hospitality suites" where unofficial parties pop up. These unsanctioned party spots not only lose the organization revenue, they also add liability. The resulting court case following the "Tailhook Scandal" (in which a female cadet was groped in the hallway at a military meeting at the Las Vegas Hilton), set a precedent that a hotel can no longer claim that it does not know what is going on within the property. Liquor Laws vary from state to state and county to county. Always check the laws in your specific location. For example:
- In Las Vegas liquor can be sold 24/7
- In California, liquor cannot be sold between 2 am and 6 am
- In South Carolina, liquor is sold in airline size bottles
- In Atlanta, liquor may not be served until noon on Sundays
- In some states, liquor may not be sold at all on Sundays.

There are generally four types of illegal sales, wherever you are located:
- Sale to minors
- Sale to intoxicated persons
- Sales outside legal hours
- Improper liquor license.

There are different types of liquor licenses. There are On Sale Licenses, Off Sale Licenses, and Beer and Wine Licenses. Licenses are assigned to the property. For example, if a hotel has a liquor license, it is not valid in the public park across the street. A special temporary permit would need to be obtained.

Room Set-ups for Food Functions:
The set up of the room is a critically important area to consider. The set-up can affect

the flow of service, the amount of food and beverage that is consumed, and even the mood of the guests. The atmosphere can "make or break" a meal function, whether it's a continental breakfast or a seated dinner.

Room set-up includes tables, chairs, decor and other equipment such as portable bars, stages, and audio-visual equipment. It is vital to communicate precisely how the room is to be set up to the banquet manager. This is accomplished on the Banquet Event Order (BEO), and by using readily available room layout software that allows you to place tables, chairs and other equipment into a meeting room.

Many facilities charge room rental. Sometimes these fees can be waived, depending upon the venue and the dollar value of the event. If the event is part of a convention with room nights at the hotel, it is easier to negotiate away the room charge. However, there may be a minimum sales amount on the room. The organization may have to spend $50,000 to secure a ballroom for an event, which often means that attendees eat extremely well.

At event venues, also known as an off-premises site, whether room rental fees can be waived depends on how the venue has set up its charge/profit schedule. Most event venues charge fees. Some charge a room rental fee, some an admission fee per guest and a few charge both. Then, the catering, rentals and service costs are added on. It almost always depends on how profitable the event is for the site. Everything is negotiable.

TABLES			
Rounds	60" Round = 72" Round = 66" Round =	5 Foot Diameter = 6 Foot Diameter = compromise size	Round of 8 Round of 10 Seats 8 to 10
Rectangle	6' Long 8' Long	30" Wide 30" Wide	Banquet 6 Banquet 8
Schoolroom/ Classroom	6' or 8' Long	18" or 24" Wide	
Half Moon Table	Half of a Round Table 1/4 Hollowed		
Serpentine	Round Table		

It is important to include aisles. They allow people to move easily around the room without squeezing through chairs and disconcerting seated guests. Aisles also provide a buffer between the seating areas, and the food and beverage service areas. Aisles between tables and around food and beverage stations should be a minimum of 36" wide (three feet). It would be preferable to have 48". Leave at least a three foot aisle around the perimeter of room. Large events should have cross aisles at least six feet wide. Check with the local fire marshal for local rules and regulations. In some jurisdictions, a fire marshal must check and approve any layout for 200 or more people.

Allow 10 square feet per person at rectangle banquet tables. Allow 12-1/2 square feet per person at rounds. This assumes the facility is using standard 20" x 20" chairs

SPACE REQUIREMENTS FOR RECEPTIONS	
Minimum (tight)	5 1/2 to 6 square feet per person
Comfortably crowded	7 1/2 square feet per person
Ample room	10+ square feet per person

Don't forget to deduct space taken up for furniture before calculating the number of guests that a room will accommodate. This includes large sofas found in some hospitality suites, buffet tables, portable bars, plants, decor and props, and check-in tables.

Tablescapes

The tabletop is a stage. It sets expectations, and should reflect the theme of the event. Once seated, the focal point is the tabletop, so it is essential that it not be ignored. The centerpiece should not block sight lines for people sitting across the table from each other. Centerpieces should be low or – if high – should have a Lucite or slender pole in the middle portion so as not to obstruct vision.

The cover is the place setting, and includes placement of flatware, china, and glassware.

Napery is the term to include all table linens, including table cloths, overlays, napkins and table skirting. Props can be rented from prop houses, service contractors, and party stores, or owned by the hotel or convention center.

Staffing

Service is a critical component of any event. Many outstanding meals are spoiled by poor service. Meal service levels can run from one server per eight guests, to one server per 40 guests. Most hotel staffing guides allow for 1:32, but most show managers prefer 1:20, or 1:16 with poured wine or French service.

Show managers prefer at least:
• Rounds of 10 - 1 server for every 2 tables
• Rounds of 8 - 1 server for every 5 tables
• 1 busser for every 3 servers.

With poured wine or French Service
• Round of 10 - 2 servers for every 3 tables
• Round of 8 - 1 server for every 2 tables
• Buffets 1/40

One room captain, and one section captain for every 250 guests (25 rounds of 10) should be provided, as well as:
• 1 busser for every 4 servers
• 1 runner per 100-125 guests

French or Russian
• Rounds of 8 or 10 and 1 server per table
• 1 busser per 3 tables

Set Over Guarantee:

This is negotiable. It is the percentage of guests that the hotel will prepare for beyond the guarantee in case additional, unexpected people show up. The average overset is five percent, but it is necessary to look at the total numbers, not just the percentages. The most accurate overset percentages are a function of the total number of guests. For example:

100 guests = 10% overset

100-1000 guests = 5% overset

Over 1000 guests = 3% overset

Cocktail servers can only carry from 12 to 16 drinks per trip. Counting the time to take the order, the time to wait for the drinks at the service bar, and the time it takes to find the guest and deliver the drink, each trip to the bar takes at least 15 minutes. This only makes it possible to serve from 48 to 64 drinks per hour. Cocktail servers are usually only used at small or VIP functions.

SUMMARY

Food and beverages are an essential part of most conventions. Intelligent planning can save a remarkable amount of money. Knowing what is negotiable, and how to negotiate, is important. Food and beverage events create memories, and provide a necessary service and more than just a refueling stop. While most attendees do not give food and beverage events as a reason for attending a meeting, when asked later about the meeting, they will often rave (or complain) about these events. Catered events can set the tone of the meeting, and create great memories that can result in future convention attendance.

QUESTIONS FOR DISCUSSION

① Why do show organizers need to worry about how attendees will be fed?

② Do you think food at a catered event is likely to be better than or worse than restaurant food and why?

③ What is the largest party you or your family has ever hosted and what is your best tip for managing large numbers of people?

Chapter 5
Budgeting and Financial Planning

*"I continue to find my greatest pleasure,
and so my reward, in the work that
precedes what the world calls success."*

– Thomas A. Edison

Section IV: Show Planning

OBJECTIVES: IN THIS CHAPTER YOU WILL LEARN

- Why an understanding of budget and finance leads to a more strategic role in any organization
- How to speak knowledgeably regarding exhibition revenue and expense items
- To develop and recommend registration and exhibit fee structures
- To construct a zero-based budget
- How to understand and manage cash flow
- Why it is important to calculate return on investment

INTRODUCTION

You conducted research. You assessed your competitors. You performed market analysis. You identified a venue. The sponsoring organization thinks the exhibition is a good idea. However, before giving the go ahead to proceed, the sponsoring organization wants evidence to show that the exhibition will meet financial objectives. This chapter presents background information necessary to understand financial matters concerning the exhibition, tools and information on creating a budget, and financial help useful in planning any segment of the exhibition that involves handling monetary funds.

CONTRIBUTOR

Mary Ann Bobrow, CAE, CMP, Bobrow & Associates

Accounting Fundamentals

The show manager's role is easier if the individual has a basic understanding of accounting terms and functions. Organizations now demand more strategic thinking on the part of their employees and consultants. The greater the understanding of finance by show managers, the better equipped they will be in assuming more strategic roles within their organizations.

Basic Accounting Principles – Cash or Accrual Accounting?

Most organizations prefer using the accrual accounting method instead of the cash accounting method. Cash accounting is a system that counts revenue and expenses at the time they are received, while accrual accounting counts revenue and expenses at the time they are committed. Because it is necessary to count revenue and expense items during the same year in which the show is held, show managers use the accrual accounting method.

For example, consider an exhibition that is held during the first part of September for an organization whose fiscal year is October 1 through September 30. The final bill for food and beverage will not arrive until one week after the fiscal year ends. Using the cash accounting method, the bill would be paid in October, even though it is an expense attributable to the prior fiscal year. The accrual accounting method allows for a financial process called *journal entry*, whereby the amount paid could be moved into the fiscal year just closed – even though the bill would be paid in October. Using this process, the financial statements for that fiscal year will reveal the true profit picture for the exhibition held within that fiscal year.

Financial Statements

There was a time when for-profit and not-for-profit entities used the same names for their financial statements. That is no longer true. Not-for-profit organizations have changed the names of their most frequently used financial reports – even though the content of the reports are the same as their for-profit counterparts. The names shown in parentheses are those now commonly used by not-for-profit organizations.

• Balance Sheet (Statement of Financial Position)

• Income Statement [or Profit and Loss Statement] (Statement of Activities)

• Budget (Functional Expense Report)

• Cash Flow Statement (Statement of Cash Flows)

The Income Statement, the Budget, and the Cash Flow Statement are important tools for the show manager. The budget is the first item to create as it provides estimates of expected revenues and expenses in producing the exhibition. Prepare reports that compare budgeted amounts to actual amounts, and discuss the reasons for variances. Prepare these reports so that they illustrate the cash difference between the budgeted and actual amounts, or percentage differences.

EXAMPLE:				
Expense	Budgeted Amount	Actual Amount	Variance	Notes
Food and beverage	75,000	81,000	6,000	Catering guarantees increased due to higher than anticipated # of attendees
Pipe and Drape	4,000	3,750	<250>	More custom booths used than projected

Knowing why items vary from projections will enhance the show manager's professionalism in the eyes of superiors.

Technology Tips and Tools

Different organizations have various types of accounting software to assist in the preparation of these financial reports. They may even have an accounting department that will prepare the statements. Often, the reports from these software programs can be exported to more user-friendly software, like Microsoft Excel, where a comments section can be added to address issues and answer any questions readers may have as they review the reports.

The Income (or Profit and Loss) Statement is the second statement that is used frequently throughout an exhibition's life cycle. These statements can be presented in various formats, including showing status of the financials for a current month, year-to-date, or prior year comparison. If this is the first year the exhibition will be held, obviously there will be no prior year's data. If the exhibition has been held previously, using a prior year comparison is recommended.

For instance, a simplified Income Statement might look like this:

SAMPLE INCOME AND EXPENSE STATEMENT

INCOME	This Month	Year-to-Date	Prior Year
Registration Fees	$10,000	$75,000	$65,000
Exhibit Sales	50,000	125,000	110,000
Sponsorships	15,000	25,000	15,000
Total	$75,000	$225,000	$185,000

EXPENSES	This Month	Year-to-Date	Prior Year
Official Services Contractor	$1,000	$35,000	$32,000
Food and Beverage	0	75,000	72,000
Marketing	25,000	40,000	50,000
Total	$26,000	$150,000	$154,000
NET INCOME	$49,000	$75,000	$31,000

This simple statement readily illustrates that this year's experience compared to last year's is positive, with a substantial increase in net income over the prior year. Production of these kinds of statements provides a *picture* of the financial health of the exhibition to interested parties.]

Prepare to Budget

A budget is the process of identifying anticipated revenue and expenses for the exhibition. This process is an *educated* guess based on research that the show manager conducts, including but not limited to contacting a general service contractor to get a reasonable estimate of what costs will be for pipe and drape, as well as getting estimates for the cost of security, food and beverage and lodging. Additional research will include finding out what comparable exhibitions charge attendees, exhibitors and other sources of potential revenue. All of this research will aid a show manager's efforts to development a budget for the exhibition.

If this is the first time this exhibition is being produced, the show manager will need to use zero-based budgeting, since the show has no history. If this exhibition has been produced in the past, use prior year figures to help construct the budget. This process simply increases the prior year's budget by some pre-determined percentage. Incremental budgeting is not as exacting as zero-based budgeting, because it does not utilize the same level of scrutiny when researching and examining revenue and expense items. The format of the budget depends on what is most important to the show manager and the organization. It can be constructed so that all fixed costs, variable costs, and indirect costs are grouped together. This type of formatting facilitates the calculation of attendee and exhibitor fees. The format can be constructed as a functional budget, where like items are grouped together, which makes it easier to monitor costs.

Remember that the budget is only a guide, and actual numbers may vary. Monitor the budget as the exhibition opening date approaches, and track where exceptions occur – noting the reasons for such exceptions. For instance, if the budget estimates attendance at 2,000, and that food and beverage will cost $125 per person, this projects a cost of $250,000. However, what if 2,100 people actually attend? The food and beverage costs would be $262,500, or $12,500 more than budgeted. By making a notation of the increased number of attendees (referred to as a *budget diary*), anyone questioning the additional expense would read the note and find that the revenue for attendee registration fees has increased by one hundred registrations.

Developing the Budget

Before a show manager begins to develop a budget, it is important to know what the sponsoring organization's budget philosophy is. There are three primary budget philosophies:

• Make a profit
• Break-even
• Lose money.

To make a profit, the exhibition's revenues must exceed its expenses. The break-even point is where revenues and expenses are equal. An event loses money when the expenses exceed revenues. Why would an organization intentionally set out to lose money? It does so when the purpose for which an event, including an exhibition, is not financially motivated. For instance, an organization may wish to hold a conference and exhibition because the group's members require advanced education. In preparing its budget, the organization is more concerned with keeping booth and attendee fees low to maximize attendance than with the fact that its net profit results in a loss. As long as the organization maximizes attendance, it will have realized its objectives – including the financial objective of losing money.

Once the budget philosophy is decided, it is time to start creating the exhibition budget.

Begin with Expenses

In order to set attendee and exhibitor fees, it is necessary to know how what the expenses will be to ensure that revenue received will offset them. Begin by obtaining bids or estimates from all potential vendors. Expenses that might be included in the exhibition include:

• Advertising and Public Relations
• Audiovisual
• Awards
• Credit card processing fees
• Desired Profit
• Event Insurance
• Facility
  ◦ Rental

- ○ Permits
- ○ Janitorial
- Food and Beverage
- General Service Contractor
  - ○ Drayage
  - ○ Electrical
  - ○ Equipment
  - ○ Pipe and Drape
- Marketing and Promotion
  - ○ Brochures
  - ○ Directories
  - ○ Programs
- Postage and Delivery
- Printing and Reproduction
- Registration
  - ○ Badges and Ribbons
  - ○ Equipment Rental
  - ○ Online registration fees
  - ○ Photographer
  - ○ Registration Staff
- Special Events
- Security
- Telephone/Fax
- Transportation
- Web site Design and Maintenance

Project Revenue

Once reasonable projections for any anticipated expenses have been determined, put them into the spreadsheet and total them. This provides a good idea as to what the revenue needs to be in order to break even. See the Registration and Exhibit Fees section below for some guidelines about how to forecast revenue items for the exhibition. Typical revenue items include:

- Advertising Sales
- Exhibit Sales
  - ○ Islands and Peninsulas
  - ○ Standard
  - ○ Additional Exhibitor Badges
  - ○ Booth Cancellation Fees

- Registration Fees
  - Early
  - Advance
  - On-site
- Special Event Ticket Sales
- Sponsorship

Once the anticipated revenue and expense items have been entered in a spreadsheet software like Microsoft's Excel, - it is possible to manipulate the registration and exhibit fees, and any other sources of income until an acceptable budget emerges. Once registration and exhibit fees have been determined, compare them to competitors' to ensure that they are neither too low nor too high. Either situation can result in a negative perception about your exhibition.

Registration and Exhibit Fees

There are many factors to consider when deciding what to charge as fees for the exhibition. Depending on the type of organization and its budget philosophy, the exhibition may charge attendee registration fees and exhibit/exhibitor fees. Points to consider when deciding what, if anything, to charge attendees are:

- Will there be early, advance and on-site registration fees?
  - If so, what will the deadlines be for receipt of those fees?
- Will single day registrations be permitted? If so, what procedures will be in place to ensure that these attendees participate only on the day for which they are registered? The example below illustrates the costs associated with each participant; having attendees register for one day, but participate fully in the event, will negatively impact the budget.
- Will members from the same organization (multiple registrations) receive a discount? If so, will the full fee be charged for the first registrant, and a discount be extended to the remaining registrants?
- Will speakers, members of the media, VIPs, and others be afforded complimentary registrations to the exhibition and any ancillary functions or special events? (Note that these ancillary functions or special events are those that are bundled with the "full"l registration fee, but can be purchased separately. They do not include ancillary events such as a golf tournament so frequently organized in conjunction with an exhibition that are paid for separate from the "full" registration fee.)
- If so, include an expense line item in the budget to account for these complimentary registrations.
  - For instance, that the value of one attendee registration (including all ancillary functions and special events) is valued at $375, and 25 complimentary registrations will be extended, the "complimentary registration" expense line item entry will be $9,375.

- Is there a fair and concisely-written refund policy? Some organizations allow a full refund up until a certain date, while others charge an administrative fee and refund the balance after that fee is deducted. Some also have a declining scale of refunds available by certain dates. For example, some allow for a 75 per cent refund if requested by Date X, 50 percent if requested by Date Y, and so on.

  - Best practices recommend that whatever the policy is, that it be stated on your Web site (if you have one), on all registration materials (including any receipts for payment issued) and at the on-site registration desk.

  - Best practices also dictate that any requests for refunds must be received *in writing* by the date specified based on when the final income (profit and loss) statement must be furnished. It is important to specify "in writing" to avoid situations where people say they "spoke with someone in the show office" or that they left a voice mail message canceling their registration prior to the *no refund* cancellation date.

  - Is there a separate (perhaps even unwritten) policy dealing with emergencies (death in the family or other crisis or emergency)?

These issues must all be decided in advance of sending out any registration materials so that you will have policies in place to deal with them.

- Is a refund/cancellation policy in place for exhibitors? Will booth fees and/or additional badge fees be refunded to exhibitors who cancel? If so, is there a date after which no refunds will be given? Usually, this date will be prior to publishing any printed, on-site program so that those who cancel are *not* included in the on-site program.

The answers to all of these questions will affect the budget and must be answered before the budget to be used for the exhibition is finalized.

Calculating the Attendee Registration Fee

Exhibition expenses can be described as fixed costs, variable costs, or indirect costs. Fixed costs do not change depending on the number of attendees, while variable costs do. Indirect costs can be either fixed or variable, and are not tied to attendee registration fees.

An example of a fixed cost would be the amount being charged for the audio-visual equipment needed for the exhibition. Whether there are ten attendees or ten thousand attendees, the need for audio-visual equipment does not change. Because the number of attendees does not influence the cost, the expense does not change.

An example of a variable cost is the cost of food and beverage for the exhibition. If lunch on day one costs $19 per person inclusive, then that number will be multiplied by the number of anticipated attendees. If that number were 10, then the cost would be $190. If that number were 1,000, then the cost would be $19,000. The cost *varies* with the number of attendees.

An example of an indirect cost is staff wages. Although staff may not be paid to specifically process attendee registrations, but if a portion of their time is spent doing so, that equals an *indirect* cost.

When calculating an attendee registration fee, construct it to the break-even point. There are two ways to calculate an attendee registration fee: when the number of attendees is known (or projected), and when the fee is not known (or projected).

To calculate the attendee registration fee when the number of attendees is known:
1. Determine the fixed costs.
   ◦ Be sure to include the desired profit as an expense line item.
2. Determine the variable costs using the following formula:
   ◦ Variable costs = variable costs per person times number of attendees
3. Add the total fixed costs plus the total variable costs
4. Calculate the break-even fee by dividing total costs by the number of attendees.

REGISTRATION EXAMPLE ONE

STEP ONE: Calculate fixed costs

Fixed Costs	
Audio-visual Equipment	$ 15,700.00
Exhibition Web site Development	25,000.00
Marketing Costs	48,000.00
Event Signage	11,300.00
Total Fixed Costs	**$100,000.00**

STEP TWO: Calculate variable costs

Variable Costs	
Food and Beverage	$ 75,000.00
On-site Attendee Program	25,000.00
Speaker/VIP lodging (75 people, 3 days or 225 sleeping nights)	45,000.00
Total Variable Costs	**$145,000.00**

STEP THREE: Add Fixed Costs and Variable Costs

Total Fixed Costs:	$100,000.00
Total Variable Costs:	145,000.00
Total:	**$245,000.00**

STEP FOUR: Divide total costs by number of attendees (Assume 1,000 attendees)

$245,000.00 divided by 1,000 = **$245.00 per attendee**

From this number, make a decision as to a logical fee to charge for registration that is equal or above this calculation. Remember, $245 is equal to the amount needed to break even on the cost of having one attendee participate in the exhibition.

Calculating the Attendee Registration Fee

To calculate the break-even number of attendees when the registration fee is known (Assume that the attendee registration fee will be $245 per person):

1. Subtract the per person variable costs from the registration fee to arrive at the contribution margin.

2. Then divide total fixed costs by the contribution margin to arrive at the number of attendees needed to break even.

REGISTRATION EXAMPLE TWO

In this example, we know the following:
Registration Fee   = $245.00
Variable Costs   = $145.00
Total Fixed Costs = $100,000.00

STEP ONE: Subtract per person variable costs from registration fee to arrive at the contribution margin.

Registration Fee	−	Per person variable costs	=	Contribution Margin
$245.00	−	$145.00	=	$100.00

STEP TWO: Divide total fixed costs by the contribution margin

Total Fixed Costs	÷	Contribution Margin	=	Break-even # of Attendees
$100,000.00	÷	$100.00	=	1,000 attendees

Establishing Exhibit/Exhibitor Fees

Use the same types of formulas in calculating exhibition fees to arrive at attendee registration fees. Fixed costs will include such things as security, exhibit space rental, and other exhibition related costs. Variable costs will include such things as the cost of pipe and drape based on projected number of booths in the exhibition, lead retrieval equipment (if included in the cost of booth space rental), and similar exhibition related costs. The show manager should also decide how many exhibitors will be included in the cost of booth space rental and then, using the costs arrived at for attendees, use this same formula to decide how much to charge for additional exhibitor badges.

Once these fees are established, decide what to charge attendees and exhibitors. Early, advance, on-site, and/or group discounted registration fees might be offered to attendees. For exhibitors, different fees may be charged depending on booth location such as islands, peninsulas, and corner booths. The opportunity to have additional exhibitors in their booth at no additional charge is sometimes offered to exhibitors. If so, insert a line item in the budget to account for this additional expense.

A Sample Exhibition Budget

Please note that this simplified budget is based on 1,000 attendees, 75 VIPs and speakers, 250 booths, 10 sponsors, and 50 additional exhibitor badges. No group discounts, special or ancillary events are factored into this budget. This sample is not representative of all revenue and cost items one might expect to find in an exhibition budget.

REVENUE			
Tradeshow Income			
Standard, In-line Booths	100 @ $ 00.00	=	$90,000.00
Corner/Peninsula booths	100 @ $1,100.00	=	110,000.00
Island Booths	50 @ $1,300.00	=	65,000.00
Add'l Exhibitor Badges	50 @ $ 150.00	=	7,500.00
Sponsorship Income		=	100,000.00
Total Tradeshow Income		**=**	**$440,000.00**
Attendee Registration			
Early Registration	500 @ $ 245.00	=	$122,500.00
Advance Registration	400 @ $ 260.00	=	104,000.00
On-site Registration	100 @ $ 275.00	=	27,500.00
Total Attendee Registration Income		**=**	**$254,000.00**
TOTAL REVENUE		**=**	**$694,000.00**

EXPENSES	
Fixed Costs	
Desired Profit	$ 200,000.00
Contingency	40,000.00
Exhibition space rental	58,500.00
Marketing	75,000.00
Security	8,000.00
Audio-visual equipment	15,700.00
Exhibition Web site development	25,000.00
Event signage	11,300.00
Total, Fixed Costs	**$433,500.00**

Variable Costs	
Food and beverage	$75,000.00
On-site attendee program	25,000.00
Speaker/VIP lodging (225 nights @ $200/per night)	45,000.00
Exhibit Hall Pipe and Drape (300 booths @ $15/each)	4,500.00
Lead retrieval equipment (300 units @ $200/each)	60,000.00
On-site Registration Staff	3,000.00
Total Variable Costs	**$212,500.00**
Indirect Costs	
Staff Wages (45% of 100,000.00)	$45,000.00
Telephone Service (excluding long distance charges)	3,000.00
Total Indirect Costs	**$48,000.00**
TOTAL EXPENSES	**$694,000.00**

Managing the Master Account

Proper management of the master account is important to the financial success of any exhibition. Whether the show manager personally supervises the exhibition's master account, or delegates it to a staff member, policies and procedures for establishing, reviewing and reconciling the master account must be in place.

Ensuring there are some simple controls in place on the master account will help to control costs and keep them within budgetary guidelines. These controls include:

- Listing all charges eligible to be posted to the master account
- Identifying those individuals authorized to sign for charges that will post to the master account. Be sure anyone authorized to sign for charges understands the budgetary guidelines,. and does not sign for extraordinary charges not anticipated in the budget.
- Scheduling time each day during the exhibition to review the master account to ensure there are no unusual or unauthorized charges posted to it.
- Requesting detailed documentation to support charges posted to the master account.

Once the final billing is received, reconcile the master account. Be sure to dispute and resolve any questionable charges within the time allotted for remitting payment on the master account.

Technology Tips and Tools

Whether the final billing is large or small, reconciling it can be like looking for that missing penny when balancing a bank statement. Spreadsheet software like Microsoft Excel can help make the reconciliation process quick and simple. Set up the first worksheet of Excel to replicate the master account summary. The summary might look like this:

Audio-visual equipment	$ 10,000.00
Food and beverage	85,000.00
Lodging	45,000.00
Subtotal	$140,000.00
Less room rebate	<1,200.00>
Balance Due	**$138,800.00**

Then set up additional Excel Worksheets for the separate categories, and plot the charges applicable to each of them, verifying them against the show's own records. Verify that all the charges were authorized, and that there were no duplicate charges. For instance, was an audio-visual package ordered for a full day, yet charged separately for a meeting held in that same room later in the day? Plotting all charges into a spreadsheet will reveal such duplication readily.

Once all the charges have been entered on the spreadsheets, total each worksheet to see if the total agrees with that shown on the final billing. If not, locate disputed charges and enter them in a disputed charges section on the first worksheet so they are readily accessible. Discuss any disputed charges and resolve them quickly so that payment can be submitted on a timely basis. These same procedures should be followed in paying all exhibition-related bills to ensure their accuracy and the timely payment of them.

Managing and Controlling Cash

How the receipt of cash and other funds is handled depends on anticipated revenues. The show manager may wish to transfer funds from one bank account to another, higher yield account if the forecasted revenues are significant, and will be held for months at a time. This is particularly true when registration options include online registration, with fees automatically being deposited to a bank account as they are received.

No matter how successful the exhibition is, unless the cash balances, the show's organizers will be displeased. Cash handling procedures may already be in place within the organization for other purposes; these may be adaptable for the handling of cash before, during, and after the exhibition. If not, it is essential to develop procedures to ensure the responsible handling of all cash, checks, credit cards, and other methods of payment. Best practices dictate that anyone responsible for handling receipts should be bonded, particularly the person in charge of receiving and reconciling monies received on- site during the event. Best practices also prescribe that pre-numbered receipts be used, with a minimum of two copies, more if other departments within the organization require copies. Include in any written procedures for cash management that all pre-numbered receipts must be retained – even those that are voided.

Working with International Currency

An exhibition may or may not include an international component. If it does, consider the impact of the foreign currency exchange rate (the number of one currency needed to buy another) will have on the budget. While best practices require that payment be asked for in the currency of the country in which the exhibition is to be held, it is important to know that there are fees involved with currency exchange, and how the country's currency compares with other countries.

> **TECHNOLOGY TIPS AND TOOLS**
> The Internet features easily-accessible, up-to-date tools to help with currency conversation. Search engines can locate currency converters and other helpful Web sites.

Managing Cash Flow

Once the budget has been developed and approved, it is important to chart the flow of cash in and out of bank accounts (called *inflows* and *outflows*). Using the information acquired while developing the budget, determine how much money should be received (*inflows*) and in what month, as well as what expenses will be incurred, and when those expenses will come due. Once all this information has been entered, look for months when *outflows* exceed *inflows*. When considering whether to transfer money to high-yield accounts, allow for the months where a negative cash flow will need to be addressed.

> **TECHNOLOGY TIPS AND TOOLS**
> If an organization does not have accounting software that can produce cash flow reports, use a spreadsheet software like Microsoft Excel to plot cash flow.

Here is an example of a simple cash flow, using selected revenue and expense items. The facts are:

Revenue

- The event takes place in November
- There are 200 booths, each priced at $1,500.
  - 50 will be sold in March
  - 50 will be sold in April

- 50 will be sold in May
- 25 sold in June
- 15 sold in July
- 7 sold in August
- 3 sold in September
- Attendee registration fees are set at $200 each. Two thousand attendees will register as follows:
  - 500 in June
  - 500 in July
  - 500 in August
  - 300 in September
  - 150 in October
  - 50 on site
- Sponsorships total $75,000, all paid in March

Expenses

- Five speakers are booked. Each will cost $1,500 including honorarium and travel costs.
- Marketing and promotion expenses are projected to be $85,000
- Food and beverage costs are $100,000
- Exhibit booth expenses are $4,000
- Security costs are anticipated at $3,250
- Program production and development is $35,000

CASH FLOW STATEMENT

	Jan.	Feb.	Mar.	Apr.	May	June	July	Aug.	Sept.	Oct.	Nov.	Dec.	Total
REVENUE													
Booth Sales			$75,000	$75,000	$75,000	$37,500	$22,500	$10,500	$4,500				$300,000
Attendee Reg.Fees						100,000	100,000	100,000	60,000	30,000	10,000		400,000
Sponsors			75,000										75,000
Total Revenue			150,000	75,000	75,000	137,500	122,500	110,500	64,500	30,000	10,000		**$775,000**
EXPENSE													
Speakers			4,500										4,500
Mktg./Prom.			5,000	5,000	10,000	10,000	15,000	15,000	10,000	15,000			85,000
F & B									25,000		75,000		100,000
Exhibits											4,000		4,000
Security											3,250		3,250
Program			5,000						10,000	20,000			35,000
Total Expenses			14,500	5,000	10,000	10,000	15,000	15,000	45,000	35,000	82,250		**$231,750**

REVENUE OVER EXPENSES			135,500	70,000	65,000	127,500	107,500	95,500	19,500	-5,000	-72,250		**$543,250**
CASH FLOW CUMULATIVE			135,500	205,500	270,500	398,000	505,500	601,000	620,500	615,500	543,250		

In this example, the early receipt of revenue means that – despite the fact that more will be spent in October and November than is taken in – no money will need to be borrowed during the life cycle of the exhibition. If the earlier months had indicated a negative cash flow, the how manager would need to arrange to have money available to pay expenses until the cumulative cash flow exceeded total expenses to date.

Monitoring the Budget

Whether a show manager is solely responsible for development and production of an exhibition budget, or works with financial professionals within the organization, it is important to periodically monitor revenue and expenses. Taking a close look at revenue and expenses on a monthly basis allows the show manager to make any necessary adjustments or modifications to ensure that everyone stays within the established budget wherever possible. For instance, consider the following example of income being reported four months prior to the exhibition:

ORDINARY INCOME/EXPENSE

Income	Jan-Dec 200__	Budget	% of Budget
Tradeshow Income			
Booth Sales			
Islands and Peninsulas	$125,800.00	$125,800.00	100.00%
Standard Booths	287,100.00	308,850.00	92.96%
Additional Exhibitor Badges	800.00	3,000.00	26.67%
Booth Cancellation Fees	850.00	3,625.00	23.45%
Total Booth Sales	414,550.00	441,275.00	93.94%
Total 4000 · Tradeshow Income	**$414,550.00**	**$441,275.00**	**93.94%**

Not realizing 100 per cent of the booth and exhibitor badge revenues four months in advance is not typically a cause for concern. On the other hand, if the event's revenue and expenses looked like this one month prior to the show, that might be cause for concern.

Now consider an event's revenue and expenses that look like this four months ahead:

Exhibition Expenses	Jan-Dec 200__	Budget	% of Budget
Exhibit Hall Pipe & Drape	$3,876.50	$4,080.00	95.01%
Licenses, Permits and Fees	35.00	400.00	8.75%
Exhibition Signage/Decorations	5,764.00	4,000.00	144.10%
Exhibition Food & Beverage			
Exhibition Hall Breaks	0.00	42,000.00	0.00%
Exhibition Hall Lunches	0.00	73,500.00	0.00%
Total Exhibition Food & Beverage	0.00	115,500.00	0.00%
Marketing Expenses			
Collateral Materials Design	93.50		
Collateral Materials Printing	1,720.93	3,000.00	57.36%
Collateral Materials Postage and Delivery	567.59	945.00	60.06%
Collateral Materials Expenses	2,382.02	3,945.00	60.38%
Security	3,645.00		
Lead Retrieval	9,000.00	35,500.00	25.35%
Janitorial	1,500.00	2,000.00	75.00%
Total Exhibition Expenses	**$26,202.52**	**$165,425.00**	**15.84%**

The entries that are substantially below expected budget line items may not be cause for concern because the event has not occurred, and the organization has not been billed yet for exhibition hall food and breaks. The line item for exhibition signage and decorations – some 44.1 per cent above budget, with four months remaining until the start of the event, requires investigation and explanation.

Post-Event Analysis

The primary purposes of post-event analysis and reporting is to wrap up details of the existing exhibition, and to make informed assumptions on future exhibitions based on the current year's performance. The budget diary will be helpful, because it contains ongoing comments as to why certain revenue and expense items resulted in positive and/or negative variances. Also essential to this process is the reconciliation of the master account billing discussed earlier in this chapter. Once these items have been evaluated, reports are prepared that include recommendations for improvements to future exhibitions, including enhanced financial policies and procedures.

Return on Investment is defined as *a financial ratio indicating the degree of profitability*. The basic calculation is:

Net Profit divided by Net Worth.

At its most basic level, if the exhibition makes a profit, then it has realized a positive ROI. In some instances, the evaluation may not be based on financial or monetary returns, but rather on how well the sponsoring organization's objectives were met. For a sponsoring organization that chooses to break even or lose money, realization of objectives is the primary return.

However, there is more to ROI than just the achievement of the sponsoring organization's financial goals. There is also ROI for attendees, exhibitors, sponsors, and other stakeholders. For the attendee, the return is whether any registration fees paid are perceived to have been well spent in return for the educational value received from attending. For exhibitors and sponsors, it is whether the money expended to exhibit or sponsor results in sales or the provision of services. Exhibitors and sponsors may also evaluate return on objectives, where they perceive value in an increased number of qualified leads. The evaluation process does not start and end at the conclusion of an exhibition. Indeed, in order to finalize results, measurements are taken, and this collected data is analyzed months after the event has ended.

SUMMARY

An enhanced understanding of budget and finance matters enables a show manager to assume a more strategic role in his or her organization, usually leading to promotion. This is accomplished by acquiring the knowledge necessary to identify, define, and otherwise manage all aspects of the exhibition's revenue and expenses. Included in these newly-acquired skills is the ability to calculate and recommend fee structures for exhibit booth sales and attendee registration fees. Additional skills are the ability to create a zero-based budget, to manage cash flow, and to handle post-event evaluation processes, including the calculation of return on investment. The ability to demonstrate proficiency in these areas will ensure that the show organizer is viewed not only as a valuable member of the organization but also as a strategic thinker.

QUESTIONS FOR DISCUSSION

① Why do you think some show managers dread the task of budgeting?
② If you have a personal budget, explain what categories you use and how you monitor it.
③ Why do you think ROI is one of the most common terms heard in the exhibition industry?

Section IV: Show Planning

Chapter 6
Specifications & Work Orders

*"Part of the inhumanity of the computer is that,
once it is competently programmed and
working smoothly, it is completely honest."*

– Isaac Asimov

Section IV: Show Planning

IN THIS CHAPTER YOU WILL LEARN

- Why standardization is important
- What steps have been taken towards standardization
- Where to get more information for your own events

INTRODUCTION

Great strides have been made towards standardization by the Convention Industry Council (CIC), which is a federation of 32 associations in the hospitality, exhibition, meeting and convention industry. CIC has developed industry-wide voluntary standards, also known as accepted practices. The initiative has been titled Accepted Practices Exchange (APEX). This chapter provides an overview of this important work but a detailed status on future initiatives, various templates and forms, and updates to the existing work can be found at www.conventionindustry.org.

CONTRIBUTORS

This chapter was compiled by the IAEM staff and the Art of the Show editor.

Why Standardize?

Standardization is important because of the large volume of tasks and individuals involved in producing an event. An event coordinator at a large convention center or an account executive for an official services contractor can be processing work orders from a half dozen different events simultaneously. As well, a show organizer or meeting planner can be creating work orders for different events simultaneously. A convention services manager at a hotel can be juggling function information for dozens of events on any given day. Plus, the largest events can create hundreds of pages of specification sheets and they all need to be distributed among a dozen different people who may all be in different cities.

One of the challenges the industry has encountered has been a lack of standards for transferring this type of information between show organizers, hotels and exhibition facilities and service contractors. Each segment and even each person has their own processes and systems so changes are rampant. Inconsistency in information flow can result in miscommunication, and may compromises customer service between suppliers and the organizer, or the organizer and their attendees and exhibitors. Fortunately, the APEX initiative has tackled this problem

Getting Input

City Discussion Groups (CDGs) played a vital role in the APEX Initiative. Located in cities throughout the US and Canada, the original groups of volunteers met regularly to review and provide feedback to the recommendations of the seven APEX industry panels. CDGs were developed to provide a sounding board for the APEX panels, as well as offer an opportunity for increased industry involvement on a local level.

City Discussion Groups came completed their feedback on the Contracts Panel Preliminary Report in early Spring of 2006. While the main goal of CDGs has been met, CIC has encouraged these volunteer groups to continue their role in bringing an increased awareness of APEX to the meetings, conventions and exhibition industry by planning ongoing education sessions.

Some of the benefits that are derived from accepted practices include:

- Seamless transfer of data between computer systems, which reduces duplication of efforts, increases efficiencies of operations, and results in cost-savings
- Streamlined systems and processes that result in time and resource savings
- Enhanced quality of services provided to customers, including event attendees and exhibitors
- Acknowledged measures of comparison and evaluation for improved decision-making
- Consistent employee training resulting in increased professionalism industry-wide

APEX addresses how business is conducted and how information is exchanged, as well as providing suggestions on what historical information is to be shared and stored about events.

Terminology

No glossaries or list of industry specific terms has been included in this text because APEX has developed the definitive source of terms and definitions for the meeting, convention and exhibition industry. This glossary can be found at the CIC Web site.

History and Post-Event Reports

A report of the details and activities of an event is called a Post Event Report (PER). A collection of PERs over time will provide the complete history for an event. CIC recommends that the post-event meeting should include the completion of a Post Event Report to be filed with each venue and facility. The APEX Post-Event Report template provides detailed recommendations for this process. The most recent PER for an event can then accompany any request for proposal (RFP) for future events. Templates for PER reports can be found at the CIC Web site.

Resumes and Work Orders

The Event Specification Guide (ESG) template is the industry's official format for delivering information clearly and accurately to facilities and suppliers, and contains all of the host organization's requirements for an event. It includes three sections:

1. Narrative
2. Function Schedule
3. Function Set-up Order.

Because tracking specific bits of information can become complex, especially after changes between multiple parties, the ESG requires:

- Every function must have its own Function Set-up Order.
- Every function must have a number.
- Items such as diagrams, photos, and sign copy must refer to the function number at all times.
- When a new function is added, it is at the discretion of the planner whether to order in sequence, or to use "intermediate numbers." Anything other than whole numbers must be formatted as 1a, 1b, 1c and so on.
- When a function in sequence is cancelled, the function number should not be reassigned.
- Every section may not apply for every event.
- Changes & Revisions: ESGs should be shared in a way that, when changes are made, they can be properly tracked and identified. Specifically, when a change is

made from the original published document, a revised date should be inserted, and any change should be highlighted and dated within the document.

- The Function Set-up Order (Exhibitor Version) should be used by exhibitors to communicate booth/stand needs to show management and other vendors. Additionally, show managers can use the form to guide exhibitors through the process of determining and relaying their set-up requirement.

See the example below and/or to download the entire template go the CIC Web site.

EVENT SPECIFICATIONS GUIDE TEMPLATE

Date Originated*: _____

Date Revised*: _____

Repeat for additional revisions as necessary.

A. EVENT PROFILE

Event Name*: _____

Event Organizer/Host Organization: _____

Event Organizer/Host Organization Phone*: _____

Event Organizer/Host Organization Mailing Address Line 1*: _____

Event Organizer/Host Organization Mailing Address Line 2: _____

Event Organizer/Host Organization City*: _____

Event Organizer/Host Organization State/Province*: _____

Event Organizer/Host Organization Postal/Zip Code*: _____

Event Organizer/Host Organization Country*: _____

Event Organizer/Host Organization Web Address: _____

Event Web Address: _____

Event Organizer/Host Organization Overview (mission, philosophy, etc.): _____

Event Objectives: _____

Event Scope: Drop Down Options:
                 ☐ Citywide
                 ☐ Single Venue
                 ☐ Multiple Venue
                 ☐ Other: _____

Event Type*:   Drop Down Options:

☐ Board Meeting

☐ Committee Meeting

☐ Customer Event

☐ Educational Meeting

☐ General Business Meeting

☐ Incentive Travel

☐ Local Employee Gathering

☐ Product Launch

☐ Public/Consumer Show

☐ Sales Meeting

☐ Shareholders Meeting

☐ Special Event

☐ Team-Building Event

☐ Training Meeting

☐ Trade Show

☐ Video Conference

☐ Other: _____

Event Frequency: Drop Down Options:

☐ One Time Only

☐ Biennial

☐ Annual

☐ Semi-Annual

☐ Quarterly

☐ Monthly

☐ Other: _____

Event is mandatory for attendees: ☐ Yes ☐ No

Spouses & Guests are invited to attend: ☐ Yes ☐ No

Children are invited to attend: ☐ Yes ☐ No

Other Event Profile Comments: _____

B. KEY DATES, TIMES, & LOCATIONS

Refer to the complete Schedule of Events (Part II of the ESG) for complete details on all functions and scheduled activities.

Primary Event Facility Name: _____

Event Location City: _____

State/Province: _____ Country: _____

Published Event Start Date*: _____

Published Event End Date*: _____

Pre-Event Meeting

  Day & Date*: _____

  Time* (US & Military via auto calc): _____

  Location*: _____

  Attendees*: _____

Post-Event Meeting

  Day & Date*: _____

  Time* (US & Military via auto calc): _____

  Location*: _____

  Attendees*: _____

Pre-Event Move-in & Set-up Required: ☐ Yes ☐ No

  If Yes, Specific Schedule Will Be Provided By: _____ (e.g. name of contractor)

Other Dates & Times Comments: _____

  (e.g. registration desk hours, daily review meetings)

C. KEY EVENT CONTACTS

Use this section to list all key personnel for the event (e.g. staff, exhibits manager, general services contractor, A/V company, security company, preferred shipper).

Event Organizer/Host Organization Contacts

Name Title Company	Address Telephone Fax Email Mobile Phone	Description of Responsibilities	Location During Event	Emergency Contact?
Contact1 Name* Contact1 Title* Contact1 Company*	Contact1 Address* Contact1 Telephone* Contact1 Fax* Contact1 Email* Contact1 Mobile Phone*	Contact1 Responsibilities*	☐ On-Site* ☐ Off-site*	☐ Yes ☐ No
Repeat for additional Contacts as necessary.				

Supplier Partner Contacts

Name Title Company	Address Telephone Fax Email Mobile Phone	Description of Responsibilities	Location During Event
Contact1 Name* Contact1 Title* Contact1 Company*	Contact1 Address* Contact1 Telephone* Contact1 Fax* Contact1 Email* Contact1 Mobile Phone*	Contact1 Responsibilities*	☐ On-Site* ☐ Off-site*
Repeat for additional Contacts as necessary.			

Other Event Contacts Comments: _____

D. ATTENDEE PROFILE

See Section E for the Exhibitor Profile.

Expected Total Event Attendance: _____

Number of Pre-Registered Attendees: _____

Number of Domestic Attendees: _____
   Note: Domestic Attendees live in the same country where the event is held

Number of International Attendees: _____

Demographics Profile (Attendees Only): _____

Accessibility/Special Needs*: _____
   Note: Use this section to outline any special needs the group has.

Other Attendee Profile Comments: _____

E. EXHIBITOR PROFILE

Number of Exhibitors Attending: _____

Number of Domestic Exhibitors: _____
   Note: Domestic Exhibitors live in the same country where the event is held

Number of International Exhibitors: _____

Demographics Profile (Exhibitors Only): _____

Number of Exhibiting Companies/Organizations Represented: _____

Accessibility/Special Needs*: _____
   Note: Use this section to outline any special needs the group has.

Other Exhibitor Profile Comments: _____

F. ARRIVAL/DEPARTURE INFORMATION

Major Arrivals: _____

Major Departures: _____

Group Arrivals/Departures: _____

Porterage/Luggage Delivery Requirements: _____

Luggage Storage Requirements: _____

Drive-in and Parking Instructions: _____

Fly-in Instructions: _____

Other Arrival/Departure Comments: _____

G. HOUSING

Room Block(s)*:

For a multi-hotel/housing facility event, name all housing facilities and specify the headquarters

Facility Name	HQ Hotel?	Day 1	Day 2	Day 3	Additional days as necessary
Facility Name1	☐ Yes ☐ No	Final Room Block #	Final Room Block #	Final Room Block #	
Additional facilities as necessary					

Reservation method*: _____

Third-Party Housing Provider Used: ☐ Yes   ☐ No

  If Yes, Housing Provider Company Name: _____

Suites: _____

Double/Single Occupancy: _____

Accessibility/Special Needs Rooms*: _____

Amenities: _____

In-room deliveries: _____

Room Drops (outside doors): _____

Other Housing Comments: _____

  Note: See Section D for VIP information

H. VIPs – VERY IMPORTANT PERSONS

Name	Title	Employer	Arrival Date & Time	Departure Date & Time	Amenities	Upgrades	Relationship to the Event	Comments *e.g. special billing, airport transfers*
VIP1								
VIP2								
Repeat for additional VIPs as necessary.								

I. FUNCTION SPACE

Use this section to address any special issues or situations that apply to the event.

Off-site Venue(s): _____

Function Rooms: _____

Message Center: _____

Office(s): _____

Registration Area(s): _____

Lounge(s): _____

Speaker Ready Room(s): _____

Press Room: _____

Storage: _____

General Reader Board Information: _____

Other Function Space Comments: _____

J. EXHIBITS

Location(s) of Exhibits: _____

Exhibitor Registration Location(s): _____

Number of Exhibits: _____

Gross Square Feet Used: _____ Gross Square Meters Used: _____

Net Square Feet Used: _____ Net Square Meters Used: _____

Exhibit Rules & Regulations Attached: ☐ Yes ☐ No

Show Dates and Times:

Day/Date	Show Hours	Show Hours	Show Hours

Storage Needs: _____

Anticipated POV (Privately Owned Vehicle) Deliveries (#): _____

Exhibitor Schedule

Move-in Begin Date: _____ Move-in End Date: _____

Move-in Begin Time: _____

Move-out Begin Date: _____ Move-out End Date: _____

Move-out End Time: _____

Service Contractor Schedule

Move-in Begin Date: _____ Move-in End Date: _____

Move-in Begin Time: _____

Move-out Begin Date: _____ Move-out End Date: _____

Move-out End Time: _____

See Section B: Dates & Times for Targeted Move-in Information

Other Exhibits Comments: _____

K. UTILITIES

Use this section to describe any special situations in regard to Engineering, Rigging, Electrical, Water, Telecommunications, etc.

L. SAFETY, SECURITY & FIRST-AID

Medical/Emergency Instructions*: _____

Key Event Organizer/Host Organization Contact in Case of Emergency/Crisis*: _____

Crisis & Emergency Instructions*: _____

On-site Communications Protocol*: _____

General Security/Surveillance: ☐ Not Required   ☐ Group To Provide   ☐ Venue To Provide

☐ Outside Vendor To Provide: _____ (company name)

Day/Date	Location	Hours (start & end)	Hours (start & end)	Hours (start & end)

First-Aid Services: ☐ Not Required   ☐ Group To Provide   ☐ Venue To Provide

☐ Outside Vendor To Provide: _____ (company name)

Day/Date	Location	Hours (start & end)

Keys

Location	Function Name	Start Day & Time	End Day & Time	# of Keys Required	Key Type
					☐ House/Standard ☐ Re-Keyed

VIP and/or Police Escorted Movements: _____

Other Security Comments: _____

M. FOOD & BEVERAGE

Special Requirements*: _____

Catered Food & Beverage Total Expected Attendance*

	Day 1	Day 2	Day 3	Day 4	Repeat for additional days as necessary.
Breakfast(s)	#	#	#	#	
AM Break(s)	#	#	#	#	
Lunch(s)	#	#	#	#	
PM Break(s)	#	#	#	#	
Reception(s)	#	#	#	#	
Dinner(s)	#	#	#	#	

On-Site F&B Description: _____

Off-Site F&B Description: _____

Anticipated Outlet/Concession Usage: _____

Other Food & Beverage Comments: _____

N. SPECIAL ACTIVITIES
Recreational Activities: _____

Guest Programs: _____

Tours: _____

Pre- & Post-Event Programs: _____

Entertainment: _____

Children's Programs: _____

Other Special Activities Comments: _____

O. AUDIO/VISUAL REQUIREMENTS
Use this section to address any special issues or situations that apply to the event.

P. TRANSPORTATION
Attendee Shuttle Provided*: ☐ Yes   ☐ No

  If Yes, complete the following:

Day & Date (i.e., Monday, mm/dd/yyyy)	Route Name	Start Time	End Time	Frequency
Repeat for additional occurrences as necessary.				

Transportation Provider: _____

Shuttle(s) Provided for Off-Site Events: ☐ Yes   ☐ No
If Yes, complete the following:

	Off-Site Function 1	Off-Site Function 2	Off-Site Function 3	Off-Site Function 4	Additional Off-Site Functions as Necessary
Departure Location					
Departure Date/Time					
Drop-off Location					
Drop-off Date/Time					
Return Location					
Return Date/time					
Transportation Provider					

Other Transportation Comments: _____

Q. IN CONJUNCTION WITH (ICW) GROUPS
Use this section to list and describe any In Conjunction With (ICW) groups of which suppliers for this event should be aware. Full contact information for the main point of contact should also be included. Additionally, note any important rules and regulations regarding these groups.

R. MEDIA/PRESS

Use this section to address any special issues or situations that apply to the event (e.g. contact information for the person to whom all media inquiries should be sent).

S. SHIPPING/RECEIVING

From:	To:	Shipper:	# of Items:	Expected Delivery Date
(contact and address)	(contact and address)			

Expected Outbound Shipping Requirements*: _____

Dock Usage: _____

Freight Elevator Usage: _____

Drayage To Be Handled By: _____

Other Shipping/Receiving Comments: _____

T. HOUSEKEEPING INSTRUCTIONS

Use this section to address any special issues or situations that apply to the event.

U. FRONT DESK INSTRUCTIONS

Use this section to address any special issues or situations that apply to the event.

V. OTHER REQUIREMENTS

W. BILLING INSTRUCTIONS

Final Bill to Be Provided to*: _____ (contact name)

Final Bill to Be Sent to*: _____ (mailing address)

Special Concessions and Negotiated Items/Services*

Description
Item/Service1
Item/Service2
Repeat for additional items/services as necessary.

On-Site Bill Review Instructions: _____

Third-Party Billing Instructions: _____

Use this section to give specific instructions for goods & services that the event organizer is not responsible for (e.g. contractors expenses, etc.)

Group is tax-exempt*: ☐ Yes   ☐ No

   If yes, Tax Exempt ID #: _____

Room & Tax to Master*: ☐ Yes   ☐ No

Incidentals to Master*: ☐ Yes   ☐ No

Guests Pay on Own*: ☐ Yes   ☐ No

X. AUTHORIZED SIGNATORIES

Full Name	Title	Approval Authority
Signatory1 Full Name*	Signatory1 Title*	Indicate Approval Authority Instructions*
Repeat for additional Signatories as necessary.		

Housing and Registration

In addition to collecting, reporting, and retrieving complete data, APEX attempted to address specific housing issues such as housing providers, Internet access, international housing and disclosure. A secondary charge was to recommend industry-accepted practices around housing issues such as third party housing providers, Internet services, international reservations and disclosure of commissions. In its work, the Panel considered a number of existing accepted practices and identified other best practices throughout the industry, including those summarized in the Convention Industry Council's *Project Attrition Final Report*. The complete ESC for Housing and Registration can be found on the CIC Web site.

Request for Proposals (RFP) Templates

The purpose of the APEX RFP templates is to develop recommended industry accepted practices for consistent and thorough RFPs that address core information and unique needs. There are APEX RFP templates for the following services on the CIC Web site:

- Audio Visual
- Destination Management
- Official Service Contractor
- Single Facility Space Availability
- Transportation

Section IV: Show Planning

SUMMARY

In short, accepted practices will make the industry more efficient, freeing up valuable time to devote collaborative energies to broader, more pressing industry issues. The initiative is ongoing and all updated information may be found at http://www.conventionindustry.org.

QUESTIONS FOR DISCUSSION

① What do you think were some of the problems faced by APEX in determining standard industry practices?

② Do you think the exhibition industry needs standards when every event is unique from every other event and host organizations vary widely?

③ What would you do if your boss wanted information prepared in a format different from the recommended APEX templates?

Chapter 1
Official Services Contractors

*"To have an outstanding exhibition, you must have
an outstanding general service contractor."*

– David Yowell, Society of Exploration Geophysicists

October 16, 2006

Dear Future Exhibition Industry Leader,

This section focuses on the role of contractors in the exhibitions and events industry. As our industry evolves, the role of contractors continues to change; this change provides new challenges as well as opportunities to grow our businesses.

Official service contractors such as GES are no longer just providers of pipe and drape, floral arrangements, audio visual equipment or carpet – we are creators of temporary marketing environments designed to attract and inform an increasing global audience.

To best serve our clients, both show organizers and exhibitors, the contractor must be a consultative partner. By understanding our clients' goals, we are able to contribute to the planning and execution of successful shows.

In today's environment, contractors must use their experience, innovation, creativity and technology to help show organizers grow their events and provide ROI to exhibitors. Exhibitor value is key to the future growth of a show, and offering innovative services that assist exhibitors will continue to be a priority.

This section will introduce you to the behind the scenes teams who play a vital role in the success of the show – contractors, show organizers and event producers.

From the entire GES team, we welcome you to this dynamic industry.

Kevin Rabbitt
President and CEO
GES Exposition Services

Chapter 1 — Official Services Contractors

IN THIS CHAPTER YOU WILL LEARN
- The role of decorators in the early exhibition industry
- What an official services contractor (OSC) does
- How to issue an RFP for an OSC
- What goes into an exhibitor kit
- Why relationships with contractors are crucial

INTRODUCTION

Without the services of a wide range of companies, an exhibition would never happen. A successful exhibition depends on a network of contractors, each in the business of producing a different segment. Overseeing the coordination of all these segments is the official services contractor (OSC), the vendor with whom you will work most closely. Your relationship with the OSC and other contractors will often span many years, so arriving at an understanding of what each does is a critical task for the show organizer.

CONTRIBUTOR

Julia Smith, CEM, Vice President of Sales, GES Exposition Services

A SHORT HISTORY OF SERVICE CONTRACTING FOR EXHIBITIONS
(compiled by Sandra Morrow, Editor, 2nd Edition, Art of the Show)

From the early 1800s through the 1920s, exhibitions were largely self-sufficient. There were no specialty contractors to bring in and set up pipe and drape, furniture or floral arrangements. For example, when the Franklin Institute hosted its first tradeshow in Philadelphia in 1824, organizers brought furniture and fixtures from home. As late as the early 20th century, it was standard practice to either bring furniture from home or the office, or rent basic wooden desks, chairs, hat racks and other needed items from a local furniture dealer or office supply store.

How did the exhibition contractor industry come into being? According to the late Harry Katz, one of the founders of United Exposition Services, the industry happened by accident. Usually, there was a single vendor in the host city for each needed service – one office furniture rental company, one sign painter, and so on. These companies supplemented the labor, equipment and service needs of the local hotel or hall where the exhibitions were held.

According to industry veteran James Howe, the equipment and services offered for the first convention service contractors were very limited. Rental equipment consisted of wooden office furniture – straight chairs, armchairs, swivel chairs, conference tables and desks. Hotel-supplied tables were covered with white sheets. A brass spittoon – polished and partially filled with water – was rented for smokers and tobacco chewers. Florists, photographers, models, signs and drape cleaning were all handled by individual service companies.

The 1930s ushered in a significant change to the exhibition service contracting business. Many conventions moved into larger buildings being built expressly for this purpose. The rental of wicker furniture was initiated because it was light, had removable cushions and could be painted quickly to supply the colors exhibitors desired. Drapery materials were often fastened to hard wall panels that were set up in modular pieces. Around this time, a new product called duvetyn was beginning to join colored paper as a prevalent material for draping. Made of cotton, duvetyn came on 100-yard rolls in a wide range of colors. Grass mats were often used as a floor covering, and were always green. Wilton Carpets, in pre-cut rolls of burgundy, blue, green and beige were the deluxe floor coverings of the day.

The 1930s also saw the introduction of specialized labor contractors to the exhibition services industry. For example, window trimmers installed the paper or duvetyn after the hard walls were set up, usually by carpenters. General labor then delivered the furniture and carpets. In 1936, Royle Chrome Manufacturing introduced a table with chrome legs, as well as an all-chrome frame product line of chairs, settees, straight chairs and lounge chairs with red or blue upholstered cushions. Special colors were rare. Although hard wall booths and wooden side rails were still the basic booth components, additional wall coverings like velour were introduced. These specialty fabrics were hand-fastened to the wall panels with tack hammers.

In each city, labor jurisdictions were established based on available or pre-determined manpower. For instance, at Chicago's Navy Pier, the longshoremen had jurisdiction; in New York, it was the exposition workers. In major cities, companies evolved as the industry grew. Many of the companies entering the business were family-owned, and had year-round business centered on holiday decorating, street parades and state fairs. Auto shows were the primary source of revenue in the early years. Services were expanded based upon customer demand.

In the 1940s the first major convention center opened in Atlantic City, and a new era for the industry began. Several new companies were created to service the newly-expanded region. After World War II, the development of forty foot long trailers and interstate highways made the transport of contractor and exhibitor equipment from city to city possible.

With the ability to transport supplies across interstate highways came the need for "knockdown" booth equipment which would fit in trucks. Pipe and drape, pioneered by industry pioneer Bill Brede (who founded an early decorating company), became the industry standard, and wood paneling was phased out of fashion.

Today's version of the convention service contractor company evolved in the early 1960s, when the modern approach to bidding and pricing came into being. This industry milestone precipitated the development of national companies with teams of suppliers and subcontractors that traveled with events and enabled them to provide a wide range of services for the same show in multiple locations around the country.

Definition of an Official Services Contractor

The Exhibition Services & Contractors Association (ESCA) is the professional organization of firms engaged in the provision of material and/or services for tradeshows, conventions, exhibitions and sales meetings. ESCA defines an official services contractor (OSC) as "an organization that provides show management and exhibitors with a wide range of services, sometimes including, but not limited to, installation & dismantling (I&D), creating and hanging signage and banners, laying carpet, material handling, and providing booth furniture." The official services contractor is sometimes also referred to as a decorator, which was the generic name for such companies until the late 20th century.

OSC Functions and Services

As the ESCA definition indicates, the official services contractor (OSC) may provide any of the following services:

- Floorplan development
- Designs
- Signs, graphics and banners
- Aisle carpet
- Aisle signs
- Entrance treatments and décor
- Modular rental booths
- Custom fabricated booths
- Rental furnishings
- Exhibitor order-processing
- Freight receipt and handling
- Warehousing of materials
- Floor marking and taping
- Cleaning of booth and aisle carpet
- Sign hanging
- Installation and dismantling labor
- Lighting package installation
- Electrical and plumbing
- Staging needs
- Special event requirements
- Custom drapery
- Coordination with specialty contractors
- Post- event evaluation

Once selected, the official services contractor agrees to provide an established list of services to an exhibition or event. While some of the services are presumed to be supplied exclusively by the OSC, others are discretionary, or optional, and can be provided either by the OSC or another contractor selected by show management or exhibitors.

Photo courtesy of GES Exposition Services

Exclusive Services
Exclusive services may include the following:
- Material handling
- Rental of standard furnishings

- Rigging and/or sign hanging (when not an exclusive service of the facility)
- Forklift labor
- Electrical and plumbing (when not an exclusive service of the facility)
- Cleaning (unless exclusive to the facility)
- Standard carpet rental
- Modular booth rental

These services and others can be ordered through the exhibitors' service manual or kit, which is provided either in print, via PDF files, on a CD, online, or through a combination of these media.

Services are deemed "exclusive" for a number of reasons. First, in order for an OSC to provide show management with guaranteed rates for the products and services needed to install the show, and to absorb the costs of the labor and materials to do so, they must be able to expect a certain percentage of the overall revenue available on the show.

Secondly, the OSC assumes certain liabilities affiliated with working within a facility. If an unlimited number of contractors were allowed to operate forklifts and other mechanized equipment such as scissor lifts, it would be difficult to ensure the safety of individuals, and to protect the facility from damage.

Photo courtesy of GES Exposition Services

Finally, to ensure an orderly and on-time set-up and dismantling of an event, a single contractor must maintain control of the primary logistics on-site, including the dock areas and freight elevators, often called drayage.

Drayage originally meant "to transport by a sideless cart," but drayage now describes a logistical service in the shipping industry. Drayage service is mandatory in tradeshows where a large number of vendors gather in a large exhibition area with a large number of products. Because of the sheer volume of goods, it would create mass confusion if the individual vendors transported their own goods and equipment into the site. Exhibition facilities and hotels do not have the space, equipment, or manpower to manage the receiving and storing of all the exhibit freight. Thus, the exhibit sponsor would assign and recommend a drayage service for the entering and exiting of freight and products.

Drayage service is usually provided by a national trucking or shipping company, or an international shipment brokerage firm in addition to the transportation of the freight to and from the exhibit site. Drayage service provides for:

1. Completing inbound carrier's receiving documents.
2. Unloading and delivery of the goods to a booth/stand from the receiving dock
3. Storing of empty cartons/crates and extra products at a on/near-site warehouse
4. Pickup of the goods from a booth/stand to the receiving dock and loading back into the carrier
5. Completing outbound carrier's shipping documents.

This is also the case with many malls and so-called "shopping streets" where there are many retailers gathered in the same building or street, and it would be too difficult for a delivery company like UPS or FedEx to maneuver their vehicles to all the locations because of parking restrictions or pedestrian paradises. The mall or street association has a drayage area, in a convenient location, where all packages from the tenants and couriers will be collected and distributed by a service by the association. This is similar to a "mail room" facility at large corporations.

Discretionary Services

Discretionary, or optional services, are often available through the OSC, but under set circumstances (observing any rules and regulations set by the facility or show management), may be obtained through outside contractors as well. Such services include, but are not limited to:

- Signs and graphics
- Installation and dismantling labor
- Freight transportation/shipping
- Booth construction
- Custom carpet rental
- Specialty furniture rental
- Prop rental

There are pros and cons to using an outside contractor for discretionary services or products. For example, exhibitors may be able to get better pricing through companies with whom they have established relationships. On the other hand, services such as the rental of custom carpet or furniture through vendors other than the official services contractor may include material handling charges when delivered to the show site, whereas the cost when rented through the OSC typically includes delivery and installation labor. In addition, the OSC is likely to have better access to resources on site or in their local office in case there are problems, such as an incorrect logo on a sign, or a damaged booth panel.

Exhibitor-Appointed Contractors (EACs)

When an exhibitor selects a contractor other than the OSC or one of the specialty services contractors recommended in the OSC kit, the contractor is called an exhibitor-appointed contractor, or EAC. When an EAC is hired by an exhibitor at an exhibition, the EAC is held to the same rules and regulations as the OSC. For example, the EAC must carry the minimum liability insurance coverage and any applicable permits required by the work they are performing. If unions claim jurisdiction over certain types of work in the local area, EAC workers must be members of the appropriate unions.

Prior to the first day of move-in, show managers typically require that exhibitors provide the names of companies and individuals who will be servicing their booths, as well as proof of insurance coverage.

Unless permission is granted by show management for a satellite service area (useful when one EAC is servicing a large number of exhibitors located in various areas of the exhibit hall), they are expected to conduct their business within the confines of their clients' booths, since EACs are generally restricted from soliciting new business on the show floor.

Subcontractors to the OSC

For various reasons including low demand, low inventory or requiring specialized equipment, an OSC may use a subcontractor to provide certain services, even when not exclusive to the facility. Examples of this include:

- **Specialty furniture** (often office, residential or special event furniture): Usually entrusted to an outside contractor with the means to update inventory more regularly to include new design trends, as well as the ability to warehouse and maintain a larger selection of specialty items.
- **Cleaning:** Typically handled by an outside subcontractor with ready access to a temporary local labor force, and other cleaning supplies.
- **Custom carpet:** Often handled by a custom carpet company that cuts the carpet to order, delivers, and may even install the plush carpet orders.
- **Logistics:** Commonly assigned to a van line, freight or common carrier with whom the OSC has a relationship. Moving exhibits and materials from the OSC's warehouse to the show site, however, is usually handled by the OSC's own

drivers and trucks.

Specialty Contractors

There are a number of additional services that exhibitors may require to complete their booth experience. If the OSC does not provide these services or products, a specialty contractor is selected by show management, often with the recommendation of the OSC, the facility staff, the local convention bureau or other show organizers. These recommended contractors can also offer their specialty services through the exhibitor's services manual, through mailings and telemarketing to the exhibitor list. Recommended contractors may include:

- Florists
- Photographers
- Temporary booth personnel
- Promotional item suppliers
- Marketing support
- Audio-visual suppliers

The specialty contractor will always have a representative at the service center at shows with a large number of exhibitors. At other shows, exhibitors will be directed to a toll-free or local number posted for last minute sales or service.

Other key contractors are discussed in other chapters. They usually compete for business through a bid process, often in response to an RFP generated by show management.

Facility Contractors

Hotels tend to offer more exclusive services due to the nature of their business and the likelihood that they have guests needing the services (such as engineering) year-round, regardless of whether there is an exhibition in house. On the other hand, exhibition facility business can be very sporadic, especially in less frequently booked locales. Because it can be difficult to carry staff on payroll every week when needs fluctuate, these venues often find it is more cost-effective to either subcontract or outsource certain services. Even in major destinations, as exhibition facilities and hotels seek additional revenue streams, many services traditionally handled by the OSC are now provided by the facility. Some facilities are even acting as labor dispatchers for contractors working within their halls, controlling who works inside their facilities, and well as claiming a portion of the revenue generated.

There are a few facilities within the United States who require exclusive, in-house contracting relationships with potential exhibitors, either via their own company, or through an affiliated contractor. While these venues may be able to offer potential exhibitors a contractor who knows the facility, and offer price breaks due to efficiencies gained through an in-house arrangement, many show managers prefer to work with OSCs and other contractors whom they have selected through a competitive bid process, and which often travel with the show from city to city.

Food service is typically exclusive in all types of facilities, because the in-house company maintains a full time kitchen and staff within the building. Catering services especially for large functions may or may not be an exclusive service of the in-house company.

Other facilities (often large convention hotels or privately owned exhibition halls) have recommended or preferred relationships with contractors. Often in return for a percentage of the contractor's revenue, the facility will encourage clients booked into the facility to use the contractor.

Choosing an Official Services Contractor

Many factors can influence a show organizer's selection of an official services contractor. The organization may have a long-term relationship with a contractor who knows the event, the exhibitors, and its needs. Local and national resources, reputation and recommendations may also come into play. Pricing is certainly a factor, as is creativity, attention to detail and other capabilities. To ensure an educated and informed decision during the selection process, preparing a thorough RFP is essential.

Include as much of the following detail and history as possible when preparing an RFP for an OSC:

- Name of the exhibition
- Owner(s) and sponsor(s)
- Event's purpose and history
- Location of past events
- Location of future event(s)
- Show dates and times
- Move-in and move-out dates
- Anticipated size of exhibition
- Number and profile of exhibitors
- Previous year's floorplan
- Anticipated attendance
- Exhibitor packages, if any
- Special events
- General session decor
- Anticipated number of signs
- Required aisle carpet
- Meeting room requirements
- Management freight needs
- Exhibitor services needed

Information which should be included by the OSC in a proposal:
- Experience
- References
- Company information
- Insurance coverage
- Financial health of the company
- Floorplan and drafting capabilities
- Sample floorplans

- Sample designs
- Sample service manual
- Clarification of what is to be provided by the OSC and what is to be subcontracted
- Management services cost estimates (response to the RFP specifics)
- Biographies of key staff; organizational charts

A well-done RFP for an OSC should generate proposals that clearly demonstrate a contractor's ability to meet the exhibition's requirements. With this information, show organizers can be more confident about selecting a OSC that can become a long term partner.

The Exhibitor Service Manual

The Exhibitor Service Manual is one of the primary methods of communication between show organizers and exhibitors. Although manuals have traditionally been printed, collated, and mailed either in a folder or a binder, many show organizers and contractors are moving toward electronic formats. Many exhibitors prefer less cumbersome ways of sharing information, such as email, PDF files, CDs and web-based systems, all of which are often easier and more convenient for the exhibitor to access, especially while traveling.

Regardless of the method used to transmit the information, the essential contents remain relatively constant. At a minimum, most include an overview of the show, general information and the show's rules and regulations, all of which is provided by show management. There are also catalogs and order forms from contractors and the facility. Order forms generally offer financial incentives for placing orders prior to a set discount date; early orders help contractors plan their labor and equipment needs more efficiently, thus saving them money.

The manual or "kit" may be compiled and distributed by the show sponsor, or by the OSC. The manual is then sent to all paid exhibitors, generally about three to six months prior to the show. Complex shows may distribute kits as early; smaller shows or package shows (where the cost of booth space automatically includes most of the services an exhibitor will need) may distribute the kits closer to the show. Some show organizers require exhibitors to confirm receipt of the exhibitor kit, in order to avoid missed deadlines and show site problems with rules and regulations blamed on "never having received the information".

Suggestions for content to be provided by Show Management:
- Show name, dates and location
- Schedule of events
- Schedule of set-up and tear down
- Display rules and regulations

- Hotel information
- Transportation information
- Registration forms
- Marketing opportunities
- Future dates and location
- Catering menus from the in-house food purveyor
- Sponsorship opportunities

Suggestions for content provided by the OSC:
- Payment information
- Limits of liability
- Order forms
- Local labor rules and jurisdictions
- Color "slicks" showing the product lines
- Shipping information
- Shipping labels
- Grids for plotting electrical distribution
- Targeted floorplans
- Marshalling yard maps and addresses

The Exhibitor Service Center

The Exhibitor Service Center or service "desk" is the hub of contractor activity. Installed and staffed by the official services contractor, the service center also includes counters for other contractors and facility services. Service center activities include order taking and processing, labor dispatch, freight tracking and arrangements for outbound shipments, invoice preparation, and answering exhibitor questions.

Photo courtesy of GES Exposition Services

Some official services contractors are shifting their focus, taking the service and order-taking capabilities out on the floor to the exhibitors. From touch-screen kiosks, to hand-held wireless order units carried by floor staff, the goal is to keep exhibitors from standing in line at the service desks. Technological developments will no doubt continue to change the way business is conducted on the show floor.

Labor Unions

By its nature, the exhibition industry can be cyclical. The need for labor ebbs and flows as exhibition business rotates from location to location. These needs are more easily met if there is a source for qualified labor, such as a union. As the exhibition industry developed, the involvement of trade unions grew. Carpenters, decorators, stagehands, riggers, teamsters, drapers, electricians and other members of the building and construction trades provided labor for the growing industry, and began to claim jurisdiction for various activities in different parts of the country. Today, the major official services contractors may be signatory to over 100 individual labor agreements to provide labor to events around the country. Collective bargaining is the process through which unions negotiate with multiple employers such as an OSC in setting jurisdictions (what kind of work is done by what type of laborer), and establishing wages, benefits, employer contributions, training and other specifics.

In markets that are "right to work," it can be challenging to fill labor calls (the number of worked requested at any given time) with qualified labor. The Taft-Hartley Act allowed states to pass right-to-work laws prohibiting closed shops (where one must be a union member to get work). Right-to-work states have provisions making it illegal to require union membership as a condition of employment. However, even if an event takes place in a right-to-work state, if a union contractor is involved, union personnel may still be used to perform some types of work. If the OSC or one of the other show contractors is signatory to a union or unions claiming jurisdiction for certain types of work, those work rules will be enforced at the event. Sometimes, a facility will promote itself as a non-union facility. However, this actually pertains only to the facility's own employees.

Labor issues and labor management can be very complicated. The OSC should keep clients informed of jurisdictional issues, as well as any pending labor concerns, including expiration dates of all union agreements to verify that there are no potential labor strikes.

Local labor rules should be included in the exhibitors' service manual, so that exhibitors may plan and budget accordingly.

Contracts and Agreements

It is vital that agreements with contractors be carefully executed in written form. Some agreements can be in letter format. Contracts are preferable. The show organizer's job is to detail the non-legal portions of the agreement. Quantities, minimums, schedules, deadlines, deliverables, prices, surcharges, and staffing expectations should be as specific as possible. Most official and support contractors will write the initial contract because they have standard applicable language. The show organizer can then have this contract reviewed, approved or altered by their organization's own attorneys until agreement is reached.

SUMMARY

No other contractor has as much history in the exhibition industry or bears as much responsibility for an exhibition as the OSC. According to their own organization, ESCA, "Your success is their success." The best show organizers establish solid working relationships with this essential partner. When selecting the OSC, in addition to evaluating proposals for pricing of both show management and exhibitor services, careful examination of experience, references and capabilities is in order. Labor union issues will be managed smoothly when all parties understand and comply with existing agreements and stay abreast of changing circumstances.

QUESTIONS FOR DISCUSSION

① Do you or anyone in your family belong to a labor union? What are the benefits and what are the disadvantages?

② Have you visited an exhibition recently where the main entrance includes an elaborate display of some type, possibly including signage, lights and plants? Which contractors were most likely involved in creating it?

③ In addition to parties, corporate meetings, and ground breakings, name some other types of events for which official services contractors could provide services.

Section V: Contractors

Chapter 2
Registration & Data Management

*"He who every morning plans the transaction of the day and
follows out that plan, carries a thread that will guide him
through the maze of the most busy life. But where no plan is laid,
where the disposal of time is surrendered merely to the
chance of incidence, chaos will soon reign."*

– Victor Hugo

Section V: Contractors

IN THIS CHAPTER YOU WILL LEARN

- Key components required for a registration system
- Options in technology and software applications.
- How to create a registration form
- Techniques for on-site crowd control
- About various value added services

INTRODUCTION

Regardless of the type of event, some form of registration or enrollment will take place. At a public show, it may be as simple as paying admission at the door or purchasing a ticket. At conventions, educational programs, expositions, or an event that is a combination of these, the registration process usually entails filling out a comprehensive registration form. The registration process may also integrate a qualification process. The registration process for events has never been easier. Technology allows you to determine the timeline for the registration process, and offers attendees a multitude of choices on how to accomplish this task.

CONTRIBUTOR

Susan Bennett, Mgr, Strategic Account Sales and Industry Relations, ExpoExchange, LLC.

Components of a Registration System

Registration by definition is (1) the act of enrolling, (2) the body of people who register or enroll, (3) a document certifying an act of registration. In essence, registration is the process of accurately capturing demographic and profile data from those individuals who choose to participate in an event. The pre-registration and on-site registration processes set the tone and influence the attendees' experience at the event. Because attendees need to prove the value of participating in the event, they are increasingly motivated by interaction and education. They are also demanding a more personalized experience. A positive registration experience has proven to lead to better interaction with exhibitors, better participation in educational programs and social functions, and fewer complaints overall.

To determine the comprehensive registration process that will meet the events needs, first determine the types of services, systems, and reports that would be beneficial to the goals of the event. Once this list has been developed, create a list of requirements, or "must have" list. Finally, determine a list of value-added services, or a "nice to have" list. Use this information to develop a registration process for the event's attendees.

Review and analyze the organization's historical performance. The historical performance is a good guideline to determine the budget, effectiveness of marketing objectives, the date to open pre-registration, the preferred method used to pre-register by past attendees (Internet, email, fax, telephone, or mail), the financial payment categories, the types of educational and social functions offered, the demographic data captured, and the flow of on-site registration and arrival.

Depending on the size of the organization's staff and the physical constraints of the system, managing registration can easily be a full-time process that includes doing data entry, answering telephone inquiries, and maintaining the Web site. The registration operation requires individuals who can translate and interpret data, use statistical and survey methods effectively, and integrate marketing strategies with the pre-registration process to create an efficient on-site operation and synthesize post-show reports.

Outsourcing

Determine whether or not to completely outsource the registration service from pre-registration through post show registration. Some show managers elect to perform some of the pre-registration functions within their organizations, and then have a registration vendor handle the credentials, remaining reporting, and on-site registration. Others elect to manage the entire registration process in house.

Improvements and efficiencies in technology are being developed with lightning speed. Organizations and individuals not working within the data management software environment on a regular basis are challenged to keep pace with all of the innovations in the marketplace. For example, the integration of event and housing registration allows an attendee to register for your event and make a housing reservation on the same Web site, and receive a real time confirmation detailing their entire event itinerary.

Registration vendors today are specialists in their field. They are able to stay current, and are constantly looking ahead to determine how the latest technology offerings can be deployed in the marketplace. Registration vendors have experience with a number of events and can provide practical guidance and suggestions for an event.

In-House Registration

Organizations that elect to perform some or all of the registration process themselves often leverage an association management software package with a registration component. They generally do so because they have the resources to manage the process, desire to maintain full control over the process, and/or due to the economies of scale with outsourcing the process.

There are a variety of registration software programs available for small to mid-size events (less then 5,000 attendees). These registration software programs, by their very nature, have less flexibility and depth than a customized registration system, and do not come with full technical support. There are other software applications such as ACCESS that organizations can use to customize their database and generate a sufficient – though somewhat limited – registration process.

Those organizations that elect to perform some of the pre-registration function may choose to utilize or license registration software from a registration vendor. Budgets and resources such as personnel and time should be a consideration when determining which registration functions to outsource and which to manage in house.

Designing a Registration Form

A crucial first step in achieving overall event success is the collection of complete attendee information, and the distribution of accurate data, before, during, and after the event. Ease of registration will establish a positive foundation for the successful event. Careful planning and design of the registration form is paramount to the registration process, and should be clear and concise. Design and implement an easy-to-use registration form that is also optimal for capturing important data. The registration form may be produced on paper or electronically, and should be designed to reflect the look and feel of the event or organization. Today, nearly half of the pre-registrants processed are on-line, and many events are experiencing a much higher on-line percentage. Review the organization's historical performance and determine the preferred method of registration (Internet, fax, email, telephone, and fax).

There are a variety of methods used to distribute printed registration forms, including publications, direct mail campaigns, and as a downloadable PDF file through the organization's or event's Web site. Using a different color paper or heavier stock for printed forms will help make them stand out. It is essential that the form separates easily from the other collateral, and can be fed easily through a fax machine. When providing the option to download the form from your organization or event site, the form should be in a PDF file to prevent editing of key information or layout.

A well-designed registration form should be no larger then an 8.5" x 11" sheet of paper. Registration forms should include enough room to hand write information. Procedures and instructions for attendees should be included on the same page as the form to be completed. If this is not possible, the procedures and instructions should be on the page facing or immediately preceding the form.

Those data elements that are required for the event should be designated with an asterisk (*), and a notation should be made on the form that these fields are required in order for the form to be processed. If event registration and housing is integrated, the registration form and the housing form can be combined if the processes are not too complex.

APEX (Accepted Practices Exchange) Event Registration Form Template*

*Copyright by Convention Industry Council

APEX EVENT REGISTRATION FORM TEMPLATE

HEADER

At a minimum, the following information should be included in this area:

• Event Name

• Event Dates in – Month Name, Start Date-End Date, Year – Format

• Name of Primary Event Facility

• Event City, State/Province, Country

• Deadline for Submitting the Event Registration Form & Receiving Event-Specific Rates

Additional form header content may include:

Event Logo

Event Organizer Logo

Other pertinent information determined by the event organizer]

ATTENDEE INFORMATION

*These fields are required in order for this form to be processed.

Prefix (Mr., Ms., Dr., etc.): _____ Given Name/First Name: _____ Middle Name/Initial: _____

Family Name (as appears on passport): _____ Suffix(s) (Jr., MD, CPA, etc.): _____

Preferred Name (for badge): _____

Employer/Organization: _____ Job Title: _____

Preferred Mailing Address:

Address1: _____ Address2: _____

City: _____ State/Province: _____ Zip/Postal Code: _____ Country: _____

Employer/Organization Mailing Address: ☐ Same As Preferred Mailing Address

If different from preferred address, complete the following:

Address1: _____ Address2: _____

City: _____ State/Province: _____ Zip/Postal Code: _____ Country: _____

Preferred Phone: _____ (Include appropriate country, city, and area codes)

Mobile Phone: _____ (Include appropriate country, city, and area codes)

Fax: _____ (Include appropriate country, city, and area codes)

Preferred Method for Receiving Acknowledgement of Registration: ☐ E-mail ☐ Fax ☐ Mail

Would you like to be contacted by event sponsors and exhibitors prior to the event?

☐ Yes By E-mail ☐ Yes By Fax ☐ Yes By Mail ☐ No

Attendee Type (List all attendee categories the Event Organizer desires to track, for example, Member, Speaker, Exhibitor, Guest):

☐ [Attendee Type 1]

☐ [Attendee Type 2]

☐ Additional Attendee Types As Necessary

Do you have any special physical disability, dietary (for example, vegetarian, kosher), or other needs: ☐ Yes ☐ No

If yes, please describe: _____

[Event-Specific Attendee Information – Use this section to add additional questions that are specific to this event. For example: Are you a first-time attendee for the XYZ Conference? ☐ Yes ☐ No and, If No, How many times have you attended? _____

ON-SITE EMERGENCY INFORMATION

Where are you staying during the event? _____ (for example, name of hotel, with a family member, at home)

In Case of Emergency:

Name of Person to Contact: _____

Phone: _____ (Include appropriate country, city, and area codes)

Relationship to You: _____

REGISTRATION FEES

All fees are in (note type of currency). Note if any functions are limited by space or other requirement.

	Before [Date]	After [Date]	Additional Date Categories As Necessary
[Attendee Type1]			
[Fee Type1]	☐ [$ Amount]	☐ [$ Amount]	☐ [$ Amount]
[Fee Type2]	☐ [$ Amount]	☐ [$ Amount]	☐ [$ Amount]
Additional Fee Types As Necessary			
[Attendee Type2]			
[Fee Type1]	☐ [$ Amount]	☐ [$ Amount]	☐ [$ Amount]
[Fee Type2]	☐ [$ Amount]	☐ [$ Amount]	☐ [$ Amount]
Additional Fee Types As Necessary			
Additional Attendee Types as Necessary			

Note any discounts that are available.

Total Cost – Payment Due $ _____ $ _____ $ _____

[An event's Fee Types could be Full Registration, One-Day Registration, Special Session/Event #1, etc.]

PAYMENT INFORMATION

Please … only one form of payment per registration!

[Include any special event-specific instructions (for example, Any registration form received without a valid deposit will not be processed). Indicate all methods of payment that are applicable to the event including, but not limited to:]

☐ Check   ☐ Money Order

If paying by check or money order, make it payable to [Payee] and mail with this form to: [Payee], [Mailing Address], [City], [State/Province], [Postal/Zip Code], [Country].

☐ [Card Type Accepted1]   ☐ [Card Type Accepted2]   ☐ [Card Type Accepted3]   ☐ Additional card types as necessary

Credit Card Number: _____

Expiration Date: _____ (NOTE: All credit cards must be valid through the dates of the event.)

Card's Security Code: _____

Cardholder's Name: _____

Cardholder's Signature: _____

Today's Date: _____

Billing Address (If Different from Preferred Mailing Address):

Address1: _____ Address2: _____

City: _____ State/Province: _____ Zip/Postal Code: _____ Country: _____

☐ Additional Forms of Payment as Necessary (such as wire transfers or purchase orders)

ACKNOWLEDGEMENTS

[Reiterate all policies outlined in the Registration Procedures regarding acknowledgements.]

SEND COMPLETED REGISTRATION FORMS TO:

[Reiterate all methods by which reservations can be made as outlined in the Registration Procedures.]

NOTE: On the APEX Event Registration Form template, any information enclosed in [brackets] are instructions to the person developing the form, and should be deleted once the form has been developed and is ready for public distribution. The show organizer may also add event-specific information that is required for the effective planning and implementation of each event.

The "$" symbol is a currency placeholder only. There is no requirement that all funds be in dollars.

All sections of the APEX Event Registration Form will not apply to every event. Any section that does not apply should not be included.

Event Registration Can Be Completed By:

Please use only one method to complete your event registration:

[Indicate all methods that are applicable to the event including, but not limited to:]

• Telephone: [Note if the attendee should call the event organizer, or other entity. Include 1) the name of the person/company to call, 2) days and hours of operation, and 3) the telephone number(s) with appropriate country/city/area codes. Note if there are different procedures for international attendees.]

• Fax: Complete this form and send it via fax to [fax number(s) with appropriate country/city/area codes]. [If appropriate, add instructions to include "ATTN: Person or Department" so that the form is efficiently delivered.]

• Internet: Complete this form on a secure connection at [URL]. [Note what should be expected in the way of confirmation in order to ensure completion of the on-line form.]

• Mail: Complete this form and mail it with payment to: [Note mailing instructions including 1) Event Name, 2) Mailing Address, 3) City, 4) State/Province, 5) Postal/Zip Code, and 6) Country. If appropriate, add instructions to include "ATTN: Person or Department" so that the form is efficiently delivered.]

Acknowledgement of Event Registration:
[Note whether or not acknowledgements of registrations will be sent to attendees, and if they will be, indicate the procedure. (For example, The XYZ Conference will send an acknowledgement of your registration via within one day of your reservation being received. Your badge and credentials will be sent by mail three weeks prior to the start of the event). If you require attendees to provide an address, or other contact information in order to receive their acknowledgements, state so here and indicate that requirement on the Event Registration Form with an asterisk (*).]

Fees & Deadlines:
[Describe all types and categories of registration fees offered, indicating the time frame during which they are offered, and the functions and services (for example, shuttle service) that are included in each fee. This section should describe any discounts offered for multiple attendees from the same company or organization. Additionally, make note of: 1) any functions that are NOT included in the general registration fee, indicating the fee for each of these items; 2) the type of currency in which all fees must be paid; 3) the final deadline for registration; and, 4) whether or not registration will be available on-site at the event. Disclose any information the attendee should know about the registration fees (For example, $10 is included in the registration fees to offset direct costs including shuttle service).]

Payment Methods Accepted:
[Include event-specific payment instructions (For example, Any registration form received without a valid payment will not be processed or Selection of an incorrect registration category may require rate adjustment.)] Indicate all acceptable methods of payment, and any related fees that are applicable such as check, money order, credit card (indicate types), wire transfer (indicate associated fees charged), or purchase order. Specify the name of the merchant that will be noted on credit card statements for all charges.]

Changes, Cancellations, & Refunds:
[Clearly state the applicable policies and dates regarding the making, modifying or canceling of an event registration. Note: 1) any fees charged for canceling, and when they will be charged; 2) if the cancellation fee increases the closer a cancellation is made to the event start date; 3) how and when refunds will be made; 4) if refunds will not be given on cancellations made after a specific date, the process for substituting attendees (for example, if a company can pay one registration fee and a different person comes each day, or if one person registers and another comes in his or her place; and, 5) exactly how requests for changes, cancellations, and/or refunds should be made (for example, requests must be made in writing and received by the Event Organizer by <<Date>>)]

Deadlines & Reminders:
[Include event-specific information and reminders here (For example, "Don't forget to fill out your Housing Form!" or state how and when badges/tickets will be distributed.)]. Additional examples of information to be included here are the deadline dates for: cancellation with full

refund; making housing reservations at the discounted event rate; making changes and cancellations to registration; receiving discounted registration fees; being listed in the registration directory; and/or cancellation with partial refund.]

[Add Additional Event-Specific Sections to the Registration Procedures as Required.]

Financial Processing

If the event requires a form of payment, be sure to provide enough room on the registration form for the credit card type, credit card number, expiration date, printed name on credit card, as well as the written signature. The policy for acceptance of other forms of payment, like checks and purchases orders, should be clearly stated. The more *a la carte* the event pricing, the more time consuming and confusing the registration process can become. Keep the pricing model as simple and inclusive as possible.

If the event requires a form of payment, determine if an existing bank account can be used to deposit checks, or if a new account opened specifically for the event needs to be arranged. Some show managers elect to establish a lock box system, or provide their registration vendor with "deposit only" rights to the event bank account.

When using a lock box system, the registration forms and checks will go directly to the bank, and the checks will be directly deposited into the account. The registration vendor or the organization will then be sent the registration forms for data entry. When using a deposit only account, the registration form and checks will go to the registration vendor or the organization for data entry and depositing of the funds.

Credit card payments can be processed in real time using the organization's merchant account. The credit card payments will be made directly to the organization through the real time system and the registrant's statement will reflect the organization's identifier. By processing the credit card payments in real time, declined or disputed charges are minimized. In addition, financial reports from the registration vendor can be easily balanced against the event's bank account statement.

Demographics

The demographic information collected on the attendees will be significant in helping to compile event statistics, analyze the success of the event and for use in future marketing of the event. Data on the buying power of attendees will be significant information for prospective targeted exhibitors, and will help the show organizer better prepare educational sessions, social functions, and housing packages. An accurate, up-to-date database is essential for promoting expositions, conferences, and other related programs.

Registrants are busy professionals, so when developing the demographic questions, keep it simple, minimize the number of questions to no more than five to seven questions, include closed-ended questions that require a "yes" or "no" answer, or multiple choice answers. Answers should be structured to be synthesized and reported easily.

The registration form developed for pre-registration print and on-line formats will need to be adapted for on-site registration. Consistency is key, as the data collected in pre-registration must be comparable to the data collected on site.

On-line Registration

Many attendees take access to the Internet for granted. Therefore, the event's on-line presence will need to provide easy-to-use, detailed Web sites to meet their expectations. Web technology can offer the attendees convenient "anytime, anyplace" registration, up until and throughout the event. Attendees can pre-register for an event from their homes, offices, hotels or any Web-enabled computer. On-line registration page(s) should be consistent with the printed registration form(s), and accessible on a secure Web site to allow real time registration for the event. The registration screen logic should be customized, and follow all the business rules established for the event. The on-line registration page(s) should allow for all registration types, discounts, and multiple registrations as designated for the event.

Confirmations

Once a registrant has been entered into the event database, it is important to confirm the transaction. All attendees registering on-line should receive a personalized, detailed, real time confirmation generated at the time of the registration. A confirmation should include the registrant's contact information, registration/event information, payments and convey any additional event-specific information that will enhance their event experience.

All attendees registering by fax, mail, email, or telephone should also receive a personalized and detailed confirmation. The preferred method should be via email, then by fax, and then by mail.

Badges

One of the primary components of registration is the badge. Consideration must be given to design, development, production and fulfillment for the pre-registration process as well as the on-site process. Consider the purpose of the badge when designing it. The badge will not only be used to display the registrant's name, title, organization and other basic information; it will be used as a tool for security. In addition, it may be used for attendance verification, lead retrieval, message centers, product locators, continuing education, and reporting. Ensure that the font and size of the information can be easily read, and that important registration categories can be easily identified.

Attendee and exhibitor badges can be mailed prior to the event until a pre-determined deadline. Badge holders can also be mailed prior to the event, but it is recommended that they be distributed on site. This will save mailing costs, help avoid damage/loss in mailing, and provide the opportunity to verify attendance as attendees and exhibitors arrive to pick up their holders on site.

After the pre-registration deadline, registration requests can still be accepted and processed; however, the badges will need to be picked up on site. For training purposes, the show manager may elect to have temporary, on-site personnel process any forms or requests that were received after the deadline.

Reporting

Technological solutions for registration can vary from company to company. One significant element of registration is Web site technology. Selecting a registration vendor with this capability allows access to the event registration database twenty-four hours a day, seven days a week (24/7). In addition, the show manager can participate in the registration process and generation of reports as much or as little as he or she chooses. As an attendee pre-registers, the show manager is able to view their information, run a report on the information collected, and generate a confirmation.

The full benefit of careful data collection and management is found in the reports that can be produced for the event. The registration vendor should partner with show managers to develop a reporting schedule that addresses both content and frequency. Standard reports usually include registration counts, accounting information, balance due/credit due reports, and demographic counts. Reports can also be of assistance in balancing credit card and bank statements. They can also provide insight into how registration is proceeding, so that marketing plans and budgets can be adjusted as necessary.

On-Site Registration and Layout

The registration vendor will be able to recommend a number of options when it comes to the physical layout of the on-site registration system. Based on the physical plant, pre-registration requests, on-site registration hours and the capabilities of the vendor's software and hardware, the system will be configured for optimal use and minimal wait times.

Wait time is the amount of time an attendee will wait for service before forming a negative impression of the service received. Typically, an attendee may become anxious and develop a less than favorable attitude after approximately 20 minutes of waiting to receive their badge, directory, and other show materials. In order to avoid long wait times, proper planning and communication between the show organizers and the registration vendor are essential

A well-planned registration area should be attractive, provide ample space to accommodate varying attendee levels, and adequate staff so that attendees and exhibitors are not kept waiting for any prolonged length of time. Photo courtesy of Professional Golfers Association of America, Palm Beach Gardens, FL.

Time and speed of registration are a concern no matter what system is being used. Staff must work at peak efficiency at all times, and efficiency often suffers when traffic volume increases. Any time loss per attendee due to staff support issues, design of the registration process or the need to re-verify information will cause traffic congestion, and the effect can become compounded in short order.

While registration technology is definitely here to stay, show managers need to decide whether outsourcing this function, or bringing in technology to handle it in house, is the better choice for their event. Answering this question involves issues of control and finance, and can only be answered with careful regard to the organization's individual circumstances.

The Registration Planning Process

The Pre-Registration Processing Time Line

This timeline assumes that the organization has already selected a particular registration vendor to work with – a sample RFP appears on the next two pages – or is planning to manage all or a portion of the registration process:

Step One

- Determine the audience and their means of response, budget historical performance, the goals of the event, the type of data to be collected by the end of the event and reports and the databases to be used – for example, member file and past attendee file.
- Develop the pre-registration and on-site registration forms and business rules, review payment policies, procedures, and deadlines, and design the confirmation.
- Develop the educational content, the space limits for events and the badge allotment criteria for certain groups such as exhibitors, media, and affiliate organizations.
- Design and order credential supplies, inserts, ribbons, and any other materials needed.

Step Two

- Develop marketing strategy.
- Establish mailing dates for promotional materials.
- Based on marketing and mail dates, format a timeline for creation, development, and production of collateral materials.

Step Three

- Ensure that all methods of accepting registration forms and requests are operational.

Step Four

- Mail all materials via traditional mail or electronically.

Step Five

- Accept and process registration forms by mail, fax, email, telephone or on-line
- Generate confirmations.

Step Six

- Process and mail credentials and badges up to a fixed time before the event if it has been decided to mail credentials to pre-registered attendees.

Step Seven

- Analyze and integrate demographic data with existing marketing strategies and operational planning.

Step Eight

- Establish on-site registration physical layout and requirements.
- Reserve temporary personnel and determine training schedules

- Re-confirm materials, electricity, counters, telephone lines, Internet connections, and security.

Step Nine

- Review reports and reporting times scheduled for on-site show management.

Step Ten

- Review and re-establish shipment schedules and on-site delivery destinations for registration equipment and materials.
- Work closely with the registration vendor to establish schedule.

Step Eleven

- Re-confirm registration layout and set-up on site, using your site plan.
- Ensure that registration vendor double checks all registration equipment
- Double check all counters, signage, chairs, waste management plans, collateral materials and other details.
- Continually monitor availability of badge stock, badge holders and other collateral.
- Continually monitor wait times and traffic patterns.

Step Twelve

- Oversee post-show evaluation and critique of the entire registration program and services.

SAMPLE REQUEST FOR PROPOSAL (RFP) FOR REGISTRATION SERVICES

I. Requesting/Client Organization

A. Contact Information: Event Organizer, Key Contact

B. Event Profile: Event Name, Type, Location, Objectives, Web Address, Anticipated number of pre-registered and on-site attendees, history, demographics, registration hours, event move-in and move-out dates, and future dates.

C. Requirements: Pre-Registration, On-site Registration, Membership Verification, Event tracking with Limited Space, Ticket Generation, Customer Service, Reporting, Credential Production, Staffing and Equipment. Describe how current pre-registration and on-site process works.

D. Proposal Specifications: Information as to who questions should be directed, Decision Making Process, Key Decision Factors, Instructions for Responding, and Competition.

E. Proposal Content: Name/Address of Respondent, Individual Contact, Experience with events last three years, Year Company Founded, Scope of Services, Member of Industry Organizations, Services Directly Providing and those Sub-Contracting, Exhibitor Services, Expenses to Organizer, Equipment, Staffing, Respondent Requirements, Union Labor Requirements, Insurance Coverage, References, and Attachments (For example, a lead order form sample.)

II. Vendor Responding to RFP

A. Contact Information: Company History, Depth of Experience, Key Contact

B. Event Profile (Incorporate information from RFP)

C. Requirements (Incorporate answers from RFP and outline technical aspects of the registration software and hardware configurations and the benefits of this system to the client.)

D. Proposal Specifications (Incorporate information from RFP.)

E. Proposal Content (Incorporate answers from RFP.)

1. What services and types of reports are offered by the vendor for pre-registration, on-site, and post show?

2. How much control can the organizer maintain over the pre-registration process?

3. Can the reports be customized and is there an additional fee to do so?

4. How does the vendor process pre-registration payments? What types of reports accompany these payments?

5. Can individuals register for special events, education programs and another other add-on activities? Can the vendor track Continuing Education Units (CEUs)? Can the vendor track space-limited events and close them out once they are sold out?

6. How are registration confirmations handled?

7. What are the customer service offerings that can be used by the organization? Hours of department operation? Contact by email and phone?

8. What is the suggested timeline for deployment of services by vendor?

9. Does the vendor provide value-added services such as product locator, message center and Internet café?

10. What type of lead retrieval services and products can the vendor supply?

11. What services are handled by the vendor and what services do they subcontract?

12. How much staff will the vendor supply to support the event? What are their areas of responsibility?

13. Can the vendor's registration program be integrated with housing services, or can they work in tandem with a specific housing vendor?

14. Provide an outline and preliminary estimate of costs for the services provided in the proposal and those not included. (For example, per diem, hotel, airfare, supplies, and shipping.)

15. Provide insurance coverage and references.

Supplemental Registration Components
Lead Retrieval Systems

Registration can be integrated easily with lead retrieval systems, Internet cafes, message centers, exhibitor locators, product locators, session directories, CEU managers, and survey centers. These components are readily identifiable, and are primarily used on site at the event. When considering the complete registration package for the organization, consider including these additional components in the package plan.

Lead Retrieval systems vary. They are designed to enable exhibiting companies to record and follow up on prospective customers who visited their booth, expressed an interest in their products, or fit the buying criteria of their customer base. The most common forms of lead retrieval are bar code, magnetic stripe cards, and RFID (Radio Frequency Identification).

A one or two-dimensional bar code can be printed on the badge at the time of production. The one-dimensional bar code includes a unique identification number that is tied back to the attendee's registration record. The two-dimensional bar code includes the unique identification number as well as contact information and demographics provided at the time of registration.

The magnetic stripe cards, commonly referred to as "mag" stripe, are a plastic card that can be custom-designed based on the look and feel of the event. They also offer the event organizer the ability to obtain sponsorship. The magnetic stripe card can be used as the badge, or it can be used in conjunction with a paper badge. The magnetic stripe card includes a unique identification number, as well as the contact information and demographics provided at the time of registration.

The show organizer can determine what data is to be encoded and shared with the exhibitors. The exhibitor then rents a lead retrieval unit that allows them to scan the bar code or read the mag stripe card, further qualifying the attendee who has indicated interest in their products and/or services. In some instances, the exhibitor can also ask additional customized demographic questions. The information can be provided to the exhibitor in paper format, electronic format (example, pen drive or diskette), and on-line. The lead retrieval units typically are desk-top or hand-held units.

Many vendors also offer the ability for exhibitors to connect the lead retrieval unit to a laptop, allowing them to populate the information directly into their own software lead management system.

It is important to note that the vendor selected for registration services will most often provide lead retrieval services as well.

Message Centers

All of the standard reasons for coming to an exhibition have one major element in common: they all involve *communication*. Bulletin boards with push pins holding messages were once the norm for interpersonal communication on site. In the early 1980's, the industry saw the first electronic message service developed to enable attendees to communicate among themselves, and with their offices, families, and colleagues. The communication and organization tools available today are much more sophisticated, helping to create more productive attendees and exhibitors who stay on the show floor longer. A message center connects attendees with exhibitors and with each other. When an attendee or exhibitor needs to get a message to another event participant or the event organizer, the message center is the tool of choice. Recipients can be notified by scrolling screens or upon log-in to let them know they have messages or to display other important announcements.

Internet Cafes

An Internet café is an area – usually in a visible public space – which is set with a number of computers with Internet access which allows attendees to access the Web to check email, travel arrangements or do other business. Often these computers are arranged side by side on shelves that are counter height, which allows only standing usage, in order to discourages long work sessions. Some events provide more comfortable Internet Café areas for certain segments of the attendee/exhibitor population, such as VIPs or in an exhibitor lounge. Generally there is no charge for Internet access to the user and the show organizer either pays for the set up and the Internet connection, or finds corporate sponsorship.

Product Locators

An exhibitor locator or product locator allows attendees to easily find the booth number of specific exhibitors by company name or by product type. Some events publish a booklet-type product locator and either hand it out at registration or distribute it near the exhibit hall. Many shows still create these in print form and they look like large signs posted in strategic points near all of the entrances to the exhibit hall. A product locator can also be an elaborate custom-built stand, either incorporating back-lit signage or a computer terminal for touch screen access to the search. When locators are provided on the Web site in advance, the attendees can search for products before leaving home, upon entering the exhibits on arrival at the show, or while walking the show floor. On-line and electronic locators offer the best opportunity to have all details as accurate as possible as changes can be posted in real time right up to show opening.

By incorporating a short survey which must be answered prior to accessing an electronic locators, a show organizer can gain additional vital information. Also, by integrating registration with these services when offered in advance, the show organizer can develop pre-show leads for the exhibitors, and some even offer match-making systems which will schedule appointments between the exhibitor and the pre-qualified attendees who have expressed interest in visiting that exhibitor's booth.

Session Directory

A session directory allows attendees to locate a specific session or educational opportunity that fits their schedules and to plan each day's activities in advance. Many session directory systems allow the registrants to search by title, date, speaker, category, or location. Usually this information is accessed on the Internet prior to departure for the event, but is also available on site at an Internet Café or downloads to a PDA or other Web-enabled device.

CEU Tracking

If an event offers CEUs, session tracking and management of the CEU process may be an additional service provided by the registration vendor. One method of session tracking is the placement of lead retrieval units at the door or entrance ways of each session. The attendee's bar code or mag stripe card are scanned as attendees enter or leave. The data can then be used for reporting, issuance of CEU certificates, and planning for future events.

Another method is the use of an on-line system that puts the control of individual session verification, tracking, and certificate production in the hands of the attendee. The registrant is able to record the sessions they attended and validate attendance to produce their certificate either on site or after the show themselves.

Radio Waves as Data Tools

Radio Frequency Identification, or RFID, is a generic term for technologies that use radio waves to transmit the identity of people or objects wirelessly. A number of vendors offer services using RFID technology. As equipment and tag prices continue to decrease, and the technology continues to standardize, it is reasonable to assume that usage will accelerate. Show managers should monitor developments and request regular technology updates from vendors implementing RFID technology.

There are several methods of identification. The most common is to store a unique serial number that identifies that person or object on a microchip that is attached to an antennae. The chip and the antennae together are called an RFID transponder, or RFID tag. The antennae enables the chip to transmit the identification number to a reader. The reader converts the radio waves reflected back from the RFID tag into digital form, and passes it to a computer system. Vendors using RFID technology are able to filter that information into a usable format for a variety of purposes.

RFID technology is not new, but previously, its cost limited its use. RFID is popular not only in the event marketplace but also in commerce. The implementation of RFID by major retail chains, advances in frequency systems, and the ongoing development of RFID industry standards have all contributed to advances in this technology.

Applications

Show organizers must evaluate the current level of technology and its practical applications before implementing it. In the event marketplace, the most common uses for RFID technology have been general event tracking, session tracking, traffic flow analysis, and lead retrieval.

Medium or long-range RFID technologies can offer a less invasive method of tracking attendees. Medium or long-range RFID technologies require that the RFID tag assigned to the attendee pass within one foot to 300 feet of an antennae. This less invasive tracking can provide faster entry at events with large attendance, such as an opening general session, or at high-traffic points such as entrances to the exhibit floor.

Short-range RFID technologies require that the RFID tag assigned to the attendee pass within three feet of an antennae. The short-range technologies can be used for lead retrieval, and can provide easier scanning capabilities than line-of-sight technologies such as bar coding. The proximity of the tag to the reader ensures security to the attendee that their information will only be provided to those exhibitors whom they choose to engage on the exhibit floor.

Current Challenges

Because RFID technology does not have a long history in the exhibition industry, there are several challenges to the show organizer besides expense. Privacy, health, security, and accuracy are all issues to evaluate.

The use of the information provided during registration for an event as it relates to the registrant's privacy and security can be an issue. Show organizers may want to inform attendees that RFID is being used in the same manner as barcode and magnetic stripe technology, but that it will enhance their event experience by making it more efficient and user-friendly.

One method to ensure the security of the information is to use only the unique serial number on the RFID as the link between reading of the tag and the registration information. Information on how the RFID technology works can also be provided to attendees. There are no studies that RFID technology is harmful or causes any health risks. RFID uses the low-end of the electromagnetic spectrum, and operates on a frequency similar to a car radio or cellular phone.

There are physical factors that affect the performance and accuracy of RFID technology depending on the range and frequency used by the vendor. Water and metal are particularly challenging to a tag. Radio waves can be absorbed by water, and the human body is mostly made up of water. One method to increase the accuracy rate is to design the badge holder with an air gap between the tag and the registrant. Radio waves may not penetrate metal, yet badge holders are often designed with a metal clip. Designing the badge holder with plastic clips will increase the performance.

Deploying an RFID system involves more than using RFID tags and installing readers. One benefit of using RFID technology is the ability to generate data that was not previously available. To get value from the data collected, the registration vendor must filter the information collected into a usable format that can assist show organizers in analyzing the data.

Registration Procedures
Pre-registration Process

Pre-registration is the process of gathering data on attendees in advance, and serves to streamline on-site registration. Most professional and trade organizations attempt to pre-register attendees for their event. Consumer or public events often attempt to pre-sell admission tickets as a form of registration.

It is to the show manager's advantage to offer attendees and exhibitors the option for registering for an event well in advance. First, industry studies have consistently shown that pre-registration is a key element in the ultimate decision to attend. Second, it provides an early indication of the sponsoring organization's marketing strengths and weaknesses, specifically as they relate to actual response level, geographic representation, and quality of the prospective attendee. Third, supplemental exhibit space sales are often bolstered or thwarted by the demand and excitement a show may demonstrate by the strengths and weaknesses in pre-registration numbers.

The percentage of attendees that take advantage of pre-registration depends on the event. For some events, it is less than 20 percent; for others, it may be 80 percent or more. Typically, medical and scientific conventions and tradeshows have extensive educational programs, and the attendees are professionals who depend on receiving CEUs in order to keep their status, licenses or degrees in good standing. As a result, pre-registration may be at or near 90 percent, and will be maintained on-site. The more attendees who pre-register, the lower the number who will need to go through the process on site.

Based on the registration process and system selected, attendance verification and badge distribution can be set up separately from on-site registration for new participants. This creates a number of efficiencies in traffic flow, significant reduction in wait times, and ultimately succeeds in getting attendees to the show floor or into educational sessions quickly.

Other types of tradeshows without educational programming may not fair as well, depending on the purpose of the event. If the event is significant in its related industry, and a large number of transactions take place between buyers and sellers, then an educational component may not be essential in its success. Subsequently, if an aggressive marketing strategy is employed, pre-registration numbers can be high because the potential attendee knows the value of the time saved in pre-registering for the event.

Site selection can also affect pre-registration numbers. If the destination for the event is popular and in-demand, then housing and pre-registration will be completed by the attendees early. If the destination can also be viewed as a vacation or can accommodate families, then the overall attendance has the potential to increase. Stays will also tend to be longer. It is recommended that the show organizer review any historical information if the event had previously been held at the destination.

Another means of encouraging attendees to pre-register is by offering an incentive or benefit if they pre-register. In the case of events that charge for registration, the fee to register in advance may be discounted up to a deadline. After the deadline, the fees are raised. Other suggestions include discounts off future events and first access to in- demand sessions.

Benefits of a pre-registration campaign include gaining advance information and profiles on attendees, and an opportunity to adjust for on-site registration requirements and logistics. For those events that charge a registration fee, pre-registration monies can be used toward up-front registration and event costs should the sponsoring organization want to take advantage of that pre-event cash flow.

As stated earlier, pre-registration data provides pivotal information as to the effectiveness of the show's marketing efforts. If, at a pre-determined cut-off date, pre-registration is well below historical averages for an established event, or the expected figures for a new program are not where they need to be, the marketing plan needs to be re-evaluated to determine if:
• The mail dates of promotional materials did not coincide with prior year mailings
• Supplemental programs and events are not valuable to the show's target market
• The venue of the event is not generating excitement or interest
• Promotional materials are not conveying the right message.

Pre-registration is a valuable assessment tool that can be used to redirect, enhance, or completely change the event's marketing, promotional, and event activities. It can also be effective inducement in selling booth space at the last minute to potential exhibitors who may have been previously reluctant to exhibit at the event.

Exhibitor Pre-registration
Pre-registration for exhibitors is a different process than for attendees. Most show organizers provide exhibitor badges based on the size of the booth purchased for the event, and then charge a fee for every badge in excess of that allotment.

It will sometimes be necessary to limit the number of exhibiting personnel for the following reasons:

- To ensure the appropriate ratio of buyers to sellers on the show floor
- To keep exhibitors from ordering badges for customers (who might otherwise register as attendees)
- To keep exhibitors from ordering badges for individuals who might not otherwise be authorized to attend the event
- To ensure fairness to smaller exhibiting companies that do not have the large sales staff and to prevent them from being overwhelmed by competitors

There can also be a surcharge for late exhibitor registrations. The show organizer must determine whether to collect excess badge fees on site before exhibiting companies can retrieve any of their additional badges, or to bill for additional badges after the event. It is exceedingly difficult to collect fees once the event is closed.

Exhibitor personnel who pre-registered before the badge mailing cut-off may elect either to have their badges mailed in bulk to the main contact for the booth to distribute, or mailed to each individual. If badges are not mailed prior to the event, the on-site layout should take into consideration the on-site pick up of all badges by exhibitors.

On-site Registration

Not everyone who plans to attend will actually walk through the door, and many will not plan to attend until immediately prior to the event. For most shows, in order to accurately credential and count all participants, all attendees, exhibitors, media, special guests, and others will register on site in one form or another. Even those who have pre-registered may be required to present their badges to be verified in order to receive additional materials such as badge holders, the event program and any other materials.

Depending upon the registration system, it may or may not be necessary to provide a separate area for pre-registered attendees who still need to pick up their credentials and other event materials. Some systems are so efficient that the small amount of additional wait time for a pre-registered attendee in the on-site registration area is inconsequential, and it is not worth establishing a separate area for that purpose.

Exhibitors typically arrive before the registration area is open to begin set-up of their booth. In that case, the show organizer will need to distribute temporary set-up badges (paper or sometimes wrist bands) to allow access to the show floor before the registration area is open for business and exhibitors can register officially. Some shows also want to credential all union labor and other workers on the exhibit floor. One benefit to opening registration early as the exhibitors arrive is that they will not need to re-enter the on-site registration area during peak hours. Additionally, temporary on-site registration personnel gain additional training time under 1 less stressful circumstances, and are then able to better manage challenges during busy times.

The process for on-site distribution of event materials and collateral once attendees and exhibitors arrive should be established in advance of the event. One method is to prepare packets for each attendee or exhibitor to pick up; however, this may be impractical at mid-size or large events. Depending on the registration vendor chosen, the "print-on-demand" capability of their system could prove to be more efficient than distributing packets on-site. A second method is to arrange for badge holders and other materials to be picked up at centers outside of the main registration area.

The on-site registration layout and process can be either a "one stop shop," where attendees register, receive their credentials, and all collateral material at one counter, or a system that directs attendees to a badge pick-up area following registration. Logistically, if badge holder pick-up and verification for pre-registrants is kept separate from the on-site registration area, traffic flow is faster.

Attendees who have been to the event in the past but have not pre-registered may be able to approach on-site registration a bit differently than attendees registering for the first time. Most registration databases can be used to look up the prior attendee's name or membership file on the previous year's list. The attendee can update any new information in the database, and pick up his or her badge.

Self-Registration and Staffed Registration

Self-registration and self-will call systems are quick and efficient processes that allow registrants to obtain their credentials with minimal staff interaction. Many different types of registrants can use the self-registration process effectively at events that do not mail badges ahead of time, for events that have a large number of attendees who register after the mailing deadline, and for events with a straightforward registration process for new registrants.

The advent of "scan & go" allows advance registrants to access the self-will call system by scanning a bar code printed on their confirmations. Other forms of access include the entry of the registrant's last name or a unique identification number. Once the system is accessed, registrants can view their information, validate it and submit it to be printed. The efficiency of self-registration systems increases when linked to a member, alumni or other pre-loaded database of participants. Once the registrant accesses the system, the registration information can be populated from the database, expediting the registration process.

Staffed registration is recommended for events with a more complicated registration process, and those requiring a more personalized registration experience. The registration process is handled entirely by temporary registration personnel supervised by the vendor or the show manager. The comfort level of the event's audience with technology should be considered when evaluating the use of self-registration versus staffed registration.

Self-registration and self will-call software works best if it follows the common practices and functionality created for on-line registration and other common software applications. The verbiage used in the application, how the forms are displayed and operated, and the use of touch screen or mouse-driven applications all contribute to the ease of use.

Evaluate historical data, know the audience, and – if outsourcing on-site registration – work with your vendor to determine the right combination and use of self-registration and/or staffed registration.

Validation of Credentials
Show organizers typically require some form of identification to be presented when registering on site. Once an exhibitor's or attendee's identification has been validated, they are able to register for the event. Validation of credentials is important for determining whether or not the attendee has the right to attend the event, that they are in fact who they say they are, and to help re-confirm the registration category to which they belong. This is especially useful for individuals attending the event for the first time.

Acceptable identification is usually a driver's license, company photo identification, business license, copy of a tax ID number, and/or a letter of introduction on company letterhead. On-site show staff should be available to answer questions, clarify information and interview prospective attendees prior to admittance to the event.

Based on the facility, estimated traffic flow and historical information from previous events, show organizers may want to consider separating on-site registration from those registrants who simply need to verify their attendance and pick up their badge holders. For registrants who have pre-registered and received their credentials in the mail, the registration process can be completed on site at a verification counter by scanning a barcode, scanning a magnetic stripe card, or by dropping off a verification stub mailed with their badge.

Layout of an Effective On-site Registration Area

On-site registration requirements need to be considered during the initial site inspection. The registration area should be easily located and accessible by all attendees. Factors that need immediate consideration:

- The event must meet the requirements of the Americans with Disabilities Act (ADA) and all related amendments. It is the show organizer's responsibility to ensure that access to registration is ADA compliant.

- The event's layout must abide by the fire marshal's rules, regulations, and constraints for the facility.

- Determine the network abilities of the facility, such as telephone, cable, fiber optic, and Internet connections.

- Determine where the network and electrical services and outlets are located in relation to the proposed registration area(s).

- Determine where the registration freight is off-loaded and stored.

- Determine the expected pedestrian traffic flow through the registration area(s).

- If the event collects cash and checks on site as part of the registration process, determine where the armored service enter the property, accesses receipts, and exits the facility.

The show manager works with the official services contractor (OSC), registration vendor, and facilities customer service representative to lay out the location and design of the registration area(s). In today's event environment, registration can be located in a variety of unrelated locations within the facility, and – in some cases – in other facilities. This again depends on the registration vendor selected, and the abilities of the facility. The OSC, the registration vendor, and the facilities customer service representative can recommend where the telephone cable, network connections, electric, counters and signage can be placed based on the restrictions and characteristics of the facility.

Once the layout of the registration area(s) is/are determined, the layout should be drawn to scale reflecting the placement of all counters, kiosks, equipment, electric, telephone cables, snake lines, temporary staff, and collateral distribution such as badge holders, directories and event bags.

The OSC will submit the layout of the registration area(s) to the local fire marshal for approval. This is required before any plans can be finalized, and typically cannot be deviated from once approved.

Directional and informational signage requirements and placement depend on the facility, the types of attendees such as international or special needs, and anticipated attendee traffic patterns. When estimating traffic patterns, consider the various entry points to the facility, shuttle bus drop off areas, and heavily-used parking areas. Good signage should be designed to create excitement about the event, be consistent with pre-promotion materials, and present clear and concise directional information.

Traffic Patterns and Flow

Review historical information on the event during the on-site registration planning process. If this is a first time event, plan the on-site registration based on anticipated attendance for the event. Once the number of attendees can be estimated more accurately, begin to plan for the demands that will most likely be placed on the registration process from start to finish. Logic dictates that any event will experience a rush in attendees to either register or verify their attendance just prior to the featured event, which may be the tradeshow, a strongly-promoted opening general session, or special entertainment.

Queues or snake lines can be established based on the amount of physical space and the anticipated attendance for the event. Crowd and traffic flow should be taken into consideration when designing the process. Counters can be designated for specific registration types, and queues or snake lines can be created by using ropes and stanchions. The use of queues allows for all registrants to enter specific lines, and – when they reach the front of the line – be directed to the next available person to help them complete the registration process.

Another layout design for registration counters is a multi-sided registration pod placed in various locations throughout the general registration area. One flow technique with the pod design allows individuals to approach one of the three sides of the pod, be processed, and move to the fourth side to pick up their badge and event materials. No ropes or stanchions need to be used.

Soft Openings

Pedestrian traffic at the event can be managed, and the impact of the first hours of registration prior to the event's immediate start can be controlled. As long as the registration area is up and running, attendees and exhibitors should be able to register at any time prior to the event's official start. This will depend, in part, on the policies and procedures the organization has about soft openings, as well what groups of attendees will be permitted to obtain their badges prior to the official start.

Soft openings allow the temporary registration personnel to gain additional training time under less stressful circumstances, and allow for any final glitches in the registration process to be worked out. It allows anxious attendees and exhibitors an opportunity to complete their registration prior to the official opening. Simply put, soft openings remove potentially distracting elements from the on-site registration process, thus eliminating some of the challenges that might have been experienced at the crucial time period.

Off-Site Registration

If shuttle buses are being used at an event, the show manager has the option of placing remote registration areas or self service terminals at the hotels serving as pick up points for shuttle service or at hotels with large numbers of early arrivals due to educational sessions held prior to the show opening. Another option is to control the flow of arrivals at the exhibit facility by directing the buses to registration areas or entrances that are less crowded during peak registration times.

Measurements for Time in Line

One of the on-site measurements taken is "time in line," or how long it takes for an attendee to go through the registration process. A few minutes delay in the process can cause an immediate backlog, which is then compounded as the day goes on. One way to determine time in line is to hand an on-site registrant a card indicating the time they entered the registration line. The card is then turned in at registration, and the time difference is noted. Done on a regular basis during both the peak and slow times, an accurate measurement of the processing time based on the number of attendees can be determined. This information can be used to determine staff scheduling requirements, the inclusion of additional registration counters, and the streamlining of the process at future events.

Registration Personnel

It is essential that the people selected to greet attendees, provide directions and information are amiable, speak clearly, and are knowledgeable about the basic event layout. They are the first impression attendees have of the event, and will significantly influence their general attitude for their entire stay.

Registration personnel can be found through various sources. Provided there is enough staff and the organization can afford it, show organizers can recruit in-house personnel to work the event. Typically, however, show organizers utilize the temporary personnel services provided by the local convention and visitors bureau. Another popular alternative is to use temporary personnel services provided by private personnel service companies in the industry.

Temporary personnel services are usually offered at a competitive hourly rate that reflects the skill level and responsibility of those individuals required to do the job. For example, supervisors are paid more than data entry clerks, who may be paid more than someone hired to be a line monitor.

Show organizers work in conjunction with the personnel agency or convention and visitors bureau, and with input from the registration vendor, to determine the number of individuals required for the event. Remember to consider training, peak registration hours, shift changes, breaks, and meals when planning for the appropriate number of personnel. As the number of attendees requiring registration services diminishes over the course of the event, the schedule of personnel should be reduced so as not to waste money on staff that is not needed.

Supervision, Control and Troubleshooting

Although the show organizer is ultimately responsible for the smooth-running operation of the entire event, it is still important to identify qualified individuals who can act on the organization's behalf throughout the event. Temporary registration personnel are typically supervised by one or more senior members of the core on-site team. Registration supervisors will work closely with the registration vendor to address personnel training, requirements, and re-scheduling if necessary. The registration supervisor and the registration vendor can recommend personnel reductions and summarize the personnel used.

The event's controller, accountant, or designated staff person will most likely be responsible for overseeing cash collection and accounting in registration. This individual may handle the daily distribution of cash drawers and other accounting documentation used by the organization, as well as receive reports from the selected registration vendor.

Data Management and Marketing

In planning the exhibition, decisions will have to be made about the data collected via the registration process. In addition, show organizers may take other measurements during the event to gauge the successes and disappointments from both the attendees' and exhibitors' points of view. The data management process not only collects data on the attendees; it also provides an effective planning tool for future events. Often, the data collected will provide invaluable information about the event, its attendees, and the marketplace. The database should be a living document that is constantly updated to accurately reflect what is happening to the event in particular and the industry in general.

The data is critical in analyzing attendance for the event. Registration data for the current event should include the following, and be used in conjunction with historical data from the past three to five years:

- Advance Registration Count and Verified Advance Registration and By Category (Examples: Member, Non-Member, Conference, Expo Only, Exhibitor, VIP, Spouse, Press)
- On-site Registration Count, By Day, By Hour, and By Category

- Educational and Social Functions Count
- Total Verified Advance Registrants and On-site Registrants
- Total Advance Registrations Not Verified
- Demographic Count (Examples: Job Title, Industry Classification, Buying Power)
- Geographic Count (Examples state, country, and/or defined regional areas)

The registration process is the primary research tool, and should be used to full advantage to develop an accurate profile of the event attendee and exhibitor base. Because many show organizers sell or rent their attendee database to their exhibitors to help market the event, the information provided must be as accurate as possible, and can be verified by a reputable outside source. Many show organizers use professional services companies to audit the attendance at their event.

An additional source of revenue can be derived from providing exhibitors with access to lists of attendees' they may have missed during the event. On-line matchmaking tools are another example of how exhibitors can access potential buyers utilizing the organization's data and the organization can generate additional revenue.

SUMMARY

A comprehensive registration management system is instrumental to the success of any event. Many decisions have to be made in advance, beginning with whether to manage registration in-house or through a registration vendor. A show organizer also has to have some knowledge of the range of registration technologies and the demographics of the attendees and exhibitors in order to choose the best fit for each show. Expertise in techniques of crowd control and managing traffic flow efficiently are also important. Data collected in the registration process is often important in making key marketing decisions and promoting future events.

QUESTIONS FOR DISCUSSION

① What is the longest you have ever stood in line and what was your reaction to the experience?

② What are the pros and cons of self service registration terminals or kiosks?

③ Why is it important for the exhibit manager to register all workers on the exhibit floor, even if they are not exhibitors?

Resources & References

RFID Journal, Inc., "What is RFID?," www.rfidjournal.com/article/articleprint/1339/ -1/129/

RFID Journal, Inc., "The Basics of RFID Technology," www.rfidjournal.com/article/articleprint/1337/-1/129/

RFID Journal, Inc., "RFID Components and Costs," www.rfidjournal.com/article/articleprint/1336/-1/129/

Lucke, Bob, "Advances in RFID Driving Event ROI," *Event ROI*, Fall 2005 .

Braley, Sarah, "It's In The Badge," *Meetings And Conventions*, February 2005.

Stevens, Ruth, "5 Web Site Success Stories," *Expo*, June 2005

Kirkwood, Heather, "Tradeshows 2010: Attracting Tomorrow's Attendees Today," *Expo*, October 2005

Convention Industry Council, "APEX Housing & Registration Accepted Practices," August 10, 2005

Chapter 3
Housing Management

"The saying 'Getting there is half the fun'
became obsolete with the advent of commercial airlines."

– Henry J. Tillman

Section V: Contractors

IN THIS CHAPTER YOU WILL LEARN

- Why a housing management system is critical to most events
- Various ways to provide housing services
- The historical and current role of convention & visitor bureaus
- How to acquire blocks of hotel rooms for your attendees & exhibitors
- Some of the most critical hotel contract issues

INTRODUCTION

Behind the scenes in exhibition management are a series of tasks that, on the surface, appear to have little relevance to exhibitions. These tasks are all service-related, and usually include offering hotel accommodations at negotiated rates. If exhibitors and attendees do not experience an acceptable level of service in making hotel reservations, the true business of the show will be tainted. Their perceptions of the show itself may even take a back seat until these issues are resolved to their satisfaction.

CONTRIBUTOR

Penny Kent, CEM, Director of Marketing, Travel Planners, Inc.

Options in Managing the Hotel Reservation Process

In spite of some predictions that organized housing will fade away as Web-based retail travel services take over, allowing attendees and exhibitors to fend for themselves is not widely considered to be a viable option. First, without managed housing, there is no guarantee that there will be a sufficient number of rooms available for attendees over any specific dates, especially if they book only a few weeks prior to the event – which is very common. Secondly, there is no way to know the demand from other business and leisure travelers at any given hotel over the event dates. Finally, convention facilities in most major cities accommodate multiple events. Those events' attendees could easily get to the most desirable hotels to make reservations first. There are also major sporting events and corporate conferences which could be scheduled near or over the event's dates, and use up much of the hotel inventory that appeared to be available when the event was first planned and the dates confirmed.

Finally, without any system in place, or depending solely on the Internet retailers to provide sufficient rooms, there is the possibility that rates could increase to a point much higher than negotiated group rates would be, simply because of the high demand anticipated because the event is on the books. Therefore, another important reason to plan hotel accommodations in advance is to guarantee rates.

Early in the planning process – usually 18 months out – the options for providing a housing system for the event should be examined. A decision should be made no later than 12 months prior to the event, preferably before hotel contracts have been signed. Sometimes, however, a show organizer must negotiate a hotel contract before deciding on a housing management system. When this happens, there should be a clause saying that the method of reserving rooms will be determined at a later date, and the contract should only quote tentative rates, not confirm final ones.

Many show organizers are frustrated by not being able to confirm hotel room rates at the same time as they commit to a facility. Generally, hotels are willing to commit inventory and hold room blocks far in advance, but will not confirm exact rates until about 12 months in advance. This delay in confirming actual rates is probably advantageous on both sides, since the event's most recent history is not typically available before then. In addition, there are likely to be ups and downs in market conditions which will be more evident closer to the event's dates.

If the number of sleeping rooms needed is very minimal, it is possible to let attendees and exhibitors find their own housing. However, even if the number of rooms is so small that housing is needed only for staff and a few out-of-town exhibitors – a common scenario for regional consumer shows, for instance – there are benefits to formally managing the housing arrangements. For example, even a room block of 20 rooms over a three-night stay (which is the same as 60 room nights), all located in the same hotel, and all at the negotiated show rate, would likely be rewarded by the hotel with one "comp" (a complimentary or free) night. This is a small but potentially significant benefit to the bottom line. Also, in most cases, group rates are among the lowest available.

Following are the various ways a show organizer might opt to provide a housing management system.

The Direct Approach

After the site inspection, the show organizer negotiates room rates and availability, and contracts with several hotels. Then, the hotel names, rates and telephone numbers are published in all of the event publicity. The attendee or exhibitor is then responsible for making his or her own reservation directly with the hotel, or with the hotel's Web site or toll-free phone service.

This system works best when a very small number of hotel rooms is required. For example, the direct approach is most efficient when only one hotel is needed, when only one hotel in each of several, distinct price ranges or locations within the city is needed, or when the hotel agrees not to hold the show organizer liable for how many rooms are used.

For example, when attendees at a conference place such a high value on networking that they strongly prefer all being in the same one or two hotels, the direct approach works very well. Another example of when this method is preferable is when attendees at local professional meetings either stay in their own homes, or have long established local hotel preferences. The only down side to this system is that show management will not be aware of any problems with housing that might affect attendance.

Housing In-House

Depending on internal staffing resources, managing housing in house may be a good option, especially for events that require labor intensive handling of many sub-blocks (or special arrangements to housing certain groups together). For events where attendees are housed as delegations, such as political, fraternal and educational groups that elect state delegations, doing housing in-house can be the best way to ensure that all parties are housed according to the rules, and that someone in authority is always in touch with delegates.

Some groups also have a large number of VIP constituencies that require a great deal of personal communication with staff. In these types of cases, after selecting hotels and negotiating group rates and contracts, the show organizer would direct the attendee or exhibitor to send housing requests to staff members, who would then screen the requests and sends them to the hotels for confirmation to the attendee. Attendees and exhibitors then make any changes or cancellations directly with the hotels. Note that hotels are sometimes not able to honor the negotiated group rate inside the cut-off date, which is usually 30 days in advance of the event. Therefore, the negotiated and publicized rate might not be available if attendees procrastinate in making reservations.

Local Convention and Visitor Bureaus

Each city that has a local bureau offers some form of assistance with housing, ranging from Web site information and hotel links, to a fully-staffed housing department. The range of services is wide, and has changed significantly over the past decades.

A SHORT HISTORY OF BUREAU HOUSING

During the 1950s, local convention and visitor bureaus began offering housing services as a means of making their destinations more attractive. As the tradeshow industry grew, show managers and meeting planners came to expect that a convention city would provide housing services at no cost to the event organizers. Local bureaus then became major processors of hotel reservations. Many purchased special computer software designed just for bureaus that would handle a large volume of calls. Phones were usually staffed by local temporary workers.

As competition increased among destinations, the sophistication of housing services grew. By the early 1990s, bureaus in most second and third-tier destinations offered a toll-free telephone reservation service. Although show organizers were not paying for these services, the cost to the bureaus to provide housing services escalated. Driving the rising cost to the local bureaus was the increased volume of business from show organizers, and the demand for faster and more complex services – especially for exhibitors and other groups.

In the mid 1990s, several of the larger bureaus formed a national consortium called the Convention Housing Reservation Services (CHRS) to handle city-wide and convention housing nationwide under the umbrella of the International Association of Convention and Visitor Bureaus. Formerly known as the IACVB, this organization – now called Destination Marketing Association International – provided services through a private vendor from the tourism industry. This effort, however, was abandoned in 1995, and bureaus began to experiment with a variety of other options.

Many local bureaus now outsource housing management to companies that are the convention housing specialists for that city. In most cities, these "official" and recommended (but not exclusive) housing providers are paid a transaction fee – which is calculated either per room night or per reservation – that is negotiated by the bureau but paid by the local hotels. The amount varies from city to city. These costs may or may not be reflected in negotiated group rates, depending on the many variable factors that influence all hotel contract negotiations, but there is no direct charge to the sponsoring organization. In addition, some bureaus still maintain telephone support for housing issues, and often have staff that coordinates services between the outsourced company and the show organizer.

Even if they choose another housing management system, many show managers use local bureaus to find out if enough rooms are available in a city before committing definitely to dates in that city. Bureau staff queries all member hotels who respond with tentative room block commitments for the dates in question. This advance assurance that sufficient rooms are available is critical to the decision process. In addition, organizers sometimes use the bureau as a central source to communicate their other requirements (suites and meeting room space) to all of the hotels holding tentative room blocks. Bureaus also keep show organizers informed of changes in the hotel market in their cities, such as when there is new construction of a hotel, when hotels change ownership, or when hotels holding group commitments enter into renovation projects.

Third Party Housing Providers

In the early 1980s, private companies began offering housing services similar to those offered by local bureaus. As local bureaus began to discontinue housing services, the number of companies offering housing services increased dramatically, and show managers now have many companies to choose from.

Now commonly called third party housing providers, these private companies are in the business of providing housing services to show organizers, almost always at no cost to them. Some also provide registration and meeting planning services. Often show organizers contract with a third party housing provider for multiple years, because they prefer to work with the same company in every city. Other benefits to this option include the opportunity for customized services and advance booking for future events.

When a show organizer does choose to work with a third party housing provider that is not affiliated with the local bureau, the hotels pay the housing company instead of the bureau. Some of these companies grew out of the travel agency business, which has traditionally been paid on a commission basis, so the most common compensation structure is commission (a fixed percentage of the hotel's rate). Just as when housing services are provided by a local bureau or their official provider, these costs may or may not be reflected in the final room rates. As full time convention housing specialists usually working in all major cities simultaneously, many claim to be able to assist show organizers with negotiating advantageous rates.

Travel Agencies and Incentive Houses

Many show organizers have relationships with travel agencies and business incentive and travel companies who provide travel services for the staff's routine business travel, or for employee incentive programs. Depending on the size of the room block and the dynamics of the host city, these companies can also be effective in managing housing for certain types of events. However, since the travel agents handling corporate or staff travel are usually not familiar with the dynamics of handling complex sub-blocks, some degree of special expertise is required for events with large numbers of exhibitors. Travel agencies and incentive houses are most effective when the attendees are a homogenous group who can be directed to make arrangements in a specific way. For example, corporate annual meetings or private tradeshows, software user groups, or specialty meetings with large numbers of international attendees are likely to use an agency or incentive house for housing, even for large numbers of attendees. Travel agencies have traditionally worked on a commission basis.

WHO PAYS FOR ALL THIS?

There is usually no direct cost to a show organizer for a housing management system unless there are expenditures incurred in building an in-house system. But because – whether working with a bureau, a third party housing provider or a travel agency – transaction fees and commissions may or may not be absorbed in the group room rate, some show managers feel that it is necessary to inform the attendees that "a portion of your hotel room rate is being used to provide a centralized housing service." This statement usually goes on the Web page or direct mail piece that announces the availability of the official housing system, describes the hotels and lists the negotiated rates.

Some hotels offer a commission to show organizers as an incentive to use their facility; others offer a commission to site selection companies. Site selection companies, however, do not manage the housing process, as their responsibilities end after the hotel and organizer have signed a contract. There is also some debate on whether these types of revenue generators should be disclosed.

Another issue often debated is that of revenue-sharing. This generally means that the housing provider "shares" a portion of the revenue it earns from the hotels for handling the reservation process with the show organizer. Honest communication and familiarity with standard business practices are the only answers to these sometimes complex issues.

Housing on the Web

Competition between all types of housing providers has resulted in sophisticated call centers and a wide range of online services. Some groups find that the majority of the reservations for their events are now made and managed online, including complex transactions for large staff blocks, online reporting for the meeting planner (and in some cases for the participating hotels) and the option for large and complex group blocks – such as exhibitors who bring a large staff to an event – to make all of their changes online. Very busy exhibit managers (professionals whose job it is to take a company's exhibit to a large number of shows each year) who are often traveling, have found that 24/7 availability of their group blocks is one of the biggest advantages of the advent of Web-based convention housing.

Most show organizers now create a Web "show page" for each event, and link multiple other services from that site, including housing and travel arrangements. The housing page generally lists all hotels participating in the official housing program, and offers descriptions and photos of each, along with the negotiated group rate. The sponsoring organization will usually be responsible for the initial housing information page, and often gives separate instructions and links for booking to attendees and exhibitors. As soon as users click on a link, they are directed to the housing provider's site. This transaction, however, is usually so transparent that users do not realize the difference, and the provider's name is not conspicuous. The responsibility for hosting the reservation site and all of the technical details of how reservations are made falls to the housing provider.

Considering the many other ways an attendee can choose to make a reservation, keeping as many hotel reservations in the official housing program as possible is a common challenge. Many show organizers also post various incentives for attendees and exhibitors to book through the official program on the initial housing page, including an explanation of the potential benefits to the sponsoring organization, and recognition that higher benefits could reflect positively on the organization's dues structure.

The Accepted Practices Exchange (APEX) has put together recommendations on incentives to encourage attendees and exhibitors to make hotel reservations within the contracted block for an event. Many show organizers have contributed ideas and some of these include:

- Offering "value-adds" such as free breakfast and complimentary fitness center access for early-bird housing, or for anyone who books through the official housing program at any time

- Access to a negotiated early-bird rate in the contract. For example, rooms booked and pre-paid 60 days prior to the event will have a different rate than all other rooms in the contracted block. A discounted rate on the housing and/or registration can be implemented to encourage early booking

- Offering discounted or free additional registrations for exhibitors who book through the official housing procedures. Invite group block managers (usually exhibitors) to a welcoming reception. Give them a package of their block's name badges and materials, and offer them an opportunity to make changes to their registrations at that time
- Providing positive incentives for exhibitor pick-up, such as higher housing booth selection priority points for picking up a high percentage of a group block
- Requiring participation in the contracted room block to access the shuttle bus system by providing a special badge or shuttle pass which must be shown before boarding the event shuttle bus.

More about recommended APEX practices can be found at www.conventionindustry.org.

Although primarily contracted to handle hotel reservations, many housing providers also provide the following Web-based services to different degrees and in different ways:

- Hotel Confirmations in Real Time: Ability to provide instant confirmation of a transaction, although some providers still accumulate reservation requests daily, process overnight and respond with a confirmation by email the next day
- Group Reservations: (Generally defined as 10 rooms or more.) Allows groups of internal or external coordinators for exhibitors and other important groups, such as speakers, board members, staffers and other VIPs, to request reservations online. Group coordinators then receive some type of password for access to their assigned room block for later changes.
- Online reporting: Allows show organizers and sometimes hoteliers to check progress of room pick up – how many reservations have been made to date in the hotel – in order to monitor the progress of reservations for their event and customize reports .
- Travel services: Links to booking engines for airline and rental car reservations, where negotiated discounts or group rates can be displayed.

Putting Together a Room Block

Addressing housing and transportation issues requires knowing who is going to be attending the event. If available, the attendee and exhibitor profiles created from the data collected during previous registration efforts will make the selection of appropriate hotels easier by knowing what types of accommodations the attendees and exhibitors prefer. For instance, are they budget conscious, or status and amenity conscious? Do they require large suites for entertainment after hours? Are they walkers, or is there a significant population who prefer not to walk? All of these factors and more go should contribute to the choice of hotels to participate in the event's official housing program. During the first inspection of the exhibit hall or convention center in a new city, there should also be a thorough inspection of the nearby hotels.

The group history (how many rooms used on which nights at which hotels, which is part of the documentation of the economic impact of an event) is also critical. The creator of a first-time event faces substantial challenges in acquiring hotel commitments without prior history, especially in high-demand cities.

Histories are most credible when they come directly from the previous hotel. Hotels are sometimes tardy in providing these important final numbers, so some show managers routinely write into the hotel contract that final payment of the master bill will be delayed until such reports are provided. Some shows regularly file histories with the Destination Marketing Association (formerly the IACVB), which keeps a database available to all hotels and bureaus expressly for this purpose.

Once the hotels to be included have been selected, and those hotels have agreed to hold a number of rooms in a tentative block (which means with no contractual obligation to the organizer), the contract may be processed immediately. In some cases, the processing of the contract can be deferred as long as several years, provided a Letter of Agreement is in place to document the tentative hold on the agreed-upon block.

At what point a hotel will request a formal contract usually depends on other pressures on the hotel. For instance, if there is another group requesting rooms over the same dates, the hotel will propose a deadline for signing the contract. The rooms will be released if contract terms have not been agreed to by this deadline. Show organizers may also initiate the signing of the contract in order to ensure room availability prior to beginning to promote the exhibition.

Negotiating the Hotel Contract

Whether the hotel contracts are negotiated by exhibition management, or by a third party housing provider acting on its behalf, it is important to be educated on basic legal issues as well as the issues unique to group hotel contracts.

Because the financial repercussions to the sponsoring organization as well as to the attendees and exhibitors can be substantial, it is important that the contracting process be given as much attention as the many other tasks involved in producing an event. Some event organizers work for organizations that have either in-house attorneys or outside legal counsel review all of their hotel contracts. After enough years of experience, however, an event organizer should be able to negotiate with a hotel salesperson in order to obtain the most advantageous deal possible.

There are many continuing education opportunities in the meeting and tradeshow industry for learning about hotel contract negotiation. The list of negotiable issues is substantial, and varies from hotel to hotel and city to city, but indeed *"everything is negotiable."*. However, the amount to which this is true relates back eventually to determining the room rate to be paid by the attendees and exhibitors. The hotel is interested in total revenue for the property, whether recovered from room rates, catering, food and beverage outlets, health spa fees or Internet access charges. Savvy show organizers will research the total value of the business they bring to the hotel, and understand the relative strength that each party brings to the negotiation. The "win-win" philosophy must apply to any successful hotel contract negotiation.

Attrition will always be a challenge for the meetings, conventions and exhibitions industry. But thanks to Project Attrition, planners and suppliers now have a comprehensive toolbox and resources to combat the problem.

Project Attrition, an initiative of the Convention Industry Council funded also by the ASAE Foundation, the American Hotel & Lodging Educational Foundation, the MPI Foundation, and the PCMA Education Foundation, was born in response to the industry's growing concerns over attrition. Finalized in 2004, this short-term industry collaboration was designed to help educate members of the meetings, conventions and exhibitions industry on the issue while pursuing solutions to minimize the impact of the problem.

The Project Attrition Final Report, which details the work of the Project Attrition Task Force and includes tools developed to assist planners and suppliers alike, is now available on-line at www.conventionindustry.org. The direct link to the report is: http://www.conventionindustry.org/projects/project_attrition_report11204.pdf

---

Two of the most important contractual issues an event organizer will deal in negotiating hotel contracts are attrition and cancellation.

Attrition refers to a situation in which fewer rooms were used than anticipated in the hotel contract. Because it is rarely possible to accurately predict the number of hotel rooms required as far in advance as is necessary to sign a hotel contract, even the savviest planners are at risk for what can be significant attrition charges. On the other hand, hotels agree to take sellable inventory off the market far in advance of the actual dates, and are at risk of not being able to re-sell that inventory if the show organizer does not produce the anticipated demand for those rooms.

The successful negotiation is one in which both sides evaluate the circumstances and agree to jointly and fairly apportion the risk. The best answer to reducing exposure to attrition penalties is by carefully managing the room inventory and a show organizer's comfort with this exposure. The need for outside assistance in managing the hotel room inventory may be one of the factors that help determine which method of housing management will be used.

Attrition can be defined as anything less than 100 percent of the "total room night" commitment in the contract. For events using multiple hotels – often called city-wide events, even if they are not strictly using every hotel in the city – hotels commonly want a clause in the contract that reimburses them in some way if 20 percent or more of the room nights are not utilized. This means the rooms are not just reserved, but paid for and occupied. In other words, if a group uses at least 80 percent of the room nights the show organizer has committed to, attrition charges will probably not be applicable.

Although attrition can be calculated in many ways, the most common way is to multiply the group room rate by the number of nights (not including taxes). Hotels may also ask for attrition penalties if a show's catered events do not meet the numbers initially predicted.

Cancellation relates to penalties for the cancellation of the entire contract. Occasionally, circumstances require either the hotel or the event organizer to cancel. When such action is contemplated, each party should understand its rights and responsibilities. The closer to the contracted dates the cancellation occurs, the larger the percentage in liquidated damages – the amount of financial recovery owed to the injured party, usually the lost profits – the hotel will require. As a rule, the parties should agree ahead of time to the grounds and remedies for cancellation. Although not all parties will agree to include any or all of these clauses, some of the more common scenarios that might be addressed in a cancellation clause include:

- A hotel contract can be canceled at any time if there are disruptions in transportation, such as strikes or similar events that would prevent the exhibition from being held at the hotel
- The contract can be canceled if the event itself is canceled or if the exhibition facility becomes unavailable
- If the attendance at the event increases more rapidly than anticipated, the contract can be canceled if the hotel is not equipped to handle the larger meeting and provided adequate notice is given.

Most contracts today also include a *Force Majeure* (or "Acts of God") clause which relieves both parties of any liability to the other when uncontrollable events such as natural disasters, terrorism or other unforeseen events make it impossible to hold the event.

Determining the Rate

The rate paid for a guest room is one of the single most significant factors an attendee or exhibitor will consider when booking a room. When negotiating a group rate, a good negotiator will know how many nights the typical attendee or exhibitor will be staying, whether they will be utilizing single or double rooms (or triple or quads), local sales tax, and the bed or tourism tax (yet an additional charge) that will be applied to the rate.

Many factors affect the rate you will be able to negotiate, and there are many continuing education opportunities to learn more about the art of negotiation. One key element is the time of year the rooms are needed. If rooms are booked during a slow season, rates will be more negotiable than during a high or peak season when demand for that hotel is at the highest point of the calendar year, and rates are high also. If booking during a peak time, the best leverage may be large "room night" volumes, and/or using as few hotels as possible to maximize the size of the room block in each.

Another factor affecting rate is the days of the week for your event. In a resort area, the weekends will most likely be busy, and not available for discounted group rates. In a downtown hotel, the majority of business is normally during the middle of the week. Therefore, requesting the weekends could produce some better rates.

Everyone wants to negotiate a good rate, but sometimes a higher rate is a better option if the rate results in a better overall contract for the show organizer. Sometimes, free meeting space, audio-visual equipment and services, and complimentary group refreshment breaks can be included in the contract. Quite often, meeting room rental rates are based on a sliding scale; the more sleeping rooms booked, the lower the charges. Items such as parking charges, health club fees, and golf greens fees can sometimes be negotiated as well. These options can be advertised to attendees as an attractive value-added package, which in turn may encourage increased attendance and room pick-up.

Marketing the Housing Program

All destination bureaus and most major hotel chains and third party housing providers offer assistance with promoting the official housing system. Standard options include "canned" content for the show page, links to local attractions and transportation information, and other assistance with e-marketing efforts and expenses. Although any e-marketing campaign must be carefully coordinated with other communications from the sponsoring organization, show organizers are increasingly turning to this technology to promote both their events and the official housing system.

Since many housing providers now either offer registration services themselves, or have systems that share data with major registration vendors, merge/purge data comparisons are not difficult, and are used to carefully target email messages to the right recipients. There are also telephone marketing vendors whose software can send pre-recorded phone messages to prospective attendees reminding them to register for the meeting and to book their housing.

Section V: Contractors

Logistics On-Site

Best laid plans often go astray, and multiple factors affect housing logistics on site. Again, the best medicine is prevention, and a carefully planned housing management system goes a long way toward eliminating surprises on site. Generally, most housing problems begin showing symptoms weeks or months before the first arrival date, and can be dealt with early enough to alleviate problems once the event begins.

Supply and demand are the critical issues in determining the potential for a walk (when a room reservation is not honored by the hotel at the time of the guest's arrival). Since the number of changes in hotel reservations is often significant, hotels sometimes second guess actual occupancy by over selling their room inventory (taking more reservations than there are rooms available). When their estimate is off the mark, a certain number of guests must be accommodated in other hotels. Most hotel contracts contain provisions related to how a guest must be treated if walked (such as free transportation to the other hotel, reimbursement for the room rate, or a guaranteed return to the host hotel the next night.).

There is no absolute way to guarantee that this situation will never happen. Some show organizers recommend that when signs indicate that a hotel will be close to 100 percent occupancy on a given night (or more, as some hotels gamble that a certain percentage of guests will not show up and sell over 100 percent of capacity), it is wise is to review the arrival list with the hotel's front office manager. At that point, it is possible to request that guests identified as being with the exhibition are the last to be walked.

Many exhibitions run a housing assistance desk near the registration area on site, staffed by a member of the housing reservations management staff. This desk services any attendees who arrive on site without a reservation, those who want to inquire about possible changes, and those encountering problems of any kind. Some shows also provide a locator system by which attendees and exhibitors can locate colleagues by hotel.

Another on-site housing management tool is the survey. Some event organizers request housing information on the registration form and compare these answers to the information received through the official housing management system. The intention is to determine how many of the attendees and exhibitors are using other means to obtain housing accommodations. This information supplements the information obtained by the official system plus any information gained by auditing the official hotels.

Large exhibitions sometimes either allow or ask exhibitors to indicate housing requirements for the following year while on site for the current year's show. This is often tied to a seniority point system for exhibit space selection, and is usually only a preliminary system to ensure that key and returning exhibitors are accommodated.

Show organizers also need to stay in touch with key individuals at all of the hotels which are housing attendees and exhibitors throughout the entire period, from arrival to departure. This task may be delegated to someone from the housing management system, either in the sponsoring organization, with the local bureau, or from the third party housing provider. Daily checks as to room pick-up and occupancy of each hotel demonstrate interest to the hotel, and assure that surprises and complaints are kept to a minimum. There are also times that information from hotels is required to make adjustments to shuttle schedules based on heavier or lighter than anticipated usage from any given pick-up point.

A master bill will only be generated from hotels where expenses were billed to the sponsoring organization. Many show organizers request a face-to-face meeting with the front office or convention services manager of each hotel prior to departure from the city in order to review billing. At that time, pick-up reports can be mutually scrutinized, and any discrepancies can be negotiated while the circumstances are fresh in everyone's mind.

Auditing

As soon as the event is over and as part of the evaluation process, all of the hotels in the official hotel program – and sometimes those who were not – should be requested to report exactly how many room nights were occupied. This request becomes critical if your hotel contracts include attrition liability.

Although some hoteliers operate under corporate policy which prohibits sharing information about individual guests, auditing software has been developed which can be used on site at the hotel, and which protects the guest's privacy. Without software, the audit is also possible if the show organizer is willing to take a list of registrants to the hotel, and manually compare hotel occupants against this list for each relevant date.

Audits are often quite successful in increasing the number of room nights credited to an event because they turn up guests who made a room reservation – either through a hotel's national reservation toll-free number or corporate Web site, or even through a Web discounter – without mentioning they were attending the event in question. Before the numbers are finalized, it is important to capture an accurate snapshot of the event's usage of the entire hotel inventory in the city in order to maintain an accurate history of your event.

Section V: Contractors

SUMMARY

The number of options for a housing management system has increased significantly over the years. Although not providing an official housing system is still an option, it is now possible to choose from a wide range of other options, from handling housing in-house, to working with local bureaus, to soliciting proposals from numerous competitive third- party housing providers. Above all, the housing process must be actively managed in order to produce the best possible exhibition.

QUESTIONS FOR DISCUSSION

① What are the benefits to the host organization when attendees and exhibitors book their hotel rooms inside the official housing program?

② What are the reasons exhibitors are likely to book their hotel rooms outside the official housing program? Do you think these are valid?

③ What are the advantages and disadvantages to hotels for participating in large city-wide housing programs?

④ What online site do you use most frequently to book hotel rooms and why?

Chapter 4
Air & Ground Transportation

"Travel is only glamorous in retrospect."
– Paul Theroux

Section V: Contractors

IN THIS CHAPTER YOU WILL LEARN

- How to obtain negotiated airfares
- What to expect in an airline contract
- Why ground transportation is one of show management's responsibilities
- How to assess the need for shuttle systems
- How to hire a convention shuttle company

INTRODUCTION

Because everyone has to get to the exhibition in some way, site selection is often influenced by the cost and accessibility of air travel from areas with large numbers of potential attendees. Ground transportation, or how attendees get from their hotels to the event, can also significantly impact the success of an exhibition. If the exhibitors and attendees cannot easily, efficiently and economically get from their homes to the exhibition, it will be more difficult to attract them to and retain them at the event.

CONTRIBUTORS

For air travel, Garet Roberson, Airline Manager, Travel Planners Inc. For ground transportation, Jeffrey Ducate, Vice President of Sales, CMAC

The exhibition is a service product. The exhibition manager is a service provider. While the most important service they provide is the production of the exhibition, show organizers must never lose sight of the fact that attendees and exhibitors have expectations for all of the services involved, including getting them to and from the event. Transportation is a service for which expectations are high, and unfortunately its delivery is not directly under the show manager's control.

Airline Travel for Conventions

Many airlines offer convention and group discounts. The terms of the contracts vary by airline, and sometimes by event location. Gone are the days of competitive bidding for convention business. But in return for being named the official carrier for a specific event – especially a high profile one – there are still opportunities to obtain a percentage off the retail ticket price, plus complimentary tickets for staff travel and even airline incentive points. With prominent placement in all collateral materials and promotion of the discounts, a show has the potential to earn significant travel rewards that can directly affect the travel budget while also providing a service to attendees and exhibitors.

In order to obtain these benefits, travelers must reference a specific discount code so that the airline can credit the show. However, tracking these purchases has long been a challenge. Most airline Web sites do not have a place to enter a convention discount code. So until recent years, travelers had to call the airline or a travel agency to book at the discount. But with the advent of specialized Web booking engines that accept the airline codes, online processing of convention discounts has become possible, making tracking easier and leading to better benefits to the show organizer.

There are two types of group discounts:
- A convention discount is applicable to more than ten travelers traveling from various points to a specific city between specific dates (usually from a week or so prior to the event to a few days following it). Many airlines will not allow one-way travel, as the one-way travel may be fraudulent for travel originating in the meeting city.
- A group discount is applicable when ten or more people traveling are on the same flight. The benefit to a group discount is that often fares can be locked in, and a sufficient number of seats can be blocked far in advance for all travelers at one time. In return, the event organizer agrees to provide a list of the travelers' names and payment for all by a given date. This type of contract is most often used for corporate meetings than convention travel.

Both of these types of discounts require a contract which is usually written for only one year, or only one event. Due to budget cuts and repositioning of their markets, most of the major airlines maintain a Groups or Meetings Desk. Staff in these offices are responsible for these contracts, and for maintaining relationships with event organizers. An event organizer could research the host city or consult the local bureau to determine which airlines provide the most service (or "lift") into the host city for their event.

SAMPLE EMAIL COPY FOR CONVENTION AIRLINE DISCOUNT PROMOTION

American Airlines is offering discounted zone fares to San Diego, California. These special fares allow for midweek travel and do not require a Saturday-night stay - plus they qualify for AAdvantage and Oneworld mileage programs and upgrades. **To book your reservation on American, call your travel agent, or American at +1(800) 433-1790, and reference STARfile: AXXN6XX**

Have you searched the web and found a great American Airlines rate on an Internet Web site? Before you book the flight over the Internet, call American Airlines at +1(800) 433-1790 and reference STARfile: **AXXN6XX**. Our American Airlines agreement gives you an additional 5% off the lowest applicable fare. These fares are valid for travel 26 November through 2 December 2006.

Book your flight NOW!

Airline Travel for Other Business

Whether for site inspections, contractor selection or visiting competitive events, a show manager is often in the air. Occasionally this type of business travel is managed under the umbrella of the airline contract discussed above, especially if the event is producing a large number of complimentary tickets or obtaining other benefits. Some show organizers utilize retail travel sites on the Web for their year-round travel, and use their earned complimentary tickets for travel to and from the event itself. However, many organizations require employees to book their own travel using either in-house resources, or local retail travel agencies with whom the organization has contracted. This allows the organization or agency to enforce travel policies and monitor expenditures, although the agency will charge a transaction fee for each ticket. Many convention housing companies also offer all of the services of a retail travel agency, including car rentals and train tickets.

Ground Transportation

The key to effective and successful ground transportation services is to start early, plan well and pay close attention to the details and fine print. Given the complexity of local regulations including labor and union issues, transportation surcharges, city taxes, state licensing or access fees, fuel, oil and labor costs, and considering the fact that a single route on a large or city-wide event may be 50 miles round trip, requiring hundreds of buses needed over a very short time span, most exhibition managers with events utilizing a large number of hotels outsource to a ground transportation specialist with experience in the exhibition industry. There are many companies that specialize in these services. Some work only in their own cities; others work nationally, utilizing local equipment and drivers. As in selecting other vendors, making a good match for the event's unique characteristics will require research and good business practices.

SEE FIGURE 1a and 1b

Advance Work

Ground transportation needs should be thoroughly investigated during the early site selection process. To ensure all the necessary services are available, research must be done on all transportation options to or from the airport, the exhibit hall and hotels, as well as to various tourist destinations within the city: taxi, commuter trains, trolleys, city transit, courtesy vans, water taxis, in-city rapid transit or subways, and walking where possible. Test runs should be done on the same days and during the same hours at which the event is to be held. Although traffic patterns in most cities are heaviest on weekdays in the early morning and mid-afternoon to early evening, the volume and patterns shift dramatically on weekends in many areas. If the event is held on a weekday, and show hours coincide with the city's normal rush-hour traffic patterns, attendees could be in line for long waits for and on shuttle buses trying to navigate clogged city arteries, and more expensive taxi rides. Assessing transportation needs during event days and times will reveal how much public parking might be available to those who choose to travel to the event by car.

Consider Options

The second step in planning ground transportation services is to decide if dedicated transportation services are actually needed between host hotels and the exhibition site. What are the factors that determine whether or not walking is a good option?

• **Safety**: During the initial site inspection, a thorough walk-through of the areas that attendees may use to access the exhibition site is useful. Feedback from the facility staff, the security contractor or local police can be helpful.

• **Location**: If the majority of hotels are only a five or ten minute walk from the exhibit hall, most show organizers encourage walking. A short walk is not usually perceived as a hardship by attendees. In fact, many enjoy the brief physical exercise. However, even if the majority of attendees will be walkers, there is usually at least a minimal shuttle service, primarily for disabled or other attendees unable to walk that distance. Often, hotel courtesy vehicles can be appropriated for this purpose.

• **Weather**: If the hotels are located within a ten minute walk, and local weather conditions are favorable year-round, encourage walking. Always have a plan for inclement weather.

FIGURE 1a

SEMICON®
West2006

SHUTTLE BUS INFORMATION

Complimentary service will be provided to and from official hotels as follows:

ROUTES 1 - 8

	Inbound to Moscone Center Every 15-20 Minutes	To/From Hotels Departing Moscone Ctr. Every 25-30 Minutes	Return to Hotels Every 15-20 Minutes
Tues.	8:00am - 11:00am	11:00am - 3:30pm	3:30pm - 6:30pm
Wed.	8:00am - 11:00am	11:00am - 3:30pm	3:30pm - 6:30pm
Thurs.	8:00am - 11:00am	11:00am - 3:30pm	3:30pm - 5:00pm

ROUTE 9

	Inbound to Moscone Center Every 30 Minutes	To/From San Mateo Departing Moscone Ctr. Every 30 Minutes	Return to San Mateo Every 30 Minutes
Tues.	8:00am - 11:00am	11:00am - 3:30pm	3:30pm - 6:30pm
Wed.	8:00am - 11:00am	11:00am - 3:30pm	3:30pm - 6:30pm
Thurs.	8:00am - 11:00am	11:00am - 3:30pm	3:30pm - 5:00pm

Subject to weather and traffic conditions.

Shuttle Service Desk Hours:
(North, South and West Hall Entrances)

Tuesday, July 11	7:30am - 7:00pm
Wednesday, July 12	7:30am - 7:00pm
Thursday, July 13	7:30am - 5:30pm

Special Services:

Shuttle Service between Caltrain Station and Moscone Center: Service begins at 8:00am, with continuous service every 20-30 minutes. The last daily shuttle will depart Moscone Center at 6:30pm on July 11-12, and 5:00pm on July 13. *Schedule information is subject to change.*

Shuttle Service between San Mateo County Event Center and Moscone Center: Complimentary shuttle service between Moscone Center and the San Mateo County Event Center will be available on SHOW DAYS ONLY (July 11-13). Parking will be approximately $7.00 per car, per day. Route 9 shuttles will run every 30 minutes beginning at 8:00am.

Shuttle Service between San Francisco and San Jose: Route 10 shuttles will depart from the SEMI Headquarters at 3081 Zanker Road, San Jose. Departure times are 7:30am, 9:00am, 10:30am, & 12:00pm from San Jose. Return times are 2:30pm, 4:00pm, 5:30pm, & 7:00pm.

 For hotel shuttle information or special needs transportation, **please call toll free 1.888.933.3300.** Accessible equipment is available during scheduled shuttle hours. Please request service at least 30 minutes in advance of desired pick up time.

This information is current as of May 22, 2006. For complete, up-to-date schedule and boarding information, please see the sign in your official SEMICON West show hotel lobby.

FIGURE 1b

HOTEL LOCATOR

Note: UPPERCASE indicates Boarding Location
WD indicates Walking Distance

HOTEL	ROUTE #	BOARDING POINT
Argent Hotel	WD	Walking Distance
BEST WESTERN AMERICANIA	5	7th Street
Best Western Carriage Inn	5	At Best Western Americana
Caltrain Station	8	Townsend and 4th Street
Chancellor Hotel Union Station	2	At Westin St. Francis
Clift Hotel	1	At Hilton San Francisco
Commodore Hotel	2	At Westin St. Francis
Courtyard by Marriott San Francisco	WD	Walking Distance
Crowne Plaza Union Square	2	At Westin St. Francis
Fairmont San Francisco	4	At InterContinental Mark Hopkins
Four Seasons	WD	Walking Distance
GRAND HYATT SAN FRANCISCO	3	Sutter Street
Handlery Union Square	2	At Westin St. Francis
HILTON FINANCIAL	6	Kearny Street
HILTON SAN FRANCISCO	1	Taylor Street
Hotel Adagio	1	At Hilton San Francisco
Hotel Britton	5	At Best Western Americana
Hotel Diva	1	At Hilton San Francisco
Hotel Metropolis	1	At Renaissance Parc 55
Hotel Milano	WD	Walking Distance
Hotel Monaco	1	At Hilton San Francisco
Hotel Nikko	1	At Renaissance Parc 55
Hotel Palomar	WD	Walking Distance
Hotel Rex	2	At Westin St. Francis
Hotel Triton	3	At Grand Hyatt San Francisco
Hotel Union Square	1	At Renaissance Parc 55
Huntington Hotel	4	At InterContinental Mark Hopkins
HYATT FISHERMAN'S WHARF	7	North Point Street
HYATT REGENCY	6	Drumm Street
INTERCONTINENTAL MARK HOPKINS	4	California Street
JW Marriott (formerly Pan Pacific)	2	At Westin St. Francis
Kensington Park Hotel	2	At Westin St. Francis
King George Hotel	1	At Hilton San Francisco
LE MERIDIEN (formerly Park Hyatt)	6	Battery Street
Marriott San Francisco	WD	Walking Distance
Maxwell Hotel	2	At Westin St. Francis
Monticello Inn	1	At Renaissance Parc 55
Mosser Hotel	WD	Walking Distance
OMNI	4	Montgomery Street
PALACE HOTEL	2	New Montgomery Street
Pickwick Hotel	WD	Walking Distance
Prescott Hotel	2	At Westin St. Francis
Radisson Fisherman's Wharf	7	At Hyatt Fisherman's Wharf
RENAISSANCE PARC 55	1	Cyril Magnin Street
San Mateo County Event Center	9	San Mateo County Event Center
Serrano Hotel	1	At Hilton San Francisco
Sir Francis Drake Hotel	2	At Westin St. Francis
St. Regis Hotel	WD	Walking Distance
Villa Florence	2	At Westin St. Francis
W San Francisco	WD	Walking Distance
WESTIN ST. FRANCIS	2	Post Street

Shuttle Managed by **cmac** 1.401.826.4100

For some events, a walking program is a good way to encourage a degree of physical exercise for all attendees, and help the show's bottom line. A walking promotion may be incorporated into a corporate sponsorship program that will cost the event little or nothing, and give the sponsor a highly visible, interactive marketing opportunity. In short, it's possible to make a walking program a value-added component of the event.

If there are a limited number of hotels, or there is a need to minimize the cost of the service, one option is to offer shuttle service on a limited basis. Careful scheduling and planning will be necessary to ensure punctuality. Attendees and exhibitors must be well informed that the shuttle bus will run only at certain times on certain days, such as just once in the morning and once in the afternoon. Schedules should be published in all promotional material, and be highly visible via signage at both the exhibit hall and hotels.

Other events utilizing a limited number of hotels, or hotels in close proximity to the exhibit hall, might run on clock schedules such as every 15-20 minutes or on the half hour. This type of scheduling builds in waiting time at either end of the route, as well as time for minor traffic delays. For example, a transportation unit (usually a bus or van) would be leaving the exhibit hall on the hour. After making the 10-12 minute journey to the hotel, the transportation unit would load waiting passengers, wait until the appointed time, and then head out again.

Dedicated Shuttle Service

Because thousands of people will expect to have easy access to the exhibit hall in a timely and efficient manner, ground transportation needs for large events often present some of the biggest logistical challenges a show organizer can face. Ultimately, the show organizer will have to decide what level of services will be required, and who will pay for it. Some show managers restrict shuttle usage to those staying in official hotels, and even to only those who have booked their hotel reservations through the official housing system. Enforcement can be tricky, as attendees have to show a specially- imprinted hotel key card or some other identifier before being allowed to board a bus.

Despite the cost, most large exhibitions provide shuttle transportation as a complimentary service, either through direct absorption of the cost – including it in registration and/or exhibit fees – or by having a corporation underwrite the cost of the service through a sponsorship agreement. The level of service offered depends on the number of hotels that are being used by attendees and exhibitors, the complexity of the program, and the expectations and demographics of the attendees.

When using multiple hotels, how many transportation units needed and the ultimate cost of the entire system depends primarily on how much the show organizer is willing to spend to make the ride time for each attendee as short as possible. Multiple options can create a complicated decision grid, and also make it difficult to predict the final cost. Will the buses pick up at multiple hotels, but make a return trip to a single designated hotel? Will they pick up at multiple hotels, and make multiple stops on the return also? How many attendees will want to depart from each hotel early in the day vs. later? How many people will be exiting the exhibit hall immediately after the show closes each day? Each bus and each stop will decrease the total riding time of the route, but increase the total cost of the system. Determining these variables are the reason many show organizers – particularly those with city-wide events – often outsource the management of the shuttle bus system to an experienced contractor.

In addition to anticipating potential ridership and planning the transportation routes, the shuttle contractor must also plan for emergencies and other circumstances which could disrupt transportation plans. The shuttle contractor must ensure that alternate routes have been planned that can be easily and efficiently put into place with minimal disruptions to attendees.

Special Event Transportation

Special events are becoming a common occurrence with exhibition programs. Some of the more common special events are golf tournaments, opening receptions held at a famous local landmark, restaurant "dine-arounds" and pub crawls. Transportation for special events is in addition to the daily shuttle system planned to transport guests to and from the exhibit hall, and may be run by the daily shuttle contractor, or by show staff, or by a destination management company. Separate information and schedules must be posted at all pick-up points.

There are several guidelines that can help make planning for special event transportation easier:

• List expectations and budget constraints at the outset of the negotiations with the shuttle contractor or other service provider for the event(s).

• Do a site inspection of the special event venue. Ascertain whether or not the site will accommodate buses. If this scenario proves highly difficult, what other options are there? (Smaller buses, vans or limousine service are some of the options).

• Are there any other transportation needs for this special event? What about VIPS or entertainers and their equipment?

• If there is a large group to move, does the city have adequate vehicles to handle it? Have you used up all available buses with the regular shuttle service?

• Schedules must be planned so that guests have adequate time to get from the exhibit hall back to their hotels before heading out to a special event. If time is a concern, this issue can be eliminated by providing service from the exhibition hall directly to the event.

- Will guests want to move in and out at one time, or will there be waves over the period of several minutes or hours? It will be important to be able to predict the guests' tolerance level for waiting, and have a schedule that will meet the needs of guests throughout the event, including early departures.
- For a large group, crowd control is a critical issue. Load lines, adequate signage, special traffic control (city police units) and lots of space for both people and buses in the staging areas may be needed.

Equipment needs – and therefore costs – will be significantly affected by how quickly and how often the guests are to be transported. Transportation costs are directly proportional to the time it takes to transport people from Point A to Point B.

Choosing a Ground Transportation Provider

Choosing a qualified ground transportation provider is crucial to the overall success of a transportation plan, and the exhibition itself. Using the same format and criteria as used for other contractors, develop an RFP that outlines the event's needs, budget, nature of the clientele, and type and level of services required. Some of the essential details that should be included in a ground transportation RFP include:

- **Costs and Formula for Calculation**: Ask what the anticipated cost of the services is, and how these costs are calculated. How the shuttle contractor being compensated?
- **Minimums**: Four-hour and five-hour minimum rates are quite common in major cities, especially when dealing with bus transportation. Will minimum rental rates apply? Ask for a detailed breakdown of costs.
- **Number, Condition & Availability**: How many and in what condition are the available ground transportation units, such as buses, vans, and motor coaches? Ask to see a copy of the company's maintenance schedule, as well as its policy on unit upgrades and repairs. Ask for a policy regarding back-up units in case of breakdowns or accidents.
- **Reputation**: Ask for references from representatives of groups who have had similar scheduling needs, for events of similar size and duration.
- **Experience and Expertise**: How adept is this provider at moving large or small groups of people? Again, asking for specific requests is a good idea.
- **Special Services/Compliance**: Does the provider offer any special services? Are they able to comply with ADA legislation?
- **Fulfillment**: Can the company handle the contract in house? If subcontracting will be required, how will show management's interests be protected?
- **Insurance**: What is the status of the company's insurance coverage? How comprehensive is it? Is it adequate for the scope of service needed and the size of the event?
- **Operator Experience**: Ask for operator abstracts. Find out if they are used to operating the equipment being hired. Are they familiar with the city and locale, or

have they been brought in from other cities or areas? If so, what training provisions have been put in place to ensure they can meet the needs of the event? Ask for a list of clients whose requirements were similar to the anticipated needs of the event.

- **Labor Contracts:** When are operator contracts up for renewal? Are there any contract restrictions or requirements that may impact the service levels needed for the upcoming event? Does the transportation union have contract stipulations regarding driver work schedules, overtime, waiting time, or similar issues?

- **Surcharges:** Does the host city or the service provider have a series of transportation surcharges that are to be added onto or hidden in the contract price? City taxes, state licensing or access fees, fuel, oil & labor surcharges are all add-ons that could end up being included in the event's ground transportation billing. Ensure that the proposal states that all such costs are included in the original price quote.

- **Subsidies:** Does the host city offer subsidies to groups? It never hurts to ask the local convention and visitor bureau whether you qualify.

Everything with respect to pricing and service levels should be in writing and fully executed in a contract. Ground transportation costs have been known to spiral completely out of control because the show manager did not ensure that all additional costs were included in the contract.

SUMMARY

Whether planning airline travel or ground transportation, the show manager must be well informed about all options. Ensuring that attendees and exhibitors can easily and economically access the event will encourage increased and repeat attendance. Booking air travel and utilizing ground transportation is, in many instances, an attendee's first experience with an exhibition, in much the same way a hotel guest's first experience is at the front desk upon checking in: it must be positive.

QUESTIONS FOR DISCUSSION

① Which is likely to be a better deal when purchasing an airline ticket to attend a convention: 5 percent off a coach fare purchased six months in advance, or an Internet fare purchased 5 days in advance?

② What type of show would be most likely to decide that attendees would appreciate the opportunity to walk to and from their hotels to the exhibit hall? Least likely?

③ What are the differences between city transportation system busses and busses used for long trips (called coaches)? Which type are most likely to be used for convention shuttle programs and why?

Section V: Contractors

Chapter 5
Audio-Visual Services

"The Internet is the most important single development in the history of human communication since the invention of call waiting."

– Dave Barry

Section V: Contractors

IN THIS CHAPTER YOU WILL LEARN

- Services audio-visual contractors provide
- How to determine your AV needs during a site inspection
- How to guide your speakers towards their best presentations
- Some tips on video conferencing and electronic presentations

INTRODUCTION

In addition to producing the exhibition, a show organizer may also be responsible for the logistics for meeting rooms, general sessions and entertainment functions, all of which usually require audio-visual equipment (AV). Audio-visual contractors supply technical support, and rent AV equipment ranging from simple projector screens to full-scale productions, including live talent. In some cases, it is not unusual to have multiple AV contractors or production companies involved, each specializing in one service area. Selecting the appropriate contractor to manage each one of these technically-demanding tasks is a critical decision, and requires some very specialized knowledge.

CONTRIBUTOR

Gary Clark, Vice President, Communications, AVW-TELAV Audio-visual Solutions

Who Provides Audio-Visual Support Services

"Attention to details. Attention to details." This is a useful mantra for anyone involved in producing an event, but especially when planning for audio-visual services. The use of AV in an event can vary in scope from a small video monitor playing a taped presentation in an exhibit booth, to having a major production extravaganza in a general session venue. The key to successfully producing any AV-based event regardless of size is proactive planning.

In planning for the event, a show organizer must analyze the facilities, the vendor options and the program goals of the functions. All these must blend to satisfy budget considerations, and the overall objectives for the event. Working through all the checklists and timelines can become a tedious logistical challenge, leaving little time and energy for the "look and feel" of the attendee experience. However, it is important to step back and take a "big picture" look at the project and ask the questions: "Why are we doing this?" What is the purpose and goal we want to achieve?" Then, turn on the creative juices for the fun part, and visualize the look and feel that attendees should experience as they participate in the event.

While service contractors and facilities are unique, and some facilities require use of an exclusive in-house contractor, smooth interaction between the facility and the contractor is important when planning and producing an event. However, regardless of the event site, certain factors always come into play when integrating facility and AV production support.

Services Typically Provided by the AV Contractor

- Meeting room AV equipment and labor
- General session staging
- Tradeshow exhibit AV rentals and production
- Computer hardware rentals
- Webcasting and Podcasting services
- Video conferencing and satellite remotes (distance learning)
- Simultaneous interpretation services
- Presentation management systems
- Program capture and archival services
- Entertainment booking
- Design logistics and preplanning support
- Audio systems
- Lighting systems and rigging
- Video program production and presentation
- Advanced presentation technologies

- Audience Response Systems
- Program content creation and aggregation

Audio-visual services providers may offer some or all of the products above. The show organizer should become fully aware of a particular provider's capabilities to ensure proper event support.

In-House or Outsourced

The division of labor between facilities and an AV contractor can be confusing. Many meeting facilities, such as hotels, convention centers, resort conference centers and expo centers, have various forms of in-house audio-visual services. Some may be wholly-owned, managed and operated by full time staff, while others may be outsourced or contracted vendors who are representing the facility by wearing the facility uniform and acting on behalf of the venue. In either case, the amount of in-house AV service that is provided varies widely from property to property. It is important for the show organizer to get a clear and definite understanding from the facility representative of what is considered "exclusive," "preferred" or "unrestricted" audio-visual services.

Making a Good Match

Show organizers develop beneficial working partnerships with service contractors while producing events. Over a period of time, these relationships fuse the staff and support techs into a production team that eliminates the need to "reinvent the wheel" for each show. For many large conventions with large exhibits and a complex meeting schedule, bringing in a traveling contractor partner to produce the event is often considered mandatory. At the same time, facilities with in-house services available are anxious to have their own departments participate in the event production, and can present compelling financial reasons to do so. A show organizer must review each event on its own merit, size, complexity and degree of difficulty to determine which contractor to use when.

In many cases, smaller remote events can be handled satisfactorily by an in-house AV provider, while larger annual conventions and tradeshows may be best served by the extended staff of the show organizer's traveling contractor partners. Even for small meetings, however, it might be prudent to bring in the traveling partner to focus exclusively on the specific event. In a larger hotel or convention center facility, the in-house staff may have several concurrent events to handle, causing a dilution of technical support.

Union Labor

In large city facilities that have a strong union labor presence, the technical support staff may have a minimum- number-of-hours requirement. A show organizer may have a session scheduled for two-and-a-half hours, but the AV labor to support the session will be charged at a four-hour—and sometimes eight-hour— minimum. By asking these questions in the pre-planning process, the budget can be appropriately developed in order to avoid "invoice shock." In many cases, the AV contractor will accept responsibility for monitoring and minimizing union charges and for strategically determining how to make the best use of union labor.

Vendor Selection

The sample RFP in this chapter offers the show organizer the opportunity to consistently share relevant information about AV needs at an event with prospective vendors. The more detailed the RFP is, the easier it is for vendors to respond with relevant information about themselves and their capabilities. If budget is a factor, vendors usually appreciate knowing parameters in advance so as to prepare a compatible estimate of costs. There should also be a procedure for responding to questions from vendors throughout the RFP process, and some open-ended questions in the RFP will encourage the vendor to demonstrate their expertise.

Although everyone is concerned with cost, cost does not always value. The lowest dollar bid may not be totally comprehensive, especially concerning associated expenses (billed direct by another party), and can actually end up costing more in the end. To avoid this situation, a show organizer should expect a full explanation of services and costs from the contractor. Cost estimates and equipment price lists are much like the sticker price on a new car; they serve as a point from which to negotiate. Seek a fair settlement that satisfies all parties.

Facility Contractors

In some instances, facilities may impose restrictions or surcharges when a show organizer outsources some services to another production partner rather than the in-house vendor. When selecting a site for an event, show organizers should be aware of facility contracts that may affect their ability to work with chosen suppliers and negotiate appropriately:

- Know all terms before signing a contract
- Make sure outside contractors have access to the building
- Be aware of rigging restrictions
- Determine electrical services
- Ask if there are restrictive Audio Patch fees
- Is there a vendor Storage Area?
- Are there security/supervision fees?
- Are there commissions, access fees and/or surcharges?
- Ability to keep options open during the planning process?

It's always good practice to ask fellow show organizers about their experiences with prospective contractors or facility-specified providers. The more information available, the better the final selection decision is likely to be.

Internet Connections

In the recent past, computer rental agencies were regarded as separate vendors. With the ubiquitous use of laptop computers and presentation video projectors as primary display devices, the division between computers and traditional AV equipment has vanished. Typically, an AV provider now offers a full line of computer rentals as part of the standard inventory, and has staff technicians who perform as both IT (information technology/computer) specialists and AV technicians. In most newer facilities, and older ones that are renovating, Internet access infrastructure is available either through in-wall wired ports or wireless Internet.

The management and operation of these Internet services began as an offshoot of the telecommunications department, and remains in that domain in many facilities. Some are outsourced to IT management contractors in much the same way as in-house AV services are. However, these Internet services are typically exclusive services, much like electrical and catering in a facility.

Looking at Facilities from the AV Perspective

Questions to Ask...

... At a Site Visit:

- Does the facility have a contract with a particular AV supplier?
- What are the labor union jurisdictions?
- Are there charges for set-up and move-out days?
- If a 24-hour hold is made on a room, is there an extra charge?
- Who locks and unlocks rooms? When? Is there full time security?
- Is there an engineer on staff, or is engineering contracted?
- When are rooms normally set-up?
- Is there an accessible dock and elevator for contractors bringing in equipment and staging? How big are they?
- What is normally provided by the facility as part of the room? (Microphones, Flipcharts, Lecterns.)
- What is the "true" ceiling clearance? Measure "Clear Ceiling Height."
- What is the potential effect of low-hanging chandeliers, columns and other obstructions on usable space?
- Are there mirrors in the area? What impact might they have on the set-up or program?
- Are there windows? If so, can they be blacked out?

- If there is a house phone in the room, can it be disconnected?
- If there are portable walls, how soundproof are they?
- Where are the entrances and exits? What can be blocked?
- Do doors squeak? Close completely? Automatically lock?
- What is the "true" meeting space?
- Is there room for AV set-up and a control console?
- Does the room have a Permanent Stage? Does it have stage lighting?

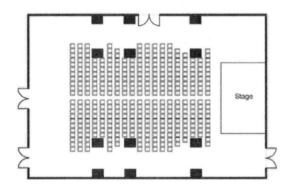

Don't believe the room sizes listed in the facility's brochure. In most cases, the capacities are based on total square footage, not the usable space. In this example, the brochure says that the room's theater-style capacity is 600, but for practical usage with an AV set up, 450 is more accurate. Furthermore, some seats fall behind the columns and are not useful, making the room's capacity even less than 450.

Section V: Contractors

... Electrical Services
- Where does the electrical service originate in the room?
- Who provides hook-up service?
- What is the cost for hook-up and use?
- Flat rate?
- Metered charge?
- Local government surcharge?

... About Sound Systems:
- Who handles the sound in the facility? Is there a patch fee?
- Is there a sound system already in the room? Ask for a demonstration to determine its quality.
- Is there a portable sound system? Are there sound lecterns?
- Can the rooms be patched for audio recording from a central location?

... Lighting Capabilities
- Where are the House Lighting Controls?
- Are they able to be remote controlled?
- Can the room lighting be divided into sections?
- Are Follow Spotlights available? At what cost?
- If stage lighting is to be hung from ceiling, what are the restrictions?
- Where can it be hung? Who can do the work?

... Rigging Restrictions

- Are there rigging restrictions, such as weight load or types of equipment that can be rigged?
- Are there any exclusive agreements for operation of rigging equipment?
- Are there scissor lifts or basket lifts available from the facility?
- Are covered wheels permitted on carpeted surfaces?
- Must the rigging be removed from the room prior to event?
- Is there a way for the crew to exit the room after set up?

Understanding Presenter Needs

Any event that has educational content ("programming") will involve speakers or presenters. Professional speakers will usually communicate their AV needs clearly. Most presenters, however, are volunteers. While flattered by the opportunity to present, most will not be trained in presentation techniques. Therefore, expect that these volunteer presenters may not be fully aware of what they will require or may not be precise about what to ask for. Many show managers provide a standard set of presentation tools which specify exactly what can be provided, including the fact that no special requests can be accommodated; others decide to give each speaker anything he or she requests. Which route the show manager chooses is often driven by the budget. Keep in mind that there are multiple methods of communicating in a meeting room environment, and each comes at a different cost to the show organizer:

- "Just plain talk" (no AV support)
- Using props
- Visuals (Microsoft PowerPoint, videos)
- Enhanced environment (Stage sets, décor)

If a show organizer decides to honor requests, he or she may want to develop a Speaker Support Checklist. This tool is designed to ask presenters what type of support they expect from the event planner. In today's presentation environment, a PowerPoint style presentation is common, taking the place of the slide projector supported talks of the past.

Questions for Presenters

- If they plan to use PowerPoint, what version of the software are they using?
- Will there be video embedded in the PowerPoint? (This can cause challenges with a video projection system if not addressed in advance.)
- Will they need a computer to be provided, or will they bring their own? (If a computer will need to be rented, does the presenter prefer a PC or a Mac? Ask the presenter to specify any additional information on type, speed, memory, and any external disk drives that will be needed.)

- What resolution works best? (VGA, SVGA, XGA, SXGA, or UXGA)
- Is more than one computer being used?
- Is more than one screen needed?
- Is a local monitor required?
- Is an Internet connection needed? (Do they really need it? Internet connections have become more readily available but can come at a hefty price. In many cases, presenters can convert their talks to CD-based presentations and eliminate costly "live" sessions.)
- Will there be any audio played by the computer during the presentation? (This requires a connection to the sound system).

Suggestions for Presenters
- Bring power supplies if using a laptop.
- Bring all adapters normally used in the office or home.
- Arrive well before the meeting to test the computer with AV gear.
- Bring backup of presentation.
- If using a Web site, back it up on a CD, an external drive, on the hard drive.

For P resenters Using Video
- What format will they be using? (VHS, SVHS, ?", Betacam, MiniDV, DVD)
- What color standard will they be using? (US (NTSC) or European (PAL / SECAM).)
- Do they want to control the playback or do they need an operator?

Keep in mind that everyone needs back-up copies of any tape or disc that is critical to an event. In addition, always be sure that the operators of any AV or house equipment coordinate cues with speakers in advance.

Working with Speakers
Although some show organizers hire professional speakers, most exhibition industry speakers are volunteers who are either members of or VIPs in the host organization. It is important to do everything possible to help them succeed. Here are some things a show organizer can do to get more effective presentations from these types of speakers:

- Explain the meeting goals and objectives. Speakers who understand the goals of the meeting will help to achieve them.
- Provide an executive teleprompter. A teleprompter will make the speaker more comfortable in front of the audience, and help keep the speaker on topic—resulting in a more effective presentation.

- Use electronic cues. An operator signal system is a low cost way to allow speakers to more effectively operate computer graphics or video. Having a signal transmitter that cues an operator to advance a graphic or video clip keeps the speaker's presentation flowing more smoothly and evenly.
- Alert speakers about time limits. A timer allows a presenter to know how much time he or she has to speak, and can help keep a meeting on schedule.
- Provide guidelines for graphics. Well-presented graphics on screen should support the spoken word and emphasize key points. Remind presenters of these accepted standards for presentation graphics:
  - ° Try not to use more than two fonts in a presentation
  - ° Keep fonts consistent throughout the presentation
- Fonts should be no smaller than 24 point
- Never reduce the font size to fit all the words of a sentence on one slide. Convert complete sentences into bullet points or create another slide
- Use drop shadows. They tend to make the letters stand out, making them more readable from a distance.
- Use contrasting colors when choosing backgrounds and text styles. If you have a dark background, use light text and use dark text if you have a light background
- When projecting a presentation, never use red text. It almost always appears over-saturated. White and yellow text work best for projection
- Avoid animation if the computer is not fast enough to allow smooth movement.
- Ensure that type in a PowerPoint presentation is large enough to read from the last row in the audience by standing ten feet back from the monitor. If text can be read at this distance, attendees in the last row will be able to see it.

Section V: Contractors

SUMMARY

As technology becomes a bigger and bigger part of everyday life, so do the technical requirements for producing an exhibition expand every year. Deciding which AV services can and should be handled in house, and which should be outsourced is only the first step. Selecting the right contractor for the programs associated with the event as well as one that can service the exhibitors is the next challenge for a show organizer. Keeping up with presentation and staging technology is a specialty and often best delegated to the many specialists in the exhibition industry.

QUESTIONS FOR DISCUSSION

① Are you familiar with PowerPoint or other presentation technology? If not, consider that its use has become standard in the meetings and exhibition industry, and determine how you will become proficient. If yes, what is your favorite PowerPoint trick or tip?

② What would you expect to be the piece of AV equipment most requested by exhibitors and why?

③ What types of conventions require the most meeting room AV equipment?

Chapter 6
Exhibition Shipping

"Neither snow, nor rain, nor heat, nor gloom of night stays these couriers from the swift completion of their appointed rounds."

– Inscription, New York City Post Office,
adapted from Herodotus (Greek historian)

Section V: Contractors

IN THIS CHAPTER YOU WILL LEARN

- What is takes to get a booth to an exhibition
- What kinds of contractors are involved
- The importance of fl• awless shipping to an event
- How procedures in the US differ from other countries

INTRODUCTION

Whether it's called material handling, freight forwarding or shipping, it is another critical aspect of exhibition logistics. Substantial investment by the exhibitor of time and money in booth space, marketing materials, product development, planning, travel and hotel are wasted if the exhibitor's booth, sample products, machinery or collateral material do not arrive at the right booth, on time, and in good condition. Furthermore, even one empty space or one unhappy exhibitor detracts from the success of an event, and can negatively impact its future.

CONTRIBUTOR

Mike Kovac, Director, Sales and Marketing, Fairs & Exhibitions, Rock-It Cargo LLC

By definition, an exhibition is a temporary event. Large quantities of exhibit materials – sometimes millions of pounds of freight – must be moved in and out of a venue in a very short period of time. The official services contractor bears the burden of coordinating a large portion of these logistics, including control of the dock during move-in and move- out, and control of the truck, forklift and other vehicle traffic on the show floor itself. However, the official services contractor has little control over whether all of this freight arrives and departs the facility in a timely manner. It's no wonder that an entire segment of the industry has evolved to handle these unique challenges.

Unlike the type of business-to-business deliveries that occur daily, shipping of exhibit materials has some unique challenges. Deliveries and pick-ups must be made from large and complex facilities, often in congested city centers, often with multiple crowded docks, and always within a very narrow timeframe. In addition, some exhibit materials are unusually fragile, and require special handling and packing in large and cumbersome crates or pallets. Exhibits often go directly from one show to another with little time in between, leaving practically no tolerance for error or late deliveries. And on top of those complications, many exhibitors ship their booths dozens or even hundreds of times each year, both within the US and internationally.

For these reasons, most show organizers who expect the participation of international exhibitors will select and recommend an "official international freight forwarder," one with specialized experience in exhibition forwarding. This vendor will have agents in the participating countries who are also exhibition forwarders, and who are experienced in the particular industry or industries related to the event, such as medical equipment or heavy machinery. Exhibitors are usually encouraged to use the official freight forwarder, in order to reduce the chance of the many problems which can occur when using a general freight forwarder who is not familiar with the exhibition industry.

For the same reasons, many organizers of US exhibitions will recommend an "official common carrier" with divisions specializing in domestic exhibition transportation. When appropriate, they will also recommend an "official exhibition van line" and an "official exhibition air freight forwarder," all of whom have experience in the unique and demanding process of moving an exhibitor's materials from origin to the booth in good and usable condition, exactly on time. This can make the difference between a successful and not-so-successful exhibition for an exhibitor.

Therefore, in order to ensure satisfied exhibitors, the show organizer must be familiar with the complex logistical details of shipping and forwarding in order to select the best contractors. Complicated as they might be, shipping and transportation are some of those event-related services that must go right for an event to be successful.

What an Exhibitor Must Do

Shipping to an exhibition within or to the United States or Canada is a two-part process. First, the exhibitor's materials must be shipped from point-of-origin to the official services contractor, either directly to the site, or to the official services contractor's Advanced Receiving Warehouse (ARWH). Next, the materials must be delivered by the official services contractor to the booth.

Offloading the exhibit materials from the delivery vehicle, and delivering them to the booth is one part of what is called "on-site material handling" or drayage. On-site material handling also includes the positioning of the materials if necessary, removal, storage and return of empty boxes, crates, and cases, re-delivery from the booth to the venue dock, and reloading the material onto the pick up vehicle.

The exhibitor can deliver to the official services contractor's ARWH usually about 30 days before the beginning of move-in for an exhibition, but not after one week prior to the beginning of move-in (without penalty). The official services contractor then delivers the materials to the dock at the venue on the first day of move-in, offloads the materials, and delivers to the booth. This alternative allows the official services contractor to move all materials in their warehouse to the site in an orderly way during regular business hours before more urgent "direct to site" deliveries begin. In addition, it is easier – and sometimes less expensive – to ship to the warehouse, since there is usually no waiting time for the exhibitor's carrier and the marshalling yard process can be avoided.

The marshalling yard is an area near the site where delivery vehicles must register their arrival with the official services contractor, and wait for permission to move to the venue dock to be offloaded. Unloading at the venue dock can take many hours, incurring additional costs. Also, the official services contractor charges more for on- site material handling when storing exhibit materials in their warehouse prior to delivery to the site. This extra cost can also be substantial, depending on the weight and size of the exhibitor's materials.

The decision to ship to the ARWH or direct to site is directly related to the decision of how to ship. There are a number of choices when shipping from within the United States to an exhibition in the US. Those choices include private or common motor carriers, independent trucking companies, integrated couriers, van lines, indirect air carriers (IACs), freight brokers, freight forwarders, and shippers themselves or shipper-owned vehicles.

Common carriers are asset-based; in other words, they own their equipment. Trucking companies who specialize in LTL or "Less Than Truckload" shipments, use regular routes based on a hub system. Independent trucking companies also own their own equipment, and normally specialize in FTL or "Full Truckload" systems. Integrated couriers specialize in the expedited transport of documents and small packages, also using a hub system. Van lines specialize in uncrated freight, such as large booth components which require special handling and usually include pad or blanket wrapping services. Indirect air carriers specialize in expedited air freight. Freight brokers specialize in matching shippers with a particular carrier which meets the shipper's needs. Freight forwarders normally specialize in international and transborder transportation.

There are numerous factors that influence which type of transportation or transportation company the exhibitor chooses to ship their exhibit materials to and from exhibitions in the United States. These include type of packing unit (such as boxes, crates, cases, pallets or uncrated booth components), the number, weight, and dimensions of packing units, the origin of the shipment, the destination, the length of available time to ship, and costs. Finally, the decision whether to ship direct to site or to the official services contractor's advanced receiving warehouse will also influence the method or mode of transportation chosen.

Shipping within the United States

The process for shipping to an exhibition or event within the United States differs varies depending on the circumstances and the mode of transportation selected. However, the exhibitor must:

- Decide which items and materials will be shipped to the exhibition and how they will be packed. It important that durable and protective packing materials are chosen because exhibition materials must arrive not only on time but in good condition, and they may be loaded and unloaded frequently, or exposed to harsh weather conditions.

- Provide a packing list to the carrier and obtain a cost estimate. A packing or crate list is a description of the shipment which lists the number, dimensions and weights of each shipment. Most motor carriers charge either by the actual weight or by the truckload. Depending on the mode of transportation, most indirect air carriers, integrated couriers and freight forwarders will charge by the actual weight, or by the dimensional weight, whichever is greater. As part of the quotation process, the exhibitor will advise the carrier of the required delivery address and delivery date. For larger exhibitions, and for shipments made direct to site, official services contractors often establish "targeted" move-in dates, depending on the exhibitor's location in the exhibit hall. Before obtaining and approving a cost estimate, the exhibitor will need to tell the carrier exactly when their materials will be ready to ship, as well as the requested or required move-in date. In addition to approving the cost estimate, the exhibitor must confirm the pick-up date and time.

- Prepare the exhibit materials for shipping. When the materials are packed, labels must be attached to the packing units. All labels for shipments within the United States or Canada should show the name of the exhibition, name and booth number of the exhibiting company, the name of the consignee (usually the official services contractor) and the delivery address. Also, each label should include a "piece count" showing the number of each piece, and the total number of pieces in the shipment. Two labels should be attached to each packing unit, preferably on the sides.

- Prepare the bill of lading. Simply stated, a bill of lading is the contract between the shipper (exhibitor) and the carrier for the transportation of goods from one point to another. It normally includes the name of the shipper, the pick-up address, the consignee (receiver of the goods), the delivery address, and the details (normally, number of pieces, weights, and dimensions) of the goods being shipped.

A critical aspect of the bill of lading is the terms and conditions of the carrier, freight forwarder or broker. Normally, these terms and conditions are printed on the back of every bill of lading. Their primary purpose is to describe the limits of liability of the carrier. A shipping company's or carrier's liabilities for lost, damaged, stolen or delayed goods is severely limited by law in the United States, and the shipper and the exhibitor should be aware of these limitations. To protect against this liability, exhibitors can purchase excess declared value liability or "cargo insurance" from the carrier or shipping company.

The exhibitor is also required to advise the official services contractor of the size of the shipment, the name of the carrier, and its estimated time of arrival. Normally, standard forms are provided to the exhibitor for this purpose.

Finally, the carrier or the carrier's cartage agent will arrive at the point of origin to pick up the cargo, and begin the transport of the exhibit materials to the exhibition. Signatures of the shipper and the driver are required on the bill of lading, a copy of which is normally attached to and travels with the goods. Copies are distributed to the shipper, the carrier and any other parties involved in the process.

Advance Freight

During the first days of the exhibition move-in period at the site, the official services contractor will load all advance shipments on their vehicles and deliver them to the dock at the site. At the dock, labor hired and managed by the official services contractor offloads the goods, and delivers them to the appropriate booth or stand. The driver's copy of the bill of lading is signed by the warehouse personnel who offloaded the exhibit materials. The date and time are noted, as are any exceptions in the number of pieces received. The condition of the cargo is also noted on the bill of lading.

Direct Freight

At the marshalling yard or at the venue's dock control point, the driver must provide a copy of the bill of lading showing the exhibitor name and booth number. In many cases, the driver must present a certified weight ticket showing the weight of the truck both with and without the exhibition goods being delivered. Depending on space availability, the driver must then wait in line until the official services contractor grants permission to move to the unloading bays, where union personnel offload and deliver the exhibit materials to the exhibitor's booth or stand. When this process is completed, dock personnel sign a copy of the bill of lading, indicating the date and time of delivery, and noting any exception to the number of pieces or their condition.

Move-In and Move-Out

Exhibitors arrive, unpack their materials and set up their booths/stands, or supervise union labor or other installation and dismantle company personnel (often called I&D companies or exhibitor appointed contractors). When this process is finished, empty packing units are labeled and picked up for storage prior to the beginning of the exhibition. After the close of the exhibition, the empties are returned, and the exhibitors repack and re-label their materials with return shipping labels. Before leaving the venue, exhibitors must fill out, sign, and attach the carrier's bill of lading to one of the packing units. They must also fill out, sign, and return to the service desk the official services contractor's material handling form or outbound bill of lading. This document governs the movement of the exhibit materials from the booth or stand to the site dock, and from the reloading onto the vehicle of the carrier responsible for the return shipment.

The material handling form includes several critical pieces of information: the exhibitor name and booth number, the name of the show, the number and types of packing units and their weights, the name of the company receiving the goods, the delivery address, and the carrier name and mode of transportation to be used. One of the most important fields on the official services contractor's material handling form concerns instructions for the shipment of any cargo or exhibit material which is not picked up by the exhibitor's carrier. In the event their materials are left on the exhibition floor, the exhibitor is given the choice to either have their goods returned to the official services contractor's warehouse and stored until other arrangements can be made, or have their goods returned by the official services contractor or the official carrier for the exhibition. Once the official services contractor's material handling form is signed and returned to the service desk, the exhibitor can leave and return of the exhibit materials – or the forwarding to another exhibition – can begin.

International Shipping or Outside the United States

The modes of transportation, processes and terms for international exhibition shipping are similar in many ways to those for US events with several important exceptions. Nearly all international shipments are handled by freight forwarders or integrated couriers. International exhibition shipping can and often does include shipping by ocean which – although slower than air freight – is much less expensive for heavier or larger cargo. Also, international exhibition forwarding involves Customs authorities and procedures, in both the origin and destination countries. Because of this, international shipments require additional documentation. In almost all countries of the world, except the United States and Canada, the shipping and on-site material handling processes are combined.

Freight forwarders generally offer surface or truck transportation, air freight transportation and ocean transportation services, as well as Customs formalities and brokerage services in the origin and destination countries. Because the import and export formalities governing international exhibition forwarding differ in major ways from those pertaining to US freight forwarding, many exhibitors choose to work with exhibition freight forwarders.

One significant way that international exhibition forwarding differs from procedures in the US is that the overwhelming majority of goods shipped by normal freight forwarders are permanent or definitive imports. In other words, these goods stay in the destination country, and are subject to duties and taxes in the country. On the other hand, the overwhelming majority of exhibition goods are temporary imports that are shipped to the destination country and then returned to the origin country; therefore, they should not be subject to duties and taxes.

There are three ways to import goods on a temporary basis and avoid the payment of duties and taxes: temporary import bonds, ATA carnets and trade fair bonds. There are advantages and disadvantages to all three of these methods, depending on the destination country or countries, the type and value of commodities being shipped and the amount of available time prior to shipping. An experienced exhibition forwarder can and normally does advise the international exhibitor which of these methods is best and most cost effective.

An ATA carnet is best described as a passport for cargo, which allows the listed cargo to be imported temporarily in participating countries without the payment of duties and taxes. It is a very formalized packet of documents which include a front page listing the owner of the goods and the carnet, the intended destinations, agents authorized to present the carnet to customs authorities, a general list describing the contents of the shipment, and detachable vouchers for use by Customs authorities when goods enter and leave the countries involved in the shipment. Fees for an ATA carnet include payment of a surety bond based on the value of the goods being shipped.

For all other temporary imports, a commercial invoice or packing list must be used, and a temporary import or trade fair bond fee paid. A commercial invoice or packing list describes each packing unit and its contents, specifically the quantity of items being shipped, a description of the items being shipped, the country of manufacture, the HTS number of the item, and a value for Customs. (The HTS or Harmonized Tariff System number is a worldwide classification system for goods which are imported and exported whose primary function is to identify the commodity or item being shipped for the purposes of tax assessment, as well as to determine any ancillary documentation requirements, such as a certificate of origin or FDA forms.) The commercial invoice also includes the shipper's name and address, the consignee and consignee's address, the name of the show and the booth number.

Deliveries to international tradeshow destinations do not involve a marshalling yard or official services contractor. In addition, international venues are often spread out over large areas, and can include many buildings or sometimes two floors. An exhibition freight forwarder is often recommended, because most general or commercial freight forwarders are neither familiar with the procedures for making timely deliveries to these venues, nor do they provide on-site material handling services. General or commercial freight forwarders typically do not know how to arrange this service for exhibitors.

On-site material handling services at international exhibitions also include organizing the return shipment. Before the close of an international event, the exhibition freight forwarder will meet with the exhibitor at the booth, and confirm the method, destination, and details of the return shipment. Based on this interview, they will ask the exhibitor to sign the disposal or return instructions. They will then return with the appropriate shipping labels and a signed copy of the instructions, which are also sent to the exhibition forwarder who handled the inbound portion of the movement.

Show Organizer Freight

When setting up to do business for a week or two at a convention center or other exhibition venue, the show organizer will usually need to ship office materials, files, brochures and other support materials to the show site. In some cases, computers will need to be shipped as well. If the show organizer represents an association with membership, there will also be additional materials to support the work of various departments during meetings and program sessions, as well as a myriad of other things that will also have to be shipped to the show site.

Just as for the exhibitor's materials, it is imperative that these shipments arrive on time and at the right location. If quantities are limited, it is possible to ship by normal business carriers such as UPS or FedEx. If quantities are large, shipments can sometimes be transported by the official services contractor. But if quantities are substantial, some arrangement will need to be made either with a common carrier, or through an exhibition freight company. Close coordination with the official services contractor will ensure that once the materials are delivered to the facility, they are sorted and distributed to the right location in the building early in the move in period.

SUMMARY

Arranging for shipping of the booth is one of the many tasks exhibitors face. This can sometimes be one of the most frustrating, since the procedures and the rules can be both complicated and variable between the US and other counties. A successful show organizer will assist the exhibitors by making participation in the event as easy as possible, and this can include selection of contractors who are specialists in shipping and handling exhibition materials.

QUESTIONS FOR DISCUSSION

① Why would an exhibitor choose to ship directly to the venue if shipping to the Advance Receiving Warehouse is cheaper?

② Right to Work laws in many states (for example Texas) allow exhibitors to unpack and set up their own booths, and other states (for example Illinois) require the use of union labor. Discuss the pros and cons of each situation from the exhibitor's perspective.

③ Long ago, a teamster was a person who drove a wagon lead by oxen, horses or mules. How does this definition fit the kind of work teamsters do today?

Section V: Contractors

Chapter 1
Staffing & Communications

"Speak properly, and in as few words as you can,
but always plainly; for the end of speech
is not ostentation, but to be understood."

– William Penn

Section VI: On-site

IN THIS CHAPTER YOU WILL LEARN

- Various ways of staffing for an event
- Roles of the various contractors on site
- How to communicate the event requirements to all parties
- About pre-cons and post-cons
- Why it's called "show biz"

INTRODUCTION

Exhibition management is to many people a logistical science. The multitude of details, the facts, the figures, the planning ... all must be addressed within a logical, sequential framework in order for a successful event to take place. To others, exhibition management is a "people business." The daily interaction with contractors, attendees, exhibitors and staff requires a high degree of effective communication skill. After months of planning, when everything culminates with the arrival at the show site and the management of the event, most would say it is both – and more.

CONTRIBUTOR

Sue Hueg, CEM, CMP, Business Development, National Business Media, Inc

Arrival at the Facility

Depending upon the size of the building, the facility person handling the event may be an event coordinator (large convention centers), the general manager (smaller convention centers and other facilities) or even a convention services or sales manager (hotel exhibition space or conference centers). In any case, this person will be the main source to help get things done within the building in a quick and efficient manner. In short, this person will become the show manager's "new best friend" in the coming week to ten days while on site.

Since the show manager is actually one of the first to arrive, the first day on site is the best time to check the condition of the building to make certain that there have been no changes to the infrastructure since the last planning visit. This can be done with or without the official services contractor or the facility event coordinator. This is also a good time to check for cleanliness, and make special housekeeping or refurbishing requests. Look for pre-existing damage, documenting any issues that arise (with photos, if possible) and reporting them to the facility immediately.

The other early arrival at the show site is usually the official services contractor. Therefore, another initial task for the show organizer is to meet with the account executive or other key contact to go over last-minute details, updates and changes. Most show managers are on site anywhere from one to two weeks. Moving into the headquarters area, getting organized and establishing good communications with all key players early is a good practice.

Staffing and On-Site Needs

Depending upon the type of host organization, the show staff can range from a couple individuals to dozens of people, and can vary in size during the planning cycle. There may be a group of staff who are dedicated to the meetings or events department, and work together all year. Or, at the other end of the spectrum, there may be a group of volunteers who are involved only while the event is on site. In either case or anywhere in the middle, it is important to understand the needs and the talents of the on-site staff in order to bring an event to a successful conclusion.

Even if there are other departments or volunteers involved in an event on site, there will be a core event team who will handle any last-minute changes, and make recommendations for any decisions which affect the event. These are the exhibition professionals. In addition to the show manager, members of the core team include key meetings and exhibition staff from the event sponsor, the official services contractor's account executive, and the facility's event coordinator. It is a good idea to meet with this staff as soon as possible upon arriving on site, and arrange the timing for briefing sessions with all of them to clarify the limits of authority for each individual.

Section VI: On-site

In addition to the core event team, there will be other individuals who are key to the success of the event. When determining how communications will flow while on site, consider the following:

- Are daily meetings necessary to go over each day's schedule, or can responsibilities simply be assigned to specific individuals?
- Will a complete daily schedule for each staff person be designed with hourly tasks, or will each individual handle this themselves?
- What will be the protocol for answering questions? Which issues will need authorization from which individuals?

SAMPLE STAFF SCHEDULE

When?	#	Wednesday, June 9 Seminar Title (What?)	Where?	Who?
7:45 am - 8:15 am	201	Troubleshooting Customer Files (for Beginners)	104-A	
7:45 am - 8:15 am	301	Advanced: Making It Ready	104-B	
8:45 am - 9:15 am	10	Basic Application	203-A	
11:45 am - 12:15 pm	13	Small Business Sales Strategies	203-A	
11:45 am - 12:15 pm	15	What's New	203-C	
12:45 pm - 1:15 pm	101	Selling Applications	104-C	
1:45 pm - 2:15 pm	A.	Workshop	201-B	
2:45 pm - 3:15 pm	16	Basic Printing	203-B	
2:45 pm - 3:15 pm	17	Automotive Airbrush	203-C	

When?	#	Thursday, June 10 Seminar Title (What?)	Where?	Who?
7:45 am - 8:15 am	202	Making It Ready (for Beginners)	104-B	
7:45 am - 8:15 am	302	Advanced Troubleshooting Customer Files	104-A	
8:45 am - 9:15 am	18	Production Techniques	203-A	
8:45 am - 9:15 am	19	How to	203-B	
8:45 am - 9:15 am	40	Basic Design Clinic	202-C	
8:45 am - 9:15 am	B.	Workshop	201-B	
11:45 am - 12:15 pm	20	Installation Techniques	203-A	
11:45 am - 12:15 pm	21	Design & Application	203-B	
11:45 am - 12:15 pm	22	Let's Make More Money!	203-C	
12:45 pm - 1:15 pm	102	Pricing	104-C	
1:45 pm - 2:15 pm	41	Clinic	202-B	
1:45 pm - 2:15 pm	C.	Workshop	202-A	
2:45 pm - 3:15 pm	23	Computer	203-A	
2:45 pm - 3:15 pm	24	Causes & Cures	203-B	

When?	#	Friday, June 11 Seminar Title (What?)	Where?	Who?
7:45 am - 8:15 am	103	Finish Solutions	104-C	
8:45 am - 9:15 am	25	Hand-Lettering Techniques	203-A	
8:45 am - 9:15 am	26	3rd Dimension	203-B	
8:45 am - 9:15 am	27	Developing Relationships for Lifelong Sales	203-C	
8:45 am - 9:15 am	D.	Techniques Workshop	201-B	
8:45 am - 9:15 am	42	Basic Computer	202-C	
8:45 am - 9:15 am	E.	Screen Printing on Signs All-day Workshop	202-B	
9:45 am - 10:15 am	104	Installing Large-Format Graphics for Maximum Impact	104-C	
11:45 am - 12:15 pm	28	High Payback Marketing Ideas	203-A	
11:45 am - 12:15 pm	29	BeginningTechniques	203-B	
11:45 am - 12:15 pm	30	Advanced Design Principles	203-C	
1:45 pm - 2:15 pm	F.	Application	202-A	
2:45 pm - 3:15 pm	31	Commercial Strategies	203-A	
2:45 pm - 3:15 pm	32	Introduction	203-B	

When?	#	Saturday, June 12 Seminar Title (What?)	Where?	Who?
8:45 am - 9:15 am	33	Installation	203-B	
8:45 am - 9:15 am	34	Simple Installation Techniques	203-A	
8:45 am - 9:15 am	G.	Techniques	202-A	
8:45 am - 9:15 am	H.	Workshop	202-B	
8:45 am - 9:15 am	I.	Workshop	104-B	
11:45 am - 12:15 pm	35	Troubleshooting	203-A	
11:45 am - 12:15 pm	36	Marketing	203-B	
1:45 pm - 2:15 pm	J.	Beginning Workshop	201-B	

Other Key Staff Often Required:

Registration Management

One of the most important members of the on-site team is the registration manager. Since the registration area is usually one of the first interactions by attendees and visitors, the person managing it should be capable, steady and efficient. This person is responsible for overseeing the registration set-up, training of regular and temporary staff and daily management of the entire registration process. Whether registration of exhibitors and attendees is handled in house or outsourced, the registration manager is the liaison between event and registration staff, and will direct their efforts.

Unless the sponsoring organization brings a large number of their own people to the event, the registration manager usually works with the local convention bureau or a local agency to hire temporary workers to assist with data entry, cashiers and badge checkers. It is often suggested that this manager schedule a training day where specifics about the group, the event and registration rules and procedures will be covered. Daily management of this group includes scheduling of the staff, making certain that each person gets adequate meal and other breaks, monitoring and tracking on-site attendee flows, answering question, and ensuring that computers stay in working order. Some bureaus often have convention services managers who are the key contact for providing temporary staff.

Educational Program Management

Depending upon the size of the event, the monitoring of the educational program can be managed by a single individual, or by an entire fleet of workers, either from the sponsoring organization, or hired for the event (sometimes called "room checkers" or "monitors"). Sometimes the audio-visual contractor will assist with this function. Responsibilities for room monitors include working with the speakers (assisting in the "Ready Room" where speakers check in and rehearse presentations), assembling and distributing handouts, posting signage outside of meeting rooms, double-checking room set-ups for correct capacity and speaker requirements. Some groups now post workers to monitor attendance by "counting heads," or utilizing badge scanners.

Exhibit Hall Management

The exhibit manager has total management responsibility within the exhibit hall, and in many cases, is also the show manager for the entire event. Depending on the type of sponsoring organization, this person might actually be the show manager, an individual who reports to the show manager, director of meetings and conventions or even the executive director or CEO of the host organization.

Some shows also employ floor managers who report directly to the exhibit manager, freeing up the exhibit manager by acting as their "eyes and ears" on the show floor.

Often hired on a temporary basis, the responsibilities of floor managers can vary greatly depending on the type of show and the personal style of the exhibit manager. In addition to many types of problem-solving, they may include monitoring and enforcing the rules and regulations, handling exhibitors' special needs and requests, and acting as liaison for exhibitors with the official services contractor and the facility's event coordinator.

Advance Sale of Booth Space

Sometimes, show organizers will offer booths for the next show for sale during the current one. When this occurs, the organizer often has specific staff assigned to handle this process, sometimes in conjunction with a housing company who will take requests for future blocks of hotel rooms at the same time. This may be staff pulled from other departments, or on large shows, a dedicated sales staff who are working to sell booth space year-round will handle the process. Large shows that are in high demand often schedule specific appointments for exhibitors on a seniority or other priority basis. When this is the case, an exhibitor is obligated to appear at the appointed time to select next year's space, or fall to the bottom of the priority list. Other shows simply make the next year's floorplan available by posting it in places such as the show management office or exhibitor lounge, and interested exhibitors come to the show manager with questions or to submit applications for future booth space.

These staffing assignments vary widely. Depending upon the size of the event, separate individuals may handle each of these tasks, or the show manager or an assistant may handle all of the tasks.

Working with Contractors
Official Services Contractor

One of the most important contractors the show manager works with is the official services contractor. Each event is usually assigned to an account executive who will work directly with the show and/or the exhibit manager, as well as collaborate with all subcontractors who will assist in the actual production of the show. This vendor's main job is to translate directives from show management into decorating, signage and all other logistics inside the exhibit hall on time and correctly. Because familiarity with the unique aspects of a show is usually advantageous to all parties, many show managers prefer that the same account executive produce an event year after year.

Event Security

The responsibility of these officers is the overall protection of the event once the show organizer takes occupancy of the facility. The show manager usually meets with the officer in charge, along with any supervisors and key staff to finalize duty stations and review event rules and regulations. In addition, there must be coordination with facility security to review procedures for dealing with emergencies.

This group is also responsible for checking badges to ensure that only properly-credentialed individuals are allowed access to the exhibit hall and meeting rooms.

Food Service and Catering
This staff person is responsible for any scheduled meal functions and special receptions, as well as concessions and staff meal needs. Often they will be the liaison with an in-house caterer or concessionaire.

Transportation
If it is a large event and a special contractor has been hired to manage the shuttle bus operation, the key contact from that company will serve as liaison with show management, as well as be responsible for scheduling, signage and on-time performance. In the absence of a specialty contractor, this position may fall either to the show manager, or to one of his or her permanent staff people. There will probably be a final on-site meeting to review schedules, late changes in routes and to assess contingency plans for traffic accidents or delays. It may also be necessary to confirm that limousine procedures are in place for VIPs.

Floral
Often specialists in the convention industry, their personnel will fill all orders from exhibitors as well as provide plants and flowers ordered by show management for entrance ways, staging, registration areas and any special events like banquets or entertainment.

Cleaning
While some facilities include cleaning in their contracts, some require the services of outside contractors who are typically hired by the official services contractor. In some cases, there may even be a separate contractor who handles just vacuuming of the booth and aisle carpet. Arrangements vary around the country.

Shipping/Freight/Drayage
Working along with the official services contractor, these transportation specialists will manage the traffic arriving at the dock with deliveries for the show, supervise the unloading of freight and delivery of materials to each booth, store empty crates and return them to the right booth at the end of the show, and load up and supervise everything in reverse as the show moves out. The show organizer will also have freight deliveries which need to be carefully tracked.

Audio-Visual
Many show managers work with the same audio-visual provider year after year, but most facilities also provide in-house services which are sufficient for less complex events. In some cities, union personnel must be used in the meeting rooms, as well as for any general session or special entertainment events. In these cases, the

audio-visual contractor will complement the union personnel with staff of their own. As with other key contractors, there is likely to be an account executive who will be the primary liaison to show management.

Lead Retrieval

If registration is outsourced, staff from the registration company will either work directly with the event's registration manager, or will report directly to the show manager to register attendees and exhibitors. Their duties will probably also include providing a system for exhibitor lead retrieval, including distributing the equipment prior to the show opening, collecting it promptly at show close and assisting exhibitors with data management.

Destination Management Company (DMC)

When an event includes a large number of guest activities or tours, the account executive or a company principal will want to do a final review of plans and briefing on tickets sold to date. An emerging trend for some shows with large family attendance is for a DMC or other specialized contractor to provide childcare programs either at the convention center or off site.

Working with Facility Staff

General Manager

This is the person responsible for the overall management of the facility, whether it is a convention center, a hotel or a conference center. Interaction between this person and show management generally depends on the size of the event. In some cases, the general manager will provide a welcome to the on-site staff, and periodically check with the show manager for an indication of how well the event is going.

Event Coordinator

This person will be the main "go-to" source for all facility- related questions and concerns. Most facilities assign coordinators who have experience with other events of the same type and size; these individuals can be a great resource for borrowing new ideas from other show organizers. When working in a hotel exhibition hall, this function may be handled by a convention services manager or even a floor manager.

Security

In some cases, an outside company will have been contracted to take on overall security of the facility and the event. If not, there may be separate contacts for facility and event security. The responsibility of the facility security is the overall protection of the building. Review procedures and patrol schedules. Early in the planning process, both sides should outline any areas of concern, such as late-night events, VIP guests, and parades, review emergency procedures and protocols, and establish an event emergency plan.

First Aid

During the planning phase, the show manager will have determined if the facility has an Emergency Medical Technician (EMT) on staff, or if one or more will need to be hired as an outside contractor. No matter who is providing this important function, the key event staff must know the location of the first aid room, how to reach the EMT (usually by portable radio or direct cell phone) and that the communication system is in working order. It is generally accepted that the most dangerous time for an event with exhibits is move-in and move-out, so first aid staffing should be provided during these important times in addition to during show hours.

Catering

Most large facilities have an in-house catering staff who will review all food and beverage requirements – including special meals for staff and guests, concessions, and coffee breaks – far in advance, and again upon arrival at the facility. When confirming final orders, pay special attention to delivery times and placement of tables and carts. Also, this is a good time to review procedures for additional orders, letting the catering manager know who is authorized to change orders on site, or to place new orders without your direct approval.

Housekeeping or Operations

The event coordinator may be the liaison for this function, but when dealing directly with the housekeeping staff, it is helpful to review general cleaning requirements for the show office or staff rooms, as well as when cleaning will be most convenient. Certain events also require special accommodations, such as when most or all attendees are female and some of the restrooms usually reserved for men are temporarily converted by the housekeeping staff for use by women to increase the number of facilities available.

Parking and Traffic Control

Large events can have a huge impact on the traffic in the immediate vicinity of the facility. Because all factors may not be under the direct jurisdiction of the convention center, move-in is a good time to ask the facility staff to check with the city traffic department to make sure there are no surprises. Sometimes reserved parking or special parking passes can be obtained for show management staff

Engineering Department/Phone Installation/Electrical Utilities

In addition to any changes to show management requirements, a final review meeting (or the "pre-con") might include requirements for the event lighting (timing of "on and off" lighting in the exhibit hall), the current need for air conditioning for the exhibit hall (sometimes not included in facility rentals), and updates and changes including the latest projection of attendance in the meeting rooms.

Other Host City Contacts

If working with a salesperson at the local convention and visitors bureau to select the host city for an event, that person will most likely be in touch as soon as the show management arrives on site for the event. This individual will also be able to offer assistance with any last-minute requests or issues that cannot be resolved elsewhere. The public relations person at the local bureau can provide lists for local media, and assist with press releases or other local media coverage. Larger bureaus that are providing temporary staffing will usually have a convention services person who will be liaison between the event manager and the on-site supervisor of their personnel.

For certain events, it is common for the mayor or other city official to appear at an opening session or ribbon-cutting to provide a welcome to the city or a proclamation of welcome. In any case, staff from the mayor's office would be included in the planning process, and would provide an on-site contact person.

Written Communications

With the advent of the hospitality industry's initiative in standardizing many areas of communication between show organizers, facilities and contractors (APEX), creating templates for communication among all parties is becoming more standardized, although many variations still exist in content and format.

Event Specification Guide is now the preferred term for the comprehensive document that outlines the complete requirements and instructions for an event. Sometimes still called a Staging Guide, a Resume, or a "Spec" Book, this document is typically authored by the show manager and is shared with all appropriate contractors in advance of move-in (usually about 30 days out). It contains detailed information on all aspects of the exhibition, general and specific. If not transmitted electronically, most event books take the form of three-ring binders. They are portable, it is easy to insert or remove pages, and a tab system makes it easy to locate specific information in a hurry.

As a general rule, there will need to be one copy and version of the event book for each member of the core event team. Typically, an event book will also be prepared for the official services contractor and the facility's event coordinator. Each version of the book should contain the information specific to that person's area of responsibility, and any that overlap with other contractors. For example, the requirements to the official services contractor might include specifications for all entrance decorations, the number of registration counters and placement, signage placement (although sign copy will have been submitted separately), requirements for carpeting certain areas, providing masking drape, setting up lounges, draping in meeting rooms, and show management booths in the exhibit hall. A Facility Event Book would include overall schedules, the requirements for all meeting areas, plus orders for staff food and beverage, and a recap of advance orders for facility services, including utilities, phone and electrical, plus security.

ITEMS TO INCLUDE IN AN EVENT SPECIFICATION GUIDE

• Emergency Information
• Important phone numbers(All event staff and contractors)
• Facility floorplans, staff phone numbers and contracts
• Hotel contracts, staff and VIP room confirmation numbers and Food and Beverage contracts
• Contracts and schedules for official services contractor and other vendors
• Itinerary, schedule at event and personal information for all event staff
• List of exhibitors and any pertinent correspondence, alpha and numerical listings
• Several copies of the floorplans
• Daily Staff Schedule
• Education Schedule
• Speaker contracts & schedule, travel itineraries, hotel information and personal information
• Promotional materials

Electronic Communications

The size of the event will dictate whether to use radios, cell phones or pagers for key staff. Decide which system will work best for the event, and review the plan for communications. If the plan is to use radios as the main source of communication, assign radios to key event staff at registration, education, AV, and childcare, as well as to any floor managers. In addition, the official services contractor's account executive, the event coordinator and security supervisor should be on radio with show management as well. Use one channel for staff communication and another channel for communication with the event coordinator and official services contractor. Ensure that all event staff understand who will have radios, and where they can be located in case of questions or an emergency. See next page for Radio Rules and Etiquette.

Pre- and Post-convention Meetings

Planning and follow-up meetings, sometimes called a "pre-con" or a "post-con," are often scheduled with the facility and individual hotel. The pre-con meeting is the time to meet face-to-face with everyone who will plays a role in the success of the upcoming event, and serves to focus attention on the special requirements of this specific event. For large events, there might be a general pre-con to which the sales and front office personnel from each hotel with a large room block are invited, along with representatives from the convention center. Usually arranged by a third party housing provider, the event coordinator or the local convention and visitors bureau, pre-cons range from laboriously detailed problem-discussing forums to hospitality events.

Radio Rules

1. Pick up your radio in the staff office every morning.
2. Keep your radio on **at all times** – headphones & ear pieces will be available for staff so the noise will not disrupt any sessions or meetings you may step into.
3. If you will be in a meeting or unable to respond for a length of time, please announce to all staff that you will be "off-radio" for X amount of time.
4. Return your radio to the staff office at the end of each day to recharge.

Radio Etiquette

1. Keep the lines clear as much as possible. If your conversation is lengthy either meet the person you are talking with or go to another channel. Just know that when you tell someone to switch to another channel, everyone else will switch there too, just to hear what you have to say. *NOTHING IS PRIVATE.*
2. If you do go to another channel, remember to switch back after your conversation.
3. Do not say anything negative about staff, exhibitors, members or vendors over the radio. At least 20 people will hear you and you never know who is in hearing range of the other users. You might as well publish it in Expo Magazine.
4. **Never** say 'fire' or 'bomb'.
5. **Emergency Codes (new):**

Code	Description
Blue	Medical emergency. Doctor or ambulance urgently needed. Announce code and location. Make sure that that security hears the message – "security did you copy" – and that I have heard it.
Green	Minor medical. Announce code and location. Need first aid attention.
Red	Fire or Smoke. Announce code and location. Be sure that security hears the message and that exhibition staff are alerted.
Grey	Security Emergency. Announce code and location. Again, be sure that security hears the message and that exhibition staff are alerted.

If the building has other codes they want us to use we will update you on-site.

6. Be sure to push the button and wait a full second before talking. Otherwise your first words will not be heard.
7. Wait till other people are done talking before you start (this works in real life, too.)
8. Be sure to charge your radio each night. Carrying around a dead radio is as useful as carrying a brick and is equally frustrating for people trying to reach you.
9. Identify yourself when you call someone. "Jeremy to Karen, come in."
10. Goofy code words that come in handy:

Code	Definition	Jargon	Definition
10-4	Ok	What's your 20?	Where are you?
10-10	Negative	Did you copy?	Understand?
10-17	On my way	Come back	Repeat please
10-18	Urgent	Negatory	No
10-20	Location	Eat 'em up	Restaurant
10-24	Assignment Complete	Rest 'em up	Hotel room
10-25	Meet me at...	Good buddy	Your radio friend
10-100	Bathroom Break	Got your ears on?	Are you there?

Although quite different in tone and agenda, the post-convention meeting is often held with just the core event team, the event coordinator and the official services contractor. The goal is to review successes and discuss opportunities for improvement at future shows. Post-con meetings with hoteliers are usually held one-on-one in order to recap room pick-up or to conduct an audit.

On-site at the Event

Show Opening

Early to arrive and early to depart, the show manager walks the exhibit hall many times while on-site, but the most important walk is the last one before the doors open. Usually taken jointly with the official services contractor, the final walk guarantees that the exhibit hall is set properly, there are no crates left in the aisles, all masking drape is up, and that there are no empty booths due to exhibitors who did not arrive in time. (Planning in advance for this contingency will assist in camouflaging the exhibitor's absence. For example, unoccupied booths are often made into mini lounges with simple furnishings.)

Immediately prior to the show opening, there may also be a check-in with the event coordinator to ensure that paging mikes are on and working, event hours are confirmed for lighting and air conditioning purposes, and that all food and beverage stations are placed correctly and ready to open. The facility staff will also want to confirm policy for opening each day, such as exactly when each set of doors will be unlocked, and whether opening and closing announcements will be made each day.

Some events stage a formal ribbon-cutting in the moments prior to the opening of the exhibit hall. This usually includes VIPs from the show organizer such an association president, plus any local dignitaries or celebrities. As this is a public relations activity, other staff typically conduct the festivities; the show manager is usually responsible only for providing the needed equipment.

Show Days

When all is in place – or even if it is not – exhibitors arrive, the show opens and attendees will pour through the doors. Because the best show managers arrive before anyone else and leave only when the building is empty, long working hours are the rule during show days. Generally, the event coordinator will either keep the same hours as the show manager, or delegate another contact person when he or she is unavailable.

Experienced show managers know that comfortable but appropriate clothing and especially good walking shoes are essential to stamina. Some host organizations may require and furnish staff uniforms. Many host organizations also provide breakfast and lunch for staff during show days, especially if the food and beverage outlets at the facility are likely to be busy with attendees, and there are few accessible options outside the facility. Coffee and other beverages are often provided for exhibitors in an exhibitor lounge so that they have a place out of the eye of attendees to take short breaks.

There should be a master communications and emergency list of all staff at the event, listing hotels, cell phones or pagers and emergency family contact numbers distributed to all parties. Staff should be clearly instructed as to when they are expected to be at their various posts and the policy for taking lunch and other breaks.

Move-Out

Move-out should be as well planned as move-in. Last-minute booth communications – either by public address system before show opening on the last day, or fliers dropped in every booth – are often used to ensure that all exhibitors are familiar with rules, regulations and timing of move-out procedures. Because safety and security are a major concern during move-out, extra meetings with both in-house and contractor security are often necessary. To keep theft to a minimum – a major concern for many exhibitors – some shows allow only hand-carried items to be removed from the show floor on the final day. Others impose limitations on the staging of personal vehicles arriving to load up exhibit materials. Whatever the special circumstances, creating an orderly process is mandatory to ensure that the show is out of the building by the contracted time – and often time is short.

Before leaving the building for the final time, a show manager will often complete a final walk-through and check for damage, covering all the same locations as toured on arrival with the event coordinator and the official services contractor. Use the notes made during initial inspection to determine if there is any liability, and make extensive notes or take photos.

After bidding farewell and shaking hands with the many parties involved in staffing the event, the show manager will walk out the door with a huge sense of satisfaction. Very few other occupations provide such moments of gratification.

SUMMARY

It's an odd variety of "show business," but just like a theatrical performance, an exhibition definitely includes performances by a wide variety of people performing for an audience under the duress of time. The show manager bears ultimate responsibility for all parties working smoothly together on-site. Mastery of all the interrelated factors, and knowledge of the appropriate scope of responsibility for each contractor, is also key to an event's success.

QUESTIONS FOR DISCUSSION:

① What are the benefits and disadvantages of producing the Event Staging Guide electronically?

② Why might stamina and physical fitness be important to an organization's core event team?

③ What are some of the factors that make move-in and move-out periods so dangerous?

Chapter 2
Crisis Management & Security

"There cannot be a crisis next week.
My schedule is already full."

– Henry Kissinger

Section VI: On-site

IN THIS CHAPTER YOU WILL LEARN

- Various types of crises that can happen
- What goes into a crisis management plan
- Who to put on a crisis management team

INTRODUCTION

Exhibition management includes the art of planning for the unexpected. It also includes the exacting science of managing risks, which involves a host of business issues. This chapter will explore the planning for a single element within the overall risk management portfolio, which is on-site crisis or emergency planning management, the single element most often ignored or neglected by show managers.

CONTRIBUTOR

Jennifer Hoff, CEM, Vice President of Operations & Conferences, National Trade Productions, Inc.

A crisis, according to a variety of dictionary definitions, is "a decisive moment; a time of danger or great difficulty; a turning point; a critical situation whose outcome decides whether good or bad consequences will follow". A blended definition works best. Viewed from an on-site perspective, a crisis may be defined as "any unplanned event that can cause deaths or significant injuries to employees, members, or the public; or a) can shut down or disrupt the exhibition or event, b) cause physical or environmental damage, c) or threaten the event's financial standing or public image."

On-Site Crisis Situations

What kinds of on-site crisis situations must be planned for? As a rule of thumb, on-site crisis situations generally fall into two broad categories:

Health and Safety

The health and safety category is by far the larger of the two. Within this category, there are several situation-specific categories. These include:

1. Medical emergencies: Simple fainting spells, sun stroke, heart attack, or being overcome by noxious fumes.
2. Fire.
3. Natural disasters and weather related occurrences: Tornadoes, blizzards, hurricanes, and earthquakes.
4. Criminal activities: Robbery of attendees and/or box offices, vandalism, assault and weapons offenses.
5. Terrorism: Bomb threats and/or hostage-taking.

If you are working in the international arena, a seventh type of crisis may need to be considered: politics and/or government interference. Politics and/or government interference have played a prominent role in expositions in parts of Europe, Asia, Africa and the Middle East.

Policy and Situational

This type of crisis includes:

1. Demands for compensation and/or retribution by attendees and/or exhibitors.
2. Contractual issues with exhibitors, contractors and/or sub-contractors.
3. Labor issues and/or disputes: Strikes, work to rule campaigns, union jurisdiction disputes.
4. Cancellation by a major speaker or entertainment act.
5. Discrimination.

It is obvious from reviewing these lists that it is almost impossible to predict what may happen at any given event. The key, therefore, becomes one of good planning for unexpected outcomes, whatever they may be.

Section VI: On-site

Natural Disasters

There are possibilities for property and bodily risk due to natural disasters in every US state where exhibitions are produced. For example, the northern and midwestern states are prone to blizzards and winter storms. Midwestern states and the plains states are susceptible to tornadoes, and floods may occur in any region. Many halls in the midwest have tornado "cellars" for evacuation and safety of attendees, as well as special alerts which are put into effect in the event of tornadoes. Weather bureaus along the East Coast, Gulf Coast and in Florida are of invaluable assistance in the event of weather emergencies in the form of tropical storms which may develop and proceed toward land.

Because of their intensity and the possibility of wide-spread damage, earthquake emergencies need to be considered and planned for in any area where there is a risk of seismic activity. If an exhibition is being hosted in a city where earthquakes are likely to occur, contact the Office of Public Safety or the Office of Emergency Services for specific information regarding earthquake preparedness and disaster plans. Most facilities in earthquake-prone zones have stringent construction codes which must be met by exhibitors during the construction and installation of their displays. Floorplans must be developed with aisle and exit areas which comply with local earthquake-dictated codes.

Make sure to be thoroughly briefed on all of these alerts during the site inspection. Additional information is available from service organizations such as the American Red Cross, Federal Emergency Management Agency (FEMA) and the US Geological Survey; among others.

Man-Made Disasters

While it is impossible to plan for every situation, there are some man-made disasters and violent acts for which it is possible to plan in the hope of minimizing their occurrence.

Food Poisoning

Perhaps the most common man-made disaster that occurs wherever many people gather is food poisoning. While food poisoning is the result of the food and beverage contractor not doing a job properly, it is a situation where the show manager must take immediate action. Have a contingency plan in place in the event of a food poisoning incident. Develop a plan in consultation with local health officials to ensure that all their requirements are met in addition to your own. Control and reporting are crucial functions that need to be considered in this type of emergency.

One of the first lines of defense against food poising is a thorough inspection of the kitchen, either at the facility or the off-site caterer, if applicable. Check with the local health and sanitation officials as to the record of the food and beverage service contractor. Conduct a thorough check of references during the initial site inspection and on subsequent visits.

Fire

Fire is perhaps the next most common man-made disaster. All public facilities must adhere to a set of regulations regarding fire safety. In addition, the show manager is bound to abide by the local, state and federal fire codes with respect to the production of your exhibition. A fire safety checklist like the one prepared for general use by IAEM is a must during site inspections. Every exhibitor manual should reference fire safety requirements, and every attendee should be given a fire safety brochure by the hotel they are using when they check in. Consider including such a brochure in attendee registration packages.

Acts of Violence

Acts of violence can range from pick-pocketing, assault and harassment to rioting or a terrorist bomb threat. Awareness of the crime rate where the event is being hosted and looking at the previous history of crime patterns when exhibitions are in town are good places to start developing a crisis management plan. Check with local police and the FBI if necessary to get the history of crime in an area. Be very cognizant of the exhibition's security needs during all hours of the event, and at all locations programmed activities are occurring.

Demonstrations

Demonstrations are organized public displays of opinion against a perceived offending policy or person. Demonstrators are usually very vocal, carry signs and banners, and frequently hand out literature in support of their cause. Demonstrations are legal in some jurisdictions, provided the demonstrators do not interfere with the normal business of the event and a permit has been obtained. The permit may restrict how close the demonstrators can come to the building. If a controversial speaker has been hired, or if a VIP guest who has been embroiled in a recent controversy will be on-site, a demonstration may result. Additional security for the event will be necessary to ensure that no harm comes to the guests or any of the attendees.

Confrontations

A confrontation is a one-on-one interaction that is intended to disrupt the normal business of a meeting or event. Many confrontations arise from demonstrations, so plan well in advance to ensure that any known demonstration does not get out of control. If it is known in advance that a demonstration is going to happen, it is wiser to hire a security expert who is trained in dealing with these types of situations. Make the expert a part of the crisis management team, and heed the advice given.

Additional security staff may be necessary to ensure that guests and attendees are adequately protected, or call upon the local police force for assistance.

Developing a Crisis Management Plan

When an assessment of all the possible emergency situations has been completed, the next step is to create a working document. The purpose of a crisis management plan is to assist staff and management in making quality decisions during a stressful time. Failure to respond responsibly to a crisis situation could have broad-reaching ramifications.

A crisis management plan will be based on a series of decisions aimed at avoiding or minimizing injury to people, the show in total and valuable assets individually. Obviously, the priority of protection should be in that sequence: people, show, assets. Because every organization faces a unique combination of potential crisis situations, planning should be tailored to the specific organization.

Given the bombing of the World Trade Center in New York and the Federal Building in Oklahoma City, show managers can no longer afford to assume that their exhibitions will not be impacted by even the most extreme types of crisis situations. A show manager cannot assume that it is not necessary to plan for all eventualities. A crisis management plan has to be comprehensive enough to ensure that all possibilities are, at the very least, acknowledged, paid the respect due to them, and addressed in writing. A comprehensive crisis management plan is grounded in the four basic principles of:

- preparedness
- mitigation
- response
- reporting

Preparedness is based on the theory of planned avoidance. In other words, the show manager must do everything possible during the planning and execution of an event to reduce the risk of something occurring.

Mitigation usually refers to a series of rules, regulations or guidelines that are put in place and enforced to limit the possibility of a situation developing, and – if a situation does occur – to lessen the damage. It also includes being aware of the smallest detail so that if something out of the ordinary occurs, its effect on the event will be limited.

Response includes elements of what to do during a situation and immediately following to lessen the damage.

Reporting is about paperwork. It is about creating a "paper trail" that documents what happened when a crisis situation occurs. The second reporting form is the efficient and timely reporting of the incident to the proper authorities, such as police, fire, and medical. Again, pre-planning and effective communications are the cornerstones on which effective reporting is based.

The steps in creating a basic crisis management plan are as follows:

1. Identity the crisis management team, a team leader and two or three competent assistants.
2. Prioritize the various emergency situations and the possible responses. Detail the responses in writing in the plan. The response should include who assumes responsibility, the communication protocols to be followed, the reporting procedures and the actions of all staff.
3. Outline an internal communications plan that details how to get information immediately to on-site staff and medical personnel, security, and local emergency officials. The plan should include the use of some form of remote communication system such as two-way radios or cell phones.
4. Create a reporting system that ensures the collection of necessary data during and after the incident.
5. Identify and develop a response to any situations that may result from the city's geographic location, event timing, and/or controversial speakers.
6. Train all staff members on how to respond to an emergency situation. Conduct practice sessions before the show opens.
7. Have adequate insurance coverage. Clearly understand the deciding point at which the interruption/cancellation coverage will cover a claim. Consult with the insurance company representative and legal counsel when making the decision to postpone or cancel an event. Not doing so may complicate a claim.
8. Plan for every eventuality. Never take anything for granted.
9. Make sure that the facility's emergency plans coordinate with the one developed for the exhibition. Understand who is responsible for determining if an event must be evacuated, postponed or cancelled.
10. Create a detailed evacuation plan with a designated meeting area depending on the venue.

Evaluating a Crisis Management Plan

A crisis management plan should be a working document; in other words, it should be continually updated as the industry, the world and the organization changes. It is imperative to assess the value of the plan, both during the crisis and once it is over. This two-pronged approach will allow time for reflection, refinement and change to various procedures and protocols in order to further enhance the safety and well-being of future event attendees. When evaluating a crisis management plan, keep these twelve questions in mind:

1. How well defined is the notion of what constitutes a crisis?
2. Is there a well-prepared crisis management team? Is the crisis response procedure well publicized?
3. Is there a crisis reporting mechanism? Is it distributed?
4. Is there a chart defining reporting responsibilities? Are names and phone numbers listed? Is a spokesperson identified?
5. Is there a procedure for telephone calls?
6. How will the information be gathered? What information will be gathered? Will a statement be issued? How will the news be disseminated to media?
7. When and how will the media be dealt with, and by whom?
8. What if there is a death or serious injury?
9. What about facilities? Is there an area that can serve as a briefing/media room?
10. What about evaluation once the crisis is over?
11. Does the crisis management team meet regularly?

While no two events are exactly the same, all crisis management plans should have certain key components. The show manager who has viable answers to these questions should be in a good position to deal with crisis situation if it arises.

Exhibition Specific Planning

Some portions of a crisis management plan should be developed to address potential areas of concern specific to the exhibition and exhibitors.

Site Selection

Because it is the show manager's responsibility to choose a safe venue, conduct a safety review during the site selection process. Choosing a safe site means more than just doing a physical inspection. Ask direct questions to ensure that the site being considered is indeed safe in terms of the facility's compliance with federal, state and local ordinances.

Use the *National Safety Council's Safety Questionnaire and Statement of Warranty* as a guideline during the site inspection. The questionnaire is broken down into three categories: documentation/inspection, personnel training, and facility coverage.

**National
Safety
Council**

ADA Compliance Questionnaire
and
Allocation of Responsibility

Hotel _____

City _____

Date_____

The following questionnaire has been developed to provide an overview of the hotel facilities as they relate to accommodating a disabled guest means covers all possible compliance items, nor is it presented as an absolute measure of compliance suitability by the hotel. Nothing contain hotel's answer shall be deemed to impose any responsibility or liability on the Council.

Please answer each question and provide any additional comments which will help the Council determine the level of compliance reached at th well as future plans for compliance.

Further, without any further action by the Council or the hotel, the Allocation of Responsibility clause contained in this questionnaire will be inc by reference and made a part of any agreement reached by the Council and the hotel.

A. Public Areas

Indicate which of the following services are *currently* in place.

	Yes	No	Not Applicable
1) Parking Lots: Sufficient parking spaces designated for disabled (in accordance with applicable regulations), allowing sufficient area for wheelchair maneuvering into a car.	___	___	___
2) Hotel entrance:			
a) Wheelchair access through main doors.	___	___	___
b) Automatic doors at main entrance (i.e., sliding doors).	___	___	___
c) Ramps to entrance with gradual slope, handrail and top and bottom platforms.	___	___	___
3) Walkways:			
a) Nonslip	___	___	___
b) 4' minimum width	___	___	___
4) If staircases exist, one smooth handrail available at each.	___	___	___
5) Front Desk:			
a) Lowered counter area for wheelchair accessibility	___	___	___
b) Concierge/guest service desk check in/out	___	___	___
6) Elevators:			
a) Wheelchair access from main entrance	___	___	___
b) Lowered control panel (40-54" from floor)	___	___	___
c) Braille floor numbers	___	___	___
d) Voice annunciation of floors	___	___	___
7) Public Phones:			
a) Wheelchair accessible	___	___	___
b) Maximum of 48" from floor	___	___	___
c) Sound amplifier built into receiver	___	___	___
8) Fire alarm pulls at a maximum of 48" from floor.	___	___	___
9) Signage:			
a) Block lettering used for offices and rooms.	___	___	___
b) Lettering at a maximum of 60" from floor.	___	___	___
c) Braille translation	___	___	___

	Yes	No	Ap
10) Recreation facilities:			
a) Wheelchair accessible	___	___	
b) For locker facilities, proper grab bars and seating equipment available in shower stalls.	___		
11) Restaurants:			
a) Wheelchair accessible to room	___	___	
b) Wheelchair accessible to buffet stations	___	___	
c) Braille menus	___	___	
12) Meeting space:			
a) Wheelchair accessible to all meeting space	___	___	
b) Stage ramps available	___	___	
c) Sound system equipment for hearing impaired	___	___	.
13) Other:			
a) Wheelchair access to public restrooms	___	___	.
b) Lowered water fountains	___	___	.

B. GUEST ROOMS
(Reserved for Disabled Guests)

	Yes	No	Ap
1) Doors:			
a) Entry threshold flush with hallway floor.	___	___	.
b) 32" minimum width (entry and bathroom)	___	___	.
c) Handle door levers	___	___	
2) Connecting sleeping room for traveling companion	___	___	
3) Bathrooms:			
a) Sink with narrow apron for wheelchair clearance	___	___	
b) Bathtub grab rails	___	___	.
c) Hand-held shower faucet	___	___	.
d) Levered water controls	___	___	.

	Yes	No	Not Applicable
4) Accessible room appointments lowered to a maximum of 40" from floor.			
shelves	___	___	___
closet rods	___	___	___
mirrors	___	___	___
light switches	___	___	___
door security chair	___	___	___
door security "peep" hole	___	___	___
5) Close-captioned TV			
6) Braille room service menu			
7) Telephones:			
a) Flashing light indicating incoming calls	___	___	___
b) Equipment for hearing impaired	___	___	___
8) Emergency Notification:			
a) Strobing fire alarm light	___	___	___
b) Announcement speaker	___	___	___

C. ADA COMPLIANCE PROGRAM

Please answer the following questions in paragraph form and attach them to this questionnaire.

1) Briefly describe the procedures, committees and programs currently established to survey current needs and develop implementation programs.

2) Briefly describe the personnel training procedures established to assist disabled guests. Include front and back-of-house programs.

3) Describe any structural changes planned between now and the Council's meeting dates being discussed.

4) Describe evacuation procedures for disabled guests.

ALLOCATION OF RESPONSIBILITY CLAUSE

1. Americans with Disabilities Act Compliance - Hotel shall be responsible for complying with the public accommodations requirements of the Americans with Disabilities Act ("ADA") not otherwise allocated to the group in this agreement, including: (i) the "readily achievable" removal of physical barriers to access to the meetings rooms (e.g., speakers' platform and public address systems), sleeping rooms, and common areas (e.g., restaurants, rest rooms, and public telephones); (ii) the provision of auxiliary aids and services where necessary to ensure that no disabled individual is treated differently by Hotel than other individuals (e.g., Braille room service menus or reader); and (iii) the modification of Hotel's policies, practices and procedures applicable to all guests and/or groups as necessary to provide goods and services to disabled individuals (e.g., emergency procedures and policy of holding accessible rooms for hearing and mobility impaired open for disabled until all remaining rooms are occupied).

2. Mutual Cooperation in Identifying Special Needs - The Council shall attempt to identify in advance any special needs of disabled registrants, faculty and guests requiring accommodation by hotel, and will notify Hotel of such needs for accommodation as soon as they are identified to the group. Whenever possible, the Council shall copy Hotel on correspondence with attendees who indicate special needs as covered by ADA. Hotel shall notify the Council of requests for accommodation which it may receive otherwise than through the Council to facilitate obligations or needs as required by ADA.

We hereby affirm the preceding information and accept the clause outlining the allocation of responsibility regarding ADA Compliance.

DATE_____

GENERAL MANAGER	SALES REPRESENTATIVE
SIGNATURE _____	SIGNATURE _____
PRINT NAME _____	PRINT NAME _____

	FOR THE NATIONAL SAFETY COUNCIL
DIRECTOR OF SAFETY/SECURITY	NAME _____
SIGNATURE _____	SIGNATURE _____
PRINT NAME _____	TITLE _____

Reprinted with permission, Exposition and Meeting Management Department, National Safety Council, Itasca, IL.

SAFETY AND SECURITY CHECKLIST

Expect the worst and plan accordingly. That's the bottom line when planning for the safety and security of your attendees. While it's impossible to prepare for every emergency or natural disaster, you can devise an action plan that will ensure the safety and security of your guests in the majority of unforeseen circumstances. For guidance in preparing such a plan, consult the following checklist.

PRE-PLANNING

✓ Review event insurance coverage.

✓ Prepare action plans for various situations, including natural disasters, fires, medical emergencies, demonstrations, bomb threats and terrorist threats. Consider or incorporate the facility's existing emergency and evacuation plans.

✓ Is there a written emergency plan for extreme weather conditions such as hurricanes and tornados?

✓ What transportation methods are available in the event attendees need to be moved away from the site?

✓ Know where exits are located and who to contact if an emergency arises. Make sure you exit plans include meeting and exhibit areas.

✓ Designate staff to enact the plans when necessary and delegate specific responsibilities.

✓ Give staff a copy of all action plans and designate a specific area where they can regroup in the event of an emergency.

✓ Communicate your plans to the facilities and other suppliers.

✓ Communicate your plans to the home office and establish a point of contact for staff to check in with should an emergency or natural disasters arise.

✓ Be aware of controversial content or speakers in order to anticipate demonstrations.

✓ Train staff on how to handle unregistered attendees without credentials.

✓ For international meetings and conferences, have the phone number and address of the U.S. Embassy/Consulate readily available. Be aware of any security measures when preparing and shipping meeting materials outside the U.S. so that they are not unduly delayed by customs or security. Also, be aware of limitations on attendees entering the U.S. for a meeting.

✓ Obtain the following phone numbers and addresses and post them at the registration desk and staff office:

  • Nearest hospital for emergencies
  • Nearest walk-in clinic
  • Nearest 24-hour pharmacy
  • Fire department
  • Non-emergency police number
  • Phone number of taxi company

✓ Survey attendees for information about existing medical conditions and any disability requirements. Train staff to recognize problems and respond appropriately.

✓ Notify the facility of any attendees with disabilities or special medical needs. Be aware of facility procedures in case of emergency.

✓ Include space for an emergency contact name and number on the attendee registration form.

✓ Have you hired a security company and EMT? What specific emergency areas are they responsible for and what are they trained in?

✓ Are you taking attendees off site? If so, is the transportation company bonded? Do you have hold-harmless agreements for any team-building activities?

ON-SITE

✓ Take staff on a tour of where security, EMT, and first aid are located, as well as the designated area outside the facility to meet in case of evacuation. Identify the nearest exits to the staff office, registration area, meeting rooms, and exhibit space.

✓ Keep a first aid kit and emergency radio in the staff office.

✓ Have a battery-operated radio, flashlights, glow sticks, and supply of batteries on hand, in case power is lost.

✓ Provide a printed list and download of attendee emergency contact information to registration and to your hotel contact. Keep this list with you at all times.

✓ Maintain a list of emergency phone numbers, including the facility emergency phone number, extension in the staff office, and extension in the registration area.

✓ Provide safety tips and emergency procedures as a registration addition in attendee tote bags or in the program book, including:
- Write your emergency contact information on the back of your name badge.
- Do not wear your conference badge outside the meeting area.
- Keep you luggage and personal belongings in your possession at all times.
- Consult with the hotel concierge about reputable taxi companies or car services.
- Always inquire about the closest and safest routes to walk or jog.
- Ask what time the surrounding area "shuts down" and until what time transportation will be available.
- Be alert and aware of your surroundings when outside the meeting area.
- Ask for identification of hotel staff, if there is any question, before allowing anyone into your room.
- Do not leave your personal belongings or laptop readily exposed in your guest room.

✓ Point out the nearest exits during your general session housekeeping notes.

✓ If a demonstration occurs, consider the following:
- Cordon off an area for protesters.
- Set up a press conference to address the issues or any changes in the event schedule.
- Brief staff on the organization's position and procedures on handling press inquiries.

✓ If a bomb threat occurs, consider the following:
- Record the time of the call, the exact words of the caller, who took the call, where it was received, and who has been notified.
- If possible, ask questions to keep the caller on the line to assist authorities in tracing the call. Ask why they are doing it, where the bomb is located, and when it will go off.
- Note background noises, if the voice is familiar, any accents or distinguishing vocal features.
- Write down any observations for the authorities.

GUEST ROOM AND MEETING SPACE CONSIDERATIONS

✓ Reiterate to the front desk that all guests requesting "lost" keys should promptly be asked for identification before receiving the key, and ask that employees do not speak the room number out loud to guests at any time.

✓ Does hotel staff show ID before entering rooms?

✓ What is the procedure for guests entering a room while it's being cleaned?

✓ Can guests traveling alone request an escort to their room?

✓ Verify that all guest rooms have instructions on how to contact security or 911 directly.

✓ What happens if someone calls 911 from a hotel phone?

✓ Check guest room safes. Are they secure? Is there room for a laptop, as well as other valuables? If not, is there access to a safety deposit box?

✓ Do windows in guest rooms open?

✓ Do sliding glass doors have deadbolt locks?

✓ What is follow-up procedure when wake-up calls are not answered?

✓ Where is the nearest exit from the meeting rooms and the guest rooms? Are they lit properly? Are they illuminated if an emergency or fire alarm goes off?

✓ Is there a house phone on each guest room floor and in meeting space with instructions on what number to call to report and emergency?

✓ Are smoke detectors, sprinklers, and fire extinguishers on each guest room floor? Hallways? Meeting space?

✓ Are banquet chairs interlocked in theater seating?

✓ Are there crash bars on all doors in the meeting space?

✓ Examine the condition and presence of internal lighting. When do lights go on, how well lit are the hallways and exits?

PUBLIC SPACE CONSIDERATIONS

✓ What is public access to the hotel and/or convention center? How is it monitored and controlled?

✓ What other events are going on at the same time as your function that may cause additional traffic in the building or any potential security issues?

✓ Can vehicles be driven into the building? If so, what are the rules? (i.e. disconnected battery, one-quarter tank of gas, etc.)

✓ Are some or all of the facility doors locked at night?

✓ Closely examine evacuation routes. Are they cluttered with tables, chairs, or anything else that would impede a quick exit?

✓ Is access to the parking garage restricted?

✓ Ensure that the parking lot and pathways to the hotels are well lit at night.

GENERAL FACILITY INFORMATION AND CONSIDERATIONS

✓ How often are emergency drills conducted?

✓ Are hotel staff certified or trained in CPR, first aid, and the Heimlich maneuver? Ask for a list of names and contact numbers.

✓ Does the facility own an automatic external defibrillator, and who is certified to use it?

✓ Inquire about possible union strikes and protests during the conference and how it might affect the attendees.

✓ Ask the director of security what the most prevalent incidents are in the facility and the surrounding area.

✓ Are security personnel on staff or subcontracted? If they are subcontracted, is the company bonded? Do security personnel undergo background checks prior to being hired?

✓ Does the facility have personnel who speak languages other than English? If so, how can you contact them?

✓ Who is the manager on duty while on-site, and how do you contact him/her?

✓ Is there a doctor on call 24 hours?

✓ Does the facility require an EMT during the event? If so, what is the policy and where will he/she be located on-site? What are the station's hours of operation?

✓ Is there an emergency lighting system and evacuation process in place?

✓ During power outages, do the elevators shut down automatically? Are ventilation systems turned off automatically?

✓ Are all exits clearly marked in hallways, guest rooms, and meeting space? Do all exit doors lead directly out of the building?

✓ Is there a paging or a telephone system that reaches all occupants simultaneously?

✓ What is the evacuation plan for guests with special needs? Examine the process by which impaired or disabled guests will be able to contact the front desk or security immediately.

✓ What procedures are in place to alert hearing-impaired guests to an emergency?

✓ What is the procedure if a fire alarm should sound? Is the fire department notified right away?

✓ Where is the primary location for guests to assemble during an evacuation?

✓ Ask about any ADA enhancements or exclusions that may be unique to the specific hotel or convention center.

✓ Confirm which hotel staff have keys and to what areas, including who carries the master keys.

✓ Does the hotel have the ability to do an audit on electronic door locks?

✓ What are the hotel's procedures for dealing with demonstrations and confrontations?

✓ Is security on the staff radio, or do you contact them via phone or through the convention services manager?

✓ Is the staff trained in the service of alcohol? How often? What procedures are followed if a guest becomes intoxicated?

  • If there an elevated security status nationwide, meet with the head of security and go over the management/safety of the group. What is the evacuation policy? Is the facility a designated public shelter in an emergency? Is the facility a command post for local law enforcement?

Seriously consider including in the facility rental/lease agreement, as an express condition of the contract signing date or opening day of the exposition, the section of the questionnaire that asks the facility to sign a statement of warranty with respect its compliance with all current federal, state and local health, fire and safety regulations.

Rules and Regulations

Every exposition has display rules and regulations that are used to protect the management company and attendees from risks inherent in the production of an event. Display rules and regulations are normally found within the exhibitor manual and adherence to them is referenced in the exhibitor space sales contract. Develop contracts and rules and regulations very early in the planning process, and then incorporate them into the sales production arm of the event. Establish sound, enforceable display rules and regulations *before* the first exhibit space is sold.

The International Association for Exhibition Management has developed a standard for displays for exhibitions that is helpful when developing display rules and guidelines for your event. *The Guidelines for Displays Rules and Regulations* should be incorporated into the exhibitor manual to ensure compliance with industry standards for booth construction and display. Rules which are applicable to safety and accident prevention will vary depending on the type of event, its location, and the nature of exhibits. The most common rules in exhibitor contracts deal with the prevention of possible mishaps. Most rules fall within two broad categories: site-specific and show-specific.

Site-specific Risks for Exhibitors

Site-specific risks refer to those that are directly related to either the facility or the type of exhibit. For example, exhibitors are required to conform to the local fire code; therefore, open flames, pressurized tanks, portable heating equipment, and liquid petroleum gas are either not permitted at all, or subject to inspection by the fire marshal or a qualified facility representative. Fire exits and fire equipment must be visible at all times. Furthermore, exits may not be chained at times when visitors are on the premises.

In cities like Detroit where automobiles are most likely to be displayed, there are specific safety rules requiring the use of locking gas caps, limiting the amount of gasoline in each tank, keeping a fire extinguisher in the car, disconnecting batteries, no refueling on the show floor, proper venting of exhaust if car is to be operated on the show floor, and a specified amount of liability insurance for the display. The rules regarding the displaying of equipment or machinery with fuel tanks and automobiles is relatively uniform across local, state and federal jurisdictions,

The following situations may require specialized rules and regulations to meet the exhibition's safety standards, and to comply with local, state and/or federal ordinances: fire-proofing certificates, on-site flammability tests, the storage of cartons and crates, machinery with moving parts, laser beams, specialized medical equipment such as x-ray, or where shielding from chips, sparks or toxic substances is involved.

At all major shows, electrical installations must conform to specified standards, and electrical work may be handled by qualified electricians only. Usually, all electrical equipment, cords and extensions must have an accredited laboratory approval, and must meet all city and state codes.

Construction rules are another consideration in most show rules and regulations, particularly for booths designed with a second level or with hanging signs. Refer to IAEM's *Guidelines for Display Rules and Regulations* for guidance in developing rules regarding booth construction. In general, any booth designed with a second level, stairways, or excessive height, for example, must have construction plans certified by a licensed professional engineer, and by the engineering staff of the facility in which it is to be built.

Designs for hanging signs must typically be cleared with the show manager first, and then with the engineering department of the facility in which the show is to be held. The type of clamps or other devices which will carry the weight of the sign must also meet approved safety standards.

Exhibitions are bound to comply with these and other rules and regulations as determined by local ordinances, in addition to any rules and regulations that have been developed by show management. As a rule of thumb, insert a final paragraph in any rules that indicate that questions of interpretation regarding these regulations are solely the prerogative of show management.

Show-specific Risks for Exhibitors

Show-specific risks refer to those controversies that may develop between show management and an exhibitor, or between exhibitors, regarding interpretation of the rules and regulations or conditions of the sales contract. Most show-specific risks fall under the broad umbrella of "policy" situations. As such, most situations can usually be averted by plain and definitive language in the sales contract.

For example, some booth prices are quoted in terms of "bare space," while others are quoted in "package" format. Bare space refers to a unit of space without any services attached to it, while a package unit might include draped back wall and side rails, carpet, company sign, and electrical outlet. The package offer should be clear as to whether furniture of any kind is included, and whether removal of crates, cleaning or other services is included.

Rules and regulations should be written carefully to avoid issues related to subleasing, noise control, prohibiting the use of competitive products or applications in a company's booth, distribution of food and beverages in booths, the use of drawings, contests and raffles to stimulate traffic and/or attendance, and allegations of hidden costs. Besides show rules governing these activities, there may also be state or municipal ordinances which are directed at the consumption of food and alcohol in certain premises, or gambling in any form. Spell out clearly denials of liability or liability limits in the event of theft, damage, loss or destruction of exhibits.

Along with all these various security and safety measures, there should also be a description of protection stating that a security service will be provided on a 24-hour basis. This should be closely followed by an announcement informing exhibitors about the availability of a lock-up area for after-hours use.

To avoid the potential of misinterpretation by exhibitors, and subsequent controversy and possible litigation, contracts should contain a disclaimer in one form or another that indicates that show management reserves the right to amend and interpret the terms, conditions and restrictions of the contract as deemed proper to ensure the success of the exhibition and to further the purposes of the sponsoring body.

Protecting Against Losses
Because it is impossible for show management, its contractors, the sponsoring organizations or the facility to provide blanket insurance coverage on potential losses, exhibitors are responsible for their own equipment and personnel. Individual exhibitors are expected to carry adequate insurance to protect themselves against all possible losses. It is recommended that exhibitors contact their insurance counselors to obtain riders on existing policies, or to specify new ones to ascertain proper coverage.

Show managers sometimes arrange with a reputable insurance company to issue coverage to individual exhibitors who may request it. This insurance is a type of term insurance which covers specific losses during a specific time period such as set-up, show hours and tear-down periods.

It is important to note that no insurance company will reimburse a claim – from an exhibitor or anyone else – if it is not properly and completely documented. Exhibitors who experience losses, either through theft or damage to property at the exhibition, should be directed to contact the show manager or another designated staff person immediately. At that time, an immediate investigation by a representative of security should be initiated. A written report to accompany the claim to the insurance company should be generated immediately, which will serve as important documentation in the event that the missing equipment is not ultimately located.

Section VI: On-site

Personal Security

Security is another area which must be planned carefully and thoroughly in advance. Security concerns impact site selection, protection of exhibits, and crime prevention. A registration system that controls access to the exhibit hall, helps deter crimes from occurring and provides a sense of security for all event attendees. A good security system also serves to limit access to the exhibition only by qualified attendees.

The International Association for Exhibition Management addresses several personal safety issues in its publication entitled *Guidelines for Life/Safety in the Exposition Industry.* Some areas of concern include:

Entrance and Exit Areas

Hall entries and exits need to be free from obstacles and wide enough to permit emergency access and egress. Emergency exits must never be locked during the hours when a facility is occupied by attendees. Fire fighting and emergency equipment must not be hidden or obstructed. Fire extinguishers, fire hose cabinets, alarm pull boxes and standpipes must not be hidden or obstructed in any way. Preliminary floorplans of exhibit halls should clearly indicate location of all the above.

Traffic Areas

Aisles and walkways in the exhibit hall should have a minimum width of eight feet, with an extension of ten feet for public shows. Building safety and security officials, as well as show management, should monitor all assembly situations where overflow crowds and minimal exiting alternatives exist.

Medical Emergencies

Every exhibition and/or facility should have qualified staff on hand to handle medical emergencies. In addition to briefing and preparing all staff on how to respond to medical emergencies, the show manager should have a qualified nurse or paramedic on duty during move-in, show hours and move-out. In addition to being well-versed in basic life support, injury/illness assessment, first aid, and CPR, the medical personnel must also understand and know how to use the crisis communication plan, and all of the other elements of the crisis management plan.

Developing a Crisis Management Team

Crisis preparation requires participation from many people within an organization. At a minimum, top management, public relations, operations, technical support and human resources need to be part of the planning. Employees in the field and on-site are usually the first on the scene of a crisis. Designate a staff person to analyze the show site and the surrounding area to determine where potential problems are, and how to mitigate or eliminate the risk. Management will need to review existing crisis management measures, and consider what new measures should be taken. Possible members of the crisis management team include:

- Top management
- Event host/sponsor representative
- Event management
- All staff who will go on-site
- Operations
- Media relations
- IT/technical support
- Human resources

- Finance
- Legal counsel
- Insurance consultant
- Risk analysis consultant
- Security consultant/contractor
- Facility representative
- General service contractor
- Off-site contact (back at the office)

SUMMARY

The key to a successful, crisis-free event is paying attention to details, anticipating possibilities, and planning. Many potential exhibition crises can be averted by careful communication with exhibitors. Whether dealing with natural disasters or health and safety issues, a show organizer must have a plan in place and a team ready to implement it.

QUESTIONS FOR DISCUSSION

① How much of the responsibility for the safety of attendees is the responsibility of show management and how much is the responsibility of individual attendees?

② What would be a few important criteria in determining where to locate the headquarters for EMT personnel?

③ Do you have an emergency crisis plan for your own home and family?

Section VI: On-site

Chapter 3
Green Meetings

*"When one tugs at a single thing in nature,
he finds it attached to the rest of the world."*

– John Muir

Section VI: On-site

IN THIS CHAPTER YOU WILL LEARN

- What does being "green" mean?
- How exhibitions and events can "go green"
- Some examples of changes show organizers are making
- Where to find more information and resources

INTRODUCTION

During the past few decades, environmental issues have taken on new importance in many industries, with energy consumption and minimized consumption of natural resources receiving the most public attention. Although green meetings have been an increasingly hot topic, only recently have meeting professionals begun to fully consider the importance of environmentally-friendly events.

CONTRIBUTORS

Carina Bloom, Marketing and Operations Director, IMEX; Amy Spatrisano, CMP, Meetings Strategies Worldwide & Green Meetings Industry Council

This chapter has been based largely on the IMEX environmental initiative, but attention should also be drawn to the strong campaigning record of other international tradeshows within the tourism sector, notably IT&ME (Incentive Travel and Meetings Exhibition) in Chicago, and WTM (World Travel Market) in London.

Why Be Green?

Does the environment matter? Such topics are now front and center in our newspapers and live broadcasts. Even conceding possible media exaggeration and scientific uncertainties, there is now a widespread and deepening public perception that world climatic conditions are changing. Many claim that global warming is happening; some would argue irreversibly so.

Because they use a lot of resources and can be extremely wasteful, exhibitions potentially represent a negative influence on the environment. They use large volumes of electricity, encourage the use of many travel and transportation options, and generate large amounts of waste. For example, at a recent event in the United States, a 500-stand exhibition associated with a conference attended by 8,100 visitors used the following:

- 617,000 kilowatts of electricity
- 28,000 thermos of natural gas
- 376,000 gallons of fuel

In total, over eight million tons of carbons were emitted into the atmosphere. In the UK, one estimate suggests that exhibition waste exceeds one million tons annually.

Other environmental factors to consider are water usage, and the products and services purchased to produce the show. Food and beverage service and restroom usage are the larger contributions to the water usage during an exhibition. Organizers should consider using facilities and caterers who have water conservation practices in place. The US Environmental Protection Agency estimates the average conference participant uses 846 gallons of water.

Changing Attitudes

Fears about the environment, justifiable or not, have prompted a remarkable and dramatic transformation in attitudes towards the environment, from governments down to the people. The wide variance in global environmental policies is the result of highly-disparate political agendas, contrasting cultural views and financial circumstances. In short, the leaders of some countries are more "green-minded" than others. It is easier to be eco-sensitive when a country's economy is relatively wealthy, and the average standard of living is relatively high.

For those engaged in the business of leisure or business travel, the realization has emerged that resources must be preserved and sustainability has to become a prevailing force if destinations are to remain appealing to many visitors. The new criterion for selection in holiday and corporate tourism often includes the eco-values of a location. Visitors are increasingly likely to resist the option of a compromised environment, whether the pollution is centered on land, sea or air. Many will "vote with their feet," and simply go somewhere else. Conversely, a reputation for sound environmental practices which preserve a pristine countryside and coast attracts significant interest. In the future, it seems probable that "greenness" will become if not *the* unique selling point for a property or destination, then certainly an important marketing advantage. Eco-credentials will become an increasingly important part of the entire promotional package.

A series of surveys of meetings and incentive travel industry professionals was conducted in recent years by IMEX, an organization hosting an exhibition called the Worldwide Exhibition for Incentive Travel Meetings and Events, which revealed some interesting trends. In 2003, a focus group of Europe-based MICE (Meetings, Incentive, Convention and Events) buyers called for more discussion and information about environmental issues. Not many respondents expressed concern about environmental issues. Remarks typically included statements such as, "Green is only a fad with no future," and "Eco is only for companies whose products need to be seen to be caring." Many agreed with the statement, "I am pessimistic because the countries which do the most harm are not committed to global environmental policies." Only a few said things like, "We must do something because the meetings sector produces a tremendous amount of waste, and often shows blatant disregard as to what happens after the show is over."

By the time a 2005 poll was taken, MICE buyers were reacting more thoughtfully to environmental concerns. When asked which green practices they have applied to their events, respondents (totaling 70+ from 11 countries) answered:

• Recycling of conference material: 80%
• Viewing wilderness or animal conservation areas: 73%
• Selecting a hotel known for its environmental program: 71%
• Involving an inspirational speaker on green issues: 53%
• Selecting an airline or cruise company known for its eco-credentials: 51%
• Undertaking fund-raising or other support for green causes: 41%

Furthermore, a significant majority (74%) of these buyers commented that they thought the environment would become a bigger issue in the future. This, they suggest, is because of the attention given environmental issues by the media, the role of education in fostering a generation of well-informed young people, and because of the continuing danger and destruction from industrial contamination, strip mining, and mass deforestation. Interestingly, 58% argued that delegates and participants will show their concern in the future if environmental issues are not sufficiently taken into account when planning events.

In the 2006 IMEX survey involving over 100 buyers from over 25 countries on three continents, it is clear that attitudes have become even more pro-green. Not only did a majority (56%) acknowledge that they now consistently take environmental credentials into account in event planning and destination selection, but their characteristic language had in many cases become more pointed. Comments included, "We now avoid countries with a negative media feedback on the environment," "We spot and reject environmental tokenism," and "It is no longer politically correct to stage events without a proper environmental strategy."

Economic Considerations

Despite the perception that implementing green practices can cost considerably more money for planners and suppliers, savings are actually likely to occur in the long run. According to a comprehensive report on green meetings released in 2004 by the Convention Industry Council (CIC), following the best practices for green meetings and events ultimately saves money for both show organizers and the venues in which they are held. Properties save on operating costs, including increasingly high energy charges, and both venues and planners can save from the operational efficiencies that are tied to green business practices. For example, collecting the name badges for reuse at an event in the United States with 1,300 attendees can save the organizer almost $1,000. There is a growing acknowledgment within the industry that, while it is difficult to calculate the immediate ROI of implementing green practices, the dividends are bound to pay in the long-term.

Added to monetary savings is the opportunity to savor the moral high-ground, inspire delegates and enhance the reputation of the organization. The underlying message is that greener exhibitions need not be a cause of greater workload, extra hassle, or additional cost, and have enormous opportunities within their own right.

Practical Suggestions for Green Exhibitions

The choices made by the organizers, official services contractor, facility, and exhibitors can greatly reduce the negative environmental impact that an exhibition can have. The collaboration between those players is crucial to the success of creating an exhibition or tradeshow that is environmentally responsible.

Show Organizers

Show Organizers can start by:

- Informing facilities and official services contractors of the exhibition's environmental strategies and initiatives. Ask them about their environmental practices. Include specifics like recycling, composting, and energy and water conservation.
- Informing exhibitors of the green priorities. Ask for their cooperation, or build compliance into their exhibitor contract stating their commitment to comply with the exhibition's environmental requests.

The show organizer should also plan to provide:

- Accurate attendance expected so exhibitors can bring the corresponding number of materials for distributing, cutting down on waste.

- Electronic scan cards for attendee profiles.
- A clause in the facility agreement with the facility and/or official services contractor to provide recycling services for cardboard, pallets, paper, cans, plastic, glass and other recyclable materials that are generated; and to provide clean-up crews who are trained to keep recyclable and reusable items out of the garbage.
- A clause in the exhibitor agreement to comply with the following:
  ○ Minimize the use of collateral materials.
  ○ Produce any necessary collateral materials on post- consumer paper stock, using vegetable-based inks.
  ○ Minimize packaging and participate in recycling packaging when appropriate.
  ○ Use recycled or consumable products as giveaways when possible, and do not use gift items made from endangered or threatened species.
  ○ When possible, attempt to use locally grown and/or made products.

Decisions that show organizers make about products and services can also make a considerable environmental impact. Here are some examples that were implemented at exhibitions by various show organizers:

- Name badges were printed on recycled paper and badge holders were recycled
- Conference bags were made of recycled materials.
- Programs were printed on 100 percent recycled post-consumer paper with soy-based ink.
- Approximately 31-50 percent of the food served was local and/or organic.
- All condiments were served in bulk containers, saving approximately 51-75 percent of the cost over serving individually-packaged products.

> At the recent Greenbuild Conference, exhibitors were offered a "green" booth alternative from the decorator. The carpet used in the exhibit hall for the aisles and the general session hall was recycled carpet donated called Solution Q™, which is made of 40 percent recycled materials and is recyclable.
> - 41 percent of exhibitors out of 300 used the recycled carpet in their booths.
> - 35 percent used green padding.
> - Signage was also able to be reused.

Official Services Contractor

The official services contractor company altered the way they do business permanently by incorporating the following environmentally responsible practices:

- Energy Star Saver for the registration counters
- Online exhibitor kits.
- Printed exhibitor kids made from 35 percent post-consumer recovered fiber for the binders, recycled paper and soy-based inks with printed materials

- Computer kiosks built with WoodStalk™, an engineered fiberboard made from annually-renewable wheat straw fiber that does not contain any wood species and does not use compounds containing formaldehyde.
- 50 percent of the sign boards made from Cloraplast™, a 100% recyclable board.

The official services contractor can also:

- Use recycled or recyclable tradeshow materials, or select drapes and carpets that can be cleaned in a way that is environmentally responsible.
- Use recyclable or biodegradable shipping and packing materials, paper and corrugated boxes instead of polystyrene and plastic wrap.
- Coordinate with organization to collect donated items.
- Provide carbon-offset program for shipping and freight.

Facilities

The venue where the exhibition is being held also plays a crucial role in the ability to implement environmental practices. For example, if the venue does not have a recycling program in place, minimizing the impact of waste will be virtually impossible. To ensure the exhibit hall floor reflects environmentally responsible practices, follow these recommendations: The facility should provide:

- Recycle bins on the show floor.
- Collection bins for less common materials such as batteries and vinyl table coverings.
- Information for exhibitors outlining what material is collected for recycling.
- An area to donate leftover signage, giveaways, and flowers for schools or civic organizations.
- Organization names to contact for the donated items.
- Lighting and electrical conservation practices using half-lights and no HVAC during move-in and move-out.

Exhibitors

Exhibitors should be asked to adhere to the following guidelines:

- Use soy-based ink and post-consumer recycled paper to produce the materials.
- Use recycled or consumable products as giveaways.
- Avoid bringing large quantities of collateral materials - send them upon request.
- Create tradeshow booths from sustainable or reusable materials, designing them to be as environmentally-friendly as possible.
- Minimize packaging materials and use recyclable, biodegradable shipping and packing materials.
- Purchase supplies that have minimal packaging.
- Assist move-in and move-out process by recycling cardboard, freight boxes and plastic wrap.

THE IMEX CASE STUDY

IMEX (www.imex-frankfurt.com) has a unique opportunity to influence attitudes within the MICE sector in favor of green-mindedness. Launched in 2001, the 15,000 square- meter event attracts over 3,000 exhibitors representing nearly 150 countries. These stakeholders include staff from convention bureaus, airlines, hotels and other venues, travel agencies, destination management companies, cruise lines, car rental companies, suppliers of marketing services, trade media, and others. In addition, around 7,500 visitors are attracted from 90 markets worldwide, representing the sectors of meetings, congresses, incentive travel, product launches, promotional events, training courses and sporting occasions, among others. IMEX highlights the importance of corporate social responsibility (CSR), particularly regarding the need to show concern for the environment, within a program of industry-friendly initiatives.

For example, in seeking to minimize waste, IMEX works with Messe Frankfurt to encourage re-use and recycling practices. Since material derived from exhibition stands is primarily foil, plastic, paper, cardboard, wood and carpet, the amount deemed "non-recyclable" has been reduced to around 19 percent, and a lower proportion is sought. Such targets can be set, and achieved, by all exhibitions. IMEX also circulates ideas to exhibitors for making their show presence more environmentally-friendly. Suggestions include:

- Take away your own waste
- Pre-build the stand off-site to minimize waste in the hall
- Plan for a re-useable stand they can be used for a long time by incorporating design graphics that are not time-bound
- Choose contractors with accredited eco-credentials
- Use low-energy lighting
- Substitute brochures with downloadable text (one estimate suggests that
- 60 percent of handouts at shows are thrown away.)

Rewarding Positive Action
Carbon Emission Offsets

Global warming is caused by the build up of greenhouse gases in the atmosphere from human activity, primarily the burning of fossil fuels to provide the energy and services we use every day. Fossil fuels are burned in homes and businesses, cars, airplanes and to create nearly everything consumed. "Carbon offsets" enable individuals and businesses to reduce the CO2 (carbon dioxide, a damaging greenhouse gas) emissions they are responsible for when they consume fossil fuels by offsetting, reducing or displacing the CO2 in another place, typically where it is more economical to do so. Carbon offsets typically include contributions to renewable energy, energy efficiency and reforestation projects. As more and more people are concerned about global warming and seeking to reduce their climate impact, carbon offsets, along with personal carbon reductions, provide an important solution to global warming.

Exhibitions can lead by example in sponsoring carbon emission offsets for aspects of travel associated with the event. For example, IMEX pays to neutralize the greenhouse gas cost of the 24 staff members who fly to Frankfurt, and also that arising from their global sales itineraries in a full year.

Rewards and Awards

Another opportunity is for trade fairs to reward the implementation of good green practices. As a case in point, IMEX presents environmental awards each year in recognition of achievement in green exhibiting. Undertaken jointly with professionals in the responsibility sector, such as the Green Meetings Industry

Council (GMIC) and The Wuppertal Institute, these awards seek evidence not just of worthy efforts, but in quantifiable results that minimize the environmental impact of attendance at the show. IMEX provides a focus for this environmental emphasis with a Corporate Responsibility pavilion that is staffed by specialists on the main tradeshow floor including representatives of GMIC, Green Globe 21, Louise Hall-Reider & Co, Give Instead of Take and The Wuppertal Institute. This pavilion gives both exhibitors and visitors to the exhibition a chance to increase their awareness and knowledge of environmental and social responsibility. In addition, the on-site experts give their time in helping them to set up, create or improve their CSR practices. The findings of IMEX's green research are also distributed at no cost.

In recognition of progress made by environmentally-aware buyers, IMEX now presents an annual Green Meetings Award and a Commitment to the Community Award.

Fostering Greener Meetings

While IMEX works to become a more environmentally-responsible exhibition, it is also encouraging MICE decision-makers to adopt green-minded approaches to their events. One approach is to offer tips, such as:

- Encourage buyers to choose venues where environmental strategies are top-down policy, preferably with formal accreditation, as well as to consider staging part of the conference in a setting strongly identified with conservation work.

- Feature meals which feature organically-grown food are proposed.

- Purchase carbon offset credits to neutralize the impact of delegate travel on the volume of greenhouse gas emissions.

- Examine the environmental credentials of the airlines, cruise companies and car rental firms under consideration.

- Mark the conclusion of a successful business event with a "legacy initiative." For instance, a tree could be planted or a donation made to a wildlife cause.

- Include comment cards in selected hotels to question the environmental policies of those properties.

- Recommend hotels within walking distance of the exhibition venue.

- Advise golfers that some clubs observe "greener" techniques in their course managers than others.

- Highlight partner programs that replace shopping with visits to nature reserves.

- Suggest outdoor leadership training projects that incorporate conservation work as their focus, rather than the traditional pursuits like 4 x 4-vehicle driving, shooting, or archery.

Action in the Public Arena

The most effective public relations policy tends to emerge when stakeholders in a given industry participate in developing and shaping it. Demonstrating this process in action were the IMEX surveys which invited suggestions from MICE decision-makers in an effort to offer a greener agenda for the future. A brief summary of these opinions includes the following recommendations for suggestions to governmental bodies in host countries:

- Further legislation and funding to protect the environment.

- Increased use of sustainable energy and reduction in use of fossil fuels.

- More emphasis on advising people in emerging countries on how to benefit from business tourism.

- Tighter government policies on procurement as a means of more effective management control.

- Additional sharing of best environmental practices.

Second, planners offered recommendations to the wider MICE industry:

- Become more (financially and practically) involved in the work of eco-organizations.

- Select only eco-sensitive destinations.

- Plans frequent opportunities during events to inform attendees of potential damage to environments.

- Boycott suppliers who don't appear to care.

- Convene an annual eco-conference for the meetings industry.

Future Eco-Taxation?

Apparently, MICE buyers are becoming more receptive to the idea of a destination "eco-tax" that would be invested in managing for sustainability. Forty-six percent of respondents to a 2006 poll said they would be willing to discuss the idea, commenting to the effect that "it is our generation's responsibility to preserve the environment for the future." Some cautioned that such a levy must be properly explained to visitors, and agreed with the idea in concept, "as long as we know how it is being spent." In contrast, some organizers worried that corrupt or inefficient governments will waste the money, or that their political mindsets could change. Another opinion is that an eco-tax should be a general way of life, and not an additional burden on the end-user.

SUMMARY

It is clear that managing exhibitions using environmentally-responsible practices offers a significant opportunity to minimize negative environmental impacts, as well as save money in the long-term. However, success relies on excellent communication with all parties involved, as well as ensuring that environmental strategies are incorporated in every step of the planning process. Encouragingly, even small changes can make a big difference to the "environmental bottom line," and it is this key message that organizers should keep in mind at each step of the planning process.

QUESTIONS FOR DISCUSSION:

① Do you recycle your personal household waste? Why or why not?

② Do you agree that practicing the principles of green meetings will make a difference in the future of the environment? Why or Why not?

③ What is your favorite environmental organization and why?

Case Studies, Statistics & Resources

VisitScotland's GTBS

This Green Tourism Business Scheme (www.visitscotland.com/sitewide/greentourism) encourages tourism and meeting related businesses to be environmentally friendly. Launched five years ago, it now has more than 420 members, all of whom are rigorously assessed and given Bronze, Silver or Gold awards, depending on the levels of energy-efficiency they achieve.

Coalition for Environmentally Responsible Conventions (CERC)

www.cerc04.org

The organization was formed in 2004 by 15 local Boston environmentalists in direct response to the Democratic Convention being held in Boston. CERC also targeted the Republican Convention in New York (2004) in its efforts to increase awareness and improve overall environmental education among meeting planners in the United States in general. The organization aimed to demonstrate the kinds of practices needed to reduce greenhouse gases, responsible for global warming, during conventions. Examples of its successes included:

- Boston's Fleet Center and New York's Madison Square Garden were powered by wind turbines, small scale hydro-electric facilities and landfill gases.
- An ultra-low polluting 250kw fuel cell helped to power the Boston convention's media pavilion.
- CERC persuaded the Boston Hyatt Regency to start a food waste composting program.
- 1.3 tons of waste paper products at the Boston Democratic Convention were transformed into convention posters for delegates.
- CERC persuaded 24 major convention events to use food produced on Massachusetts or New York farms.

Resources

Strict criteria for minimum best practices for show organizers and venues are prepared in the Green Meetings Report of the Convention Industry Council (www.conventionindustry.org). See also the report on the so-called Sustainable Exhibition Industry Project (SEXI) accessible via www.aeo.org.uk for further details from the British perspective on delivering responsible solutions to the challenge of waste streams at trade fairs. The Web site of the Greenbuild International Conference and Expo (www.greenbuildexpo.org) contains proposals for greater energy efficiency, such as reducing lighting at off-peak times in the exhibition hall, conserving water by serving drinking water from large containers instead of individual bottles, and encouraging participants to adjust home thermostats and unplug electrical gadgets while away.

- Convention Industry Council, Green Meeting Guidelines
  www.conventionindustry.org
  Good resource for industry accepted guidelines for exhibitions/tradeshows

- Green Meeting Industry Council
  www.greenmeetings.info
  Organization formed to provide networking and education for environmentally minded companies

- Meeting Strategies Worldwide www.meetingstrategiesworldwide.com
  Industry leaders of environmentally responsible meeting/convention practices

- Green Globe 21
  Global benchmarking, certification and improvement system for sustainable travel & tourism

- Carbon Offsetting Programs:
  www.climatecare.org
  www.CO2balance.com
  www.carbonclear.com

- Sustainable Exhibition Industry Project, UK: SEXI
www.aeo.org.uk
Through research the project has given an indication of the volume and content of the waste arising from the UK exhibition industry, made recommendations as to how the situation can be improved, and started a process of change throughout the UK exhibition industry. This has also helped encourage activity across Europe's exhibition industry.

Section VI: On-site

Chapter 4
Evaluation

*"The best way to find out what people are thinking is to ask them.
Audience feedback can be essential in determining what the
group wants, to measure comprehension, to encourage audience interest
and participation, to improve future meetings, and much more."*

– Corbin Ball

Section VI: On-site

IN THIS CHAPTER YOU WILL LEARN

- Why you need to do an evaluation
- Which groups to survey
- Some tools for gathering information
- How to apply the results of an evaluation

INTRODUCTION

Successful organizers continuously analyze their events. They rely on many sources of information and data to provide a comprehensive evaluation of all aspects of the event to determine if their internal goals and objectives are being met. This data is also invaluable in identifying ways to maintain and increase value for their attendee and exhibitor constituents. Without consistent, reliable and detailed information, the organizer is ill-equipped to make adjustments and improvements essential to ensure that the event remains healthy, vibrant and growing.

CONTRIBUTOR

Skip Cox, President, Exhibit Surveys, Inc.

Why an Evaluation Process?

Often called a post-show analysis, the evaluation process involves an in-depth look at all aspects of planning, marketing and production of an exhibition. In general, the overall objectives of the evaluation process are to:

- Determine whether the goals and objectives of the exhibition were met from the perspective of show management, as well as the event's attendees, exhibitors and suppliers.
- Identify the strengths and weaknesses of the exhibition so that improvements can be made in the future.
- Provide feedback that will help to continually refine the exhibition's strategy, planning, marketing and operations for the future.

Attendee Feedback

Attendees are the fundamental component of any successful exhibition. They are the reason companies buy exhibit space. Their attitudes about an exhibition, and the value they receive from attending, are critical to the event's success and longevity.

For exhibitions that register attendees, information gleaned from well-planned event registration forms will assess the demographic profile of the attendees. This is the first step in determining whether the exhibition attracted the targeted attendees. This information will also help show organizers to identify key attendee segments that may require more attendance promotion focus in the future.

The attendee registration demographics also provide a marketing tool for selling exhibitors, and identifying new segments of exhibitors who may benefit from key attendee segments being attracted to the show. In this case, consider an independent third-party audit of the attendee registration data.

An audit is not to be confused with a survey of a random sample of attendees (which will be addressed later.) An audit is census-based, meaning that it counts all attendee and demographic data in the registration database, and runs tests to ensure that all reported figures are correct. The third-party auditor then certifies the data for accuracy. This independent certification adds credibility to the exhibition's data when marketing to exhibitors. It can also be used as a tool to assist exhibitors in planning their participation in the exhibition.

WHAT DOES AN AUDIT LOOK LIKE?

STATEMENT OF VERIFICATION METHODOLOGY:

All conference registrants were required to pick up their badges on site before attending any conferences or visiting the exhibit hall. All advance exhibit only registrants who registered before January 14, 2005 were required to pick up their badge holders on site before they could enter the exhibit hall. All other exhibit only registrants picked up their badge on site.When a badge or badge holder is picked up the registrant is marked as verified.

AUDITED ATTENDANCE ANALYSIS:

Year	Conference Attendance	Exhibit Only	Total Conference and Exhibit Only	Speakers*	Press*	Registered Exhibitors*	Special Programs*	Grand Total
2005	1,047	4,448	5,495	139	216	1,999	513	8,362

Not audited. Provided by show organizer.

An audit might also include job functions of attendees:

JOB FUNCTION:

Job Function	Total Verified Exhibit Only & Conference Attendees	Percent of Total
Academic Head/University Faculty/Professor	81	1.5
Attorney	32	0.6
CEO	217	3.9
Chief Financial Officer	20	0.4
CIO, CTO, CSO, COO	206	3.7
Consultant	514	9.4
IT/MIS Management/Director	407	7.4
Finance – Accounting –VC	80	1.5

NUMBER OF EMPLOYEES IN COMPANY/ORGANIZATION:

Number of Employees	Total Verified Exhibit Only & Conference Attendees	Percent of Total
Under 50	1,665	30.3
50 – 99	340	6.2
100 – 499	546	9.9
500 – 999	302	5.5
1,000 – 4,999	499	9.1
5,000 – 9,999	257	4.7
10,000 or more	982	17.9
Do Not Know	624	11.3
Not Identified	280	5.1
TOTAL	**5,495**	**100.0**

Many show organizers use post-exhibition attendee surveys to provide more in-depth feedback from their attendees than basic attendee registration information can provide. Typical research objectives of these types of attendee surveys are:

- Determine motivations, reasons and expectations for attending, measure value of exhibition in meeting their expectations, and identify ways value can be improved

- Provide feedback to be used in developing future attendance promotion, and to understand the needs of specific target audience segments

- Measure activity level of attendees, such as the hours and days spent at exhibits, in the conference sessions, their attendance history and traffic density (or which locations in the exhibit hall attract the most attendees).

- Rate operational elements of exhibition to identify specific areas for improvement, including the registration process, food service, shuttle buses, for example

- Test new ideas for future exhibitions, such as a new venue or product pavilions

- Quantify buying power and quality of attendees to be used in future exhibit space sales efforts

- Evaluate the educational component of the event, and obtain feedback for improvement on topics and issues of importance and scheduling, for example

- Assess the competitive landscape, for example the attendees' perceptions of competitor exhibitions attended

Generally speaking, the survey is best conducted immediately following the event using a postal-mail, online or telephone interview survey methodology. Several of the above research objectives require that the attendee have experienced the entire event before responding. However, personal interview or self-administered electronic terminal surveys on site are a viable option depending upon the survey objectives.

In some cases, show organizers may want to explore specific issues or new ideas in more depth. Qualitative research techniques like focus groups scheduled during the exhibition are an excellent method for accomplishing these types of research objectives.

Post-show attendee surveys can be conducted in house, or by using a professional research firm that specializes in exhibitions. The advantages of using a professional research firm are elimination of potential bias in questionnaire design and analysis, credibility with exhibitors when using the information for marketing purposes and professional assistance in survey sampling, methodology and execution.

Exhibitor Feedback

Attendees are the fundamental component required for a successful exhibition, but exhibitors are generally the primary revenue source for exhibition organizers. Therefore, exhibitor evaluation is also a critical step in the evaluation process.

SAMPLE ATTENDEE SURVEY

1. Please check all previous years that you have attended XYZ Show.

   x-1 ☐ First time attending   -2 ☐ 2005   -3 ☐ 2004   -4 ☐ 2003   -5 ☐ 2002   -6 ☐ Prior to 2002

2. How many hours did you spend at the exhibits each day?

   Monday: _____ hrs.   Tuesday: _____ hrs.   Wednesday _____ hrs.   Thursday: _____ hrs.
   (xx)   (xx)   (xx)   (xx)

3. What were your main reasons for attending XYZ Show? (Check all that apply.)

   xx-1 ☐ See new products and developments   xx-1 ☐ Make a purchase
   -2 ☐ Keep up to date on industry trends/issues   -2 ☐ Attend the conference program
   -3 ☐ See specific companies/products/services   -3 ☐ Network with colleagues/vendors
   -4 ☐ Get technical information/specifications   -4 ☐ Location of show
   -5 ☐ Find a solution to a problem   -5 ☐ Other: _____
   -6 ☐ Compare products for future purchase

4. Considering your reasons for attending, what is your rating of XYZ Show in terms of the value you received compared to the time and money you spent?

   x-5 ☐ Excellent   -4 ☐ Very Good   -3 ☐ Good   -2 ☐ Fair   -1 ☐ Poor

5. What is the reason for your rating? _____

6. How did you hear about XYZ Show 2006? (Check all that apply.)

   xx-1 ☐ Direct mail from show management   xx-1 ☐ Show Web site/Internet
   -2 ☐ Mailing or invitation from exhibitor   -2 ☐ Employer
   -3 ☐ Advertisement in trade publication   -3 ☐ Friend or associate
   -4 ☐ Article/editorial/calendar in trade publication   -4 ☐ Attended a previous show
   -5 ☐ Trade association   -5 ☐ Other: _____
   -6 ☐ Email invitation

7. Check the products/services you found of interest at the show. Also check those products/services that you plan to buy in the next 12 months as a result of what you saw at the show. (Check all that apply.)

Interested	Plan to Buy		Interested	Plan to Buy	
xx-1 ☐	xx-1 ☐	X	xx-1 ☐	xx-1 ☐	X
-2 ☐	-2 ☐	X	-2 ☐	-2 ☐	X
-3 ☐	-3 ☐	X	-3 ☐	-3 ☐	X
-4 ☐	-4 ☐	X	-4 ☐	-4 ☐	X
-5 ☐	-5 ☐	X	-5 ☐	-5 ☐	X
-6 ☐	-6 ☐	X	-6 ☐	-6 ☐	X
-7 ☐	-7 ☐	X	-7 ☐	-7 ☐	X
-8 ☐	-8 ☐	X	-8 ☐	-8 ☐	X
-9 ☐	-9 ☐	X	-9 ☐	-9 ☐	X

8. What role(s) do you play in the purchase of each of the following types of products/services exhibited? (Check all that apply.)

	Final Say -1	Specify Supplier -2	Recommend -3	No Role -4
X	xx- ☐	☐	☐	☐
X	xx- ☐	☐	☐	☐
X	xx- ☐	☐	☐	☐
X	xx- ☐	☐	☐	☐
X	xx- ☐	☐	☐	☐

9. Approximately how much do you or your company anticipate spending in the next 12 months for the types of products/services exhibited as a direct result of attending this show?

x-1 ☐ $X,000 or less   -3 ☐ $X,001 to $X,000   -5 ☐ $X,001 to $X,000   -7 ☐ More than $X,000

-2 ☐ $X,001 to $X,000   -4 ☐ $X,001 to $X,000   -6 ☐ $X,001 to $X,000   -8 ☐ Don't know

10. What other conferences and exhibitions have you attended in the past 12 months?

xx-1 ☐ X   xx-1 ☐ X
-2 ☐ X   -2 ☐ X
-3 ☐ X   -3 ☐ X
-4 ☐ X   -4 ☐ X
-5 ☐ X   -5 ☐ Other: _____
-6 ☐ X   -6 ☐ No other show attended in past 12 months

11. What publications do you read regularly (3 out of 4 issues) to keep up to date in your field?

x-1 ☐ X   x-1 ☐ X   x-1 ☐ X
x-2 ☐ X   x-2 ☐ X   x-2 ☐ X
x-3 ☐ X   x-3 ☐ X   x-3 ☐ X
x-4 ☐ X   x-4 ☐ X   x-4 ☐ X
x-5 ☐ X   x-5 ☐ X   x-5 ☐ X
x-6 ☐ X   x-6 ☐ X   x-6 ☐ X
x-7 ☐ X   x-7 ☐ X   x-7 ☐ X

12. Please rate each of the following aspects of XYZ Show 2006.

	Excellent 5	Very Good 4	Good 3	Fair 2	Poor 1
Advance registration process	xx- ☐	☐	☐	☐	☐
Housing arrangements	xx- ☐	☐	☐	☐	☐
On-site registration process	xx- ☐	☐	☐	☐	☐
Location/city	xx- ☐	☐	☐	☐	☐
Conference program	xx- ☐	☐	☐	☐	☐
Show directory	xx- ☐	☐	☐	☐	☐
Convention center	xx- ☐	☐	☐	☐	☐
Show Web site	xx- ☐	☐	☐	☐	☐
Exhibit floor layout	xx- ☐	☐	☐	☐	☐
Shuttle buses	xx- ☐	☐	☐	☐	☐

13. How likely are you to attend XYZ Show next year?

xx-5 ☐ Definitely would attend   -2 ☐ Probably would not attend

-4 ☐ Probably would attend   -1 ☐ Definitely would not attend

-3 ☐ Unsure

14. What is your preferred method for obtaining information about the show before attending?

x-1 ☐ Email   -3 ☐ Phone   -5 ☐ Internet/Web site

-2 ☐ Fax   -4 ☐ Direct mail   -6 ☐ Other (specify): _____

15. How far in advance of the show do you need information to make your decision to attend?

x-1 ☐ 1-2 months   -2 ☐ 3-4 months   -3 ☐ 5-6 months   -4 ☐ More than 6 months

16. Which of the following best describes your job title/function? (Please check **one** only.)

xx-1 ☐ X	xx-1 ☐ X
-2 ☐ X	-2 ☐ X
-3 ☐ X	-3 ☐ X
-4 ☐ X	-4 ☐ X
-5 ☐ X	-5 ☐ X
-6 ☐ X	-6 ☐ X
-7 ☐ X	-7 ☐ Other: _____

17. Which of the following best describes your primary type of business? (Please check **one** only.)

xx-1 ☐ X	xx-1 ☐ X
-2 ☐ X	-2 ☐ X
-3 ☐ X	-3 ☐ X
-4 ☐ X	-4 ☐ X
-5 ☐ X	-5 ☐ X
-6 ☐ X	-6 ☐ X
-7 ☐ X	-7 ☐ Other: _____

18. What is your best estimate of the total number of employees in your company at all locations?

x-1 ☐ 1 – 19   -2 ☐ 20 – 99   -3 ☐ 100 – 499   -4 ☐ 500 – 999   -5 ☐ 1,000 or more

19. What are your organization's anticipated revenues for this year?

x-1 ☐ $X,000 or less   -3 ☐ $X,001 to $X,000   -5 ☐ $X,001 to $X,000   -7 ☐ More than $X,000

-2 ☐ $X,001 to $X,000   -4 ☐ $X,001 to $X,000   -6 ☐ $X,001 to $X,000   -8 ☐ Don't know

20. How many miles did you travel (one way) to attend XYZ Show?

x-1 ☐ 1 – 50   -2 ☐ 51 – 200   -3 ☐ 201 – 400   -4 ☐ 401 – 1,000   -5 ☐ 1,001 – 2,000   -6 ☐ Over 2,000

21. In which U.S. state or other country do you reside? _____ xx:.........

22. Do you have any suggestions or additional comments about XYZ Show 2006?

_____

_____

THANKS FOR YOUR HELP!

Please return to: Exhibit Surveys, Inc., 7 Hendrickson Avenue, Red Bank, NJ 07701 FAX: (732) 741-5704

Exhibitor evaluation begins internally. It starts by analyzing basic exhibitor trend data, such as total number of exhibitors, total exhibit space sold and ancillary revenue from exhibitor sponsorship and promotion opportunities. Other key performance indicators are exhibitor attrition rates (the number of exhibitors lost from previous event), change in space purchased by individual exhibitors (how many increased, decreased or remained the same), and sign-up rates for the next show. All of these are indicators of the health of the exhibition from the exhibitor perspective.

A post-show exhibitor survey is a valuable tool to assess exhibitor satisfaction and to identify ways to improve the show in the future. Typical measurement objectives for exhibitors include:

• Determine objectives for exhibiting and assess value of exhibition in meeting their objectives, including ways to improve value

• Rate and evaluate specific aspects of the exhibition to identify areas for performance improvement such as audience quantity, audience quality, number and quality of leads generated, attendance promotion efforts, exhibition marketing, labor, general service contractor, and venue

• Determine profiles of attendees who are most important to reach, and rate satisfaction with exhibition in delivering these market segments

• Test ideas for future exhibitions such as new venues, product pavilions, and pricing packages.

• Plans for future exhibitions, such as the likelihood of exhibiting and amount of space needed.

• Assess competitive landscape (Other exhibitions exhibited at and perceptions of competitors.)

As with attendee surveys, exhibitor surveys are best conducted after they have experienced the entire event. Postal mail, online or telephone interview surveys conducted immediately after the exhibition can be used for these types of surveys.

2006 NTI CRITICAL-CARE EXPOSITION EVALUATION FORMS

Thank you for your participation in the 2006 National Teaching Institute & Critical Care Exposition®. So we may continue to meet the needs of both exhibitors and attendees, we would appreciate you completing and returning this evaluation. All company names and individual comments are kept confidential. Please return the completed evaluation form to Exhibitor Registration or the NTI Show Office or by FAX: 949-362-2022 or mail to:

AACN, Exhibits Department, 101 Columbia, Aliso Viejo, CA 92656 - by June 16, 2006. Thank you for your feedback!

COMPANY NAME (Optional) _____

CONTACT PERSON/PHONE (Optional) _____

1. Please indicate prior NTI participation: _____ first NTI; or exhibited in NTI for _____ years

2. Was AACN material received in sufficient time for decision making? _____ Yes _____ No

3. Were AACN materials useful and complete, easy to understand, and beneficial in pre-NTI planning?

Exhibit Prospectus	☐ Yes	☐ No
"New" On-line Exhibitor Service Kit	☐ Yes	☐ No
Exhibitor Bulletins	☐ Yes	☐ No

Suggestions for improvement: _____

4. Were exposition DAYS sufficient?   ☐ Yes   ☐ No
   Were exposition HOURS sufficient?   ☐ Yes   ☐ No

How would you rate exhibit hall TRAFFIC?
(Circle your response for each day listed)

Tuesday	Excellent	Good	Fair	Poor
Wednesday	Excellent	Good	Fair	Poor
Thursday	Excellent	Good	Fair	Poor
Overall	Excellent	Good	Fair	Poor

5. How would you rate the overall success of your exhibit at the NTI & Critical Care Exposition?
   ☐ Very successful   ☐ Moderately successful   ☐ Not successful

6. How would you rate your overall satisfaction with the NTI & Critical Care Exposition as compared to other conventions where you exhibit?
   ☐ Better than most   ☐ About the same   ☐ Worse than most

   How many other conventions/ tradeshows do you participate in on an annual basis?
   ☐ Less than five   ☐ Five to Ten   ☐ More than Ten – Indicate Number _____

7. What were your objectives at the NTI & Critical Care Exposition? (Check all that apply)
   ☐ Recruiting   ☐ New Contacts
   ☐ Public Relations   ☐ New Product Introduction
   ☐ Company/Product Recognition   ☐ Education
   ☐ Sales Leads   ☐ Other _____

8. Do you feel that you attained your objectives? ☐ Yes   ☐ No

9. Of the approximately 6,500 critical care nurses in attendance, what percentage visited your booth?
   ☐ 80%–100% (approximately more than 4,800)   ☐ 20%–40% (approximately 1,201 – 2,400)
   ☐ 60%–80% (approximately 3,601 – 4,800)   ☐ 10%–20% (approximately 601 – 1,200)
   ☐ 40%–60% (approximately 2,401 – 3,600)   ☐ Less than 10% (600 or less)

10. How would you rate NTI participants' influence on decision making regarding healthcare purchasing?
    ☐ Decision makers   ☐ Strong influence on decisions   ☐ Some influence   ☐ No influence

11. Did you take part in the Exhibit/CE Program? ☐ Yes   ☐ No
If yes: Did you find the program beneficial? ☐ Yes   ☐ No Please share your comments
or recommendations to improve the Exhibit/CE Program _____

_____

12. Career Opportunity exhibitors – Will you consider offering Exhibit/CE in the future?
☐ Yes   ☐ No

13. The official contractor/decorator was Freeman. Please rate their performance.
Overall conference decor and set up of the Exposition
☐ Excellent   ☐ Good   ☐ Fair   ☐ Poor

Service provided to you on the show floor (move-in, set-up, show services, dismantle)
(if applicable)
☐ Excellent   ☐ Good   ☐ Fair   ☐ Poor

Comments: _____

14. Of the following specialty service contractors, please rate the ones you utilized.

	Excellent	Good	Fair	Poor	Did Not Use
AES (Carousel & CNN Kiosks)					
AVW (Audio Visual & Computers)					
Convention Photo by Joe Orlando					
Dan Taylor & Associates (Security)					
ExpoExchange (Lead Retrieval)					
Freeman					
Short Term Plant Rental					
SLACK (Show Advertising)					

Comments regarding your experiences with the above specialty contractors

_____

15. Did you take advantage of any of the following advertising opportunities?
☐ NTI News ☐ NTI Proceedings Book/Directory of Exhibits ☐ NTI News OnLine
☐ Sponsored Advertising (Participant Planner, Pocket Guide, Travel Guide, Map, etc.)

Do you plan to utilize any of these advertising opportunities next year? ☐ Yes   ☐ No

16. Do you plan to exhibit at the 2007 NTI in Atlanta, Georgia, May 22-24 (Exhibit Days)?
☐ Yes   ☐ No

17. Do you have specific comments regarding the 2006 NTI & Critical Care Exposition? i.e.
Show Management, the facility, transportation, hotels, city, etc.

_____

_____

18. Do you have specific suggestions for consideration at the 2007 Critical Care Exposition in Atlanta? _____

19. Was your company housing block in the NTI 2006 Official Housing Block? ☐ Yes   ☐ No

    If No, what is your main reason for not staying in the NTI 2006 Official Housing Block? (select one)
    ☐ We are / I am using one of the hotel's frequent guest points program
    ☐ Costs of hotels in the block were too high for my budget
    ☐ We are / I am from the local area and am not staying at a hotel
    ☐ We are / I am staying with friends/family who live in the area
    ☐ Our / my preferred hotels in the housing block were unavailable
    ☐ Other (please specify): _____

20. Who did your company use to make your hotel reservations?
    ☐ The AACN Housing Bureau
    ☐ Hotel's/Brand's website
    ☐ Discount or travel website (i.e. hotels.com, expedia.com, etc.)
    ☐ The hotel directory
    ☐ Other (please specify): _____

21. How many of your staff attended the Participant-Exhibitor Event at Disney's California Adventure" Park? _____

22. Please use the space below if you wish to provide a testimonial for use in NTI 2007 sales materials. Your name and company must be provided for acknowledgement.

    _____
    _____

THANK YOU FOR YOUR PARTICIPATION.
Please return by June 16. See you in Atlanta, May 19-24, 2007!

Reprinted with permission by American Association of Critical Care Nurses, 2006

Feedback from Suppliers and Staff

In addition to exhibitors and attendees, feedback should be gathered from all the companies, representatives and contractors involved in producing the exhibition. Meetings with the official services contractor and specialty contractors, facility representatives, hotel and catering personnel should be carried out immediately after the exhibition. This post-exhibition meeting is a time to review processes to see what worked and what did not. Contractors who had to implement planned tasks are the best source of information on improving processes for subsequent events.

An in-house debriefing with all staff should be conducted as the final step in the evaluation process. Staff members are the hands-on experts who execute and oversee all the planned activities associated with the exhibition. Working on the frontlines gives them a bird's-eye view of what went right and what went wrong. They are committed to the success of the exhibition, because it is a reflection of what they do. Their input is important and should be heeded.

Financial Review

No evaluation is complete without a comprehensive financial review. The budget along with the show's Profit and Loss statement provides the basis for evaluating financial success. However, the financial analysis should involve more than simply identifying bottom line success, or line items over or under budget. Focus should also be placed on identifying opportunities for cost-cutting, un-productive revenue sources and new or increased revenue opportunities such as sponsorships and promotions.

Assessing the Data

Once the evaluation process is complete, what happens to all the information gathered? The best show organizers go back to square one: the planning framework. The mission statement, aims and objectives are reviewed. Do they need revision based on the assessment of what was and was not accomplished? What changes need to be made in the overall plan, the business plan and the critical path? What strategies and tactics need to be refined or re-defined in order to make things run more efficiently and effectively next time? What about sales and show production? Were target markets saturated or is there room for improvement? What new ideas need to be incorporated? It is this process that leads to better and even more successful exhibitions in the future.

A SURVEY ON THE PERCEIVED VALUE OF EXHIBITING

Research done by Exhibit Surveys, Inc. on individual shows in the US across industries indicates that on a five-point scale (where 1 is poor, 2 is fair, 3 is good, 4 is very good and 5 is excellent), the average value rating by exhibitors in achieving their objectives relative to time and money invested is only 2.8. This means that more exhibitors are rating exhibitions poor or only fair than are rating them very good or excellent. The exhibition industry faces a problem with the perceived value among exhibitors.

Lower attendance at many exhibitions leading to lower traffic density on the show floor continues to be a nagging problem. Although attendance has increased for some exhibitions in the fourth quarter of 2003 and first quarter of 2004, traffic density continues to decline (from an average of 3.0 attendees per 100 sq. ft. in 1990 to an all time low of 2.0 in 2003). Lower density shows do make it more difficult for exhibitors to compete for the time and attention of attendees, and it impacts the perceived synergism on the show floor by both exhibitors and attendees, but exhibitors can achieve good results in lower attended and lower density shows.

The challenge to organizers (and exhibitors) is to change the mindset that heavy traffic is synonymous with success. It is unlikely that many shows will return to the attendance or density levels of the past even with an improvement in the economy and absence of any major incidents like 9/11 or SARS. Most industries are facing significant long-term structural changes in the channels of trade for their industries that are impacting their ability to attract attendees (see Growing Your Event in a Rapidly Changing Business Environment, June 2002, www.exhibitsurveys.com/whitepapers.htm).

SUMMARY

Show organizers who want to keep their exhibitions alive and growing have to make use of feedback retrieved from all vested parties, contractors, attendees and exhibitors to evaluate what works and what could work better in future events. The only way to ensure sufficient feedback is to build it into the planning process as with all other aspects of show management.

QUESTIONS FOR DISCUSSION

① What might be the two biggest challenges show organizers face in getting feedback from exhibitors and from attendees?

② What kind of feedback would you think an exhibition manager gets the most of from exhibitors: positive or negative? Why?

③ What would be the best time to ask for an attendee's feedback – while they are still at the show, or when they get back home?

Chapter 1
Exhibition Industry Certifications

Section VII: Appendices

INTRODUCTION

Credentials distinguish professional peers from one another and typically require some type of study beyond a high school diploma. A higher-level academic diploma is one type of credential; however, they are other types that measure levels or areas of professional competency. The most commonly recognized credential in the exhibition/event/hospitality-related industry is a certification. Certification programs offer individuals a means to study more in-depth their chosen profession. Many people will study and attain more than one designation, attaining several certifications over a number of years.

For the exhibition industry, a person will want to look at their core areas of experience. If the core responsibilities are focused on the exhibition, then the Certified in Exhibition Management (CEM) designation might be the point of entry. If the core experience is across all areas of meeting planning, the Certified Meeting Professional (CMP) program might be a good first certification.

In many cases, individuals will need to have a certain number of years experience in a profession, attend educational programs in the profession, demonstrate leadership skills, and voluntary involvement before applying to begin the certification process. The certification programs listed here are for all related functions of the industry, including hotel, facility, event planning, exhibitions, etc. and will help students and professionals already in the industry asses which certifications will be most beneficial to career advancement and personal growth.

CAE – CERTIFIED ASSOCIATION EXECUTIVE

Sponsoring Organization:

American Society of Association Executives

Website:

http://www.asaenet.org

A voluntary certification effort founded in 1960, the Certified Association Executive program is designed to elevate professional standards, enhance individual performance, and designate those who demonstrate knowledge essential to the practice of association management.

Requirements to Pursue:

- Chief executive officers with three years of experience as CEO of an association and a bachelor's degree or higher.
- CEOs with five years of experience without a degree.
- Association staff with five years of experience and a bachelor's degree or higher or seven years of experience without a degree.
- Employees of trade associations, professional societies, individual membership. organizations, philanthropic organizations, or association management companies.
- All must pledge to adhere to the ASAE code of conduct and have no felony convictions.

Benefits of Certification:

- Expanded knowledge into every aspect of association management, including associations events and exhibitions.
- National professional recognition - peers, staff, and volunteer leaders all value the CAE designation.
- Extensive peer-level communication - networking opportunities as a result of participating in study groups and CAE events.
- Use of certification on business cards, letters, emails, etc.

CASE – CERTIFIED ASSOCIATION SALES EXECUTIVE

Sponsoring Organization:

Professional Convention Management Association

Website:

http://www.pcma.org

CASE is an intensive nine-week course designed exclusively for sales professionals who sell to the association market. The course blends instructor-led education with online learning technology to create a unique learning opportunity. The course consists of three telephone conferences, nine Internet-based modules, an instructor-led review and exam (in Chicago at the PCMA Learning Center), and a final practicum.

Requirements to Pursue:

CASE is a course designed exclusively for association sales professionals. The content is designed to increase understanding of the trends that affect the association community.

BENEFITS OF CERTIFICATION

Provides the tools to enhance ability of selling meeting services to this segment of the meetings industry.

CEM – CERTIFIED IN EXHIBITION MANAGEMENT

Sponsoring Organization:

International Association of Exhibition Management

Website:

http://www.iaem.org

The Certified in Exhibition Management (CEM) designation was created in 1975 to provide a professional designation for individuals in the exhibition industry. The designation was formed to raise professional standards and is recognized throughout the industry as the premier mark of professional achievement. The CEM Learning Program is the cutting-edge educational opportunity designed for exhibition industry professionals to succeed. The CEM curricula, a dependable source of specific knowledge for all individuals, emphasize direct application to daily challenges. Because of the emphasis on practical knowledge, the CEM Learning Program is first, an educational program, and second, a certification program.

Requirements to Pursue:

Two to three years relevant experience in the meetings/exhibition/events industry.

Requirements to Attain

- Successfully complete all nine (9) parts, including passing the appropriate examinations within three (3) years beginning the year following you're the candidate's successful exam. Candidates have one year from the date of each course in which to take and pass the corresponding CEM exam.
- Have at least three (3) years, of full-time experience as a practitioner in exhibition management.

Benefits of Certification:

Those individuals who attend the CEM Learning Program learn to acquire and maintain a competitive edge, stay abreast in a rapidly changing industry, and respond better to customer needs.

CFBE – CERTIFIED FOOD & BEVERAGE EXECUTIVE

Sponsoring Organization:

American Hotel & Lodging Association

Website:

http://www.ei-ahla.org/

The CFBE Program focuses on developing skills that aid the candidate in providing quality service amid growing competition, technological innovation, an increasingly sophisticated and demanding clientele, and liability concerns.

Requirements to Pursue:

Current employment as an executive-level manager in hotel food and beverage administration, food and beverage director/general manager, or executive chef, with at least three years of full time experience in one or more such positions.

Benefits of Certification:

- CFBE designation may be used on letterhead, business cards and other writings.
- CFBE lapel pin and wall plaque are the visible symbols of the holder's status and achievement.

CFE – CERTIFIED FACILITIES EXECUTIVE

Sponsoring Organization:

International Association of Assembly Managers

Website:

http://www.iaam.org

The Certified Facilities Executive (CFE) program was begun by IAAM in 1976 to recognize excellence in the professional development and competence of managers of public assembly facilities.

Requirements to Pursue:

- The application forms must be submitted with attachments, outlining education, experience, program participation, publications and professional and community activities. References are requested, as well as commitment to the IAAM Code of Ethics and a written essay outlining the candidates' philosophy of facility management.
- Must have seven years of experience in a management position at a public assembly facility and be a graduate of a four-year college or university. Additional public assembly facility experience may be substituted year-for-year for the educational requirement. Work experience will be evaluated as to its quality and scope.

Benefits of Certification:

- Develops a standard of professionalism for public assembly facility managers and the International Association of Assembly Managers.
- Creates a learning process that assists the individual to understand the diversity and depth of information that lead to the creation of our profession.
- Helps the individual that undertakes the process to categorize and evaluate their professional experience.

- May increase the value (salary and position) of the job that the person currently holds and potential future jobs for the CFE.
- Creates a feeling of self-worth and self esteem to those who successfully complete the program.
- Validates the successful recipient as an extremely knowledgeable and experienced public assembly facility manager.

CGMP – CERTIFIED GLOBAL MEETING PLANNER

Sponsoring Organization:
Connected International Meeting Professionals Association

Website:
http://www.cimpa.org

Certified Global Meeting Professional (CGMP) puts emphasis on international meetings.

Requirements to Pursue:
- Minimum of two years experience in meeting management.
- Minimum of 3 international meetings for which candidate was responsible.

Benefits of Certification:
- Announces to the world that skills have been assessed by a competent body of PhD Holders and have been found to measure up to defined standards.
- Authority to use the CGMP designation on letterhead, business cards and all forms of address.
- Certificate attesting to certification.
- CIMPA will notify the employer of CGMP achievement.
- Name will be published in the official register of certified planners of professional meetings.

CHA – CERTIFIED HOTEL ADMINISTRATOR

Sponsoring Organization:
American Hotel & Lodging Association

Website:
http://www.ei-ahla.org

The CFE designation says three important things about a facility executive: he or she is a skilled manager, is committed to the industry, and is pledged to continued professional growth and development. Managers who earn the CFE designation are recognized as experts.

Requirements to Pursue:
- Minimum two to three years hospitality work experience.
- Education or work experience emphasis.

Process:

Complete and return the application form along with all supporting documentation and the application/examination fee. Supervisor completes and returns the CHA Recommendation/Employment Verification Form that comes with the application. (Owners/operators may use a CHA, regional/area director, or corporate executive as a reference.)

Because individual backgrounds vary widely in the hospitality industry, applicants may pursue the CHA designation through one of three options:

• Plan A emphasizes an education background

• Plan B emphasizes industry experience

• Plan C emphasizes early entry.

Within three weeks, the Educational Institute will review the application and send notification of acceptance.

Benefits of Certification:

• Recognized worldwide, the CHA designation is the premier symbol of professional achievement for lodging executives.

• It's an honor awarded to professionals whose leadership and managerial abilities are exemplary – professionals who, by combining education and experience with dedication to the industry, have achieved a high level of expertise.

• The CHA designation may be used on letterhead, business cards, and other writings.

• The CHA lapel pin and wall plaque are the visible symbols of the holder's status and achievement.

Recertification

CHME – CERTIFIED HOSPITALITY MARKETING EXECUTIVE

Sponsoring Organization:
Hospitality Sales & Marketing Association International

Website:
http://www.hsmai.org/

HSMAI's Certified Hospitality Marketing Executive (CHME) is a designation earned by those professionals who have effectively demonstrated the credibility, knowledge, expertise and confidence that has become increasingly necessary in today's fast-moving and ever-changing hospitality industry. The CHME program has evolved from the initial certification program developed by HSMAI in 1974 and is administered by the association's certification commission with the assistance of the Educational Institute of the American & Lodging Association.

Requirements to Pursue:

• Actively employed within the hospitality industry.

- Minimum of 250 accumulated points for written summaries based on education, association service and work experience.

Benefits of Certification:

- Being named a CHME is a prestigious honor that carries with it new opportunities and increased recognition.
- Ability to develop and execute highly successful marketing programs will be evident.
- A new level of respect and admiration from peers will also arise as a result of achieving the designation.

CHSP – CERTIFIED HOSPITALITY SALES PROFESSIONAL

Sponsoring Organization:
American Hotel & Lodging Association

Website:
http://www.ei-ahla.org/certification_chsp.asp

The Certified Hospitality Sales Professional designation elevates credibility and confidence. It emphasizes the ability to meet demanding industry standards for sales professionalism and expertise.

Requirements to Pursue:

- Minimum two to three years hospitality work experience.
- Education or work experience emphasis.

Benefits of Certification:

- The Certified Hospitality Sales Professional (CHSP) designation elevates credibility and confidence. It emphasizes the ability to meet demanding industry standards for sales professionalism and expertise.
- The CHSP designation may be used on letterhead, business cards, and other documents.
- The CHSP lapel pin and wall plaque are the visible symbols of the holder's status and achievement.

CITE – CERTIFIED INCENTIVE AND TRAVEL EXECUTIVE

Sponsoring Organization:
Society of Incentive & Travel Executives

Website:
http://www.site-intl.org/education/cite.cfm

The CITE designation signifies a high level of competency in the incentive travel industry. For those individuals worldwide who have demonstrated extensive knowledge in the industry.

Requirements to Pursue:

- Achievement of 100 points for a combination of industry experience and activities in SITE.

- Secure a mentor who is SITE member and a CITE.

Benefits of Certification:

- CITEs receive a gold lapel pin and plaque at an official SITE event to recognize their outstanding achievement amongst peers worldwide.

- Ability to add CITE to business cards, marketing materials and proposals will demonstrate to customers and partners your commitment to the incentive travel industry.

CME – CERTIFIED MANAGER OF EXHIBITS

Sponsoring Organization:

Trade Show Exhibitors Association

Website:

http://www.tsea.org/page_28.php

The Certified Manager Exhibits™ (CME®) is the only association-sponsored certification program that recognizes professionalism in exhibit management and marketing. Members of the Trade Show Exhibitors Association (TSEA) created this program to help professionals learn valuable industry recognition and advance careers. Industry peers continually monitor the certification program to ensure it meets the demands, challenges and needs of the trade show industry. From start to finish, it takes approximately three years to obtain the CME.

Requirements to Pursue:

- CME candidates are required to earn 50% of their Continuing Education Units (CEUs) from TSEA and the Healthcare Convention & Exhibitors Association, which endorses the certification program.

- A minimum of 7 CEU points. 1 CEU equals 10 hours. Programs offered through TSEA count as double points.

Benefits of Certification:

- The privilege of adding CME to your name, including business cards, e-mail signature and all other correspondences.

- Public acknowledgement through the industry press including Trade Show Ideas.

- Valuable recognition at TS2 – The Trade Show About Trade Shows®.

- A CME diploma to proudly display the accomplishment.

- A CME lapel pin to proudly wear.

CMM – CERTIFICATION IN MEETINGS MANAGEMENT

Sponsoring Organization:

Meeting Professionals International

Website:

http://www.mpiweb.org/education/cmm/

The Global Certification in Meeting Management (CMM) is the first university co-developed global professional designation for meeting professionals and focuses on strategic issues and executive decision-making.

Requirements to Pursue:

Prospective candidates likely have 10 years or more experience in the industry as a supplier, DMC, PCO and/or meeting/event planner and want to move their career to a new strategic level.

Benefits of Certification:

• Expanded knowledge in strategic meeting management and the business of meetings.

• National professional recognition from peers.

• Additional networking opportunities for CMMs held at MPI's conferences.

• The CMM designation may be used on letterhead, business cards, and other writings.

• The CMM lapel pin and certificate of attainment are the visible symbols of the holder's status and achievement.

• MPI will notify the press of your success and MPI will notify your employer of the CMM achievement.

CMP – CERTIFIED MEETING PROFESSIONAL

Sponsoring Organization:

Convention Industry Council

Website:

http://www.conventionindustry.org/cmp/index.htm

Through the CMP Program, individuals who are currently employed in meeting management have the opportunity to pursue continuing education, increased industry involvement and industry-wide recognition by achieving the CMP designation. The requirements for certification are based on professional experience and an academic examination. The CMP program was established in 1985.

Requirements to Pursue:

Prospective candidate must have:

• Minimum of three years experience in meeting management.

• Current, full-time employment in a meeting management capacity (CIC will accept applications from applicants who have been unemployed for a period less than twelve (12) months from the date his or her application is submitted).

• Responsibility and accountability for the successful completion of meetings.

On the application, candidates must attain 90 out of 150 possible points within five specific areas of meeting management:

- Experience in Meeting Management - 35 points allowed
- Management Responsibility - 50 points allowed
- Education & Continuing Education - 25 points allowed
- Membership in Professional Organizations - 10 points allowed
- Professional Contribution to the Field - 30 points allowed

Applicants are not required to score points in all areas of the application. Specific information for determining and reporting earned points in each area is included in the application form.

Benefits of Certification:

- Authority to use the CMP designation on letterhead, business cards and all forms of address.
- Receive a certificate attesting to the achievement and complimentary subscriptions to the informative quarterly newsletter: The CMP Update and the bimonthly CMP electronic newsletter.
- Recognition: your name will be released to the press and, if you wish, the Convention Industry Council will notify your employer of the CMP achievement.
- Professional Development: increased knowledge of all aspects of meeting management is gained during preparation for the CMP examination.
- Networking opportunities - become part of an elite group that shares this designation.
- Gain a competitive advantage when soliciting business as either a supplier or independent planner as proof of your professional market knowledge.

CPCE – CERTIFIED PROFESSIONAL CATERING EXECUTIVE

Sponsoring Organization:
National Association of Catering Executives

Website:
www.nace.net

This certification was designed to establish a nationally recognized standard of competence in catering and promote professional commitment to the excellence of catering. The comprehensive, three-section exam was developed in collaboration with the Educational Institute, a nonprofit foundation of the American Hotel and Lodging Association.

Requirements to Pursue:
Earn 30 points within the application form based on employment, education and NACE membership.

Benefits of Certification:

- Recognition of professional ability by fellow catering executives, employers and the public.
- Potential for increased career opportunities in the catering industry. Greater expertise in the catering profession.
- Prestige of being one of the select group who earned the right to use the CPCE designation.

CSEP – CERTIFIED SPECIAL EVENT PROFESSIONAL

Sponsoring Organization:
International Special Events Society

Website:
http://www.ises.com/CSEP/

The CSEP designation is the hallmark of professional achievement in the special events industry. It is earned through education, performance, experience, and service to the industry, and reflects a commitment to professional conduct and ethics.

Requirements to Pursue:
- Accumulate points through experience and service.
- Start self study program or study group.

Program / Course of Study:
Submit application, begin a self study program or start a study group, complete the exam application form and take the exam.

Benefits of Certification:
Awarded a CSEP pin and certificate of accomplishment.

CTSM – CERTIFIED TRADE SHOW MARKETER

Sponsoring Organization:
Exhibitor Show

Website:
http://www.exhibitornet.com/ctsm/

CTSM-Certified Trade Show Marketer-is the only university-affiliated professional certification program in the exhibit marketing industry. The CTSM program trains candidates in trade show and event marketing. Candidates are required to complete a curriculum of 28 seminars which equals 42 hours of classroom study. These sessions are available at the Exhibitor Show and ExhibitorFastTrak. Upon completion, candidates earn 4 CEUs through their university affiliate Northern Illinois University Outreach. The program started in 1992 as a "child" of Exhibitor Show, which is a branch of Exhibitor Magazine Group.

Requirements to Pursue:
- The following education/job experience qualifications are required for certification. May be working toward completing these requirements as you work on the program:
- Bachelor's degree and two (2) or more years of work experience related to trade shows.
- No degree with three (3) or more years of work experience related to trade shows.

Benefits of Certification:
- Training in the disciplines of trade show and event marketing.

- Networking with industry peers, veterans and suppliers.

- Demonstration of valuable knowledge and skills gained.

- Continuing Education Units document training.

- Many CTSM candidates experience a career advancement either during or shortly after certification.

DMCP – DESTINATION MANAGEMENT CERTIFIED PROFESSIONAL

Sponsoring Organization:

Association of Destination Management Executives

Website:

http://www.adme.org/members/DMCPCertification.asp

The purpose of the DMCP program is to increase the professionalism within the destination management industry by establishing a level of knowledge and performance necessary for certification; identifying the body of knowledge required; stimulating the art and science of destination management, increasing the value of practitioners to their employers; recognizing and raising industry standards and practices and thereby, ethics; and maximizing the value of the products and services that certified destination management professionals can provide.

Requirements to Pursue:

- Minimum of three years in the destination management industry.

- Minimum of 90 out of a possible 150 points on the application.

Benefits of Certification:

- DMCPs have the authority to use the DMCP designation on letterhead, business cards and all forms and addresses.

- They also receive a certificate attesting to their achievement as the best in the destination management industry.

- Other benefits include recognition, professional development, credibility, respect, job benefits and self esteem.

LES – LEARNING ENVIRONMENT SPECIALIST

Sponsoring Organization:

Professional Convention Management Association

Website:

http://www.pcma.org/education/distance/les/

This certificate program aids the candidate in understanding of the concept of lifelong learning and the importance of the learning environment as central to effectively plan educational events for adult learners. PCMA is not currently offering the program as they are in process of doing a major refresh of the course content. They plan to offer the program in 2006, but dates have not been set.

Requirements to Pursue:

Three and a half days are devoted to a unique educational experience that encourages innovation, interaction, and practical applications. Attendees prepare for the learning process several weeks in advance by taking a test and completing a series of assignments prior to attending the course. Peer learning is an integral part of the program, as well as problem-solving games, question-and-answer sessions, and group activities.

PMP – PROJECT MANAGEMENT PROFESSIONAL

Sponsoring Organization:

Project Management Institute

Website:

http://www.pmi.org/info/PDC_PMP.asp

The Project Management Professional (PMP®) Credential Examination measures the application of knowledge, skills, tools, and techniques that are utilized in the practice of project management. The examination specifications were established in 1997 after the Project Management Institute completed a job-analysis study.

Requirements to Pursue:

To be eligible for the PMP credential, must first meet specific education and experience requirements and agree to adhere to a code of professional conduct. Candidates applying for the PMP credential must satisfy the educational and experiential requirements for Category 1 or Category 2 and agree to abide by the Project Management Professional Code of Professional Conduct.

- For Category 1, the candidate holds a baccalaureate or global equivalent university degree and has a minimum of 4,500 hours of project management experience within the five project management process groups.

- For Category 2, the candidate does not hold a baccalaureate or global equivalent university degree, but holds a high school diploma or equivalent secondary school credential and has a minimum of 7,500 hours of project management experience within the five project management process groups.

- Candidates in either category must verify at least 35 contact hours of specific instruction that addresses learning objectives in project management.

Benefits of Certification:

By attaining the PMP credential, your name will be included in the largest and most prestigious group of certified professionals in the project management community.

OTHER MEETING INDUSTRY RELATED CERTIFICATIONS

Acronym: **CEOE**
Certification Title: **Certified Engineering Operations Executive**
Sponsoring Organization: **American Hotel & Lodging Association**
Website: **http://www.ei-ahla.org/certification_ceoe.asp**

Acronym: **CGPM**
Certification Title: **Certified Government Property Manager**
Sponsoring Organization: **American Hotel & Lodging Educational Institute**
Website: **http://www.ei-ahla.org/certification_cgpm.asp**

Acronym: **CGPS**
Certification Title: **Certified Government Property Supervisor**
Sponsoring Organization: **American Hotel & Lodging Educational Institute**
Website: **http://www.ei-ahla.org/certification_cgps.asp**

Acronym: **CGPT**
Certification Title: **Certified Government Property Technician**
Sponsoring Organization: **American Hotel & Lodging Educational Institute**
Website: **http://www.ei-ahla.org/certification_cgpt.asp**

Acronym: **CGS**
Certification Title: **Certified Gaming Supervisor**
Sponsoring Organization: **American Hotel & Lodging Educational Institute**
Website: **http://www.ei-ahla.org/certification_cgs.asp**

Acronym: **CHDT**
Certification Title: **Certified Hospitality Department Trainer**
Sponsoring Organization: **American Hotel & Lodging Educational Institute**
Website: **http://www.ei-ahla.org/certification_chdt.asp**

Acronym: **CHE**
Certification Title: **Certified Hospitality Educator**
Sponsoring Organization: **American Hotel & Lodging Association**
Website: **http://www.ei-ahla.org/certification_che.asp**

Acronym: **CHHE**
Certification Title: **Certified Hospitality Housekeeping Executive**
Sponsoring Organization: **American Hotel & Lodging Association**
Website: **http://www.ei-ahla.org/certification_chhe.asp**

Acronym: **CHI**
Certification Title: **Certified Hospitality Instructor**
Sponsoring Organization: **American Hotel & Lodging Educational Institute**
Website: **http://www.ei-ahla.org/certification_chi.asp**

Acronym: **CHRE**
Certification Title: **Certified Human Resource Executive**
Sponsoring Organization: **American Hotel & Lodging Association**
Website: **http://www.ei-ahla.org/certification_chre.asp**

Acronym: **CHS**
Certification Title: **Certified Hospitality Supervisors**
Sponsoring Organization: **American Hotel & Lodging Association**
Website: **http://www.ei-ahla.org/certification_chs.aspv**

Acronym: **CHT**
Certification Title: **Certified Hospitality Trainer**
Sponsoring Organization: **American Hotel & Lodging Educational Institute**
Website: **http://www.ei-ahla.org/certification_cht.asp**

Acronym: **CLM**
Certification Title: **Certified Lodging Manager**
Sponsoring Organization: **American Hotel & Lodging Educational Institute**
Website: **www.ei-ahla.org/certification_clm.asp**

Acronym: **CLSO**
Certification Title: **Certified Lodging Security Officer**
Sponsoring Organization: **American Hotel & Lodging Educational Institute**
Website: **http://www.ei-ahla.org/certification_clso.asp**

Acronym: **CLSS**
Certification Title: **Certified Lodging Security Supervisor**
Sponsoring Organization: **American Hotel & Lodging Educational Institute**
Website: **http://www.ei-ahla.org/certification_clss.asp**

Acronym: **CPAE**
Certification Title: **Council of Peers Award for Excellence**
Sponsoring Organization: **National Speakers Association**
Website: **http://www.nsaspeaker.org/about/cpae_hall_of_fame.shtml**

Acronym: **CRDE**
Certification Title: **Certified Room Division Executive**
Sponsoring Organization: **American Hotel & Lodging Educational Institute**
Website: **http://www.ei-ahla.org/certification_crde.asp**

Acronym: **CSP**
Certification Title: **Certified Speaking Professional**
Sponsoring Organization: **National Speakers Association**
Website: **http://www.nsaspeaker.org/competencies/csp_desg.shtml**

Acronym: **HFTP**
Certification Title: **Certified Hospitality Technology Professional**
Sponsoring Organization: **American Hotel & Lodging Educational Institute**
Website: **http://www.ei-ahla.org/certification_hftp.asp**

Acronym: **MHS**
Certification Title: **Master Hotel Supplier**
Sponsoring Organization: **American Hotel & Lodging Educational Institute**
Website: **http://www.ei-ahla.org/certification_mhs.asp**

Information compiled by:
Monica Myhill, CMP
President
Meeting Returns
3580 East Easter Avenue
Littleton, CO   80122
303-220-1920
monica@meetingreturns.com
www.meetingreturns.com

Section VII: Appendices

Chapter 2
Exhibition & Event Industry Organizations

Section VII: Appendices

Alliance of Meeting Management Companies (AMMC)
Internet: www.ammc.org

American Hotel & Lodging Association (AHLA)
Internet: www.ahla.com

American Society of Association Executives (ASAE)
Internet: www.asaenet.org

Association of Convention Marketing Executives (ACME)
Internet: www.acmenet.org

Association for Convention Operations Management (ACOM)
Internet: www.acomonline.org

Association of Exhibition Organisers (AEO)
United Kingdom
Internet: www.aeo.org.uk

Asociación de Ferias Internacionales de América (AFIDA)
Peru
Tel: + 5115660685
E-Mail: afida@feria.com.pe

Asociación Mexicana de Profesionales en Ferias, Exposciones y Convenciones, A.C.
(AMPROFEC)
Association of Mexican Exposition and Convention Professionals
Internet: www.amprofec.org.mx

Asociación de Organizadores de Congresos, Ferias, Exposciones y Afines de la República
Argentina (AOCA)
Tel: + 541148143833
E-Mail: info@viewpoint.com.ar

Canadian Association of Exposition Management (CAEM)
Internet: www.caem.ca

Center for Exhibition Industry Research (CEIR)
Internet: www.ceir.org

China Council for the Promotion of International Trade
Internet: www.ccpit.org

Convention Industry Council (CIC)
Internet: www.conventionindustry.org

Destination Marketing Association International (DMAI) Formerly IACVB
Internet: www.destinationmarketing.org

Exhibit Designers & Producers Association (EDPA)
Internet: www.edpa.com

Exhibition and Event Association of Australia (EEAA)
Internet: www.eeaa.com.au

Exhibition Association of Southern Africa (EXSA)
Internet: www.exsa.co.za

Exhibition Services & Contractors Association (ESCA)
Internet: www.esca.org

Exhibitor Appointed Contractor Association (EACA)
Internet: www.eaca.com

Fairlink Scandinavia
Internet: www.fairlink.se

Federation of Fairs and Exhibitions in the Netherlands (FBTN)
Tel: + 31102280822
E-Mail: fbtn@worldonline.nl

Financial & Insurance Conference Planners (FICP)
Internet: www.ficpnet.com

German Trade Fair Federation (AUMA)
Aussttellungs- und Messe-Ausschuss der Deutschen Wirtschaft e.V. (AUMA)
Internet: www.auma-fairs.com

Healthcare Convention & Exhibitors Association (HCEA)
Internet: www.hcea.org

Hong Kong Exhibition & Convention Industry Association (HKECIA)
Internet: www.exhibitions.org.hk

Hospitality Sales & Marketing Association International (HSMAI)
Internet: www.hsmai.org

InterEXPO
Internet: www.inter-expo.com

International Association for Exhibition Management (IAEM)
Internet: www.iaem.org

International Association for Fairs & Expositions (IAFE)
Internet: www.fairsandexpos.com

International Association of Assembly Managers (IAAM)
Internet: www.iaam.org

International Association of Conference Centers (IACC)
Internet: www.iacconline.org

International Association of Hispanic Meeting Professionals (IAHMP)
Internet: www.hispanicmeetingprofessionals.com

International Association of Professional Congress Organizers (IAPCO)
Internet: www.iapco.org

International Congress and Convention Association (ICCA)
Internet: www.iccaworld.com

International Exhibition Logistics Associates (IELA)
Internet: www.iela.org

International Special Events Society (ISES)
Internet: www.ises.com

Israel Exhibition Industry Association (IEIA)
Tel: +97236882929
E-Mail: isaac@itex.co.il

Japan Exhibition Association
Internet: www.nittenkyo.ne.jp

Korea Convention Association
Internet: www.kceia.org

Major American Trade Show Organizers (MATSO)
Internet: www.matso.org

Meeting Professionals International (MPI)
Internet: www.mpiweb.org

National Association of Consumer Shows (NACS)
Internet: www.publicshows.com

National Business Travel Association (NBTA)
Internet: www.nbta.org

National Coalition of Black Meeting Planners (NCBMP)
Internet: www.ncbmp.org

Professional Convention Management Association (PCMA)
Internet: www.pcma.org

Religious Conference Management Association (RCMA)
Internet: www.rcmaweb.org

Singapore Association of Convention & Exhibition Organisers & Suppliers (SACEOS)
Internet: www.saceos.org.sg

Society of Government Meeting Professionals
Internet: www.sgmp.org

Society of Independent Show Organizers
Internet: www.siso.org

Trade Exhibition Association (TEA)
Thailand
Internet: www.thaitradeshow.org

Trade Show Exhibitors Association
Internet: www.tsea.org

Travel Industry Association of America (TIA)
Internet: www.tia.org

ufi – The global Association of the Exhibition Industry
Union des Foires Internationales
Tel: +33142679912
E-mail: info@ufi.org
Internet: www.ufinet.org

World Trade Centers Association
Internet: www.wtca.org

Section VII: Appendices

A

Accrual accounting 323

Action item 254

Action Stations 307

Activity 254

Actual or perceived value 200

Additional Insured 187

Adult learner 285

Advertising 133

Amenity 138

Ancellation 149

Attended Buffet or Attended Cafeteria 307

Attrition 311

Audit 509

Auditory learners 286

AutoCAD 276

Average Attraction Efficiency 133

B

Barback 315

Boilerplate language 150

Brand 242

Breach 150

Break-even point 326, 330

Break-out Sessions 287

Budget diary 338

Budget philosophy 326, 328

Buffet 307

Butlered 308

Buyer 30

Buying influence 134

C

Call for Presentations 288

Cancellation 415

Cartage agent 451

Cash accounting 323

Center for Exhibition Industry Research 23

City-wide 400

Classroom 293

Cloning 55

Co-location 56

Commercial General Liability 186

Commission 410-411

Common carriers 449

Conference Style 295

Consignee 451

Consumer exhibitions 28

Continuing Education Units 283

Contribution margin 331

Convention center 199, 219

Convention center authority 220

Convention discount 423

Cost per reach 135

Crescent or Half-Rounds 296

Crime insurance 188

Crisis 471

Critical path 251

Cross aisles 267

Cut-off 395

Cut-off Dates 163, 395

D

Decorator 359

Deductible 186

Default 151

Destination Management Company (DMC) 303-304

Direct mail 121

Directing 256

Double-decker 268

Drayage 364, 448

E

Education tracks 283

End cap 266

Event Specification Guide 466

Exhibit managers 15

Exhibition 23

Exhibition freight forwarders 435

Exhibition forwarders 447

Exhibitor appointed contractors 452

Exhibitor attrition rates 515

Exhibitor prospectus 103

Exhibitor Service Center 369

Exhibitor-appointed contractor 365

Exhibitors' service manual 363

F

Fair 225

Features & Benefits 82
FedEx 364
Fixed costs 325, 329
Flighting 114
Float time 258
Floor managers 461
Force Majeure 157
Foreign currency exchange rate 335
Franchise agreement 55
Freight brokers 449
Freight forwarders 449
Functional budget 325

G

Gantt chart diagrams 249
General Sessions 287
Geographic expansion 55
Group discount 407, 423
Group history 398
Guest events 65

H

Hands-on Participation 287
Horizontal 29
Horizontal show 266
Hotel and conference centers 224
Hotel room nights 219

I

Inbound 67
Indemnification 174
Independent trucking companies 431
Indirect air carriers 449
Indirect costs 325, 329
Integrated marketing 138
Island 268

J

Joint venture 70

L

Lead generation 83
Learning objectives 284
Line of sight 268
Linear booths 268
Liquidated damages 146

Section VII: Appendices

M

Marketing mix 80
Marshalling yard 451
Material 148
Maxed out 274
Media kit 137
Media relations 127
Milestones 258
Mixed exhibition 29
Multi-purpose rooms 297
Municipal or civic center 219

N

Net rates 161
Net square feet 221

O

Official housing program 412
Organizer 30
Outbound 68
Over selling 402
Overcoming Objections 84

P

Panel Discussions 287
Peak 402
Pedestrian paradises 362
Peninsula 268
Pick up 401
Pipe-and-drape 66
Planned avoidance 476
Plenary Session 287
Positioned 96
Post-show analysis 507
Poster Session 287
Primes 255
Program objectives 284
Project plan 250
Public relations 127

R

Rack rates 161
Reception 305
Replacement value 186
Return on investment 133, 138, 338
Ridership 429
Roundtable Discussions 287

S

Sales Cycle 82
Scale 278
Seller 30
Show directory 138
Show-specific risks 486
Site selection 201
Site visit 201
Site-specific risks 485
Slippage 258
Snake lines 399
Soft openings 400
Speaker Guidelines 289
Sponsorships 133
Stand 66
Strategic Analysis 90
Sub-blocks 408

T

Tactical Analysis 90
Tactile learners 286
Tentative block 410
Termination 151
The Close 82
Theatre 294
Third party housing providers 410
Total economic impact 200
Tradeshows 29

U

U-Shape 292
U.S. Department of Commerce's International Buyer Program 245
Umbrella liability 187
Union Des Fiores Internationales 26
UPS 364

V

Value proposition 140
Van lines 449
Variable costs 325, 329
Vertical 92
Vertical show 266
Visual learners 286

Section VII: Appendices

W

Walk 425
Walked 164
Work breakdown structure 253-254
Workshops 287

Z

Zero-based budgeting 325